STEVEN HUMPHREY

Who Runs Chicago?

Who Runs Chicago?

MICHAEL KILIAN
CONNIE FLETCHER
F. RICHARD CICCONE

St. Martin's Press
New York

Copyright © 1979 by Michael Kilian, Connie Fletcher, and
F. Richard Ciccone.
All rights reserved. For information, write:
St. Martin's Press, Inc., 175 Fifth Avenue, New York, N.Y. 10010.
Manufactured in the United States of America
Library of Congress Cataloging in Publication Data

Kilian, Michael.
  Who runs Chicago?

   1. Chicago—Politics and government—1950-   2. Elite (Social sciences)
—Illinois—Chicago. I. Fletcher, Constance, joint author. II. Ciccone,
F. Richard, joint author. III. Title.
F548.52.K54   320.9'773'1104   79-9490
ISBN 0-312-87023-X

To Richard J. Daley,
who made everything possible.

Contents

Foreword

On a balmy afternoon in the summer of 1978, Time Inc.'s Lucy Nunes invited a couple hundred dear friends to a cocktail party in the lobby of the shimmering new Time-Life Building on Chicago's lakefront.

Miss Nunes, whose fluttery garden-party charm masks a machine-gun quick mind and the crafty skills of a Talleyrand, is chief flack for Time Inc. in Chicago. Her little party was to celebrate the appearance, way in the back of a forthcoming issue of *Fortune* magazine, of an article about how well politics and business mix in Chicago.

Lucy Nunes is one of the top flacks in Chicago, ranking right up there with the Edelmans, June Rosner, Ligita Dienhardt, and Mayor Byrne's Bill Griffin. She has such a genius and reputation for throwing wildly successful parties that she could easily have drawn several hundred important Chicago people to a gala celebrating some *Time* executive's hernia operation.

The people who came to Lucy Nunes' little gathering celebrating an obscure little piece in the back of *Fortune* were *the* most important people in Chicago: Mayor and Heather Bilandic, society queen Mrs. J. Harris Ward, Commonwealth Edison's Thomas Ayers, the First National Bank's A. Robert Abboud, Democratic Party

Chairman George Dunne, the Plumbers' Union's Ed Brabec, *Chicago Tribune* editorial-page editor John McCutcheon—a seemingly endless parade of big shots, and all gathered under one roof.

Such a party in New York would be unthinkable. To bring together all the people who run all the things that are run in New York under one roof, the roof would have to be that of Madison Square Garden. And hardly anyone would know anyone else.

Neither could you have such a party in Washington, although that's what Washington hostesses think they pull off every week. They don't, really. All those movers and shakers don't actually move or shake anything, they just go to parties. Washington's government establishment is run by faceless bureaucrats who go home to the suburbs every night. The city itself is run by a black subculture that hardly ever gets invited to parties.

But the kind of people at Lucy's party actually run Chicago, right down to deciding who gets promoted to police sergeant or what kind of flowers are planted in the Art Institute garden. The members of this elite *can* fit under one roof. And, they all know each other. Whether they run a plumbers' union, sell bonds, or set society fashions, they are continually running into each other at endless civic events and parties like Lucy's. And they relate to one another on a first-name basis.

The same can of course be said of the ruling elite of any of America's lesser cities: Omaha, Atlanta, San Francisco. But Chicago is not one of the nation's lesser cities. It is Omaha made good. New York may be the Big Apple, and Washington the Federal City, but Chicago is the capital of the rest of the country.

It is also, as the late Mayor Daley liked to boast, the city that works. It has never worked as well as he pretended, but it does work better than any other major city in the United States—certainly better than New York or Washington.

For some reason, the only books that ever seem to get written about Chicago are about Mayor Daley, gangsters, or historical oddities like the 1871 Chicago Fire. This book will of necessity deal with all three (the Chicago Fire is in the chapter on architects), but its purpose is to go far beyond that—into the boardrooms and back rooms, the slums and the lakefront high rises, the exclusive clubs and the Chicago Bears locker room. It will even take you under some bushes at the Saddle and Cycle Club where a Prince of Wales reportedly took a Chicago lady some fifty years ago.

This is not intended as a defense of Chicago, nor an attack upon it, but merely a good look at it. To our minds, the most penetrating and expansive view of any city is through its people, and that's what we want to show you.

Obviously, we cannot deal with all the people and all the walks of life in Chicago. We confine ourselves to those who are part of or closely relate to the city's power structure, or whose actions have a great effect on their fellow Chicagoans. For this reason, we will discuss architects, street-gang leaders, and advertising men as fully as we will political leaders, captains of industry, and society broads.

For the same reason, we will not discuss Chicago's used-car dealers, interior decorators, botanists, or actuaries. Or physicians, unless they're married to someone significant. Chicago's doctors get their hands into as many messy things as Chicago's lawyers do, but it would take even the most fiendish surgeon a lifetime of bashing spleens to cause as much damage as a Chicago lawyer can in fifteen minutes.

In addition to talking about all these people, we will also rank those at the top in their respective fields. Ranking anyone is an arbitrary and inexact business, to be sure. In 1978, author Michael H. Hart produced a list of the "100 most influential people who ever lived," and the top ten places went to Muhammad, Isaac Newton, Jesus Christ, Buddha, Confucius, Saint Paul, Tsai Lun, Johann Gutenberg, Christopher Columbus, and Albert Einstein. We simply wouldn't know why he left off such people as Karl Marx, Attila the Hun, Martin Luther, and Truman Capote.

In making our rankings, we counted not only power and influence but ability, attainment, prestige, and false impressions of power and influence. We also consulted the individuals' peers, friends, enemies, and other experts in their fields—many of whom were quite heartless in voicing their opinions.

A peculiarity of our lists is that they seem to include some rascals along with the great and noble personages, but that's how it is in a big city, especially a big city that works.

1

Dems

Mayor Daley is dead. His political machine isn't. Yet. The astonishing mayoral primary upset in which the fiery Jane Byrne ousted the bland Michael Bilandic was a phenomenon, but not the kind people read about in the magazines and newspapers. Enthusiastic in their ignorance, bright-eyed reform types seized upon the amazing election returns to proclaim that the machine was "wrecked," "killed," and otherwise ruined.

But discomfited is all it really was. The machine was stunned by Jane. It immediately rolled over like a submissive dog. But it didn't die. It couldn't. The machine is the only real political party there is in Chicago, the only real government. Jane Byrne ran against it all by herself—not to replace it with something else, but to regain her position and power within it.

Jane Byrne is certainly more attractive than Ed Kelly and Vito Marzullo, and she may have campaigned as "a woman scorned," but she proved in her first 60 days in office that she understands machine politics better than anyone believed.

In many ways, Jane Byrne's triumph was symptomatic of the city's desire, not for reform, but for a return to the old days of the maximum boss. With their music festivals, jogging, and endless

1

appearances at garden-party receptions, former Mayor Michael
and Heather Bilandic tried to bring what they saw as sophistication and glamour to Chicago, comporting themselves like a tank
town version of Prince Ranier and Princess Grace. Jane Byrne, one
of Daley's closest disciples, invoked his ghost and wrath throughout her campaign. To some, her election was Daley's hand reaching from the grave.

Daley—"Da Mare" to those who hung around City Hall—was
absolute master of Chicago and the nation's most powerful political machine for more than twenty years. He was the city's security
blanket. In 1971, as in all his elections—even when the rest of the
country was viewing him as some sort of archfiend for his role in
the 1968 convention riots—he won the support of the city's Poles,
Jews, blacks, union leaders and members, captains of industry,
liberals, and Republicans. His persona was exalted as the alchemy
that made the city that works work. His passing, predictable as it
should have been in light of a stroke and other circulatory problems, gave a new meaning to mortality. If Daley could die, everyone could. Even his most ardent Republican enemies winced at
seeing the name Michael A. Bilandic replace "Richard J. Daley" on
that huge neon welcoming sign at O'Hare.

When Daley died, many thought that was the end of the machine right there, that it would collapse from rickety old age or be
torn apart in an anything-goes struggle for power between the
party's greedy and bloody-minded ward bosses and other political
warlords. But the structure proved stronger than the individuals
who were its parts. As though Daley were still glowering over
them from his fifth-floor City Hall office, they pulled together to
maintain political stability and agreed to let a dull stalwart of
Daley's own 11th Ward named Michael Bilandic sit in the mayor's
chair—until someone more suitable could be found.

Bilandic was no Daley, even though he tried to talk like him.
He was not dynamic. He was not a protagonist. Until the great
snow of 1979, he was not even controversial. Jane Byrne's great
"greased taxi-deal" charges and the consequent scandal were ignored like another White Sox loss. And, worst of all, Bilandic was
not very political. While he and Heather went to garden parties,
others met in back rooms. Bilandic was surrounded by a circle of
Daley's leftover henchmen who made a point of sharing in his rule.
State Senator Richard M. Daley, the late mayor's son, was an

advisor. Thomas Donovan, City Hall patronage chief and political chancellor, and Edward Bedore, city budget director, at times seemed to run the city by themselves. And all, of course, were from the 11th Ward.

It soon became apparent under Bilandic that it was the machine that made the man, not vice versa. Daley had been master and molder of the machine, but it could survive without him.

The city that worked continued to work. The interdependent cliques and claques of politicians, businessmen, bankers, and labor leaders remained as friendly with each other, and City Hall, as ever. The plumes of cement dust still rose from the ever-abuilding high-rise towers that Daley so loved to see. So did fumes of corruption. The trains still ran on time, although one fell off the Loop El tracks at the height of a Christmas shopping rush hour shortly after Daley's death. The city's municipal treasure chest continued to overflow, to the envy and shame of lesser and greater cities.

Life went on as before, and no one seemed to mind Bilandic, even though he didn't really sound like Daley. Even though, like a Bridgeport version of New York's John Lindsay, he tried to change Chicago's image from the stodgy, conservative, family-oriented "city of neighborhoods" that so closely reflected Daley's personal life-style.

He and Heather, a Lake Shore Drive socialite who had met Bilandic as a City Hall patronage worker specializing in culture, tried to give Chicago culture (if jogging marathons and week-long lakefront pop music festivals can be so described).

And people seemed to enjoy it. The jogging and musicales were installed as annual affairs. The only question was whether Bilandic would continue indefinitely as the machine's bland but "fun-loving" figurehead, or whether he would be replaced in a palace coup after a term or two, perhaps with another Daley.

A coup was never needed.

On New Year's Eve, December 31, 1978, it began to snow in Chicago, and before the spring thaw finally took it all away Michael Bilandic had committed so many impolitic blunders as to make himself the most unelectable man in the country, and to make Chicago machine Democrats suffer their first mayoral defeat in history.

Jane Byrne won the Chicago Democratic mayoral primary, but she was less a winner than the only visible alternative. If lakefront liberal Bill Singer had had the luck to pick a blizzard year for his quixotic challenge, he might have won. Things were so bad in Chicago that, if the election had been held in mid-January instead of late February, Daffy Duck might have won. And many felt Daffy Duck could have handled things better.

Don Rose, a Hyde Park liberal-radical who had taken to anti-machine political campaigning like a freelance western gun slinger, was Jane's chief political strategist. Other malcontents of the liberal persuasion, such as former *Sun-Times* man Paul McGrath, flocked to her camp. Liberals and reformers, angry blacks and Slavic ethnics voted for her in droves. Some of them proclaimed her victory the coming of the millennium. It was merely the coming of Jane's revenge against those in the machine who had tossed her out after Daley's death.

Jane Byrne is the daughter of a wealthy Inland Steel Company executive. Her residence during the campaign was a luxury high rise not far from the lakefront, in fact, the same one where Heather Morgan Bilandic used to live before she married Michael Bilandic and moved to a two-flat in Bridgeport. But Jane campaigned as the quintessence of Bridgeport—and every other working-class Chicago neighborhood—right down to her trademark blue and not-at-all-Republican cloth coat.

After her election night truimph, she threw away the coat and spent four hours at Elizabeth Arden's. And she telephoned Alderman Vito Marzullo, reigning warlord of the West Side and dean of the City Council, to ask for regular organization support. That was about all the asking she had to do. In the days following the primary, party regulars from all quarters publicly declared their support. Privately, they chatted with Jane about interesting matters like patronage, the lifeblood of the organization, and they seemed pleased with the chats.

Those who had harshly denounced Jane as a dangerous nuisance were falling all over themselves to appear loving. Ed Quigley, city sewer boss and warlord of the wine-soaked and derelict-strewn precincts to the west of the Loop, at first announced he didn't need Jane Byrne and was quitting. A few days later, after Byrne explained it was going to be business as usual for the Democrats, Quigley proclaimed: "I love her!"

Party chairman George Dunne made the surrender complete by organizing a traditional party endorsement session of the Democratic committeemen, each of whom dutifully professed their loyalty to Jane, as knights did to kings in the Middle Ages. Those whose wards had been for her instead of Bilandic in the primary promised an even greater majority in the general election. Those whose wards had carried for Bilandic insisted they could and would shift their votes.

Ed Quigley had been one of the latter. He used Dunne's endorsement session to serve notice to the world that the organization was far from dead, especially in such strongholds as his. "The Twenty-seventh Ward will keep winning," he said. "Skid Row has always delivered and always will deliver."

It was the kind of political oratory to rank with the immortal line of the late Alderman Paddy Bauler, who ran the 43rd Ward from a table in his Near North Side saloon and toasted Daley's first primary victory in 1955, saying: "Chicago ain't ready for reform." He also said: "Daley's the dog with the big nuts, now that we've got him elected," but somehow that didn't catch on quite so well.

In April in the general election, the machine carried Byrne to an easy victory over Republican Wallace Johnson. Or was it Howard Johnson? Or was it Ramada Inn? Actually, the machine hadn't really failed in the February primary. The regulars turned out 400,000 votes for Bilandic, which in normal times would have been enough to win any mayoral contest in a party primary. But hordes of snow-crazed unhappy voters, who otherwise would have stayed at home, came out to give one to Jane—and stick one to Bilandic—enough to give her an 18,000-vote victory margin. No one foresaw that 800,000 ballots would be cast, the largest mayoral primary turnout in forty years.

For which Bilandic may take the credit, and the blame. Two blizzards struck the city within a month. They were considered acts of God. But Bilandic gave God some help. At the height of the snow and chaos—which some likened to that of the Russian Revolution—Bilandic went on television to announce that school parking lots throughout the city had been cleared as repositories for automobiles freed from the snowdrifts. Four days later, most of these school lots hadn't even been plowed yet. Many cars simply disappeared, to be found after the thaw piled one atop another in obscure locations.

The *Chicago Tribune* revealed that a former deputy mayor and City Hall crony, Ken Sain, had been paid ninety thousand dollars to prepare a report on how to remove snow—a report that wasn't completed until late February and read like something that could have been prepared for one hundred dollars.

When O'Hare Airport was shut down, stranding thousands and thousands of people and disrupting air travel throughout the country, Bilandic's only comment was that the airport had won the award for snow removal the previous year.

The blizzards were followed by bitter plunges in temperature that combined with ice to utterly cripple public transportation. When a lack of equipment compelled the Chicago Transit Authority to reduce rapid transit service, the CTA acted idiotically. It curtailed service in West and South Side black neighborhoods, converting some trains to suburban expresses filled with white folks that zoomed through the ghetto as black people stood freezing on platforms. All Bilandic could say was that he hadn't known about the CTA decision. Mayor Daley had known about everything.

What it came down to, as *Sun-Times* columnist Mike Royko explained to the nation after Jane's primary upset, was that Bilandic wasn't Daley. Once he had perceived the potential political disaster brewing in all that swirling snow, Daley would have had everyone from ward committeemen to National Guardsmen to State legislators out with shovels. Bilandic tried to pretend nothing was amiss until it was all over.

The crowning and crushing irony was primary election day itself. After fifty-eight days of the worst winter weather imaginable, primary day dawned bright, warm, and sunny—a wonderful opportunity for the huddled, angry masses yearning to break free of their homes and run down to the polls to send Bilandic a message.

And in April those same masses came back to tell everyone that it wasn't the machine they wanted out; it was simply Bilandic. That was Jane Byrne's message. After it was delivered, the machine was back humming along as usual, however extraordinary it might seem to have a woman at its controls.

The machine lives on, surviving and thriving long after its predecessors, imitators, and rivals in other cities have been compelled to make room for actual democracy. The Chicago that Jane Byrne is attempting to rule is not far different from the Chicago of the pre-World War I gravy days of Bathhouse John Coughlin and Hinky Dink Kenna, who then dominated the political stage

and City Council as co-possessors of the 1st Ward aldermanic
fiefdom which then, as now, included much of the business and
nightlife sections of the city.

Bathhouse and Hinky Dink established the classic pattern of
alliances in Chicago: the political apparatus linked with the business classes linked with the laboring classes linked with the criminal
classes linked with the bureaucracy.

In their case, the classes that flourished most were those involved
with gambling and prostitution. The guest register at the Everleigh
Sisters' mansion in the South Side Levee district could have then
functioned as a precursor to *Who's Who in the Midwest*. The
public servants who profited most were the policemen who were
paid off to insure the continued prosperity of all concerned.

Coughlin and Kenna also benefited from an ethnic circumstance
that has favored Irish politicians in a manner disproportionate to
their relatively small numbers even into this decade. The Irish were
lowly immigrants like all the others, but they possessed advantages.
They were among the first immigrants. They could speak English.
And, their only ethnic rivalry was with English WASPs. They were
not a party to any of the long-standing feuds and prejudices that
had forever smoldered between Europe's other nationalities.

Recurring civic outrage has periodically led to the ouster if not
incarceration of the likes of Bathhouse and Hinky Dink, but these
spasms never altered the quid pro quo pattern of making Chicago
work. When the great national experiment of Prohibition triggered
a public cleansing throughout the country, it merely gave the pols
and hoodlums greater opportunities in Chicago.

William "Big Bill" Thompson was Chicago's last Republican
mayor, and he served in the Roaring Twenties, when the city was
infested with Al Capone & Co., whose biggest overhead expendi-
tures were payoffs to politicians and cops. While other political
leaders were building formidable party organizations, Thompson
was content to put up some bridges over the Chicago River and let
the thugs run the city. The most sensible thing he did politically
was warn police officials not to "fan the mattresses" or otherwise
harass black voters in search of illicit hootch. Thompson is best
remembered today for his zany threat to punch England's King
George in the nose if he dared visit Chicago.

The present-day Democratic machine was put together at about
the same time that Al Capone's boys were inventing the one-way

ride and other American traditions. In those days, the Democrats comprised such neighborhood ethnic groups as the Irish, Germans, Polish, Bohemians, and Italians. Their ideas of political unity didn't progress much beyond getting their kind together to bust the heads of the other kind. This tactic has become more refined in subsequent years but has never totally disappeared.

Ironically, it may have been a Republican who gave this last great American-city political machine its biggest boost. Even more embarrassing, especially to some of the more bigoted ruling Irish Catholics, is the fact that the Republican was black. His name was William Dawson and, in the 1920's, he emerged as the major political leader on the South Side, where blacks were immigrating in large numbers to dilapidated housing abandoned by Irish and other white immigrants moving up the economic ladder.

Dawson, like most Negroes since the Civil War, was loyal to the party of Lincoln. Like most Chicago politicians of his era, he built up a political following and organization by taking control of the graft and criminal element in his section of town. He used his influence to purchase jobs that expanded his organization, and used favors to expand his power and popularity in his community. By the late 1920's, Dawson controlled a hefty supply of black votes that could be delivered on election day to any candidate he selected. He decided it would be to his best advantage to give those votes to the Democrats, who were forging a city-wide organization.

The Democrat then wielding the hammer was Anton Cermak, a former coal miner and leader of Chicago's Bohemian community, which has always been one of Chicago's smallest ethnic groups. But Cermak kept collecting IOUs and passing out promises until he had put together a coalition big enough to elect him mayor in 1931. The Democrats haven't let go of City Hall since.

Cermak might have held power long enough to become a Daleyesque legend of his own, but he had the misfortune to sit next to Franklin Roosevelt one day in Miami and a bullet intended for the President fatally wounded Cermak instead. One of the Democratic legends is that Cermak's supposed dying words were: "I'm glad it was me and not him." That ain't what they usually say in Chicago.

Although Cermak's reign was brief, his name lived on in Chicago politics—in the usual uncomplimentary fashion. His daughter married Otto Kerner, Jr., who became governor of Illinois and later the first federal appeals court judge ever convicted of a crime while in office. Kerner had the manners and speech of an English squire, but the soul of a Chicago Democrat. He saw nothing wrong with accepting as a gift great chunks of racetrack stock while governor. He was given the stock by a woman who owned racetracks, and whose business success depended largely on the decisions made by a racing board appointed by the governor.

The stock matter caught up with Kerner after he had left the governor's office for the federal bench. The Republican prosecutor who did him in, Jim Thompson, is now governor. The woman who gave Kerner the racetrack stock testified against him for Thompson under a federal grant of immunity.

After Cermak's death, the Democrats were taken over by Pat Nash, the chairman of the Democratic central committee made up of the committeemen from all the city's wards. The man Nash selected for mayor—(before Daley, it was considered gauche for the committee chairman and the mayor to be the same person)—was Ed Kelly, who came from the Near Southwest Side's Bridgeport neighborhood.

The Depression of the 1930's worked wonderfully for the machine. While Roosevelt's New Deal was appealing to ethnic groups of all origins, the unemployed and recently-arrived immigrants found that the only way to obtain housing, food, and jobs was through the local Democratic precinct captain. And all he ever asked of them was their vote. Dawson's growing black constituency became even more loyal as jobs and money in the private sector became scarce. By World War II, the Democrats were safe, fat, and sassy. They had put together a perpetual motion machine in Chicago that dispensed favors in return for votes, and so long as the voters knew where the favors were coming from, nothing changed.

After the war, a spasm of civic conscience interfered with Kelly's wishes for a fifth term. Colonel Jacob Arvey, a cagey Jewish lawyer who had built up a powerful organization on the then largely Jewish West Side, was party county chairman. It was he who controlled the patronage empire which supplied the committeemen with the jobs that in turn provided them with the heavy vote totals that gladdened Arvey's heart. He informed Kelly that it was time for a reform mayor, and picked another Bridgeporter, the silver-maned and silver-brained Martin Kennelly.

Kennelly served two terms. His tenure was marked by complaints from fuming Democrats that he was taking reform too seriously, and by a GOP comeback of sorts that saw (heavens!) Bridgeport's own 11th Ward aldermanic seat go to a Republican. This was particularly irritating to the Democratic county clerk at the time, another Bridgeport lad named Richard J. Daley.

In 1953, Daley shoved Arvey aside as party chairman. In 1955, he told Kennelly to move out of the mayor's chair. Kennelly refused, and had to be beaten by Daley in the mayoral primary. This was Daley's favorite victory.

This primary election was to usher in the machine's most glorious era, but, because of the seemingly limited appeal of the stout little stumble-tongued Irishman from Bridgeport, no one realized it at the time. His plurality in the general election against Republican liberal Robert Merriam was less than 120,000 votes, despite his control of a party vote-producing apparatus that still passed out half pints of wine and cast ballots on behalf of the deceased. No matter. Daley was in, and during the next twenty-one years the Republicans in the city would be made to vanish like the buffalo from the plains.

In a move then unprecedented in Democratic politics, Daley decided to hold onto the chairman's job while mayor—as in Russia, the head of the party serving as head of state. Daley intermingled the two positions so completely that for most of his reign he was the only one who really understood how that arrangement worked.

Indeed, of all the many books written about Daley, only Father Eugene Kennedy's *Himself* explained the true secret of Daley's power: his infinite capacity for and mastery of the boring, tedious details of party patronage and bureaucratic government. He knew all there was to know about who was what and what was where and which was which and why—and he never let anyone else know as much as he knew.

At first, Daley's absolutism bothered some of the committeemen who wanted to share in the rule of the city. But, after a while, they relaxed. Ultimately, they just sort of fell asleep, awakening only to shout "God bless Mayor Daley" on cue or to answer questions before a federal grand jury.

Wearing the twin crowns of mayor and party chairman, Daley had complete control over a City Hall payroll of more than thirty thousand jobs. There were no worries about public employee unions, as in New York, or of civil service protection, as in pristine Wisconsin. The city jobs were "temporary," and could be taken away as easily and instantly as they were awarded. They demanded little skill and little ardor, virtually nothing more than the delivery of precinct votes on election day.

After Daley's death, when almost every Democrat capable of speech eulogized him for his dedication to the city, the nation, the party, and mankind in general, crusty Matthew Bieszczat, one of the North Side warlords, stood up and set them straight. "You all ought to get down on your knees every night," he said, "and thank Mayor Daley for giving you a better life."

To truly understand Chicago politics, one must realize that, for most of its members, the Democratic Party in Chicago is simply a means of earning a living. The way to ensure a comfortable lifestyle is to ensure that the Democrats retain power. That's what those jobs are all about.

Daley always thought that the most powerful political subdivision in the city ought to be his own 11th Ward. So he gave a disproportionate number of jobs to the residents of that ward, who in turn produced Democratic vote totals there similar to the returns the Communist Party receives in Russian elections. All those 11th Ward jobs kept Daley's friends and relatives employed, and made certain that Bridgeport residents would entertain no silly ideas about moving to the suburbs and making way for black encroachment from neighborhoods just to the east. Daley would have let the Loop sink into Lake Michigan before he allowed his beloved Bridgeport to become part of the black ghetto.

There is a myth that the Democratic organization can just sit back and produce 250,000 or 300,000 straight-ticket votes for any election. It can, but not by sitting back. The wards that turn out the big votes do so because they have the most precinct workers, and the committeemen with the most jobs invariably produce the most votes. This is another of the self-perpetuating aspects of the machine.

Almost one of every ten city workers is a precinct captain, responsible for providing services and favors and producing votes in each of the city's three thousand precincts. Most wards have between sixty to seventy precincts. A committeeman with only 75 or 100 jobs can have only one or two people working each of his precincts. But a committeeman with 300 or 400 jobs can field five or six people for each precinct. The best precincts produce about 300 Democratic votes each and the best wards can produce nearly 20,000 votes. It doesn't take too many such wards to assure Chicago election victories for the machine.

Precinct captains who ring doorbells only at election time won't be successful. The organization's strength lies in long-standing familiarity between party workers and their neighbors—often a genuine friendship. On election day, the most major responsibility of the precinct captain is to make sure that those certain to cast favorable ballots turn up at the polls.

There is a definite orthodoxy to a precinct captain's work. He can demand a straight-ticket vote from anyone in his jurisdiction who has a city job, or who is related to or married to a jobholder. Policemen and firemen interested in promotion or not being assigned to Hegwisch are also good bets for a straight-ticket vote. With the occasional Republican, it's a little bit harder.

In presidential election years, the machine precinct captain's biggest responsibility is the Democratic primary. Not that he has many concerns about who is going to win the party nomination for President or U.S. Senator, both of which are relatively inconsequential positions to the machine. His first obligation is to reelect the Democratic ward committeeman who gave him his city job.

The second most important election for the machine foot soldier is the mayoralty. If El Supremo is not returned to office, the precinct captain's and the ward committeeman's jobs are in jeopardy. In the case of the Byrne election, the best captains—those who carried their precincts for Bilandic—were in the most trouble, but they had considerably less to worry about than they would have had had the mayor's office been won by a lakefront liberal or a Republican.

Aside from the musts of the ward committeeman and mayoral elections, the machine has a variety of other priorities, with much emphasis on the dull administrative city and county offices that never excite much interest in challengers to the machine. The county board presidency is important because it has control over an enormous amount of public funds and carries with it several thousand patronage jobs to boot. Machine possession of the county assessor's office is absolutely vital. The county clerk's office is in charge of the county election machinery, and the sheriff's office is a treasure of patronage. In the past, it has also supplied badges and guns to generous campaign contributors who enjoyed playing cops and robbers as part-time deputies.

The Cook County state's attorney's office is also quite important because it offers the Republican enemy opportunities to harass—if not actually indict—members of the machine, although the machine still has the advantage of controlling the county courts. What many characterized as Da Mare's effort to deliver (steal) Illinois for John F. Kennedy in 1960 was in actuality an all-out machine drive to oust Daley's old nemesis—Democrat turned Republican Ben Adamowski —from the state's attorney's office.

One reason Democrats haven't fared too well in state-wide elections in recent years is that party workers won't risk jeopardizing local offices by harassing a voter about his preference for Republicans on a higher level. In the 1978 general election, the GOP swept the offices of U.S. Senator, governor, and attorney general by wide margins, but the Chicago Democrats took all the lower offices from county board president on down.

The aldermanic elections, held in conjunction with the mayoral primary, are usually rather casual, pro forma affairs. Because Republicans only rarely run in them anymore, no one takes them seriously, even when Republicans do win an occasional seat. The last two Republican aldermen to serve in the City Council also allowed themselves to be persuaded to run for mayor. One of these poor souls has now moved out of town, the other is still trying to pay off a fifty-thousand-dollar campaign debt, and GOP holdings in the Council amount to zero. The machine's most earnest aldermanic struggles in recent years have been with liberal independent Democrats, but even these are becoming yawns.

Of Chicago's fifty aldermen, about one third are also ward committeemen, which makes them extremely powerful and extremely serious about their own reelections. Most of the other two thirds, not counting the occasional independent or Republican, are hand-picked by their ward committeemen. Chicago is peculiar in that seats in the state legislature or even the Congress are considered stepping stones up to the really important job of alderman. One poor fellow had to serve sixteen years in Congress before he made it to the City Council. A former president of the Illinois Senate turned down a sure shot at a seat in Congress so he could run for city treasurer. Another congressman keeps telling friends he hopes one day to come back and move up to a county office, maybe even assessor.

When Daley first took over the mayor's office, he insisted on personally approving any applicant for a job that paid more than five thousand dollars a year. By the time he died, inflation had raised the threshold of mayoral concern to jobs paying fifteen thousand a year or more.

The system of hiring, firing, demoting, and promoting has always been based on the party's needs to reward or punish. Some especially loyal or productive committeemen and aldermen have been given a remarkably free rein over all kinds of city jobs. Others have been tightly restricted, while still other positions have been traditionally reserved for the mayoral whim. In most part, each committeeman has had his own little fief and the mayor has tended to respect it.

A lawyer once visited Daley to present his credentials for a judicial post that had become vacant and that traditionally had been held by individuals from his ethnic background. Daley only shrugged. "You'll have to talk to Vito (Alderman Vito Marzullo)," he said. "That's Vito's judge."

Judicial vacancies and other local offices in which the Democrats are traditionally favored to win are for all practical purposes filled the way patronage jobs are—by the chief's personal fiat—and for the same reasons: party service and loyalty. Within the boundaries of the city and county, Daley's decisions in this regard were invariably pragmatic if not ingenious. For offices outside the home turf, they were sometimes disastrous.

But Daley's slate-making was always good show business. For endless days the would-be candidates would go before the party poobahs and, behind closed doors, profess their enduring loyalty and tell how much campaign cash they would raise. Then they'd tell the reporters clustered outside how certain they were of being selected. Then Daley would emerge with a party ticket he had decided upon months before.

It has usually worked out that Irishmen get rich plums like the assessor's office or state's attorney. The city clerk's job has become a Polish preserve. One or two seats on the Sanitary District board go to Greeks, and a few downstaters are always permitted to run for lesser state-wide offices, like secretary of state.

With a few exceptions, such as the late Paul Powell, the much-respected Alan Dixon, and Senator Adlai Stevenson, Daley's slating for state-wide office has in fact revealed an uncanny penchant for favoring the Republican cause. Maybe that's the way Daley liked it.

Republican Governors Richard Ogilvie and Jim Thompson gave Mayors Daley and Bilandic pretty much everything they wanted—including the state's first income tax and a start on the controversial Crosstown Expressway, which Jane Byrne later discarded.

Though Daley is gone, Democratic slate-making sessions are still great show biz. The 1978 session was high comedy. County Board President George Dunne, who succeeded Daley as party chairman, went to the ridiculous length of making all the proceedings public. This had the party warlords hiding their true feelings, even to the point of sitting there quietly while some character came in and harangued them for a half hour on the evils of slate-making itself, concluding by saying that he wouldn't accept the party's endorsement if they offered it to him. They didn't.

The 1978 slate-makers failed to produce a candidate for lieutenant governor because no one would volunteer for it. Daley never lacked for volunteers, even for the most suicidal missions. And Stevenson further exposed himself to party ridicule by indignantly beseeching the warlords not to run Jerome Cosentino for state treasurer because he couldn't possibly win. They ran him anyway, and, despite a Republican top-of-the-ticket landslide, he won.

The fear that was occasioned even by the mere mention of Daley's name is gone (though the mere mention of Jane Byrne's can start some nerves aquivering), but the party discipline remains. The ward dinners and political yearbook ads—dutifully attended or purchased by the patronage force that accepts such levies as employment insurance—keeps filling party coffers to the brim. One recent gala dinner for the party's county organization produced $800,000, the same neat sum the last dinner did when Daley was issuing the invitations. And, the machine is still making possible all that lucrative legal, insurance, and real-estate business that has made the dull, humdrum job of alderman so rewarding—and worth so much more than the salary.

But if the machine is still whirring and humming along without

Daley, whose hand is on the throttle? Who is running the political organization that has the most to say about the running of Chicago? Daley's rule was absolute and pervasive, influencing everything from the happiness of the commodities market to the scheduling of theatrical performances. Who now has even one tenth of that power?

Michael Bilandic sat in Daley's fifth-floor office for some two years and proved he wasn't Da Mare, even if his name had replaced Daley's on that big O'Hare Airport welcoming sign. Even Jimmy Carter's overnight visit to the Bilandic home in Bridgeport couldn't make Heather's husband a Daley. Now it's Jane Byrne's turn. But since most people call her Jane, Mrs. Byrne, or Ms. Byrne, she will have a difficult time becoming Da Mare.

Daley's longtime pal and faithful lieutenant, George Dunne, has been wearing Daley's other crown as chairman of the party, but it no longer has the same glitter. In fact, during the brief Bilandic era, when gray eminences like Donovan and Bedore were running the show, Dunne seemed in a relaxed state of semiretirement. Byrne used him skillfully after her primary victory to enlist the support of the party regulars. She has promised to restore the patronage powers taken from Dunne by the Donovan clique, which would mean a Byrne-Dunne throwback to the Kelly-Nash days of shared rule.

Although her primary victory showed Byrne to have a greater public acceptance than Bilandic ever enjoyed, she still faces a constant threat from the many factions who publicly came to her support but privately are counting the days until the 1983 mayoral election. These include some of the greediest sharks in the City Council, restless blacks, a number of hungry and powerful Irish cliques, the usual chorus of lakefront liberals, assorted drooling lone wolves, and one or more of the powerful congressmen whose Washington offices somehow seem to face toward Chicago.

As Bilandic discovered, anyone trying to succeed Mayor Richard J. Daley faces an obstacle placed there by Daley himself. In television commentator Len O'Connor's book *Requiem*, former Secretary of State Michael Howlett explained it exactly.

"With Daley," he said, "everybody else was Number Three and he was Number One."

Who was No. 2?

"Nobody," Howlett said. "That was Daley's edge."

CHICAGO'S TOP FIFTEEN DEMOCRATS

1. Nobody (as he wished it, Da Mare has not yet been replaced). His ghost has the "edge."

2. Mayor Jane Byrne

On St. Patrick's Day, 1978, Jane Margaret Burke Byrne and Jay McMullen were married. To many in the Chicago establishment, it was a marriage of losers. An Irish socialite widow who broke into Chicago politics as a fervent supporter of the late John F. Kennedy, Jane Byrne had been stripped of her party rank immediately following Daley's death and fired from her post as city consumer commissioner for the unpardonable machine sin of publicly accusing Mayor Bilandic and his friends of greasing a taxi rate-increase deal.

McMullen, an unemployed newsman with a reputation as a ladies' man, had covered City Hall for the defunct *Chicago Daily News* but was not taken aboard by the sister paper, the *Chicago Sun-Times*, when the *News* folded.

Both seemed on the permanent outs. If they watched the 1978 St. Patrick's Day parade, it was as tourists on a State Street sidewalk able to catch only glimpses of Bilandic, Dunne, and the other mighty poobahs leading the procession.

A year later, the *Sun-Times* had hired McMullen from a seniority list of laid-off *News* employees and put him to work as a real-estate writer. And Jane had become mayor of Chicago. She is the first woman mayor of Chicago and the first woman elected chief executive of one of America's great cities. She is the first North Sider to become mayor in a half century, ending forty-six years of Bridgeport City Hall rule. She is the first mayor since Republican Big Bill Thompson to win election without the endorsement of the Democratic Party.

Her ten-month campaign had little money, few volunteers, no precinct workers, and little of the traditional campaign paraphernalia such as buttons, signs, and bumper stickers. She couldn't hold big rallies because no one would come. She couldn't raise big money because even closet opponents of the Democratic regime were afraid to be labeled as traitors and punished. For campaign strategists, she had only her husband Jay and a hard-case Hyde Park liberal, Don Rose.

But she could talk about Richard J. Daley and how much she adored him. She could talk about Michael Bilandic and how much she despised him. She continued to preach that her election would restore a Daley era in Chicago. Even her radio and television commercials relied on still photographs and recordings of Daley praising Byrne.

Yet it wouldn't have meant a thing without the snowstorms, and Bilandic's arrogant, clumsy response to the problems they caused. Although more than 400,000 Chicagoans voted for Jane, few of them knew anything much about her.

She was left a widow with a baby daughter in 1958, when her husband, a Marine pilot, was killed in a jet crash at the Glenview Naval Air Station in the Chicago suburbs. She became a Kennedy zealot in the 1960's, doing anything and everything asked of her— and more.

Daley noticed this attractive, ardent young woman at several rallies and wondered why anyone so willing to work so hard for a Democratic politician wasn't a regular in his organization. After Kennedy's death, he got around to asking her why, and in an emotional meeting with her in his inner sanctum, offered her a job.

In the 1960's, there were few women other than the mayor's wife in Chicago Democratic inner circles, but the rising wave of consumerism and women's liberation prompted Daley to give Byrne the city consumer post. She also rose politically, becoming one of Daley's most shrill and strident party disciplinarians, treating the area's McGovernite Democrats in 1972 much the same way Pope Innocent III did the Albigensian heretics. Some machine Democratic pols got more abuse from her than they ever had from Republicans or lakefront liberals.

When Daley made her party "cochairman," committeemen came to resent her even more, complaining that, for all her brusque manner and sharp tongue, her only authority came from Daley's trust in her.

When Daley died in December 1976, Dunne told her that the position of cochairman no longer existed.

After that, Jane acted not merely as a woman scorned but as a rightful heir cheated out of her inheritance. She believed that Bilandic and what she called a "cabal of evil men" were usurping the power that Daley had wanted her to have, and were ruining the city Daley dearly loved.

Her taxi-deal charges provoked an avalanche of criticism, rebuttals, and scorn from the regulars, but the fact that Bilandic did agree to submit to a lie detector test and questions from a federal grand jury gave her some credibility—although nothing in the way of a criminal charge ever came of the matter.

Jane had been the staunchest of regulars, the first to leap up and applaud Daley, the first to speak and echo whatever he said, and here she was charging all her old pals with corruption and, in Bilandic's case, corruption and incompetence. People began to wonder.

But if the odd coalition of Jewish liberals, ghetto blacks, and Eastern European ethnics who helped her upset the machine thought she was going to reform Democratic politics in Chicago and sever the close ties that big business, labor, and others had with city government, they were crazy as loons. Anyone who wonders at the future of Chicago under Jane need only look back at her past. She was a staunch regular and she is still one. Her philosophy of government is to do as Daley would have done. Within days of her primary victory, she had made a public peace with practically everyone in the machine who counted and had made it clear that she was going to be a blonde Daley.

A curious irony of the election was that, despite his dragging Heather from the Gold Coast to his Bridgeport digs, Bilandic came across almost as aloof from the masses as any Lake Shore Drive baron. Yet Jane, a rich girl from the North Side who lived in a luxury high rise, seemed a symbol of the neighborhoods. Maybe Heather should have forgotten how to speak French.

Many committeemen still wonder how Jane Byrne is going to rule the city and the City Council, and whether she has the administrative skills to deal with a huge municipal budget and massive bureaucracy. Will she be as generous to public employee unions as she indicated? Will she put city money into the neighborhoods as she promised, or will she use it to keep building up downtown, the way Daley did?

As to the style with which she will govern, they have a big clue. A trademark of her campaign was her refusal to smile. She finally did on the night of her primary triumph, but that was no indication that the next four years were going to be a bundle of laughs.

3. Thomas Hynes

In Chicago politics, it doesn't necessarily follow that the man with the fewest enemies is the man with the most friends. But in the case of County Assessor Tom Hynes, it's true. A boyishly handsome man in his early forties, with curly, graying hair and those Irish blue eyes so common to successful Chicago politicians, Hynes has progressed in the period since Daley's death from a young man with potential to one of the Mighty Ones—a Mighty One with a good shot at someday becoming *The* Mighty One.

Hynes didn't get into leadership ranks through his father or uncle or because El Supremo took a shine to him, which is how so many of the others made it. Hynes did it mostly on his own, capturing a key Southwest Side committeemanship, and then a state senate seat, and then—with some help from his Springfield roommate, young State Senator Richard M. Daley—the presidency of the state senate.

A few months after that coup, the young, enigmatic Tom Tully, a close friend of Hynes and then the county assessor, startled the machine by announcing he would not seek another 'term. Before the machine sharks could get near that succulent assessor's job, Hynes made his move. He won the assessor's nomination with breathtaking ease and the general election was the merest of formalities.

Tully helped. Former Lieutenant Governor Neil Hartigan and Park District Superintendent Ed Kelly helped. Hynes didn't care who took the credit. He took the job.

Hynes was no Daniel Webster or Henry Clay in Springfield. His performance as senate president was low-key, somewhat aloof, and, most disgraceful of all, somewhat scholarly. As a politician, he has had to share some of his power in his home 19th Ward with rising talents like State Senator Jeremiah Joyce, who defeated Hynes's own choice for 19th Ward alderman in 1975 and then took over Hynes's own senate seat.

But in the nervous Byrne era, Hynes's supreme status as an important committeeman and possessor of the powerful assessor's office gives him a base that should remain constant regardless of any turmoil in the city or the party. In tranquillity, the success of his ambitions for the future is assured. Turmoil might just hasten it.

4. Ed Kelly

Park District Superintendent Ed Kelly is certain to be at the center of any power struggle during or after the Byrne administration. He is a tough political competitor—or, as some put it, ruthless and mean. He runs one of the most powerful wards on the North Side and has more patronage at his control than anyone but the mayor. Jane's failed efforts to wrest it from him was evidence of his stature. If the succession crisis that followed Daley's death hadn't been settled—by Chicago standards—so gracefully, the bald, pugnacious Kelly might well have knocked George Dunne aside as party chairman.

Despite Byrne's ascendancy and the apparent restoration of Dunne's party powers, Kelly is said to be weighing a challenge to Dunne in 1980 and is certain to be a factor in 1982, when Dunne presumably will retire. Kelly is thought of as presumptuous by some of the longer-established party princes, but he was highly respected by Daley and by the Bilandic clique, and Byrne had little but praise for him while she was rapping other Democrats.

A former boxer now in his fifties, Kelly was one of the few ward bosses Daley ever allowed to hold a big bureaucratic job. But Kelly had sagely gone after the park superintendent's post before he tried on the hat of committeeman. His ward, the Northwest Side 47th, had been one of the last big Republican wards in the city. After Kelly took over, it became anything but. It was the only North Side ward that carried for Bilandic. If Kelly succeeds in winning the party chairmanship, he would be the most likely regular to challenge Byrne in 1983, and that's the main reason she wants to shrink his political empire.

5. George Dunne

Gentlemanly George Dunne, now past the usual retirement age of sixty-five, ranks in the party hierarchy where he always has—close to the top. Since he succeeded Daley as party chairman, Dunne has revealed something about himself that had not been suspected previously. He is a kindly, considerate man.

During Bilandic's tenure, Dunne was stripped of his power. He showed no interest in the infighting required to become and stay

No. 1. Many of his friends and allies were disappointed when Dunne refused to challenge Bilandic for the mayor's office, a fight he would probably have won.

Some assumed that Dunne was just biding his time. With the party chairmanship and the mayor's office divided between two individuals for the first time in twenty-one years, the boys thrilled to the prospect of intrigue and backroom wheeling and dealing, nights of the long knives, blood, and gore. They overestimated Dunne badly.

Dunne had decided that, with Daley gone, democracy had somehow arrived in Cook County. He took to sending letters out to ward bosses, inquiring as to when they thought the primary election should be held, and if party secretaries should be given raises. The ward bosses were agog. One threw his letter away so quickly that his secretary thought it was a bomb. "I thought it was a test," the committeeman said. "That Dunne was trying to figure out who would be likely to challenge his power. I never got a letter from the chairman before, asking me what I thought. How did I know he was serious?"

Although Dunne was chairman at the time the regulars got trounced by Byrne, he also led the party to a big sweep of county offices in 1978. He must have been privately giggling the night the Bilandic-Donovan combine fell apart. Whether Byrne is serious about sharing power with Dunne could determine whether he will have to abandon his relaxed attitude toward party leadership for old-fashioned political hardball, and also whether predictions of his retirement are premature. For the moment, Byrne's victory and the fall of Bilandic has given this distinguished old gent, who also runs the Near North Side's "Roaring 42nd" Ward, a big transfusion.

6. Richard Daley, the Son

Shortly after his father's passing, young State Senator Richard M. Daley began doing something strange. He let his hair grow, eventually coming to resemble a sort of South Side-Irish version of Benjamin Franklin. Young Daley still hasn't started spouting wise Franklinesque aphorisms, or discovered electricity, but he has begun to speak in public, and to smile—a marked departure from his grim old self and one that has confounded his colleagues.

"Little Richie," as some of his enemies call him, is an enigma in that it is clear he has a future in Democratic politics, but no one, himself included, seems to know precisely what it will be. As committeeman of the almighty 11th Ward, Daley has a voice that counts heavily in party affairs. He was close to Bilandic and Donovan, but was one of the first to make peace with Byrne. There has always been a theory that Bilandic had been allowed to have the mayor's job only to serve as regent until the public could be persuaded to accept Daley the Younger.

Whatever changes, subtle or otherwise, Byrne attempts to make in the party, none should be detrimental to young Richard. Her loyalty to the Daley family was so devout she never once mentioned in her campaign that young Richard was an ally of Bilandic's. When asked, she excused any role he may have played by saying he was too busy in Springfield to take an active part in Bilandic's City Hall.

If the old guard survives in Chicago politics, young Daley will be a key factor in any fight over leadership because many committeemen are loyal to him if only because he is his father's son. There's been talk that he might be a candidate for party chairman.

But some party leaders are so tired of having been dominated for so long by 11th Ward dictates that they might combine to thwart any thrust for power made by the Daley kid, if they can.

Much might depend on whatever future role his mother designs for him. Eleanor "Sis" Daley has the total devotion of her sons. She remained an extremely private person during the years her husband ruled Chicago, but was obviously pleased to take a public part with the Bilandics in the Bridgeport welcome to Jimmy Carter in 1978. And she always draws the biggest ovation at party functions. If Mrs. Daley wants her oldest son to follow in his father's footsteps, it is not inconceivable that he might try.

7. Cecil Partee

The brilliant and sometimes tragic Cecil Partee is a man who has been toyed with often and frequently betrayed. But he could end up with the Number-One job in the city—on the day Chicago becomes ready for a black mayor.

Certainly the most eloquent statesman in the Chicago machine, the gifted black lawyer was elevated to the presidency of the state senate by Daley, mostly to quell a revolt among several key black legislators. At the time, this made Partee the highest ranking elected black state official in the nation.

Then, in one of his screwball slate-making moves, Daley made Partee the sacrificial goat in a forlorn race against the immensely popular Attorney General William Scott in 1976. Scott thrashes all Democrats and Partee proved no exception. His consolation prize was a $45,000-a-year job running the city's Human Services Department.

With that and his post as committeeman of the South Side 20th Ward, he remained a man of considerable influence. But Cecil became bored. When another black, City Treasurer Joseph Bertrand, fell from City Hall favor approximately two seconds after Daley's death, Partee saw a wonderful opportunity and maneuvered himself into line for the job, even though it meant forsaking the apparent gift of the late Ralph Metcalfe's seat in Congress. Partee was readily endorsed for the city treasurer's job and won it handily.

Now in his fifties, Partee has a strong political base. The fact that his ward, like so many black wards, failed to carry for Bilandic will not cause him problems in Jane Byrne's City Hall. Partee is now the one black Democratic regular with skill, visibility, and respect to be in the right place in the wings if the day comes that the Irish and Polish can no longer keep the mayor's office out of the hands of the blacks.

8. Wilson Frost

If Partee won't run, Frost probably will. Alderman Wilson Frost, a lawyer and committeeman of the South Side 34th Ward, actually came closer to sitting in the mayor's office than any black person might have dreamed. He was president pro tem of the City Council when Daley died and many thought he should automatically have been elevated to acting mayor. He tried, but Bilandic's Bridgeporters locked the doors to Daley's office and hid the keys until Frost agreed to step out of the succession struggle. In exchange, he was given the hefty post of City Council Finance Committee chairman, which Bilandic had held as alderman, and council floor leader.

That rebuff to Frost was a factor in the overwhelming black vote against Bilandic in the 1979 mayoral primary. And that vote has pushed Frost even closer to the reins of power. Jane Byrne will need him. Everyone need fear him.

9. Dan Rostenkowski

Congressman Daniel Rostenkowski, a handsome bear-sized man with a bear-sized zest for politics and power, is the fourth-ranking Democrat in the United States House. He is also the great Slavic hope of Chicago's Polish-Americans in their post-Daley drive to at last gain some political power proportionate to their numbers. After blacks, they're the largest ethnic group in the city.

Congressman Danny, as Daley used to introduce him at national conventions and other public gatherings, is committeeman of the Northwest Side 32nd Ward and sits in all the high party councils. If the blacks and ethnics learned from Jane Byrne's victory that they can join forces to take things away from the Irish, Rostenkowski would be a logical fellow for them to support as party chairman.

If Rostenkowski had chosen to abandon the Federal City after Daley's death and take his chances in Chicago, he might already be among the top five Democrats—or the top one. But the siren song of Capitol Hill can be sweet. With only a little more time and luck, Congressman Danny could be Speaker Danny. And who in Chicago ever gets to have breakfast with the President? Who in Chicago ever gets on *Meet the Press?*

Who in Chicago ever ran for reelection in one of the easiest congressional races imaginable, yet found it necessary to put billboards up all over the city, and buy a full-page ad in *Time* magazine? What's Danny running for anyway?

10. Tom Tully

More Chicago politicians have been wondering what young Tom Tully is going to do than philosophers ever contemplated the number of angels dancing on a pin. A blond bachelor now in his forties, Tully does have a sort of angelic look about him, but no one believed that his brains might be scrambled until he announced he was going to retire from the assessor's office. It was as astounding an event as would be the Ayatollah Khomeini's giving up religion.

The conventional wisdom at the time was that Tully, having

amassed a political war chest on the richer side of $500,000, was going to bypass the usual machine way of doing things and challenge Bilandic directly for mayor. But it didn't happen.

Then there was the Teddy theory. Tully has close connections with the Kennedy family and there was speculation that he might be willing to use his campaign cash and influence to help Teddy in 1980—if the need arises to help Teddy.

Other minds have assumed that Tully simply had a broader attention span than his old-fashioned mentor and predecessor in the assessor's job, P. J. "Parky" Cullerton, and just couldn't stand another minute of looking over ledgers and figures.

There are other things in life than assessments. Tully's law practice is one that should have him earning in the $300,000-a-year range before too long. And there is that U.S. Senate seat Adlai plans to give up in 1980. Or, if there is a Kennedy in his future, why not a nice cabinet job, like attorney general?

Like Teddy, Tully isn't saying what he wants, but with all that campaign cash in the drawer, he can be sure Chicago Democrats will be waiting to hear.

11. Stanley Kusper

County Clerk Stanley Kusper is Polish, handsome, articulate, bright, arrogant, and—unfortunately for him—a bit like a Reno blackjack dealer who's so good no one believes he's honest.

In two terms as county clerk, a job historically helpful in assuring Democratic victory what with all the county election machinery at its disposal, Kusper has modernized and streamlined the office and its many functions and won plaudits all the way around. Even the *Chicago Tribune*, which won the Pulitzer Prize for uncovering a vote-fraud scandal that centered around Kusper, ended up endorsing him for reelection in 1978. Kusper was the top vote-getter in his party that year.

With Jane Byrne in the mayor's office, Kusper shares with Tom Hynes the enviable ability to remain neutral in any ensuing conflict and keep options open for the future. He is not a committeeman and was not linked to any overt effort against Byrne. And there's nothing she could do to move him out of his office.

Ultimately, if Kusper could unite the frequently bickering Polish community behind him, he could make a formidable candidate for one of the really big-time jobs. He has a few in mind.

If Tom Hynes should leave the assessor's post, perhaps to try for the county board presidency or a major state office in 1982, suave Stanley would be a likely chap for assessor. If Hynes isn't interested in succeeding George Dunne as county board president, Stanley is. He'd need an awful lot of Polish votes to get it, but he'd have the help of the great Alderman Vito Marzullo, his longtime mentor and sponsor, provided Vito is still alive and well and boss of the West Side 25th Ward.

Vito is Stanley's political godfather, not because Vito is Polish, but because Stanley grew up in his ward. An immigrant from Italy, Vito is even more irrepressible than Stanley, and so quotable that he's actually lectured on civics at Harvard.

12. Neil Hartigan

Unlike his old chum Tom Hynes, Neil Hartigan has more enemies than friends among machine regulars. He also doesn't have a political job anymore, other than that of committeeman of the now somewhat squirrely 49th Ward, where he has trouble electing machine Democrats. His problems with machine colleagues trace back to the former lieutenant governor's public sycophancy of the late Mayor Daley, whom Neil had served loyally as deputy mayor and chief aide. Hartigan's enemies are also jealous. Daley is long gone and Hartigan is off in the world of banking and high finance, but they're still jealous.

Maybe it's just that Neil has too much luck.

His standing among Democrats was little affected by Jane Byrne's takeover, as he wasn't that much identified with one side or the other. His aspirations seem aimed at lofty levels few machine Democrats are ever interested in. He is near the head of the list (the rather long list) of those who covet Adlai Stevenson's seat in Washington.

The red-haired Hartigan is big, good-looking, bright, and Kennedyesque in a way that few machine creations ever are. Though the party's resident young idealist, he moved faster under Daley's approving gaze than many who felt they were ahead of him in line.

Elected lieutenant governor at thirty-three, Hartigan did a

superb job of making that office something of consequence in Illinois and making his own name well known. As a statewide vote-getter, he even now is considered second only in state-wide Democratic popularity to Secretary of State Alan Dixon, who also wants Stevenson's seat.

As the Walker regime in Springfield fell crashing into obscurity, Hartigan pulled out of politics to make some big bucks, as a senior vice-president of First National Bank of Chicago. But he must have kicked himself several times in 1978 for having declined the Democratic nomination to run against Republican Senator Charles Percy. Percy won that year, but barely, despite his having had a real unknown for an opponent. If Neil had taken up the challenge, Percy might likely be selling cameras for a living again.

13. Michael Madigan

When it was suggested a few years back that young State Representative Michael Madigan might become the Chicago machine's next Democratic floor leader in the Illinois House, the press-box boys giggled and guffawed into their beer and whiskey (which some have been known to sneak into that stately if not always well-behaved chamber).

Young Madigan appears on this list because the press-box boys were wrong.

Once regarded as a callow and sometimes surly youth, Madigan inherited the committeemanship of the Southwest Side 13th Ward from his father. As House Majority Leader, Madigan now has as much power as many previous House Speakers did because the present Speaker, the tiny and suburban William Redmond, holds the post only through the support of a fragile coalition that depends mightily on the Chicago Democrats led by Madigan.

Madigan's power was lessened somewhat by Jane Byrne's victory, in that his followers now feel less subject to the discipline of the awesome Daley years—when Chicago Democrats not only carried out Da Mare's every command but the mayor's every thought, even when they weren't sure what it was. Now, Madigan is constantly harried by defections.

However, he has become more of a power in his own right. He no longer has to accept City Hall decisions about legislative matters as holy writ. He rules a ward rich in regular Democratic votes.

He is thought of as a possible candidate for state's attorney, or for Congress, if he'd be willing to make the financial sacrifice, as a lot of young Democrats are not. Madigan may have made a serious mistake, however, by failing to sound enthusiastic about Byrne's transportation package with Gov. Thompson in June 1979. She publicly called him a "leader who didn't lead" and privately called him some other things.

In pondering his future, Madigan would do well to consult his two predecessors in the House floor-leader job: Gerald Shea and John Touhy, who both labored mightily and effectively for the Chicago machine in Springfield for years. Touhy's ultimate reward was being made state party chairman, which meant he had to call City Hall once a week to learn what was happening. Shea thought something like the state's attorney's office was in his future. It wasn't.

14. Phil Rock

Phil Rock slipped out of Chicago a few years ago, across Austin Boulevard into Oak Park, where he could become a suburban township committeeman, albeit one from a usually Republican township that would take years of hard work before he could bring in Democratic pluralities of the sort that would impress his machine colleagues.

At the same time, Rock, a former assistant state's attorney and one of the most respected members of the Illinois Senate, tried for the presidency of that body, and missed. It went instead to Tom Hynes. Among his other failings—candor, forthrightness, independence—Rock had declined to kiss the hand of young Richard when the mayor's son joined the assemblage in Springfield.

With Hynes rising to the assessorship, and Rock having made a sort of peace with young Daley, Rock was voted senate president last time on the first ballot.

Despite his independence and years on the outs, and his suburban status, Rock has the opportunity to become Chicago's chief legislative spokesman in Springfield. The Democrats have a comfortable margin of control in Rock's senate, but only a thin one-vote margin in the house.

Rock has a reputation for hard work, knowledge, legislative skill, and, as one Republican lawmaker put it: "When Rock is going to stick it to you, he comes to you and tells you very politely that he's going to stick it to you, and then he does it."

If the Democrats continue expanding into the suburbs as they have, Rock could be a point man for a full-fledged, county-wide machine. If he can manage not to step on the toes of good friends like Tom Hynes and Neil Hartigan, he could be running for governor in 1982. Illinois attorney general isn't an unlikely guess either.

15. Two Outcasts

Chicago has had its inseparable dynamic duos: Anselmi and Scalise of the Capone gang, Gallagher and Grimm of the Chicago Cubs gang, and Kelly and Nash of the Democratic machine gang. But there's been nothing quite like the City Council tag team of Alderman Edward Vrdolyak and Alderman Edward Burke—Fast Eddie and Flashy Eddie.

Inheritor of his father's alderman-committeeman post in the powerful South Side 14th Ward, Eddie Burke dresses like the machine's answer to Beau Brummel, except that Brummel was more sedate. Eddie Vrdolyak, alderman and boss of the steel-mill-district 10th Ward, is the machine's answer to Huckleberry Finn, if Huckleberry had known how to cut zoning deals.

Vrdolyak, a Croatian like Bilandic, and Burke were right at the top of the Democratic power structure, until Jane Byrne happened upon them. Scorned by both for her taxi-deal charges, Jane made them a sort of theme of her campaign, calling them "fast-buck artists" and citing them as prime examples of the "cabal of evil men."

They fought back, each carrying their wards for Bilandic in that losing cause. They spent the next three days fruitlessly searching the statute books for a way to run someone else against Jane in the general election. Then they capitulated, though far too late for their own good.

Before she was even installed as mayor, the City Council began stripping away the powers that Burke and Vrdolyak had piled on themselves in the wheeling and dealing that had initially put Bilandic on his fragile throne. No one loves a loser, especially the kind who had behaved the way the two Eddies had as winners. But, given the strange alliances and other mysteries that continue to occur in the machine, both could be back in power before their enemies have finished any gleeful cackling.

Vrdolyak, "Fast Eddie," was always the favorite in any political fight decided on guts alone. Now in his forties, he has dark, cunning eyes and is as brash and ambitious as Daley was, in the same ways that Daley was. Extremely, if curiously, rich, Vrdolyak is thought to be a trifle too ambitious and rash to attain any major office requiring election by the general public. As Thomas Jefferson might have put it, thumped heads are no substitute for democracy.

However, Vrdolyak is the sort of fellow who wins even when he loses. In 1974, when Daley appointed Tom Tully for the assessor's post, Vrdolyak did the unthinkable and ran against him in the Democratic primary. His challenge was so spirited that, even though it failed, Daley welcomed him back to the warmer parts of the fold—even to his own banquet table, where Eddie then had the temerity to mimic Daley's uniquely incomprehensible speaking style.

Vrdolyak was in so many camps during the scramble for power after Daley's demise that he might have been a spy. He didn't come out of that struggle with much, except the keys to figuring out the city budget. And, if Jane Byrne has now taken those away, he's sure to have kept an extra set.

If Vrdolyak is interested mostly in power within the party, Burke still has ambitions for high public office. After he and Vrdolyak became ringleaders of the City Council's Young Turk movement of the early 1970's, he thought of running for Congress. Next he toyed with running for state's attorney. Then, until Jane Byrne came along, he seemed content to carry on as a flamboyant machine spokesman with a gift for getting on radio and television.

The Byrne bunch has at least one good reason for trying to cut Eddie Burke down to very small size. He's just the kind of fellow to ignore organization dictates and go running for mayor on his own in 1983. He does have that strong ward base of his. And he has those baby-blue Irish eyes.

2

Repubs

There *are* Republicans in the
City of Chicago. One of them is Wallace Johnson, the surprisingly-
qualified GOP mayoral candidate who nevertheless lost to Jane
Byrne the way Republican mayoral candidates always lose, no
matter what their qualifications.

Another is former GOP chairman Timothy Sheehan, who has
lost to Democrats—and his fellow Republicans—so often and for
so long that he ought to have battle scars on his battle scars. Instead, the silver-haired and merry-eyed septuagenarian looks as
though he's undergone nothing more traumatic than a few bad
games of golf, not fifty years as a Republican leader in a city where
the dominance of the local Democratic machine has become part
of the American legend.

"The Republicans," Sheehan sighs, searching his memory all the
way back to the Roaring '20's, "haven't ever had any power in
Chicago."

Their best showing in the City Council since the Depression
was fifteen seats held during the Eisenhower years. Now, they hold
none, and are reduced to backing lakefront liberals in aldermanic
elections.

Eisenhower carried the city of Chicago in one of his elections, as did the phenomenal Bill Scott. But no one else has, not even Big Jim Thompson or Charles Percy, who have campaigned among Chicago black voters more than any Republicans in memory.

Race has been a major part of the problem. The defection of Abraham Lincoln's faithful black vote to the party of the New Deal in the 1930's was a crippling blow. The subsequent expansion of the black community in Chicago, and the consequent flight of middle-class whites to the suburbs, all but made the case terminal.

What remains of the GOP in the city are a few state representatives who get sent to Springfield under Illinois' unique and idiotic "cumulative voting" system, which assures minority party representation in every House district. There are fifty Republican ward committeemen in Chicago, but many are mopes who have to grub among Democratic leavings for patronage jobs. In the last city-wide judicial election, the Republicans didn't run any candidates.

If the Republicans are to Chicago what the Presbyterian Church is to the Vatican, they ought to be a powerhouse in the Cook County suburbs, which now have a larger real-estate tax base than the city does and probably a larger population. In fact, the Republicans have a big fat juicy issue with which to appeal to suburban home owners: taxation without representation.

The Cook County Board has home-rule powers to tax anything it pleases—even to tax according to wealth and distribute the revenue according to population, which is one way the machine might make suburbanites subsidize Chicago city services. The Democrats from Chicago have ten seats on the County Board; the suburban Republicans only six. But they might as well have none. The ten Democrats pushed through a rule requiring only nine votes to approve any budgetary or tax measure. The county suburbs are footing most of the county-government tax bill, but have absolutely no say as to how that money is to be spent or raised.

If the Republicans were ever to run someone for county office of the eloquent caliber of a Congressman Henry Hyde—who once would have run as the Republican nominee for the county-board presidency if he hadn't been elbowed out of the way by some incumbent GOP board members—they might get some mileage out of such compelling issues. But they seldom do run anyone like that, showing a marked preference for losers. The disastrously unsuccessful GOP candidate for county-board president in both 1970 and 1978 was Joe Woods, brother of Richard Nixon's secretary Rosemary and the lifelong recipient of the Sage of San Clemente's hand-me-down suits.

When the Republicans do manage to run someone decent, such as young legislative assistant Wayne Andersen, the GOP candidate for county treasurer in 1974, they never give them enough help, if any at all. Andersen, running in a political jurisdiction with a greater population than thirty-five states, was able to raise only ten thousand dollars in campaign funds. Two class Republicans, County Commissioners Mary McDonald and Joseph Tecson, did make it onto the County Board, but they had to do it largely on their own. And that's the only way they stay there.

Time is running out for the Republicans in the county suburbs, which are becoming increasingly independent and, in many areas, Democratic. Witness liberal Democratic Congressman Abner Mikva's victories in the supposedly Republican silk-stocking North Shore 10th District, and Democrat Martin Russo's hold on the once heavily Republican 3rd District.

It's not that the Republicans don't have the financial resources, or the organizational skills and talent. It's just that they tend to squander everything on a few big-name stars at the expense of the lesser lights.

A prime example of this occurred in 1976. Jim Thompson, light years ahead of his hapless Democratic opponent, Mike Howlett, raised more than $2.5 million for his gubernatorial race—a sum so excessive in that circumstance that he still had $500,000 left over at campaign's end. But in the meantime, the much respected Republican state comptroller, George Lindberg, was begging for money for television ads. To no avail. Lindberg, hopelessly outspent, lost by a narrow margin. Thompson won by more than 1.2 million votes.

The Democrat who beat Lindberg, feisty Mike Bakalis, went on to become Thompson's opponent for reelection in 1978. Bakalis didn't win, but he cut Thompson's victory margin down to a much less presidental 600,000 votes. Also in 1978, the comptroller's office again went to a Democrat, with Thompson's handpicked Republican candidate for the job losing.

If just one tenth of the enormous fortunes Thompson, Percy, and Scott lavished on their reelections in 1978 had gone to some key legislative races, Thompson might now have the comfort of a Republican General Assembly. When it came to the party versus individual ambitions, Mayor Daley always put first things first. With too many Republicans, the first thing is usually "me."

While glomming onto campaign cash with one hand, Republican leaders are also pretty adept at wielding a sharp knife with the other. After Thompson became governor, he thanked Cook County GOP Chairman Harold Tyrrell for his help, then dumped him from the chairmanship in favor of his own boy, Evanston Committeeman J. Robert Barr. Just for good measure, Thompson also dumped suburban Party Chairman Carl Hansen. Hansen in return used what clout he still had to have Thompson's close ally, the wealthy Harold Byron Smith, dumped as 12th District state central committeeman.

Thompson tried to get a beat on the Proposition 13 tax revolt sweeping the country by getting a meaningless advisory proposition, "the Thompson proposition," on the November 1978 ballot. It gave voters a chance to say they didn't like taxes, but had no binding effect on anyone. Former Governor Richard Ogilvie, ever the realist, called it silly. Thompson called Ogilvie some things, but not so publicly.

Ogilvie, considering himself the Republican eminence around Chicago, tried to swing the 1978 Republican nomination for county sheriff to his old crony Lou Kasper, who used to hire all the jail janitors or something when Ogilvie was sheriff. The suburban Republican committeemen said, "Hell, no," and instead gave the nod to a younger and sleeker Donald Mulack, a Bill Scott protégé. Ogilvie responded by putting his considerable weight behind the Democratic incumbent, Richard Elrod. Thompson did nothing much to help anyone. Mulack lost.

In the midst of this supposed drive to win an election, Thompson, Barr, and the whole gang tried unsuccessfully to dismantle the long respected if somewhat curmudgeony United Republican Fund, an independent money-raising organization that has often been the only source of campaign funds for rank-and-file GOP candidates.

Chicago does have some well-intentioned, principled, fair-minded, party-oriented Republicans around. Former URF president William Fetridge, retired State Senate President W. Russell Arrington, Joe Tecson, Mrs. McDonald, and the area's GOP congressman are some of them. But, instead of at party headquarters, you see them mostly at places like the Union League Club. Even that's not the Republican bastion it used to be. One of its newer members is a fellow named Neil Hartigan.

THE TOP TEN REPUBLICANS IN AND AROUND CHICAGO

1. Jim Thompson

Big Jim Thompson was only eleven years old when he decided he was going to be President of the United States one day. For a while, it seemed that ambition might prevent him from being reelected governor of Illinois. But he was reelected, somewhat handily, and so must be considered the ranking Republican in the state and the most important Republican in Chicago, where he still maintains an antique-filled townhouse on the Near North Side.

He certainly has been the most important Republican to the Chicago Democratic machine, which has made a successful point of getting along with Republican governors—sometimes better than with Democratic ones.

Thompson dictated the choice of Alderman Dennis Block, then the lone Republican in the City Council, as the GOP candidate to take on Michael Bilandic in the 1977 special mayoral election to fill Daley's vacancy. Thompson gave Block about twenty thousand dollars in campaign cash and promised to help him work the streets. But, on the day the governor was supposed to campaign with the young Republican, he instead rushed to City Hall to sign a Crosstown Expressway deal with Bilandic, whom he called a great guy. Block lost and moved out of town.

While campaigning for reelection in 1978, Thompson heard that the Democrats and real estate baron Arthur Rubloff were coming out with proposals for a massive rehabilitation of the North Loop. In no time at all, Thompson was appearing at a gala luncheon with Bilandic and Rubloff to announce that the state would do its part by buying up the old Sherman House Hotel and replacing it with a lovely $100-million new state office building.

And, when Jimmy Carter and his inflation fighters were lashing out at the Democratic-run Chicago City Council for voting itself an enormous pay raise, Thompson galloped to the rescue with a deal for legislative pay raises that took the heat off the aldermen in Chicago and put it on Thompson in Springfield—or, rather, in South Carolina, where he had gone to sun himself.

Thompson loves to travel in style. Though calling for an austerity "year of sacrifice" when he first took office, he found money for two new limousines. The only relief Bilandic had from public outrage during the Blizzard of '79 was provided by Thompson. The governor toured snow-stricken areas around the state, had an official disaster declared, and then took off for a vacation in sunny Palm Beach, Florida. When the public response quickly reached the level of shrieking outrage, he cut short his holiday and returned to the frozen wastes, saying typically and unhappily: "I was wrong."

He said the same thing in his second inaugural address about his role in the legislative pay-raise deal, and then compounded his error by calling a special session to make the legislators roll back their raises, which made them as mad at him as the taxpayers were.

The Democrats could do a lot worse than Thompson.

The Democrats, despite his public assertions to the contrary, are convinced that Thompson wants to run for President, which they consider a form of self-exile no sane Chicago politician would seek.

When Thompson was a crusading federal prosecutor putting important Democrats in jail and dropping hints about running for mayor, machine operatives began whispering nasty things about Big Jim. Once they found out he was fonder of Springfield and the Federal City than the Chicago political arena, they stopped whispering. Presidential candidates are no threat.

Thompson now has a wife, baby daughter, and three dogs, with whom he poses for photographs seemingly almost hourly. Despite his political clumsiness, he remains remarkably popular with Illinois voters. Many Illinois Republican professionals neither like him nor trust him, but as long as he's governor, he's their leader.

Posturing presidentially as though the 1980 Republican nomination was going to be accorded by *Time* magazine, Thompson abruptly pulled back from the competition, perhaps because he realized that the nomination was not going to come from *Time*. Some observers think he's trying to posit himself as a logical choice for Vice-President—although at six foot six he wouldn't be very logical for someone as diminutive as Howard Baker—but it's more likely he's being realistic and biding his time for a clearer Republican field in 1984.

Thompson is learning, and has demonstrated the foresight and skill to bring Illinois' chaotic finances under control and balance the budget without much consequent disruption three years in a row. Perhaps by 1984 he'll be able to show *Time* something more presidential than a wife, a baby daughter, and three dogs.

2. William J. Scott

Attorney General William Scott is indisputably the most popular but mysterious Illinois Republican in living memory.

His daily whereabouts have been questioned as much as his courage was when he declined to run against Adlai Stevenson for the U.S. Senate in 1970 and abandoned the governor's office to Thompson in 1976. Boyish, extremely handsome (he, too, has those baby-blue eyes), he has been called "the Scarlet Pimpernel" for his penchant for disappearing and then popping up when and where he's least expected. Some Republicans have complained that they only get to see Scott by chance, such as when he might leap out of a car on LaSalle Street or jump out from behind a tree one dark night in Springfield.

But wherever it is that Scott goes when he disappears, he does make one routine public appearance at least—every four years, on election night, when he invariably leads the GOP ticket.

In February of 1979, Scott made a public appearance that was not so routine. He showed up in Springfield and casually announced that he was running for the U.S. Senate in 1980, whether or not Adlai Stevenson stepped down from his seat. That startled the many Republicans who remembered that Scott could have run for that office in 1970 or 1974, or who remembered begging him to run for governor in 1976, when so many were skeptical of the neophyte Thompson. But, enigmatically and inexplicably, Scott decided that this was the time to make his move—just after his fourth election triumph for attorney general and just as the feds were mulling over the results of an investigation into his curious personal finances. A short while later, Scott was indicted.

Scott's decision to run for the Senate did nothing to improve his visibility. He's been seen very little since his announcement or indictment. His enemies speculate that the announcement was occasioned by the federal case, reasoning that a grand jury would take considerably more convincing to find something wrong with a U.S. Senator than it would with a mere state attorney general. Scott's admirers, and they are legion, rant and rave at such speculation. Some say privately that, even if the unthinkable happened and Scott were convicted for something, he could still beat any Democrat alive. Given the excellent record of the attorney general's office under Scott, they may be right.

Scott's finances came under investigation right in the middle of the 1978 campaign. A nasty divorce from his first wife led to a great deal of judicial and journalistic curiosity concerning fifty thousand dollars in cash that turned up in one of his safety deposit boxes during discussions of assets. Scott's explanation was typical of Chicago: "I used it for things like stamps and Christmas cards," he said.

Scott's Democratic opponent in 1978 yelled and screamed about the fifty grand throughout the campaign, but might as well have spent his days standing on his head in Daley Plaza reciting Chaucer instead. On election night, Scott once again led the ticket.

Now in his fifties, though he looks younger than Charles Percy, who looks twenty-five, Scott is not only popular in his own party but for some reason is probably the most popular politician with Illinois labor unions as well.

3. Charles Percy

Charles Percy was supposed to be President by now, but he barely made it back to the U.S. Senate seat he won so handily in 1966 and 1972. His supporters attribute his narrow 1978 election scrape to bad luck and the ascension of the New Right, but his detractors blame his personality. He is the kind of political fellow who seems always to be looking over your shoulder in search of television cameras as he engages you in a "sincere" discussion.

Conservatives disliked Percy for his unctuous liberalism, but while that hostility was occasionally evident in party polls and muttering in Springfield saloons, it never was at the polls, until 1978. Things like his refusal to recognize the Panama Canal treaties as a burning issue, and a really mean campaign by his Democratic challenger, Alex Seith, proved almost too much. If it wasn't for some last-minute Republican conscience, a galloping rescue by the news media, and a lot of television commercials, Illinois voters would have been treated to a political happening as phenomenal as Percy's upset victory over the saintly Paul Douglas in 1966.

If Republican conservatives really despised Percy the way they say they do, they would have tried to knock him off in a Republican primary long ago. But none of them had the courage to try, not even ERA foe Phyllis Schlafly, who worked her way through college during World War II testing machine guns in a St. Louis munitions plant. As it was, it was the Republican leadership of Du Page County, long the heart of Illinois conservatism, that did the most to save Percy, pulling out the troops in an all-out effort against Seith.

Percy told the voters he had learned his lesson and promised to listen to them more carefully in the future. He promised to fly out to California to talk to Howard Jarvis about taxes and what the American people had on their minds.

What the ambitious Percy has always had on his mind is success. A shrewd businessman from the very beginning, he reportedly cornered the University of Chicago student laundry market as an entrepreneur barely out of his teens and went on to the presidency of Bell & Howell while not much older. He got into politics doing odd jobs for Dwight Eisenhower and such and became the Republican candidate for governor in 1964 by beating Bill Scott in the primary. In the general election that year, he was beaten by Otto Kerner, and Barry Goldwater. In 1966, he took Douglas' Senate seat, largely by accenting his youth.

During the 1966 campaign, Percy's daughter, Valerie, was bludgeoned and stabbed to death one night in the Percys' lakefront mansion in Kenilworth. He is still devastated by that loss, and makes a point of communicating with the friends and relatives of victims of similar crimes without the usual Percy fanfare. Behind that glib political facade there probably lurks a genuinely caring person.

Percy does run an extremely effective Senate office as regards constituent services and his judicial appointments, after a clumsy start, have been absolutely brilliant, as those of Judges Prentice Marshal and Joel Flaum attest.

Percy's only real chance to attain his life's dream—the White House—was shattered by President Ford's ill-considered decision to become a candidate instead of a caretaker, scaring everyone else out of the 1976 field except Ronald Reagan. The near-miss of 1978 wrecked any plans Percy might have had to run in 1980, and, now over sixty and plagued with a hearing problem, he's no longer the stuff of boy wonders. Still, he's a survivor, and his fellow Republicans have learned to respect him as such.

4. Ed Derwinski

With the state party led by three self-centered me-firsters, and the Republicans in Chicago and suburbs lacking any real county-wide effective organization, much of the leadership of the local GOP has fallen to an amazing degree onto the shoulders of the Republican congressmen in the area. They may not mess much in county slate-making or squabbles among the top party hierarchy, but they keep a paternal eye if not firm grip on the political happenings in their own districts. When the high command's bickering or incompetence has the state GOP floundering in heavy seas, it's usually the Republican congressmen who bring it back to a safe and steady course.

The Cook County suburbs comprise five congressional districts and three of them are in the firm control of the GOP. Perhaps the most stable of these holdings is the south suburban 4th District of Representative Edward Derwinski, a veteran of two terms in the state legislature and ten in the Congress.

A huge, affable, neighborly sort of fellow in his early fifties, Derwinski is a former savings and loan president who still wears a crew cut and provides his son with NFL lunch boxes. He seems just another Kiwanis or Rotarian, but he's a major power on Capitol Hill, and his foreign policy opinions are valued by diplomats from all over the world.

As ranking Republican on the Post Office and Civil Service Committee, Derwinski was the man most responsible for blocking labor's attempts to abolish the Hatch Act and turn the federal working force into a huge patronage army. He was also the key man in getting President Carter's civil service reforms through Congress. These may seem irrelevant concerns in local terms, but not to the thousands of federal employees in Chicago. By blocking the Hatch Act repeal, Derwinski probably had an effect on local Democratic patronage even greater than Daley's in his twenty-one years as mayor.

A member of the House Foreign Affairs Committee, Derwinski

is an indefatigable junketeer and functions as a one-man lobby on behalf of the captive nations of Eastern Europe under Soviet domination (he must have winced for hours at pal Jerry Ford's "Poland is free" remark during the 1976 presidential debates). With so many ethnic Americans living in the Chicago area, Derwinski is one Republican no Democrat dare laugh at.

Derwinski and his wife, Pat, one of the most successful real estate saleswomen in the Washington area, have a home in Virginia as well as Flossmoor, but Ed's back in his district most every week, just like a freshman congressman trying to get reelected. "Anyone can get elected," he said. "It's getting reelected that's the real test."

5. Henry Hyde

No longer the lean basketball star of his Georgetown University days, Henry Hyde looks for all the world like a *New Yorker* magazine cartoon version of a congressman—right down to the silver mane and long cigar. He represents the west suburban 6th District, a jurisdiction comprising a wide variety of communities, ranging from upper-middle-class Park Ridge to liberal Oak Park to Al Capone's old haunt Cicero. It is a testament to Hyde's remarkable political skills that he does well in all of these places.

A lawyer, history buff, and constitutional scholar who wears conservative blue suits and a diamond pinkie ring, Hyde is equally at home in boardrooms and back rooms. With equal ease, he can recite long passages from *The Federalist* papers and the names of the best precinct captains in Cicero.

A longtime state legislator, Hyde worked his way up to the post of Illinois House majority leader, but was defeated in a nasty fight for the House speakership, in part done in by the likes of Governor Richard Ogilvie and other supposed friends. A later move toward the County Board presidency prompted another ambush. Hyde then turned to the 6th Congressional District, won a five-way Republican primary, and went on to stunningly defeat the terrifying Ed Hanrahan of Black Panther raid fame in the general election, and thus secure his seat for as long as he wants it.

Most of Hyde's old foes, including Ogilvie, are out of office now, and one was sent to the federal pen.

In the Illinois legislature, Hyde was known as its best orator and its leading spokesman for Catholic and conservative causes. He is rapidly gaining the same reputation on Capitol Hill, and could win a leadership role if his strident anti-abortion activities don't make him too controversial to consider.

Like Derwinski, Hyde has a great many Eastern European ethnics in his district. A junketeer as well, he wisely includes countries behind the Iron Curtain on his itineraries, and has been instrumental in freeing some of their inhabitants. He is friendly with a great many Democratic pols in his district, which is also smart.

6. Phil Crane

The handsomest and most conservative of Illinois' major Republican figures, former college professor Philip M. Crane is also what most of them can only dream of being—a contender for the 1980 GOP presidential nomination. His plan is to end up the fallback convention choice of the party's right wing, once it discovers that Ronald Reagan probably can't be elected. In fact, Reagan supporters are so nervous about losing the New Hampshire primary to Crane that some of them have been spreading scurrilous and unsubstantiated stories about Crane's sexual and drinking habits.

The author of *The Democrat's Dilemma: How the Liberal Left Captured the Democratic Party* and other works predicting that the last third of the century will be a conservative if not a Republican one, Crane leapt from academia into active politics by emerging the minority victor of an eleven-way North Shore Republican primary fight in 1969 to fill the vacancy left by superstar congressman Donald Rumsfeld when he went off to Washington to become the smartest man in the Nixon administration.

At the time, Crane's election was viewed as some sort of fluke, just as he was viewed as a right-wing loon. But he proved a most able and adept politician, easily winning reelection to Rumsfeld's seat in 1970 and then dancing into a wonderfully Republican new district created in the conservative northwest suburbs in the 1971 reapportionment. His victory ratios now routinely exceed 2 to 1.

Crane is somewhat unique on Capitol Hill for having an office staff comprised of so many nubile cuties (a circumstance which seems to have fired some of the nasty rumors in New Hampshire) and for having a sibling for a congressional colleague. His brother, Dan Crane, won Democrat George Shipley's seat in downstate

Illinois. Another brother keeps trying to get elected to Congress from Indiana.

If Crane does not become President, as Reagan supporters think likely, he has still established himself as more than a right-wing loonie charging at ideological windmills. His district constitutes the juiciest tax base in the Chicago area, and, as long as he remains popular there, politicians of both parties will have to be very, very nice to him.

7. Donald Rumsfeld

Don Rumsfeld, the man whom many think ran the country when Gerald Ford was President, is nearly as good-looking as Crane and, like Crane, in his forties. But unlike Crane, he is ever so much more the careful political moderate, and, he is out of political office. Today he spends his time running the once failing but (under Rumsfeld) now prosperous G. D. Searle drug company, making speeches on behalf of fellow Republicans everywhere, and staring out his north suburban window in the most thoughtful manner.

Rummy, as his pals in the Congress still refer to him, is one of the more thoughtful Republicans around, with a unique talent for leaving offices at precisely—almost scientifically—the right time. He left his North Shore congressional seat to become a presidential aide to Nixon when he was going nowhere in Congress and Nixon was the chief GOP somewhere. He became Nixon's wage-price czar when that was an important thing to be, but slipped out of the post before it became a disastrous thing to be.

As far as Watergate is concerned, there is this famous bit of dialogue from the period:

First Republican: "Donald Rumsfeld is the smartest politician in Washington."

Second Republican: "But Rumsfeld isn't in Washington. He went to Brussels as ambasador to NATO."

First Republican: "See."

After Nixon's denouement, Ford brought Rummy back to the capital as his chief of staff, in which position he was the man to see around the White House. After a while, he took on the less demanding job of secretary of defense, winning high praise for his administrative abilities and intelligent decisions. Some think that if Rummy had stayed on as Ford's White House chief of staff, Ford would have been the winner in 1976, but Rumsfeld probably knew better. He always does.

Rummy's great advantage in Illinois now is that he and everyone else knows he has what it takes to beat the Democrats out of most any state-wide office. He has only to wait—if not for Adlai to retire from the Senate in 1980, then for Jim Thompson to tire of being governor instead of President or for Charles Percy to tire of it all. Whichever way Rummy moves, it won't be in the wrong direction.

8. Richard Ogilvie

Tough, taciturn war hero Dick Ogilvie, former county sheriff, former county board president, former governor, and former head of the President Ford 1976 Illinois campaign, is now former Republican Party elder statesman.

If any Republican caused the Democrats fits and rages in the last two decades, it was Ogilvie. Instead of just fanning his own personal political flames in the Illinois GOP tradition, he spent his years in public office trying to build a Republican Party that could win something in Cook County, maybe even Chicago.

He didn't go about this by wearing T-shirts with Farrah Fawcett-Majors pictures on them or by posing for pictures with a wife, baby daughter, and three dogs. He did it the way he thought Daley would do it. He used patronage. He passed out jobs and he created opportunities for loyal supporters to become even more loyal by combining state business with private enterprise, and making sure friends were part of the enterprise. But in 1972, crippled by his courageous but impolitic sponsorship of the state's first —and badly needed—income tax, and opposed by a particularly ruthless Democrat, he was thrown out of office. And many of the votes against him were Republican protest votes.

A fatalist (Ogilvie lacks the ability to smile because of a World War II tank shell facial wound), the governor grimaced for a while, and then went off to the luxurious law offices of Isham, Lincoln, and Beale, where he began pulling in two hundred grand a year and plotting a comeback.

That could come, he thought and hoped, as a cabinet officer in

Gerald Ford's second administration, but Jimmy Carter got in the way of that. There was talk that he might be the Republican candidate for mayor after Daley's death, but he knew well the folly of that. Well, after all, some Republicans said, he didn't really have to come back. He could be their titular leader, because the new kid on the block, Jim Thompson, just didn't understand patronage and Ogilvie understood it better than practically anyone. So Ogilvie went along with that, puffing his ever-present pipe and keeping his options open.

But then Michael Bilandic named Ogilvie to head a committee —THE committee, the one to decide how Chicago could build a new downtown sports stadium, a project as holy to the Democratic machine at the time as a pyramid to a pharoah. Ogilvie puffed his pipe and accepted. Perhaps his future didn't lie with the GOP. Perhaps he wasn't so much of a Mr. Republican after all. Soon after, he denounced Thompson's tax referendum and swung his weight behind Democrat Elrod for sheriff. Who knew what Bilandic might have in mind for him? But then along came Jane Byrne.

Still, if anyone is interested in making the Republicans into a functioning party again, there's a man at Isham, Lincoln, and Beale who can give them some advice.

9. Bernie Carey

Grizzled old party pros might scoff at a list of top Republicans that included State's Attorney Bernard Carey. Others might say that, yes, Carey belongs on the list, but only to show to what a lowly state the party has fallen. In any case, Bernie Carey belongs on the list.

He is the only Republican who holds major office in Cook County and is likely to in the near future. And, if the state's attorney's office in the hands of a Republican is relatively powerless in the face of a Democratic machine-controlled county judiciary, it is still a major repository of local patronage for the GOP and one of its few farm teams for candidates for better things. After all, Jim Thompson used to work in the state's attorney's office—as a pornography expert, of all things.

Carey also has that wonderful political attribute shared by Bill Scott and Jim Thompson, but so few others: luck.

Something of a cherubic, fortyish patrol boy, Carey worked at an assortment of law enforcement tasks for Governor Ogilvie, but was frequently undercut by ambitious colleagues and overcut by more politically entrenched superiors.

As a sop to the Boy Scout vote in 1970, Carey was slated as the sacrificial GOP nominee for sheriff. Put up against Democrat Richard Elrod, the invalid "hero" of a violent encounter with radical Weathermen, Carey was given little in the way of meaningful campaign support and was expected by most to come in at the bottom of the ticket. To everyone's surprise, while the rest of the Republicans went swirling down the toilet along with Joe Woods and his Nixon hand-me-down suits, Bernie Carey nearly made it. He led the Republican ticket and came so close that his defeat was attributed by some to several thousand deceased voters on the West Side.

Carey's showing was so strong he was happily handed the nomination for state's attorney two years later, against that formidable Black Panther nemesis, Ed Hanrahan. But Hanrahan did some unpopular things, such as insulting Carey's wife on television and, also on television, harassing the editor of the *Chicago Tribune*. Also, Carey was lucky. He beat Hanrahan in a stunning upset while his one-time sponsor Ogilvie went down to stunning defeat.

Carey handily won reelection four years later.

In his 1972 campaign, Carey was helped greatly by anti-machine lakefront liberals and other independents. One of them, Independent Voters of Illinois Chairman Sheldon Gardner of Evanston, joined Carey as head of his office's civil division. Another liberal strategist, Hyde Park's celebrated Don Rose, almost got the job as Carey's Rasputin, but was hampered by newspaper accounts of his radical past.

But there was a Rasputin job, unfortunately, and it was ultimately filled by another Carey campaign advisor, Ralph Berkowitz, an aging but feisty, contentious, and abrasive old coot who was probably one of the smartest Republican minds in his day but who quickly gave Carey the image of a puppet helpless in the hands of a stronger man.

Berkowitz subsequently died, but the image of helplessness lingers on. If Carey overcomes it to win a third term, he may still be helpless, but he'll be a Republican giant.

10. Timothy Sheehan

Old Tim Sheehan really isn't very important anymore, but he is a Chicago Republican. He is the last Republican to have captured a major political office in Chicago. In 1956, he was a Republican congressman from the city's Northwest Side. In 1958, he ran for reelection, and lost, and no Republican has won anything of that much value in Chicago since.

Sheehan is also wise, from bitter experience. In 1959, the Republicans were as usual looking in corporate boardrooms, washrooms, taverns, and any other place they might hope to find someone to run for mayor. They found Sheehan, and persuaded him to take on the job in return for the promise of the GOP nomination for the U.S. Senate in 1960.

He ran for mayor, was clobbered by Daley, and, in 1960, was not run for the Senate. He continued on as Cook County Republican chairman for nearly a decade more until Ogilvie dumped him in favor of one of his own men. Sheehan sheds no tears for Ogilvie now.

Sheehan remains committeeman of the 41st Ward, a Polish, Italian, and Irish section that turns out heavy Republican votes for national and state candidates but finds Democrats delightful at the local level. As, some say, does Sheehan occasionally. In one recent aldermanic election, he opposed the Republican candidate in his own ward.

Honorable Mention: The 11th Ward's "Mr. Republican"

Some honorary space on this list should be set aside for the most illustrious Republican ever to hold office in Cook County. Originally a Democrat—indeed, this fellow was then secretary to one of the most powerful Democratic aldermen in the city—he found himself faced with a tantalizing opportunity in 1936: The local Republican candidate for the state legislature had suddenly died, leaving a vacancy on the ballot.

The 11th Ward's "Mr. Republican" seized the opportunity with glee, offering himself as a write-in candidate for the GOP vacancy in an election in which legions of Democrats turned out to give him those write-ins.

He won, this young fellow, and went down to Springfield to be sworn in as a Republican lawmaker when the new legislature took office the following year. He then asked permission to cross the aisle and be seated as a Democrat. It was granted. The fellow's name was Richard J. Daley.

3

Libs

Everyone has heard of Chicago's lakefront liberals—in the same way that everyone has heard of the winning 1945 Chicago Cubs or the champion 1963 Chicago Bears. The Chicago Libs were the end-all and be-all of chic politics and chic journalism in the Vietnam era—the rage of the "Days of Rage." They were the forces for good and reform that were going to rise up and smite the evil machine into extinction. The North Shore's Joe Matthewson, whose credentials as a political sage included service as WBBM-TV political editor and press secretary to Governor Ogilvie, as well as a run for Congress on his own, wrote a book called *Up Against Daley.*

It predicted the eventual demise of the machine at the hands of the crusading Libs. It came out just before one of Daley's record landslides, a victory in which Da Mare did extremely well in lakefront wards that were supposed to be sacred Lib turf.

The Libs' most spectacular if least expected achievement was the defeat of Michael and Heather Bilandic. Don Rose, the Libs' most effective hired political gun, was calling the shots for the Byrne campaign. Lib organizers worked up and down the lakefront. The Libs were as important a part in Jane's 18,000-vote victory as were all those angry black people. And, for a day or two after the primary,

50

they carried on with that heady exultation of theirs as though they had actually brought about some meaningful change in Chicago politics.

But all they had done was elect Jane Byrne, disciple of Saint Richard. The euphoria drained. After a while, some of the leading Libs got together and issued a warning to Jane, proclaiming they were not about to be betrayed. Jane kept on calling up ward bosses and labor leaders. The Libs might as well have proclaimed to a thunderstorm that they were not about to get wet.

They did have some glorious moments, though. One was in 1969, when young Billy Singer scored a dramatic aldermanic upset over a machine type in the then 44th Ward. It was as obscure an off-year election as one might have found in the nation at the time, but it made the network news.

Much more dramatic than that was the 1972 Democratic convention triumph that saw Singer and the Reverend Jesse Jackson leaping up and down before the network cameras in Miami when the vote came that clinched the ouster of Daley and his gang from the convention and the seating of "the Singer 59" in their place. That ecstatic moment almost had CBS's Mike Wallace jumping up and down.

Republican Bernie Carey's 1972 upset over the Black Panther Raid's Ed Hanrahan, with the ubiquitous Don Rose calling many of Carey's shots, was in large part an "independent" success, as was the late Ralph Metcalfe's repulse of machine attempts to purge him from Congress for his public denunciation of police brutality in Chicago.

And there was that string of legislative and aldermanic victories elsewhere along the lakefront. Indeed, as long as the University of Chicago remains in Hyde Park, and as long as there are private schools on the Near North Side for rich intellectuals' children, there will be some kind of liberal independent politics in Chicago.

But it hasn't been and won't be the wave of the future. The 1978 elections saw all the Libs' major legislative gains wiped out but one. By 1979, Lib elder Dick Simpson had wearied of being an alderman and Alderman Dennis Block—a Republican elected to the City Council with strong independent support—had fled the city. Though the Libs took their usual handful of City Council seats, they hold no city-wide office, no county-wide office, no state-wide office, and the one congressman they could claim as their own is

now becoming a federal judge. That congressman's district is likely
to be taken over by a Republican.

That isn't how it was supposed to work out.

Many lakefront liberals still can't figure out why their Glorious
Revolution fizzled, but to the experienced professional Chicago
cynic, some things are obvious. The most obvious is that what few
victories they did have were about all they could have reasonably
expected.

In addition to the machine's supreme organization, the Libs were
also up against bigotry. Most of the leaders and leading candidates
of the lakefront movement have been Jewish. As far as wards and
legislative districts in Hyde Park and on the Near North Side are
concerned, that was a plus. But to try to appeal to the entire city,
as Richard Friedman and Bill Singer tried in their hapless 1971 and
1975 mayoral candidacies, well, if one is looking for seething anti-
Semitism in a big city, Chicago's black and Polish communities are
a good place to start. This the vote totals for Friedman and Singer
clearly showed.

Commendably, the Libs are perhaps the only political group in
Chicago that involves itself in elections solely for the purpose of
doing good and helping the downtrodden. But the downtrodden
have seldom been interested, because the Libs don't hold any of
the offices from which good things traditionally come. A committeeman like Vito Marzullo can provide the poor with cash, clothes,
jobs, a roof, shortcuts through welfare agencies, and other civic
miracles. Less kindly ward bosses can threaten the poor with an
end to their welfare checks. What could Billy Singer provide? Free
lessons at the Old Town School of Folk Music?

Many of the supposedly trend-setting Lib victories were merely
flukes, even Singer's 1969 aldermanic win. Alderman Tommy Rosenberg was retiring from the 44th Ward to become a judge (the
best retirement program the machine has to offer). The late Eddie
Barrett, then county clerk and boss of the ward, was advised to
"run a Jew" as a replacement candidate and "spend the election
in Palm Springs." The ward was substantially Jewish.

Instead, the doddering Barrett picked a nondescript Irish-Catholic
protégé named James Gaughan (subsequently nicknamed "Going
Going Gaughan"), who made a seemingly anti-Semitic remark and
ran such a dreadful campaign that Bill Singer, with the help of
amazing endorsements from the Republican Party and the Chicago

Tribune, was able to squeak through with a victory margin of a few hundred votes.

The liberal orgasm in Miami in 1972 was viewed by some supposedly sane people as the end of the Daley machine, a view apparently shared by a number of otherwise sane network reporters. But Daley hadn't been thrown out of the Democratic Party; he had been thrown out of George McGovern's private little ideological rite. Even while sitting out the convention in his Michigan beach hideaway, Daley was able to keep the Singerites from gaining control of the Illinois delegation on the Democratic National Committee.

Another weakness of the Libs was the ease with which many of their number could become what strategist Don Rose calls "coopted"—succumbing to the machine's warm embrace.

Rose's own poker-playing friend and black hero, Fred Hubbard, waged an inspiring aldermanic campaign against the machine in a highly important South Side ward. And he won, only to be quickly wooed into the regular fold with a lucrative post running a jobs program. It wasn't, alas, lucrative enough. The onetime independent black hero ended his political career on the lam, having squandered large amounts of public money on his poker habits.

A more classic case of co-option was Adlai Stevenson III. Spurned by the machine in its slating for governor and senator in 1968, Adlai stood awhile by the tum tum tree in uffish thought, then suddenly emerged after the convention riots as the new hero of the war-protesting Libs. He was supposed to be their candidate for mayor in 1971 and lead them on to the Promised Land.

Then, in September of 1969, Adlai threw a little political rally and picnic on his father's famous Libertyville farm for several hundred of Chicago's and the nation's leading liberals. George McGovern, Harold Hughes, and Fred Harris showed up. So, to everyone's astonishment, did Da Mare. He came bursting out of the bushes, followed by a retinue including Congressman Danny, Mike Howlett, and all the others, looking like a blue-suited Robin Hood with his Merry Men.

Adlai hastily flung away his prepared speech with all its anti-machine remarks, and instead waxed tearfully on how happy all this unity would have made his late father. As the hundreds of kids with long hair stood with frozen gasps upon their faces, Adlai was instantly transformed into a regular again. And then came an eery lightning bolt of news. Everett Dirksen had just died, creating a wonderful new opportunity for some deserving Democrat.

Daley yawned, and handed the nomination to Adlai, who yawned, and won. In 1969, Adlai the liberal crusader had endorsed Singer in the 44th Ward. In 1971, as a man of the machine, he endorsed the machine candidate.

Yet another flaw of the Libs is that, for all their books and college degrees, they have been rather simpleminded. They viewed Daley not as the product of a political system, but as its creator. They saw him as evil incarnate, a super monster whose defeat was the key to all they desired.

Not only was Daley the last Democrat in Chicago they could possibly hope to beat, but, when the Good Lord finally took him to that great ward hall in the sky, the Libs found themselves without a real enemy, without a focal point, without a reason to get their juices up.

Their chief problem in everything, though, was their failure to grasp the real secret of success in Chicago politics: a capacity for boredom. As Father Kennedy explained so well in his book *Himself*, Mayor Daley built his awesome power mostly through mastery of all those tedious details of the patronage system and the bureaucracy. Government is basically dull, unpleasant work, but the machine never lacks for volunteers because it means a steady paycheck and many rewarding side benefits.

The Libs wanted political power, but they had no interest in boring government work. Don Rose once tried to put together a slate of Lib candidates for county offices to run against the machine in the Democratic primary. He couldn't get a single volunteer. As one unwilling prospect put it: "How can you change the world as county recorder of deeds?"

In the final summing, it must be said of Chicago's lakefront liberals that politics appealed to them only when it gave them an opportunity to get their jollies. An exciting crusade against the machine Evil One could turn them out by the thousands. When it comes to county recorder of deeds, they'd rather play backgammon.

The Great Liberal Tide was really nothing more than a spasm— a protest against the Vietnam War and against the conduct of Daley's police during the convention riots. It was a more meaningful and longer lasting protest than most, but it was no political revolution. After the war ended and the convention riots were forgotten, the Libs simply ran out of motivation. After all, it's not as though they have to depend on politics for their livelihood. Who but a machine precinct captain would have to do that?

THE TOP FIVE LIBS IN CHICAGO

1. Martin Oberman

The No. 1 spot on this list was to have gone to the greatest of living Chicago Libs, Congressman Abner Mikva. He single-handedly fought and bested the machine for twenty-three years, in Springfield and in the Congress, in Hyde Park and in the new territory he carved out for himself on the Republican North Shore. Though constantly battling for survival, he made it to the House Ways and Means Committee and became one of the most powerful congressmen in the Illinois delegation.

It was Ab Mikva who learned in a few minutes more about machine politics than some Libs have learned in a lifetime when, as a young University of Chicago student in 1948, he dropped by 8th Ward Regular Democratic Headquarters to volunteer for the Paul Douglas and Adlai Stevenson II campaign. He was told: "We don't want nobody nobody sent. We don't want nobody who don't want no job. And we don't want nobody from the University of Chicago."

But Ab is giving up the fight, lured from the Chicago political scene by President Carter's offer of a seat on the second highest court in the nation, the Federal Appeals Court of the District of Columbia.

So first place must go to Alderman Martin Oberman of the 43rd Ward, heir to Bill Singer's Near North Side independent fiefdom and now dean of the independents in the City Council.

A quintessential Near North Sider, who raises campaign funds with bicycle rallies in Lincoln Park, Oberman came into Chicago politics rather obscurely. The "Rosner Machine"—as some might refer to the Lincoln Park area liberals frequently led by June and Marvin Rosner—needed someone to replace Singer in the Council (he was running for mayor) and so chose this nice young Jewish lawyer. Since the 43rd was demonstrably Lib turf, they presumed their selection was equivalent to election, as has many a ward boss in the past.

But the machine wasn't about to let it go at that. It made use of two chess pieces in the 43rd Ward aldermanic primary: a former civic leader who drained votes from Oberman by calling himself "the true independent," and its principal candidate, Adrienne Levatino, an extremely attractive young woman who, at twenty-one, was a city planner and was serving as secretary of the huge Catholic Archdiocese's school board. She had excellent credentials and a quick mind—quick enough to march into the *Chicago Tribune* and secure its endorsement after reminding the editor that Colonel Robert McCormick had been a Chicago alderman at twenty-one, too. Adrienne ultimately lost, but gave Marty Oberman and the Rosner machine a real run for their money—a lot more money than the group had planned to spend on the campaign. Since then, Oberman has more than returned their investment.

Less scrappy than the camera-loving Singer, and not quite so scholarly as that other Lib hero, Professor Dick Simpson, Oberman's performance in the City Council has been more effective than either. He roots for all the Great Causes that Singer and Simpson did, but he has also worked hard at producing solutions to problems that bother not only ideologues but everyday Chicagoans, solutions so popular and workable that the machine dare not ignore them. If the proposed ordinances Oberman submits regularly vanish, they have come to reappear as quite similar measures with machine sponsorship. It's an odd way to get things done, but it gets things done.

Oberman easily won reelection to his aldermanic seat in the 1979 contest. Adrienne Levatino would not have fared nearly so well this time around.

2. Don Rose

Don Rose, the genius behind Jane Byrne's successful primary strategy, is rather like that fellow in the movie *Viva Zapata!* who wandered the hills of Mexico with his portable typewriter trying to stir up revolutionary trouble. With Rose, it's not the office that counts, and sometimes not even the candidate that counts. It's the fight.

He backed Jane Byrne. He backed Bernie Carey. He backed Fred Hubbard. As long as the opposition can be even vaguely linked to the machine, Rose will back almost anyone. And he's very, very good at his work.

A radical leftist back when that was considered dangerous and subversive and not yet cute and chic, Rose has more than two decades of anti-machine warfare under his belt. When he lets his beard get long and scraggly, he even looks like an anarchist. A newspaper photograph of Rose in this radical guise may have kept him out of an important post in the Carey administration. Neither did it help that Rose's resumé includes a listing as public relations man for the anti-war protesters who descended upon Chicago during the 1968 Democratic convention. He served in a similar capacity for the defendants in the Chicago Seven conspiracy trial. He would have looked funny at those Republican garden parties.

Editor of the *Hyde Park-Kenwood Voices,* a not-quite-so-successful Chicago version of New York's *Village Voice* now merged with the *Chicago Reader,* Rose is a frequent contributor to *The New Republic* and other thoughtful Lib journals. Rose is probably a frustrated newspaper reporter, though he wouldn't feel very comfortable in a newspaper business that now has little place for ideologues of any stripe.

Jane Byrne is said to feel a strong personal loyalty to Rose for what he did for her, but politics means dealing with reality and Jane is a good politician. She must work with the likes of Richie Daley and George Dunne, and they are not keen on working with the likes of Don Rose. Nor should he be with them.

So Don Rose's future will doubtless be much like his past, spent hanging out with the reporters and columnists at Riccardo's, while waiting for the next campaign.

3. *June and Marvin Rosner*

June and Marvin Rosner are the reigning husband and wife team of Chicago liberal independent politics. He is a wealthy obstetrician and she one of the ablest public relations operatives in the city. They are friends of such media stars as Channel Two's Walter Jacobson and the *Sun-Times'* Sidney Harris, and even of tonier folk like multimillionairess Abra (Rockefeller) Prentice Anderson. Guests at the Rosners' big house near Lincoln Park seem

always to have just returned from some exciting place like China
—though never from any place as exotic as Alderman Vrdolyak's
ward.

As far as the anti-machine movement is concerned, the Rosners
were there at the creation. June handled press for and helped
manage Singer's first aldermanic campaign in 1969, and performed
similar functions for the 1972 "Singer 59" convention crusade and
Singer's mayoral campaign. She and Marvin have been active in
or helped bankroll dozens of other Lib campaigns, especially those
involving their own 43rd Ward.

The Rosners have never given much thought to running for office themselves. Marvin once toyed with the amusing notion of
running for ward committeeman, so he could sit in on all those
back-room sessions, but politics—except in some Chicago circles
—doesn't pay quite so well as obstetrics as a full-time job.

As a ranking Lib and the crusading doctor who performed the
first legal abortion in Chicago, Marvin Rosner was considered
menace enough to be spied on by Mayor Daley's gumshoes. When
the courts ordered the spy files made public, Marvin discovered
that he had been suspected by someone of conspiring to blow up a
hot-dog stand. Ah, the ever-vigilant Daley.

The Rosners went up the shoreline to help out in Abner Mikva's
hard-fought 1978 reelection campaign. Working a precinct in posh
suburban New Trier Township, they were amazed to discover how
courteous and civil suburban people are in elections—even the opposition. None of this brick-through-the-headquarters-window business.

So, it may be that, like so many Chicago liberals, they may one
day soon follow the path made by Abner Mikva and find a nice
big old house in Evanston. It has a lakefront, too.

4. Dawn Clark Netsch

Perhaps the highest compliment that can be paid to State Senator
Dawn Clark Netsch is that she got into the Illinois legislature without the usual recourse to "cumulative voting."

This peculiar system, unique to Illinois, was invented by the
Chicago Tribune's Joseph Medill as a means of healing regional
divisions in the state immediately after the Civil War, when a
victorious and largely Republican northern Illinois was feeling

quite lordly over the pro-confederate Democrats of Southern Illinois. In this anachronistic system, each legislative district elects not one but three state representatives. Voters have a choice of casting one vote for each of three to be elected, or one and a half votes for each of only two of the candidates, or three votes for just one. The arrangement is supposed to assure that the minority party in each district receives at least one seat.

This worked fine in the post-Civil War era in terms of assuring Democrats that they would not be entirely shut out of state government—Rum, Romanism, and Rebellion notwithstanding. But its chief effect in recent years has been to give a great many candidates a chance to sneak into legislative office without winning anything like a majority of the vote. In some cases, state representatives have been elected with as little as 8 percent of the vote. The chief beneficiaries of this inequity in Chicago have been the Libs, whose supporters have happily cast three-vote "bullets" to get their man in, without a care as to whom the other two district seats go.

Mrs. Netsch never bothered with that. She ran as a delegate to the 1970 Illinois Constitutional Convention, won big, and made a name for herself as a prime mover in drawing up the new state charter. Then she parlayed that prominence into a run for the state senate from her Lincoln Park area, 43rd Ward district. As there is no "cumulative voting" in senate races, she had to take on her machine opponent, an incumbent, one-on-one. She beat the hell out of him, and then repeated the performance four years later.

A thin, angular lady lawyer, Mrs. Netsch is the wife of famous architect Walter Netsch. Something of a power now, with her seniority in the state senate, she is regarded as the Queen Bee of the lakefront liberals—by some, as the Catherine the Great of the lakefront liberals, for at times she can be ever so testy. She made some Libs unhappy by getting rather cozy with the Dan Walker administration in Springfield, when that was no longer a nice thing for a good Lib to do. But now, Walker's gone, and Dawn's still there.

5. Bill Singer

Bill Singer burst into Chicago politics and national fame in 1969 as the scrappy kid lawyer who tweaked Daley's nose by wresting an aldermanic seat from the machine, and who kept tweaking it in the City Council.

A decade later, Singer is not so scrappy. He holds no political office. He's divorced from his wife. He owes untold (but doubtless well counted) thousands from his failed, $1 million mayoral campaign. But if there is anyone who could still put it together for the Libs in Chicago, for any great new cause, it's the little guy with the stubby hands, squeaky voice, and electric hair.

Singer is the only independent name in the city that could still get all those housewives and college kids out onto the street corners and El stops again. He knows where the available Lib votes are and where the money is—or at least, where it's owed. He's the only Lib with any city-wide name recognition.

Despite Singer's constant City Council harassment of Daley, and his humiliation of the mayor at Miami, some of Billy's supporters at times wondered whether, if Daley had thrown his arms around Billy the way he did Adlai, Billy might only have blushed and beamed. And talked about the joys of unity, especially if such joys included a congressional seat or something.

But no one ever proved this heresy. Daley never did give Billy anything nice, and, now that Daley is dead, Singer is viewed by the machine boys as an anachronism. He was Daley's problem, not theirs.

Of course, if Congressman Sidney Yates should one soon day retire, leaving a vacancy in that nice North Side lakefront district . . . well, there are always things for out-of-office politicians to dream about, and there is the 1980 Senate race.

To pay off his debts, Singer was compelled to sell his big rambling house in the Indiana Dunes. The buyer was an old friend, Wayne Whalen, the lawyer who masterminded the legal work behind the Singer 59 credentials challenge in 1972 and the subsequent triumph when the case was later taken up by the United States Supreme Court. Whalen is also the husband of Dr. Paula Wolf, a top aide to Gov. Thompson.

In recent years, Whalen has abandoned political activism to become a six-figure-income partner in the giant law firm of Mayer, Brown, and Platt. He is one of the best bond lawyers in Chicago. Every so often, he and Singer still meet, frequently on the beach down the bluff from Singer's old house in the Dunes. They make a strange pair—the prosperous lawyer well on the way to becoming a really big figure in the Chicago establishment, and the graying, aging boy wonder turned political has-been.

A good indication of the state of the independent movement in Chicago would be whether they talk about politics, or bonds. It's probably bonds.

4

Mob

Finding out who's really who in the Chicago crime syndicate isn't easy. Chicago gangsters tend to keep a low profile—so low that the only time you ever seem to see them is when they're lying on the ground. About 1,050 unlucky thugs—and one unlucky horse—have gone public in this way since 1919, when the Chicago Crime Commission began keeping its gangster body count.

Publicity can be hazardous to the modern mobster's health. Probably the most precarious predicament for a contemporary gangster is to face a federal investigation. This raises the unpleasant possibility that he might start talking to save his own skin. An impending trial, whatever its possible outcome, usually spells impending doom. Even without a conviction, the notoriety that goes along with any trial often compels a mobster to take his much-photographed face out of town.

Consider Harry Aleman, a man ruined by publicity. Until last year, when Aleman was convicted of running a burglary ring, Harry had quite a solid reputation: he was widely believed to be one of Chicago's top enforcers. He was in a position that commands respect. When people like the late Richard Cain, the sheriff's investigator turned crook (or was it crook turned sheriff's investigator?); Bill Logan, the Teamster Union steward who balked about cooperating with the mob in cartage thefts, and Orion Williams, a mere thief who made himself a bit too visible in 1974 when he stole 36,000 pounds of beef from a railroad boxcar, went to their sudden rewards, it was wondered if Aleman might know something about it.

Aleman was happiest when unknown. The only marks against him were the "F" he earned in Civics at Crane High School and a 1971 fine of $450 levied against him, plus three years' probation, for lying on an application for a home mortgage.

Then Aleman got known. In 1977, he was tried and acquitted for the Billy Logan killing (in Chicago, it's not at all unusual for accused hit men to be acquitted—in part because hit men look so innocent without their ski masks on). Acquitted or not, Aleman wasn't lucky. A mob figure's unknown face is his fortune, after all, and Aleman's swarthy good looks had been glaring out of front page photographs throughout his trial.

Things really went bad for Aleman in 1978. That's when the activities of a West Side Club he belonged to, called the Survivors' Social and Athletic Club, came to light: besides socializing and surviving, club members allegedly planned group robbery and burglary outings in Indiana and Illinois.

Before Aleman was convicted of masterminding the operation, defense attorney Ray Smith tried to explain to the jury what a blow civilization would suffer if Aleman were sentenced simply because of a bad reputation. "It's the decision to start making exceptions that provides the crack in the judicial system that could lead to McCarthyism or to the Spanish Inquisition," Smith said, sounding like he was applying for the job of politician's speechwriter. Smith played up Aleman's stellar qualities: "Aleman has a loving family. He's been dedicated to his family. He's raised four kids. And he works as a driver for the *Illinois Sporting News*." Despite Aleman's glowing character references, the judge gave him thirty years. And because the trial brought a lot of unwelcome attention to the mob, it may want to contact Aleman before his time is up. As one state investigator put it: "Aleman has brought a lot of heat to the mob and they don't like that."

Perhaps because gangsters disappear so often (or make others disappear), some Chicagoans don't even believe the mob exists. For example, Ken Sain, aide to former Mayor Bilandic, was once overheard talking to a group of visitors from Arkansas who were touring City Hall; Sain assured them that Chicago has no crime syndicate.

More indiscreet types, less concerned with the city's image, see the mob everywhere, but no one is ever able to say precisely what's going on in it. It's amazing how often police are stumped by mob crimes. They're great at coming onto the scene, observing the well-dressed bodies stuffed into car trunks or sprawled in front of suburban carports, and speculating that the murder may have been a "gangland-style slaying." But that's about as far as investigators' deductive powers seem to go in these cases. Mostly, police wax fatalistic at the scene of gangland murders, as when the bullet-ridden body of restaurateur John Lourgos was found, and Deputy Police Superintendent John Townsend explained: "Somebody obviously wanted this guy dead."

Mob watchers depend a great deal on corporeal evidence (the bodies of discarded gangsters) to keep track of the Outfit's internal politics. This method at least allows them to speculate on who's currently out of favor. These killings still occur with great regularity, but in recent years, there's been a dull sameness to them. The mob seems to have lost its panache. It's no longer entertaining.

Chicago's old-time gangsters were a fun crowd. "Machine Gun Jack" McGurn, the chief choreographer of the St. Valentine's Day Massacre, was a walking riot. He made federal agents wait in the clubhouse until he had finished his play in the 1927 Western Open.

North Side gang leader (and florist) Dion O'Banion was once caught in the act of blowing open a safe. He simply flashed a pilfered press card at the police and explained he was covering the explosion as a reporter.

Louis Alterie, one of O'Banion's sidekicks, had a pal named Nails Morton who was a horse lover. While riding in Lincoln Park one day, Nails was thrown by the horse he had rented and fatally injured. After Nails died, Alterie went to the stables, rented the steed in question, rode it out into Lincoln Park, and shot it through the head. Later, he called the stable owner and said: "We taught that goddamned horse of yours a lesson."

The last gangster who tried to be fun was the late Sam DeStefano. What with trials for one torture murder or another, Sam was almost constantly appearing in court during the 1960's and early 1970's. He always tried to liven up the proceedings. Little things, like being carried into court on a stretcher, or haranguing courtroom crowds through a bullhorn, or ribbing witnesses with jibes, like those he once playfully tossed to government informant Fred Ackerman: "I'll put you in a sewer. I'll put out your eyeballs. I'll put icepicks in you."

Now we have thugs like "Blind Louie" Cavallaro scaring "juice loan" collectors and debtors with unimaginative threats. Cavallaro is reputed to be one of the mob's most important juice entrepreneurs. A juice loan employee (sometimes called a "shark") is a helpful type who lends money at exorbitant interest rates to people who need it fast, or can't get bank or lending company loans. "Juice" is so called because it puts the squeeze on people who are late making payments—juice collectors don't write nasty letters but break people's arms and legs to encourage prompt payment.

Fourteen years ago, Cavallaro lost his sight to diabetes. He was convicted of extortion in 1978 for threatening to cripple and blind John Clemente, a juice collector who owed Cavallaro $18,000. Cavallaro first advised Clemente that it was foolhardy of him to walk into Rush Street clubs (Cavallaro frequents Rush Street clubs) without "someone standing behind you." Then Cavallaro placed some disheartening phone calls to Clemente. One taped phone call went on in this vein: "I will have your tongue. That's all I want is your tongue, and maybe your eyes and I'll teach you how to walk like a blind man."

Cavallaro also admitted that he wanted to wear Clemente's teeth around his neck. While all this glib patter is part of any self-respecting loan shark's job, Cavallaro's "eye for an eye" policy makes mob watchers long for the days when gangsters were more subtle—when they'd show contempt with a kiss, or fold a slain enemy's hand around a nickel.

The present reputed ruling triumvirate of the Outfit: Tony Accardo, Jackie Cerone, and Gus Alex, are all elderly gents, low-profile, and mostly out of town. They're not fun. The best tough-guy talk you hear these days is done by Chicago mob investigators, who sometimes get a little carried away with their subject. The real mobsters now speak only through their lawyers.

Today's mob lacks class. Capone's syphilis was classy; Accardo's duodenal ulcer isn't. O'Banion's flower shop was classy; Tony Spilotro's Las Vegas boutique isn't. Old-time gangsters used get-away cars in hits. Now hit men sometimes use Chicago Transit Authority buses to travel to and from appointments. Gangsters used to be dumped across state lines with interesting, symbolic objects pinned on them—a comic valentine, maybe, or some money "to buy flowers." Now they're disposed of in Hefty Bags.

In the old days, there used to be public shoot-outs, cavalcades of touring cars firing Tommy guns. Now it's ski-masked men waiting in the victim's garage, or the back seat of his car. Or it's getting hit for tax evasion. Or being called before a federal grand jury and then getting hit. No wonder the late Sam Giancana hung a mat outside his door that said: "Go Away."

Another reason mobsters are less visible these days is their heavy involvement in legitimate business, semi-legitimate scams, and labor unions. To a large extent, corporate power plays and money manipulation have taken the place of a lot of old-time muscle. Peter Vaira, U.S. attorney for the eastern district of Pennsylvania and former head of the Justice Dept's organized crime strike force in Chicago, sees the new corporate mob largely as a product of the mob's success during the Depression. "In the thirties, gangsters were the only people who had a lot of money to play with and invest," Vaira said. "And a lot of bums ended up in legitimate business and the labor unions, and have been there ever since."

Their legitimate business interests haven't made gangsters give up all the old traditions, however, especially in the field of employee relations. John Dineen, president of the Federated Order of Police and a long-time mob investigator, says that the Outfit won't tolerate slipshod work: "They don't fire you. Nobody gets fired. If you don't do your job, they terminate you."

There still is a "gangland style" of murder. Ordinary killers seldom come up to the professionalism of a gangland slaying: the symbolism of bullet placement (informants get it in the throat; mobsters who take on both cop and robber roles get their two faces blown away), the ingenuity of body disposal (suburbs turn up scores of slain mobsters because the Outfit figures the suburban cops won't know what to do with them), and the invariable neatness of it all.

A suburban girl named Patricia Columbo and her boyfriend, Frank DeLuca, were convicted not long ago of murdering her parents and thirteen-year-old brother. The murder was set up to look like a mob hit. Patricia even "remembered" her father being in some trouble with mob types. But investigators instantly spotted

Patricia Columbo's ruse. Hit men don't add gratuitous gestures like rape and the repeated stabbing of bodies.

When James "Jimmy the Bomber" Catuara, scion of the stolen auto parts fencing empire, was fired last year by having a gun fired twice at his head, once at his neck, and once at the middle of his back, police knew it was a gangland job because nothing had been taken from Catuara except his life. Then Homicide Commander and now Acting Police Superintendent Joseph DiLeonardi pointed to Catuara's diamond ring and his wallet containing several hundred dollars as evidence that the mob got Catuara.

"Gangland murders are done by pros," says prosecutor Vaira, "There are no eyewitnesses, and nobody talks. Whereas in a regular murder, the guy's not a pro; he's a bungler. He leaves a trail a mile wide. But with a professional job, if somebody talks, he gets blown away. And that's why we have problems solving hits." Of those 1,050 and some gangland murders recorded since 1919, only four produced convictions.

The mob is organized largely along geographical lines in the Chicago area, a trait inherited from the territorially-minded Capone. Instead of carving up the city according to individual rackets, or vices, or even families, as other cities' gangsters have done, Chicago mobsters live by the wisdom that vice in Chicago knows no bounds. Therefore, the city has been parceled into North, South, and West (the Lake reserved for general body disposal), with each mob chieftain overseeing all the action on his individual turf.

The big mob money-makers are gambling and juice loans. The two rackets are intimately connected because, according to former U.S. Attorney Sam Skinner, "most people into juice are gamblers who got in over their heads."

Or else they're citizens who would feel embarrassed asking for a bank loan. As Jack Hawkonsen, vice investigator and head of the Confederated Order of Police, says: "Burglars can't go into a bank and say, 'We're four stickup guys. We need a loan because we're going to stick up a bank.'"

People harbor a lot of misconceptions about juice. For one thing, juice collectors don't prowl about Chicago, seeking the ruin of small debtors. According to Hawkonsen, "They don't seek out anybody. You look for them, and that's why they expect you to pay. They figure you came to them; you went through a lot of changes and a lot of routes to get to them. You knew what the deal was when you came in." Also, juice murders are rare. Loan sharks prefer breaking arms and legs to trying to collect money from a corpse.

Another big racket is the chop-shop operation, in which luxury cars are stolen, taken apart, and resold as separate, untraceable parts. It's a growth industry. Proof of its importance lies in the mounting number of gangland slayings connected with its rise.

Mobsters have also carved out a piece of the catering business. Major catering wars have been fought in Chicago since 1974, aimed chiefly at control of industrial catering. The tactics are blunt. Theresa Schaffer, the owner of the independent Thunderbird Catering Company, got a phone call shortly after her manager, Richard Crofton, had been slain. "How did you like the killing?" an unpleasant voice asked. "You're next."

The mob is also interested in film and literature. Many of Chicago's pornographic bookstore owners and sex film distributors pay protection money (usually around 50 percent of their profits) to the Outfit. Or else.

Just like the old days, cops and robbers in Chicago is a game where the players sometimes switch sides. The most notorious cop-turned-robber was Richard Cain. Cain did what everyone thought was an impressive job in the 1960's as chief investigator for then Cook County Sheriff Richard Ogilvie. He went on to do an even more impressive job for Sam Giancana. Cain's two faces got blown away in Rose's Sandwich Shop on Grand Avenue in 1973.

Another (temporarily) successful two-sider was Mark Thanasouras, the former Austin District police commander who was convicted in 1974 for shaking down West Side tavern owners for bribes. Thanasouras had his sentence reduced by testifying against other cop shakedown artists. He was slain in 1977. Mob watchers theorize that his complicated professional life made him unpopular. One federal investigator said: "He just had a propensity to pick up enemies because he burned people rather often. He was always getting involved in unsavory transactions."

Labor unions have always gotten mob attention. Unions can provide real position strength to mobsters, and this clout can be used to generate money and add muscle. Some union rolls are heavily seasoned with relatives of former or current mob figures who have been assigned part of the family trade.

The Chicago Outfit has shied away from narcotics trafficking until just recently, although not because of moral scruples. It was simply that the Mexican community had the monopoly. But now mob heavy Jackie "The Lackey" Cerone seems to have had his consciousness raised by the example of Sam Giancana, who wrested control of the "policy" or numbers racket from the blacks in the 1950's. It's reported that a Chicago mob negotiator has been making regular treks to New York to consult with the New York boys about whether some sort of drug alliance can be worked out. Now that narcotics is a proven money-maker, the Mexicans can probably be persuaded to move over.

The Outfit's organizational structure follows sound business practices. Prosecutor Vaira once summed up the new mob: "The old days of the Mustache Petes and the guys blowing up cars are over. Gangsters' m.o.'s are different now. They're using their money in different areas and getting their power by going into legitimate businesses, or by taking over legitimate businesses. They're into everything where there's money."

It's hard to rise within the mob. The most even-handed description of how thugs can get ahead was given to *Chicago Tribune* columnist Bob Wiedrich by hit man turned government informant Chuckie Crimaldi: "After you go on a few beatings with them, abuse a few people and so forth, they figure, well, we don't have to worry about this guy. He can do the job."

Staying in the mob is tough. Getting out is tougher. Few people ever renounce syndicate membership—either because the life appeals to them or simply because life appeals to them.

One old time mobster who survived voluntary retirement became a Republican ward committeeman, a job which keeps one out of the limelight.

He first became associated with the Outfit as a teenager when he got a job chauffeuring Al Capone's mother around on weekends. He left the mob and went into the more seemly work of politics after he received a revelation in a Missouri prison. Says he: "I realized that God was more powerful than the mob."

The mob hasn't recruited since 1967. Except for some low echelon jobs—numbers runners, bartenders, pizza carriers—the ranks have been closed because insiders sense that newcomers could turn out to be interested federal investigators. The present mob hierarchy is a closed shop, troubled by the infighting such a setup breeds.

There's a particularly lingering and vicious fight going on now, rivalling the feud between Capone and the O'Banion-Bugs Moran gang that culminated in the St. Valentine's Day Massacre.

The present-day fight was, in a way, started by Capone, who established a dynastic line of hand-picked lieutenants. The present reputed top dogs: Tony Accardo, Gus Alex, and mob "consultant" Joey Aiuppa, were all associated with the Capone-era mob. They were also close to the late Sam Giancana. They are considered the mob establishment, guys who knew their place in the structure and waited for the nod to move up.

On the other side are the impatient Young Turks, or, if you will, Young Italians, composed of followers of the late James "Turk" Torello and the very lively Tony Spilotro. The Young Turks want more pay and more say within the Outfit. Since there isn't a gangsters' union, some of them create job vacancies by picking off establishment thugs.

Since Richard Cain was killed on December 20, 1973, some twenty mobsters of consequence have been hit in the crossfire between the old guard and the Young Turks. The four biggest shockers were the slayings of Sam Giancana and Ned Bakes in 1975, Charles Nicoletti in 1977, and Jimmy "The Bomber" Catuara in 1978.

Giancana, then the mob's operating director, was somewhat out-of-touch with things after his long, enforced holiday in Mexico, and he was due for testimony before a federal grand jury concerning possible mob involvement with the CIA. He could have been hit by anybody for any number of reasons. In the mob, there's always a conspiracy theory.

Ned Bakes was an aging Capone-era hoodlum who used to be an important liaison between the high command and the mob's lowlifes. But Bakes hung out with an unpopular mob terrorist, served a stint in prison for extortion, and afterwards never regained his old status.

Investigators are unsure what side to tally Nicoletti's killing on. He rose from the ranks of Prohibition-era triggermen to become the Establishment mob's chief enforcer. Nicoletti had a good head for business and owned, with the late Mario DeStefano, what must have been a thriving manufacturing concern that specialized in concrete burial vault liners. Catuara's slaying has been linked to changing times—he refused to take orders from the Young Turks and declined mandatory retirement.

This continuing bloodbath has thinned mob ranks somewhat.

What we're left with are some extremely powerful old gangsters and some extremely impatient young ones. Or, as Chuckie Crimaldi put it: "The big ones are nice, gentlemanly people. The ones that are coming up are usually kind of loud-mouthed guys, impressionists, really, trying to let the whole world know that they're big tough people."

With this divisiveness running high, the following list should be read with the awareness that today's mobster biography can be tomorrow's obituary.

THE TOP TEN MOBSTERS IN CHICAGO

1. Anthony "Big Tuna" Accardo

Survival is everything in the crime syndicate. The septuagenarian Accardo has survived a lot. Today, as "elder statesman" (don't say "Godfather") of the Outfit, he directs some 300-odd fun-loving fellows. Accardo has ultimate hiring and firing authority (demotions can be permanent), responsibility for mob moves in legitimate business, and the thankless task of keeping fellow mobsters in line. Perhaps because of all this responsibility, Accardo suffers from the hallowed executive ailment, a duodenal ulcer.

Accardo spends most of his time (from October to May) in Palm Springs, living in a condominium owned by a Chicago lawyer in the exclusive Indian Wells Country Club development. Accardo must feel at home there. Many of Chicago's top mobsters escape winter and shotgun blasts in this elite California resort. "Palm Springs is like a Switzerland for organized crime," said Deputy Chief Sam Lowery of the Riverside County sheriff's office. "It's become neutral territory where mob figures can come and relax and not worry about being bumped off."

Palm Springs' less unrespectable residents feel that visitors' occupations are their own business, but the Chicago mob boys have made their presence felt. A member of the Palm Springs organized crime police intelligence unit complained to two *Tribune* reporters: "It used to be that kids in this town would try to copy people like Kirk Douglas or Jerry Lewis or Frank Sinatra. Now, they all think they're a bunch of Al Capones. They walk around acting like Mafia hit men and talking out of the sides of their mouths."

Back home in Chicago isn't quite so pleasant for Accardo. The honest mob chieftain (Accardo likes to boast that he has never spent a day in jail in his life) is plagued by the dishonesty of others. His home in suburban River Forest has been beset by thieves and FBI men carting off the valuables. In January of 1978, professional burglars broke into Accardo's suburban sanctum following a jewelry theft from a Northside jeweler. The jeweler and Accardo are believed to have known each other, and it was speculated that Accardo had ordered the loot brought to his house so that it could be returned to the original owner. The not-too-bright jewelry gang thought they could walk off with it. Since then, several burglars and fences reportedly connected with the original heist have been discovered in the trunks of cars and other pleasant places.

The FBI was next to intrude on Accardo's privacy. Their excuse was a search for clues to the disappearance of Accardo's old friend and houseman, Michael Volpe, who vanished five days after testifying before a federal grand jury regarding the January burglary of the Accardo home. The FBI didn't find Volpe, but they did find a pile of money—some $275,000 in stacks of $100 and $50 bills and two silver-plated .44 caliber pistols—sitting on Accardo's basement floor (they play Monopoly in a big way in River Forest).

The tidy arrangement of money in denominations oddly similar to those stolen from the First National Bank in 1977 led investigators to wonder if Accardo's cache was part of the unsolved $1 million heist from the bank. But wondering is often a fruitless pastime in Chicago.

Accardo is a multi-millionaire, and smart. He was once overheard spouting some mainline mob philosophy. During the Columbo family mob wars in New York, Accardo talked with a friend at length about the tough spot the New York gangs were in, then mused: "Better them than us."

2. Jackie "The Lackey" Cerone

Jackie's "Lackey" label dates from his service as Accardo's chauffeur and errand-runner in the 1920's. But there's been nothing lowly about the Lackey in more recent years. Until a prison term for an interstate gambling conviction put him out of action from 1970 to 1975, Cerone was reputedly the Outfit's operating director, the alleged head of a formidable gambling and loan shark operation, and Accardo's heir apparent. Cerone's high-standing with mob brass was hinted at in 1974, when Louis Bombacino, chief witness for the prosecution against Cerone, himself came under a mob ruling: a bomb blew up his car, scattering auto and Bombacino parts all over. Cerone also acted as Accardo's secretary of state regarding negotiations on big outside deals—a sort of ambassador with unpleasant-looking portfolio.

Now the Lackey has replaced long-time mob leader Joey "Doves" Aiuppa, who has opted for voluntary retirement. Aiuppa's retirement is unusual; it marks the first time in our history that a top guy has willingly relinquished command. Cerone, known as a tough, savvy operator, is expected to beef up mob activities.

3. Gus "Slim" Alex

Gus Alex is Greek (which may explain why he doesn't like the Young Turks) and the third member of Chicago's ruling Outfit triumvirate. Like Accardo and Jackie Cerone, both thought to be somewhat cool of blood, Alex likes to spend most of his time in warmer climes, like Fort Lauderdale.

Alex operates well long-distance. He reportedly oversees the mob's many interests in the Loop and is a top negotiator. He is believed to be behind the recent syndicate move into the janitor business. Perhaps spotting a chance to clean up, Alex and mob labor impresario Joey Glimco have allegedly asked a millionaire maintenance mogul to move over. He could be expected to comply, as no one wants to become Chicago's first "Janitor in a Drum."

4. Joseph Ferriola

Accardo, Cerone, and Alex set the tone for Chicago, represent Chicago in the high councils of the rest of the Syndicate, and serve as the highest court for erring gangsters, a court that has no appeal.

But police say the day-to-day operations of the mob are handled by Joseph Ferriola. Ferriola's lack of identifying nickname should be a tip-off that he's long been behind the scenes in the mob. Joseph Ferriola has come into his own lately; mob watchers feel that he is "the man to watch." With the death of James "Turk"

Torello from cancer, Ferriola's power base has broadened to include the Young Turks faction of the Outfit which Torello once led. Torello reportedly had been grooming Ferriola for more than a year to succeed him as the mob's top enforcer.

Ferriola reputedly had long been Torello's apprentice. According to *Sun-Times* reporter Art Petacque, Ferriola helped Torello solidify his power by providing the muscle. Under Torello's direction, Ferriola encouraged scores of independent Chicago bookmakers to join the mob, and might know about the death of six bookies who wouldn't go along. It's widely believed that Ferriola also might know something about the 1975 slaying of prominent independent bookie Anthony Reitinger, in broad daylight, in a Northwest Side restaurant.

According to *Sun-Times* mob watchers Petacque and Hugh Hough, Ferriola's first task assigned him as new chief executive officer of the Chicago Outfit was to restore internal order. What a lucky assignment. To help out, Ferriola selected his nephew, Harry Aleman. Aleman's now in jail, in solitary, and out of favor with the big bosses. Until Ferriola can come up with someone who has a way with encouraging compliance, Ferriola could find that his directives lack authority.

5. *Al Pilotto*

Pilotto is the quintessential example of the well-connected mob man. He once drove the late, great mobster boss Frank LaPorte around, and now he's a big deal in LaPorte's old territory, southern Cook and Will Counties.

Pilotto's power is centered in Chicago Heights, an area that once outranked even Chicago in the number of gangland hits and which still teems with unsavory businesses.

6. *Eddie Vogel*

Richard Cain brought the Bally slot machine to South American casinos, but it was old-timer Vogel, now in his eighties, who originally put together the Outfit's slot-machine empire. Still vital to the Chicago area gambling, Vogel, despite failing eyesight, oversees from Palm Springs. It's amazing how far you can see from Palm Springs.

7. Vincent Solano

Another symbol of the Horatio Alger ethic in the mob, Solano, now nearing sixty, used to bodyguard and do chores for the late, great Ross Prio, longtime ruler of all those lucrative North Side vice operations. When Prio died in 1972, control fell to Dominic DiBella, who handled things nicely until he succumbed to an unexpected fate—a natural death. Upward mobility came to Solano, hitherto unknown for anything bigger than aiding Prio. Now he's known all over the North Side.

8. William Dauber

Billy Dauber reportedly took over Chicago's extensive and lucrative chop-shop operation after the 1978 War of the Stolen Auto Parts left a dozen used-parts dealers shot down in the street or stashed in car trunks at O'Hare Airport. That was the war that led to the slaying of Jimmy "The Bomber" Catuara, longtime chop-shop czar.

Dauber's rise and Catuara's demise are interesting. Dauber used to work for Catuara in the auto resale business, but they had a serious falling out after Dauber began serving a sentence for mail fraud in 1973. Dauber was released from a federal prison in Terre Haute, Indiana, in the summer of 1978. Catuara suddenly decided he needed a long, long rest in his Oak Lawn home. He made the mistake of leaving it one day for an important appointment on Chicago's West Side. He was gunned down in his red Cadillac at the corner of Ogden Avenue and Hubbard Street, not far from where he and a pal and a seven-stick unexploded dynamite bomb were arrested in 1934. Forty-four years later, the neighborhood finally heard a bang.

The way now seems clear for Dauber and his Chicago Heights associate, Albert Tocco. Dauber had on-the-job training under Catuara, police say. With Catuara gone and most of the others chopped down since 1971, he's about the only one of Catuara's old associates left. Even Catuara's chauffeur is playing it smart. After Catuara's slaying, the chauffeur, who also worked for the city, told police that he never found out what it was that Catuara did for a living.

9. Larry "The Hood" Buonaguidi

Buonaguidi is one reputed mob fellow who flaunts it. A few years ago, he was arrested for not displaying a city vehicle sticker. Larry told interested police that he had retired at forty-nine, having last served as an altar boy.

He's always been a little touchy about his image. Back in 1952, when G-men were conducting a raid on the now-defunct Subway Pool Hall on North Clark Street, they overlooked Buonaguidi. When the feds left, Buonaguidi reportedly sulked. "Why didn't they arrest me?" He's supposed to have said. "I'm a hood."

10. Joseph "Doves" Aiuppa

Aiuppa was No. 2 man in the mob until he decided to retire (he's in his seventies) in July of 1979. Aiuppa, who has amassed a ton of secrets and good old gangster know-how, is being retained as a paid "consultant."

The "Doves" tag comes from Aiuppa's passion for bagging birds. In 1962, Aiuppa displeased the U.S. Fish and Wildlife Service when he and a few fellow outdoorsmen killed approximately 1,400 mourning doves on a shooting spree in Kansas. In 1965, Aiuppa and Accardo went on safari in Botswana, where the two sportsmen slaughtered some 3,200 pounds of assorted game. Now Aiuppa owns and operates a hunting club called the Yorkshire Quail Club in Kankakee County.

Many believe that Aiuppa has gone after even bigger game in his time. In the 1920's, he rose from a punk street fighter to bodyguard for Al Capone. From this post, new horizons beckoned, such as the Cicero rackets, gambling houses, and brothels. Aiuppa was talked about as "Cicero's flesh merchant," and pound for pound—he weighs at least 200 pounds and is a mere 5'6"—he's very much an Outfit heavy.

According to West Coast mobster turned informer James T. "Jimmy the Weasel" Fratianno, Aiuppa was recently assigned as a sort of time-study man concerning Mafia rackets on the West Coast.

Honorable Mentions

Other top spots in the mob reportedly are held by Anthony Grattadauro, who looks after things in Northern Indiana; Lenny Patrick, numero uno with North Side and suburban horse racing afficionados; Jimmy "Cowboy" Mirro, boss of Cicero and Chicago's Little Italy; Frank "Skid" Caruso, boss in the Loop's south end and in Chinatown; Joey DeVarco, collector of charitable contributions from porno shops; and Dominic "Libby" Nuccio, night life director for interesting parts of Rush Street, the south end of the Gold Coast, Old Town, and trendy New Town.

Joseph "Fifeky" Corngold holds a special place in the crime syndicate. Corngold was operating in Cicero before Capone discovered it. He's now considered the "oldest surviving Capone gangster," and has an honorarium from the current mob. As might be said to his younger colleagues, you should live so long.

No list would be complete without mention of the Young Turks, even though founders Torello and Spilotro have already been mentioned. We'll only focus on the late Torello and Spilotro. There are others, but not as many as there used to be. According to the *Sun-Times'* Art Petacque, most Young Turks have a reputation for being dim-witted. He quoted one investigator as saying "they can't add two and two without a calculator." But they can shoot straight. And, anyway, the late Sam Giancana tested out in prison with a sixth-grade mentality when he was 31 years old. The army judged Giancana unfit for active duty during the war because they found him to be "a constitutional psychopath and inadequate personality manifested by strong anti-social trends." The Young Turks could go far.

James "The Turk" Torello died in April, 1979 at the age of 49, but, like Al Capone and Mayor Daley, he is not forgotten. The Young Turks, now assembled under Torello's successor Joseph Ferriola, still adhere to Torello tenets and tactics. And Torello's spirit remained unvanquished during his long illness. Art Petacque reported that Torello used to appear on the porch of his Cicero home and shadowbox for a while to convince any onlooking FBI agents or eager mobsters that he wasn't through.

Torello first distinguished himself as an arm and leg breaker for the late Cicero loan shark king, Fiore "Fifi" Buccieri. His years with Buccieri earned Torello another nickname, "The Butcher." Chicago writer Bill Brashler reports that Torello didn't mind his bloody reputation. As he once told a friend, "It helps me with my collections."

Torello was taken on by the establishment in the early 1970's as the ultimate in pest control. The pests in this case were the independent bookies who had filled in the blanks left by a number of incarcerated mob gambling bosses. Torello had reportedly employed at least two hit men since 1974 to make these new businessmen feel less independent.

Torello was gambling overlord of the mob. He was also the mob's chief insurgent. It's not easy to wear two hats like that in the Outfit, but somehow Torello managed. Torello took on some of the old Buccieri boys, including Angelo Pietra and Anthony "Pineapples" Eldorado. He was Joseph Ferriola's mentor. The young crowd around Torello featured the seven mobsters indicted in 1976 by a federal grand jury for operating gambling rings in the West Side and in the western suburbs: Donald "Don Angel" Angelini (better known as "The Wizard of Odds"), Dominic Cortina, Joseph "Joe Spot" Spadavecchio, Frank "The Knife" Aureli, Salvatore Molose, Nick "Moose" Camillo, and John "Chicky" La Placa.

Despite all those Italian names in Torello's thugdom, he ran an open shop. According to the FBI, Torello also employed two veterans of the Black P Stone Nation, as well as three Oriental musclemen.

Tony Spilotro is a fellow in the versatile Richard Cain mold. He allegedly worked at unpleasant tasks for Felix "Milwaukee Phil" Alderisio, former mob extortionist extraordinaire. Spilotro also is reported to have gotten along famously with Sam De Stefano, known during his heyday as the "Marquis de Sade of the Syndicate." Spilotro was also on good terms with his Oak Park neighbor, Sam Giancana. Now Spilotro works for himself. Tony is so impressive that many authorities believe he could some soon day take over the entire mob. Now in his early forties, Spilotro has the added class of having once been arrested in Antwerp in connection with a jewel heist.

Tony has an admirable record of acquittals. He was acquitted of the 1963 torture-murder of Leo Foreman, even though Chuckie Crimaldi testified that Spilotro was an active participant in Foreman's maiming. After the trial, State's Attorney Bernard Carey made a statement worthy of Chicago. Glossing over the fact that Spilotro had gone free, Carey enthused instead over the conviction of the relatively harmless brother of Sam, Mario DeStefano. "This conviction of a trunk murderer," Carey intoned, "serves notice on the crime syndicate that the courts, juries, and citizens will no longer tolerate the killing of any individual in this city for whatever reason."

And surely the mob took note.

Spilotro, who found some digs in Las Vegas in 1971, was recently given a big say in mob operations there and points west. When he and his clients aren't tied up with other business, he likes to run his little boutique in Caesar's Palace.

If the feds, police, and other investigators know so much about gangsters, why isn't more done about them? The reason is simply that knowledge isn't evidence.

The Chicago Crime Commission compiles exhaustive annual statistics on hits. The Justice Dept's strike force and the Chicago Police Department's Vice Control Squad keep tabs on the business end of mobdom. Chicagoans know where mobsters live, what kind of cars they drive, where they eat, where they vacation. But nobody knows what move they're going to make next—and that's the only knowledge that counts.

The available information on mobsters makes better fodder for biography than for investigations. In 1973, accompanied by much press hoopla, the Police Department released its heretofore top-secret intelligence information on 35 syndicate hoodlums, turning it over to the state's attorney's office. These police dossiers detailed gangsters' addresses, habits, hangouts, heights, and weights. But State's Attorney Carey was unimpressed. "On what charges could we take these gangsters before the grand jury?" Carey asked. "For being overweight in the City of Chicago?"

Mob activities are crimes that admit of no solution. The mob has become so tightly and carefully connected to other Chicago institutions (politics, police, business) that rooting it out is impossible.

This gives rise to the peculiar Chicago cynicism and resignation that outsiders mistake for ghoulishness. Chicagoans are like the insomniac who waits for the upstairs neighbor's other shoe to drop, only they wait for more bodies.

5
Society

The trouble with society is that it is so terribly common. Every squalid corn and soybean town in central Illinois has its social elite, and—their double knits notwithstanding—they're every bit as haughty as their counterparts in Chicago. Despite the egalitarian premise on which this nation was founded, the American Dream mostly amounts to a quest for the means to establish oneself as superior to one's fellows. And everybody tries.

In Europe, people tried to maintain superior status for centuries through breeding—with rather mixed results. In Papua New Guinea, it's largely a matter of warrior skills and pig ownership.

In America, it's simply a matter of money (though with some Chicago families like the Swifts and Armours, pig ownership is involved as well).

Unlike society in Boston or Philadelphia, Chicago's upper crust came by its money and its crust rather recently. It's really only been in this century that the city ceased to be an upstart frontier boom town—perhaps the quintessential upstart frontier boom town —and its rough edges still show. Some Chicago society types make a pretense of being "old money," but theirs is really quite disgustingly new. Despite some periodic infusions of blue Eastern blood through marriage, most of the rich people wandering around the Gold Coast today are no more than three generations removed from the rascals who founded their family fortunes.

As the writings of Henry James, Somerset Maugham, and Sir Henry Channon suggest, Chicago's upstart society scored very well in Europe, especially in England, which is fond of curiosities. But in the eastern United States, the raffish Chicago image still prevails, as it did when the spectacular Mrs. Potter Palmer (a favorite of England's Edward VII, by the way) displayed her equally spectacular gold table service for fifty to a visiting Mrs. John Gardner of Boston. Said Mrs. Gardner: "And what do you use when you have a large dinner party?"

With some Newport and Southampton types, Lake Forest still means yahoo.

It must be stated that there are some members of Chicago's "prominent" families who really don't give a damn about status, locally or elsewhere. They are genuine, sincere, unpretentious people who go about their business, whether it's making money or performing good works, just like Joe Six-Pack, as Governor Pierre DuPont of Delaware once referred to the average voter.

But for others in haute Chicago, status is their whole reason for breathing, though status is becoming harder and harder to maintain. In the old days of a hundred years ago, status was very easy to maintain in Chicago because all that separated "society" from the rest of the folks was money—some of it acquired only the previous week but, in most cases, gobs of money. The city's population leapt from virtually nothing in 1840 to 112,000 in 1860 to 590,000 in 1880 to 1.8 million in 1900. If you happened to own a few acres of land or a store in the vicinity at the beginning of this boom, your immense fortune was assured.

And that money was in large part spent on anything and everything that would mark the spender as different from the rest of humanity. The handsome carriages of the Chicago rich would sweep along the public ways of the city as disdainfully as the French nobility's did through the cobbled streets of Madame Defarge's Paris. Grotesquely extravagant mansions such as the Pullmans' on Prairie Avenue, the McCormicks' on Rush Street, and the Potter Palmers' on Lake Shore Drive made the simple architectural statement: "We're rich and you ain't."

The elaborate gowns and dresses worn by nineteenth-century

Chicago grande dames were intended to make the same statement. They were simply too voluminous for the wearer to perform even the most trifling form of work, domestic or professional. And these ladies acquired their frocks (usually from Worth's of Paris) by the dozens and dozens. On a single day, Bertha Palmer might change from a dressing gown to a morning robe to an afternoon dress to a tea gown to a reception dress to a dinner dress to an evening gown. She may well have slept in the nude just for relief.

Nowadays, the things money can buy don't count for so much, because so many non-society people can afford them. Most society women shop at Saks Fifth Avenue, Stanley Korshak's, and Marshall Field's exclusive 28 Shop. So do thousands of non-society ladies. That smashingly dressed woman on Michigan Avenue might turn out to be a mere television news anchorwoman, or someone who sleeps in the nude because that's how she earns her living.

Handsome equipages are now quite commonplace. Snob doormen never know whether the sleek limousine gliding up to hand contains Mrs. Edward Byron Smith or Doug Buffone of the Chicago Bears. Or *Tribune* columnist Aaron Gold.

Lake Forest still has its ostentatious czarist lakeside palaces, but they're carefully kept from public view (or rather, the public is carefully kept from their view). In Chicago, such ostentation has vanished. Once grand Prairie Avenue is a historical district surrounded by slum. Rush Street is mostly honky-tonk. The Gold Coast is cramped with high rises containing airline stewardesses and junior advertising executives. The only mansion left on Lake Shore Drive is the old Countiss home, and that's now a surgical museum.

Mrs. Countiss, a Robinson of the Diamond Match Robinsons, copied her place after Marie Antoinette's Petit Trianon in Versailles. It was every bit as elegant as the queen's digs, except that Mrs. Countiss put in an extra floor. "If Marie Antoinette had lived in Chicago," Mrs. Countiss said, "she would have raised it [another story], too." If Marie Antoinette had lived in Chicago, the Haymarket Riots would have been even more fun.

Today, Chicago society lives mostly in high-rise apartments, and anyone can afford to live in a high rise, even on Lake Shore Drive. Mere politicians like former State Senator Bernard Neistein and former Governor Ogilvie do. So do gentlemen in dark glasses with strange business dealings in Las Vegas. In the Swearingens' building on the Drive, there was a lady resident who delighted in shouting out the door to her husband: "Bernie, don't forget the bagels!"

Anyone can have money. Of course, in the old days, anyone could have money, too. Which is how all these family fortunes got started in the first place. A remarkable characteristic of America's great wealthy families is that so many of them sprang from poverty, if not squalor.

Cornelius Vanderbilt's first maritime command was not of a yacht but of a Staten Island garbage scow. Rockenfeld, the ancestral home of the Rockefellers in Germany, was a vermin-infested collection of hovels near Bonn.

Gustavus Swift, founder of the Chicago meat packing empire, got his start in Massachusetts peddling raw meat from a cart door-to-door. Marshall Field I was a shopkeeper. Nettie McCormick was an impoverished orphan. Potter Palmer was a shopkeeper with a good eye for real estate. The only real difference between him and Chicago's present real-estate king, Arthur Rubloff, is that Rubloff is more successful and dresses better.

But if today's aristocrats have no real aristocracy in their family roots, their forebears were singular people in another and more useful sense. They generally had more intelligence, cunning, daring, ruthlessness, resourcefulness, and greed than their contemporaries. They could cope with most anything. They would have succeeded anywhere, even in Papua New Guinea. Bertha Palmer, for example, inherited $8 million from her husband. In no time at all, she managed to double that fortune through shrewd investments and skillful management of such new enterprises as a six-thousand-acre cattle ranch she bought and ran in Florida.

But few "aristocrat" descendants share these traits. Psychiatrist Roy R. Grinker of the Michael Reese Medical Center described the grandchildren and great-grandchildren of the very rich as "emotional zombies" as psychologically deprived as the children of the very poor. Calling them narcissistic, self-centered, shallow, and unable to tolerate the slightest frustration, Dr. Grinker said these rich kids lack shame, embarrassment, empathy, and tenderness. He said they easily become angry or vindictive, are chronic sufferers of boredom and depression, and have the most superficial goals and ideals, if any. Bertha Palmer had goals.

In the old days, Chicago's rich people had awesome power.

When labor unrest began leading to capitalist unrest, Marshall Field I suggested in his club one day that an army post would be a nice civic improvement, and—presto—there was Fort Sheridan, conveniently positioned on the North Shore.

Nowadays, society people haven't the power to get Fort Sheridan torn down, though some have been trying for years. Mayor Daley treated the rich with respect, but they still had to wait in line for favors just like the Polish vote, and the Plumbers Union. Society people in Chicago now get traffic tickets, just like everyone else. When Bonnie Swearingen got into a public altercation with someone's chauffeur, she was charged with disorderly conduct (though the charges were later dropped).

Perhaps the most telling illustration of the relative powerlessness of the very rich in today's Chicago is the way the foreign consulates are treated by the power structure. Only two consulates matter with Chicago society—the British and the French. Were British Consul-General John Heath to throw a little bash celebrating the discovery of one of Queen Victoria's discarded hangnails, le tout Chicago would come. Almost anything the French do is a major social occasion in Chicago, particularly if it involves the city's Alliance Française, an elite Francophile club.

How devastated these foreign consuls must have been to discover how little these slavish affections of the local elite translate into anything at all useful to them in their jobs.

The Irish consul-general, Ronan Murphy, has doors flung open for him all over City Hall. British Consul Heath has to open his own doors, unless he has Queen Elizabeth or Prince Charles with him. The British have gotten it in the neck from the Chicago news media for everything from Ulster to the Cod War with Iceland.

But the British have never failed so badly as the French, certainly not so badly as the French did on President Pompidou's state visit to Chicago in 1970. The French government had then just decided not to sell some jet fighters to Israel. The Chicago Jewish community was livid. Mayor Daley always knew where the votes were. He refused to greet Pompidou at the airport. The motorcade he had provided for a "scenic" tour of the city traveled at speeds reaching 80 miles an hour at times, and at one point, left Pompidou's car behind completely. At a gala reception for the Pompidous in the Palmer House, pro-Israel demonstrators "somehow" got through police lines, accosted the presidential couple in the lobby, and one spat on Madame Pompidou's gown. In France, it was treated as a major, shocking international incident, but not in Chicago.

The old Chicago families are still around, but few of them have anything to do with their old Chicago family businesses. An exception is Brooks McCormick, who is chairman of International Harvester, but the man who runs Marshall Field & Company isn't a Field but someone named Angelo Arena. The head of the mighty First National Bank is a Lebanese-American chap named A. Robert Abboud. John Swearingen became chairman of Standard Oil of Indiana, not as a Lake Forest polo player looking for something to do but as a lowly chemical engineer who worked his way up through the ranks.

But Chicago society still has one last rock to cling to: exclusivity. Anti-discrimination laws notwithstanding, society people still exert immense control over "exclusive" residence, membership in exclusive clubs and other institutions, and over who mixes with them socially. This enables them to maintain their own status and control that of others, or at least of those who want a piece of all that "exclusive" action.

The huge mansions may be gone, but there is still a status attendant upon real estate. The buildings along the "nicer" stretches of Lake Shore Drive look more or less the same, and the apartments tend to run in the same $250,000 to $500,000 range. But because of the people who live in them and the people who are not able to live in them, certain addresses are considered "select." As a rule, these "fashionable" addresses are in the older, seedier buildings on the Drive, not the sleek new ones.

For some reason, you don't hear many Irish jigs or smell much Italian cooking or hear people shout "Bernie, don't forget the bagels!" in the great WASP palace at 1500 North Lake Shore Drive (although you might smell cigar smoke from some of Ogilvie's politician buddies). There is a similar "correctness" to the old piles of stone at 1242 and 1540 North Lake Shore Drive, and 209 and 229 East Lake Shore Drive.

One of the nicest buildings on the street, 179 East Lake Shore Drive, where Abra (Rockefeller) Prentice Anderson has her penthouse digs, is not considered so "correct," presumably because Bernie and his bagels would be welcome there.

With some society people, address is not only important but supreme. You might have the most excellent manners, seventeen degrees in English literature, and a nomination for the Nobel Prize, but if you should admit to living, say, on Grunge Avenue in Berwyn, well, the glance flicks downward and a silence falls. If, however, you are an alcoholic child molester with a virulent venereal disease, but happen to reside at one of the right numbers on Astor Street, then you are a "nice" person with "a few problems."

This sort of residential purity is a little less evident in the suburbs, because real estate transactions concerning single family dwellings are more subject to government anti-discrimination laws than to tribal control. Still, there is an extraordinary Anglo-Saxonness to Lake Forest, Winnetka, and Kenilworth. Some rich Greek people have been moving into Lake Forest recently, but when they give parties, "no one" comes.

Another temple of exclusivity is the club. Captains of industry join the Chicago Club to escape mere lieutenants, sergeants, and privates of industry, and also to assure themselves that they *are* captains of industry. The grande dames of Lake Forest belong to country clubs not merely to have a place to play bridge and swill gin in during the afternoon, but to hold court, much as Elizabeth I did.

The Casino Club just off north Michigan Avenue is a very pleasant place to be. But even if it were an extremely unpleasant place to be—say if they used the kitchen once a week to render horses for glue—there would still be hordes of Chicagoans willing to pay huge sums of money to join. Because they can't join. And the more they hunger to join, the more they elevate the status of those who already belong.

Exclusivity is the raison d'être of the Social Register, quaint little telephone book that it pretends to be. Chicago used to have a Social Register of its own, but the publishers have gotten so cheap about things that all locales are now lumped together in a single, hefty volume not unlike Jane's Fighting Ships.

According to one society lady of our acquaintance, "Anyone can get in the Social Register." One needs only a sponsor, a second, and some letters of recommendation from people already listed.

Would "anyone" include W. Clement Stone, the peculiar multimillionaire who preaches "positive mental attitude" and who showered Richard Nixon with all that money? "Probably not," said the society lady. Would it include Chicago's extremely wealthy, philanthrophic, and social Leigh Blocks, or the Gardner Sterns? No, it does not. As another "prominent" Chicagoan, himself a registeree, put it: "Jews usually aren't admitted unless they marry someone already in the Register."

Many other groups are excluded. They include, according to the society lady, actors and actresses and people who marry actors and actresses. Richard Nixon is listed.

Perhaps the most obvious and unfortunate manifestation of the exclusivity principle in Chicago is the "important" charity. Some have the silly notion that rich people get involved in charity and civic work solely because they are interested in helping others and improving the human condition. As this notion has it, people are elevated to the boards of charities and other institutions because they have worked very hard or shown an unusual aptitude or interest in a particular area.

In some exceptional cases, this may be true. Certainly Hope Mc-Cormick, Thomas G. Ayers, and the George Ranneys don't do all the things they do because they're nervous about their status. But an unfortunately large number of people turn to charity and civic work for less altruistic reasons. Some do it out of guilt, as a means of justifying their wealth and lavish expenditure of it. Others do it because they want something to do besides playing bridge and swilling gin. Still others find such institutional work an effective means of imposing their own tastes, wills, and whims on the rest of the populace—perhaps the only effective means left to rich people.

Mrs. Potter Palmer's great haul of now priceless Impressionist paintings was in large part responsible for the Art Institute's impressive reputation today. But the dreariness of so much of the rest of the collection is directly attributable to the fact that the Chicago social set has run the place for decades, with few of its members showing Mrs. Palmer's terrific taste.

Do Chicagoans want to look at a Chagall mosaic every time they walk by the First National Bank Building? After all, most might have preferred Norman Rockwell. But Mr. and Mrs. William W. Prince decided Chagall was what they would get. Is it fitting for such an enlightened institution as the University of Chicago that its chapel be perpetually Baptist? John D. Rockefeller thought it was.

The late printing mogul Elliot Donnelley loved choo-choo trains, and had three great big ones huffing and puffing around his Liberty-ville estate. Soon after he took over the Chicago Zoological Society, there was a choo-choo train running around the Brookfield Zoo.

But an unfortunately important reason for high society's involve-ment in charities and civic organizations is to maintain its own status and control that of others. What society considers the "most prestigious" charitable or civic organizations in Chicago are the Chicago Symphony, the Art Institute, the Lyric Opera, the Chicago Historical Society, the Brookfield Zoo, the Field Museum of Natural History, Presbyterian St. Luke's Medical Center, Northwestern Memorial (Passavant) Hospital, Children's Memorial Hospital, the University of Chicago, and the Junior League.

Among the top social events of the year are the Presbyterian St. Luke's Fashion Show, the models for which are oh-so-carefully screened by a special committee; the Passavant Cotillion, a debu-tante gala that sometimes seems like something from the stage of the Radio City Music Hall; and the Lyric Opera Ball, a frequently ghastly romp that has seen the guests welcomed by costumed trumpeteers and, in 1978, by a drum and bugle corps.

The Art Institute throws dinner dances and the Children's Me-morial ladies have a big rummage sale (imagine the sort of rum-mage you get from Lake Forest). The Junior League goes out to the housing projects and teaches needlepoint to slum children.

Membership on the boards of these institutions is akin to knight-hood, or damehood. To be a governing life member of the Art Institute is what being a peer of the realm was before Harold Wilson started handing out lordships to English labor union bosses. Attendance at these organizations' social functions and business meetings is a must must. Miss too many and you're dropped. Add-ing to the unpleasantness is the fact that the seating is often ac-cording to status. You know where you stand by where you sit.

The most important work function of all these boards is raising funds, especially new funds. If the rich people who run them had to support everything with their own money, they'd soon be reduced to living in Hoffman Estates like mere mortals.

To get new money, they dangle lures: Give enough, and work enough, and you might be so lucky as to be invited into the actual home of one of the exalted board persons. In time, you might even get to be an exalted board person yourself. If you donate, say, an entire appendix removal center to one of the "important" hospitals or a new library wing to the university, you're a big leg up toward boardship. If you happen to be a member of one of Chicago's most "prominent" or "nice" families to boot, such exalted status is guaranteed.

A major problem facing those exalted ones who care about such things is how to attract new money without lowering "standards." Relegated to "lesser" charities like Clem Stone's favorite Chicago Boys Clubs, ritzy Bonnie Swearingen has shown herself to be an indefatigable worker and enormously successful fund raiser. Yet she almost never gets a crack at the big time. One of our society lady acquaintances absolutely blanched at the suggestion of Bonnie whooping it up as a board member of the venerated Antiquarian Society of the Art Institute.

It's long been recognized in Chicago that the most effective charity fund raisers in town are to be found in the city's Jewish community. Yet, for decades, Jews were routinely excluded from any meaningful role in the top charities. This unpleasant fact of life so angered a number of generous Jewish contributors to the Art Institute that they bolted and created the Museum of Contemporary Art.

The lesson was not lost. Leigh Block, one of the biggest collectors in the city, was made president of the Art Institute board.

If a nasty strain of anti-Semitism seems to run through this chapter, it's because a nasty strain of anti-Semitism has run through Chicago society. In their endless striving to appear separate, select, and superior, the means some society people sieze upon—bigotry— renders them about as separate, select, and superior as the Marquette Park Nazis.

It's unfortunately unnecessary to explain why Hanchen Stern's gala 1927 wedding (her wedding dress now hangs in the Historical Society) was held in the Standard Club and not the Casino. In this most ethnic and Catholic of cities, Irish-Catholic social events were not permitted in the big downtown hotels until just a couple of decades ago.

As for blacks, you might find one or two roaming about the Union League Club, whose hero is Abraham Lincoln. But don't search the pre-theater buffet at the Casino for chitlins.

One of the more pathetic efforts of the "old" *Chicago Tribune* some years ago was a special issue of its magazine devoted to "black society"—a separate but equal extravaganza that came across rather like Amos and Andy meet the Emperor Jones.

A decade ago, all four Chicago newspapers (there are now only two) covered society events as matters of great consequence. The *Tribune's* Eleanor Page had four full-time reporters and a full-time photographer to assist her. Now, Miss Page has retired and there's just Jon Anderson, who used to be married to Abra (Rockefeller) Prentice Anderson, lived in that big penthouse up there, and knows whereof he writes.

Miss Page, a society person in her own right, used to write chirpy little pieces like: "A large tent will go up on the fifty-one-acre Libertyville estate of . . . " Jon provides meatier stuff, such as: "In other fashionable homes, more than one elderly gentleman has been known to keep up with current trends by subscribing to *Screw* magazine."

The *Chicago Sun-Times'* society coverage now amounts mostly to an amusing weekly column in the fashion section called "Click." And it's principally written by Jon's ex-wife Abra, who keeps us informed of such things as: "Everyone has been so busy gobbling up the Chicago issue of *Town & County* this month that most have missed mention of Our Town in the back pages of *Vogue.* Check out Page 497. Exercise queen René Ettlinger is pictured ever-so-trimly demonstrating how to rid one of underarm flab."

It's said Chicago society doesn't seek publicity the way it used to.

Chicago society has always been rather sedentary, with its members prefering pursuits like gardening and needlepoint (and *Screw* magazine?) to sweatier, more vigorous endeavors. Very few of the ranking society families in the Chicago area, for example, have much to do with horses. In Lake Forest, polo seems to be looked down upon as a slob sport.

But, in recent years, society women have become a little more sweaty and vigorous in pursuit of "self-fulfillment" and a more beautiful them. In addition to exercise, face-lifts and breast-lifts have become so commonplace, said another society lady of our acquaintance, that "it's almost like having your teeth fixed."

Not everyone in Chicago society is going in for sleek good looks. As Jon Anderson recently wrote, some social functions in Lake

Forest still do resemble Margaret Rutherford look-alike contests. And, there's a rich lady in the city whose only apparent concession to a more beautiful her is to daily tape the skin of her cheeks back and then cover up the handiwork with an enormous wig.

But, otherwise, Chicago produces some really sleek numbers. It always had a few. Mrs. Potter Palmer was described in her time as being "prone to embonpoint," which was a rather arch way of saying she was built like that mansion her husband constructed for her. Mrs. Kenneth Sawyer Goodman, who started out as Marjorie Robbins and later became Mrs. James McHenry Hopkins, was a striking beauty of the 1920's and 1930's and remained almost as lovely in her eighties. The same can be said of the now-septuagenarian Mrs. Edward Byron Smith.

The sleekest numbers now, though, include the extremely dishy Diana Armour Cochrane Prince, the sort of blonde upon whom plastic surgery would be utterly wasted, and the extraordinary Christina Kemper Gidwitz, daughter of insurance mogul James Kemper and wife of Ronald (Helene Curtis) Gidwitz. And, of course, there's always Abra, who may not have the most classic profile but sure has great cleavage.

The following ranking of Chicago's top society women was accomplished only with the most arduous research and agonizing assessment. It is based on the most exact standards, including all of those used by Chicago society. Indeed, its preparation involved innumerable lunches with actual society ladies themselves, lunches featuring the most delicious little sandwiches and the most outrageous meowing.

THE TOP FIFTEEN SOCIETY WOMEN IN CHICAGO

1. Mrs. Potter Palmer

Yes, Bertha Palmer did pass on to that great drawing room in the sky in 1918, but no one since has ever come close to the style, wit, grace, spunk, and majesty with which she presided over Chicago society in its wild and woolly days. Discussing her successors is like discussing the queens who came after Elizabeth I.

One woman came closer than most—the aristocratic Mrs. Chauncey [Marion McCormick.] One of the ten richest American women of her time, the former Marion Deering was the mother of chairman Brooks McCormick, and also of the late bounder, Roger. But she, too, is up in that celestial drawing room.

With no one in Chicago approximating even Marion McCormick's stature, it seems best just to leave No. 1 in the grand if ghostly grip of Bertha Palmer.

2. Mrs. Brooks McCormick

The closest to the top at the moment is Hope McCormick, daughter-in-law of Marion McCormick, wife of chairman Brooks, and mother of rapidly socially rising Martha O. Hunt.

A Baldwin of the Bedford, New York, Baldwins, Hope had to overcome a shyness as intense as her husband's fondness for things British to occupy this place. But overcome she did, and she now performs masterfully as the perfect corporate wife, leader of society, world traveler in the grand style, and former Chicago pol.

The only other pol who says "super" as much as Hope does is Governor Jim Thompson.

Hope started out in the usual social way with things like the Epilepsy League, but fell victim to an unfortunate infatuation with local Republican politics. She served a term in that smoky den known as the Illinois General Assembly, and even became Republican national committeewoman from Illinois.

After being alternately bullied and ignored by the likes of Richard Ogilvie (whom Hope and Brooks helped into the Casino Club) at the 1976 GOP convention, it dawned on Mrs. McCormick that most of her fellow Republicans were as much interested in her money and influence as her philosophy of government. So now, instead of buying tickets to fund-raisers for candidates, she often buys clothes. She has one frock she calls her "Senate dress," in that she bought it with the one thousand dollars she saved by not going to a campaign dinner for Charles Percy.

Since fleeing from the pols, Hope is now back into social things in a very big way, having become president of the women's boards of the Lyric Opera and the Lincoln Park Zoo.

Husband Brooks, a pre-war Yalie, is active with such de rigueur charities as the Art Institute and Presbyterian St. Luke's, but commendably does his bit for less chic but deserving organizations like the Chicago Urban League. His directorships, aside from his little International Harvester Company, have included Commonwealth Edison, the First National Bank, and Esmark Corporation, as Mr. Swift's nice meat company is now known.

The McCormicks have a nifty place in the Gold Coast on North State Parkway. Their clubs include the Casino, the Chicago, the Saddle and Cycle, and the Racquet.

As a girl back in Bedford, New York, it probably never occurred to Hope that she could one day become queen of Chicago society, unless in a bad dream. But the queenship could easily be hers if she wanted it, as increasingly seems to be the case. Super.

3. Mrs. J. Harris Ward

Mrs. J. Harris Ward, now past the friendly side of seventy, no longer has a shot at the very top spot, but she's certainly worked at coming close. The widow of the late chairman of Commonwealth Edison, the former Mary Van Etten has been as busy as a buzz saw for as long as anyone can remember, often rising in her Lake Shore Drive apartment at 5:30 A.M to work her telephone as indefatigably as a bookie.

Mrs. Ward is in the business of getting charity things roaring off the runway, and she's been among the very biggest movers and shakers laboring on behalf of the University of Chicago, the Lyric Opera, the Art Institute, the Chicago Symphony, Multiple Sclerosis research and treatment, the Metropolitan Housing and Planning Council, and even the YWCA.

She was the major force behind the series of "Bright New City" lectures, which featured visiting officials from places like Detroit telling Chicagoans how lucky they are to live in Chicago. The only person who contributed more to the success of the King Tut exhibit was King Tut.

A former Vassar girl, Mrs. Ward looks the very essence of a society matron, though a trifle on the trim side. Some consider her a dreadful snob, but she's always trying to be where it's at, frequently mingling with younger folk in their fifties and wearing Gucci things.

4. Mrs. Edward Byron Smith

If the top place in Chicago society were accorded on the basis of looks, regal bearing, and manners alone, the former Louise Dewey would win with ease.

The daughter of Ambassador Charles S. Dewey and product of an old Gold Coast banking family, Mrs. Edward Byron Smith lived as a child and young woman in France. She speaks flawless French still, is very, very big with the Alliance Française, and received a medal from the French government for Francophilia or something.

A blonde turned maturer colors, she would have given Diana Prince and anyone else a real run for their money in her youth.

Louise's husband, the former chairman of the Northern Trust, is the son of Byron Laflin Smith, founder of same. Louise's nephew is the irrepressible Harold Byron Smith, who seems bent on trying somehow to become Mr. Republican Party, U.S.A.

Mrs. Smith is a Lake Forester. Her clubs include the Onwentsia Country Club, Shoreacres Country Club, Mayflower Descendants, the Arts, and the Racquet. Mr. Smith is a member of the Chicago Club, which Mrs. Smith cannot be because she is a woman. The big Smith charities include the Art Institute, Lyric Opera, Brookfield Zoo, Field Museum, Northwestern University, and, *certainement*, the Alliance Française. If a pro-Israel protester had spat on her at the Pompidou reception, Mayor Daley would *not* have liked it.

5. Abra (Rockefeller) Prentice Anderson

One of the most glamorous, richest, and, at five feet ten inches, tallest Chicago society ladies is young Abra (Rockefeller) Prentice Anderson, who makes herself even taller by wearing five-inch stiletto heels she calls her "bimbo shoes."

Abra is a Rockefeller, and not merely a parenthetical one, being a great-granddaughter of the great John D. Her grandmother, Mrs. Spellman Prentice, was so impressed with being a Rockefeller that she named Abra's father Rockefeller Prentice. He fell in love with a sweet but not at all prominent girl from Illinois, married her, and went off to make a fortune of his own dealing in artificial insemination.

Daughter Abra showed no interest in the cattle-fertility game, and went to work instead as a reporter for the *Sun-Times* in 1962, writing obits and little itsy bitsy things like that. She was crushed when she wasn't assigned to either of the political conventions in 1968, but found consolation in her marriage to a handsome Canadian *Sun-Times*man named Jon Anderson.

In 1969, the two were given the "Jon and Abra" gossip column in the *Chicago Daily News*, which was a dud, though it lasted three years. After this, they both quit to found and publish the *Chicagoan* magazine, which lasted only nine issues, though it had the potential to give Chicago its first truly sophisticated city magazine.

By then, both of Abra's parents had died, and Abra, Jon, and their three heirs were living in her parents' penthouse atop Drake Towers. Abra decided to have the place redone, startling strollers on Lake Shore Drive by having a helicopter fly building materials and things up to the building's roof.

She and Jon divorced in 1976, and now she devotes her time mostly to "Click" and being rich.

Her taste in cars runs to bright red Jaguars. Her taste in restaurants, according to *Chicago* magazine, runs to Le Perroquet (the city's best), but also to Eli's on Chicago Street, where they've named a salad for her.

Abra loves to show off the bod. As *Town & Coutnry* decorously said in its recent special issue on Chicago, "she shows off her willowly figure to perfection in low-cut or thigh-high slit evening costumes." Her 1977 Christmas card featured a "tasteful" photograph of herself and three kiddies in the buff.

When she is wearing clothes, Abra's quite active in society doings, especially on behalf of the Historical Society and the Lincoln Park Zoo. She's a big pal of Martha McCormick Hunt and recently served as cochairman of the Passavant Cotillion, which few *Sun-Times* reporters have ever done.

Her family gave the city the Prentice Women's Hospital and Maternity Center, which was very nice.

6. Mrs. Richard W. Simmons

A dame so grande as to favor flowing red evening gowns and ostrich plume party decorations, the former Charlotte Head Goodwill (not to be confused with the Good Will charity boxes) is a member of Chicago society's first rank. The Jerry Lewis of "correct" Chicago charity, Mrs. Simmons is credited with raising a record $1.6 million for the Lyric Opera while president of its women's board from 1972 to 1975.

It was Mrs. Simmons who once said: "It's harder to get extra help (for parties) during the day. So many of the waitresses and bartenders have jobs."

Her husband, the former chairman of the Midwest Stock Exchange, is one of the shrewdest estimators of stock-market performance Chicago has ever seen. If he had been around in 1929, brokers might have started jumping out of windows months earlier.

The Simmonses live in Lake Bluff, which is almost as good as Lake Forest, and belong to Shoreacres and Onwentsia, which is as good as you can get.

7. Mrs. Chauncey Hutchins

Another Lake Forester who would look quite at home in a *New Yorker* society-matron cartoon, Polly Hutchins is an elegant Wardwell of the elegant Boston Wardwells and met her Midwestern husband while their families were summering together in Maine. It's a cinch the Boston Wardwells wouldn't have been summering at Lake Geneva.

Mrs. Hutchins has been just absolutely everything with the Historical Society and Children's Memorial Hospital. Her clubs include the Casino, the Onwentsia, the Shoreacres, and the Friday. The Hutchinses also belong to the University Club, which is very egalitarian of them.

In fact, the Hutchinses may be one of the most egalitarian couples in Lake Forest. Though the son of *the* James Hutchins of the Mitchell-Hutchins brokerage firm, Polly's husband served as a mere corporal during World War II. And—on behalf of the Symphony, of course—Polly has hawked T-shirts and beach towels on radio. WFMT, of course.

8. Mrs. William H. Mitchell

Not far from the Hutchinses in Lake Forest are the Mitchells. He is a Mitchell of the Mitchell-Hutchins brokerage firm. Anne

Mitchell is the daughter of General Robert Wood, the Sears mogul.

Also a Very Important Poobah on the board of Children's Memorial, Anne Mitchell is the all-time top money raiser for the women's board of the Lyric Opera. Unlike Muhammad Ali, she does not go around saying, "I'm the greatest," though. Instead, she says: "To be effective, one can't be on dozens of boards in the city." So she confines herself mostly to these two.

The Mitchells hang out in the Onwentsia, Shoreacres, Casino, Racquet, and Arts Clubs—and he, in the Chicago. His favorite charities have included the Field Museum, Northwestern Memorial Hospital, and Richard Nixon, to whom he once gave $5,859.

9. Mrs. Bowen Blair

Pretty, toothy, and toujours gai (in the traditional sense of the term), the former Joan Smith and now Mrs. Bowen Blair is the daughter of Hastings Halpine Smith of New York and Palm Beach. Bowen is the son of the great William McCormick Blair and a partner in Pa's investment firm.

Also Lake Foresters, the Blairs belong to Onwentsia and the Casino—and he, to the Chicago. They are very big with the Art Institute and the Field Museum. Joan Blair seems fondest of all, though, of Presbyterian St. Luke's, perhaps because of all the fashion shows and fun romps. Mrs. Blair is considered by her society peers to be an accomplished musician and songwriter. She wrote one called, "Why Don't You Tell Me?" It never made it to the top of the charts but was said to be quite catchy.

Some years ago, in what was billed as a luncheon spoof to raise funds for the Extension Board of the Chicago Maternity Center, Joan played Margaret Chase Smith in a skit which entailed singing a duet with someone named Poopsie. Super!

10. Mrs. Leigh Block

Leigh Block is the retired Inland Steel mogul. Mary Block is the daughter of Albert Lasker, founder of both Lord & Thomas and modern advertising. They live on Astor Street. They would have risen quickly and high in Chicago society, but for one thing. The Blocks are Jewish.

With considerable effort, they made it anyway, through all the requisite good works and through establishing a reputation for collecting and fund raising in the art field that gave Chicago's society anti-Semites no choice. In 1970, Leigh Block became the first Jew ever to head the Art Institute. He's also a governing life member of the Chicago Orchestral Society, and a trustee of Northwestern University, the Brookfield Zoo, the Hirschhorn Museum in Washington, Michael Reese Hospital, and the University of Chicago Cancer Research Foundation.

Mary Block has been on boards of the Art Institute, the Lyric Opera, the University of Chicago, the Illinois Arts Council, the Alliance Française, the English-Speaking Union, the Chicago Historical Society, and the Rehabilitation Institute. For a time, she was also a vice-president of Foote, Cone, and Belding, which grew out of Daddy's firm.

Theirs was the first private art collection to be exhibited at the National Gallery.

Mrs. Block's approved, pre-prepared obituary proudly notes a gala party thrown for them at the Casino Club, where Jews were not always so warmly welcomed. Leigh Block belongs to the Chicago, Commercial, Executives, Tavern, Mid-Day, and Metropolitan Clubs, and the Conferie des Chevaliers de Tastevin, which is pretty nifty.

11. Mrs. Gardner Stern

Gardner and Hanchen Stern are the only other Jewish couple to have made it to the top of Chicago society. He owns Hillman's, the grocery chain that includes those elegant little Stop and Shop shops. She is a highly cultured, soft-spoken, slightly southern lady whose social success was helped by the fact that no one thought her at all pushy.

The Sterns live on the Drive just up from the Swearingens (and, no, Hanchen does not shout out the door: "Gardner, don't forget the bagels!"). Their 1927 wedding in the Standard Club still ranks as one of *the* Chicago Jewish social events of the millennium. The other wedding gowns hanging next to Hanchen's in the Historical Society are Heather Bilandic's and Mrs. Chauncey McCormick's.

The Sterns are heavily involved with Jewish charities (Rule No. 1 for members of the Standard Club). He has been a trustee of the University of Chicago and on the board of the Crusade of

Mercy. She's keen on the Chicago Boys Clubs and even more on Presbyterian St. Luke's, serving as chairman of the charity's annual fashion show.

Hanchen may well be the most fashionable woman in Chicago society. She shops at Korshak's, Saks, Field's 28 Shop, Bonwit's, I. Magnin's, and Elizabeth Arden, and she loves Dior boutique things, as don't we all.

12. Mrs. Mary McDonald

A divorcee living rather elegantly in Lincolnwood, of all places, Mary McDonald is among the most intelligent and certainly the most politically powerful women in Chicago society. Before Hope McCormick's political fling, Mary was the "Republican lady" in society circles. Now that Hope's GOP fling is flung, Mary's is the preeminent society voice in Republican politics once more.

She and blue-ribbon Joe Tecson are the only suburban county board members who ever get rave endorsements from the Chicago newspapers. Mary has also been Cook County Republican chairwoman and president of the Women's National Republican Clubs of Chicago. A good friend of W. Clement Stone, assorted North Shore industrialists, and the real powers in county Republican politics, Mary's network of contacts extends throughout the Chicago area and to Washington. Richard Nixon asked her personally to run for Donald Rumsfeld's North Shore congressional seat when Rummy left to join the White House. Just as personally, she declined.

A garden-party blonde who was one of the most photographed Chicago debutantes of the 1940's—her picture made the papers seven times one week—Mary belongs to the Casino and swings with the Antiquarian Society of the Art Institute, the Guild of the Historical Society, and the women's board of Children's Memorial Hospital. She was honorary consul for Costa Rica in Chicago for a time and is a concert harpist, which is more than most politicians can say.

13. Mrs. William W. Prince

The William W. Princes have always preferred that people refer to them as the William Wood Princes, as though they were members of the old House of Saxe-Coburg and Gotha or something. The *Chicago Tribune* has even violated its own stern stylebook rules by calling the Princes the Wood Princes, and *Town & Country* even went so far as to give them a hyphen. But the Social Register, bless it, refers to them merely as the Princes—listing them under "P." So shall we.

Mr. Prince is the adopted son of Frederick Henry Prince, the late chairman of the late Union Stock Yards, to whom he was related.

William has been named to the boards of First National Bank, Eastern Airlines, and Commonwealth Edison, and was president of the Armour Company, until a takeover by Greyhound.

Mrs. Prince has been active with the opera, the ballet, the Alliance Française, and all that, but her social reputation has also been helped by her having been friendly with the society press for so many years. She must have been photographed nearly as many times as Bonnie Swearingen has.

The Princes live grandly in a ritzy Lakeview Avenue duplex overlooking the park. They own a $100,000 clock that once graced Chicago's famous Stockyards Inn, and decorate their walls with things other than bullfight posters.

Very active with the Art Institute, the Princes were the ones who inflicted the Chagall wall and the Institute's Chagall windows on Chicago. They belong to all the right clubs and not a single wrong one. They prefer summers at Newport to those at Lake Geneva, and have their very own barge on which they cruise (pole?) the canals of France, which are certainly preferable to the Sanitary and Ship Canal and other waterways of Chicago.

14. Mrs. Pauline Palmer Wood

Pauline Palmer is rather the opposite of Mrs. W. Prince. As the granddaughter of Potter and Bertha Palmer and the wife of retired Sears chairman Arthur M. Wood, she could be at the top of this list or any other list she wanted. But Mrs. Wood shows no interest in being on lists, or doing all the things list people do. Far from being cozy with members of the society press, she often treats them as barely human creatures.

She lives quietly—as Queen Victoria lived quietly—in her imposing Lake Forest manor house, doing as she pleases. There are no signs on her lawn saying "Sailors and dogs, keep off grass," but sailors and dogs would be advised to tread carefully.

Mrs. Wood uses her money and rank the way a lot of society people would like to if they thought they could get away with it, which is to say, she does what she wants. She may well be the most genuine person of the whole bunch. No list of ranking Chicago society could be complete without her.

The Woods were among those invited to that charming little coming out party given for Dick and Pat Nixon out in Palm Desert, California, a few years ago. Mr. Wood has also been made a big man at the Art Institute. Mrs. Wood attends the more important Art Institute affairs.

When she likes.

15. Mrs. John Swearingen

Blonde Bonnie Swearingen has to be on this list because she's the only "society" woman most Chicagoans ever hear about. One of seven children of an Alabama preacher (she's fond of walking about her Lake Shore Drive apartment barefoot), she made her way to the Pasadena Playhouse and into a few minor film and television roles in the 1950's. She also worked briefly as a stockbroker.

But the biggest moments in her life, one presumes, were marriages—two to Texas oil men and one to John Swearingen, the Standard Oil oil man. As she once said of Lake Shore Drive life with John, "I love every delicious, exciting, and educational minute of it."

These delicious and exciting minutes have included some spent at White House dinners, kissing W. Clement Stone on the lips (gasp), being hugged by John Wayne, riding an elephant down State Street, wheedling a car out of Henry Ford for charity, verbally brawling with someone else's chauffeur, and telling *Town & Country* she eats honey before making love.

It's apparent that Bonnie would like to be for Chicago what Jackie O. has been for New York, but Abra (Rockefeller) Prentice Anderson and some of her crowd seem to have much more potential for the role over the long haul. Chic "W" magazine, which once declared Bonnie a Chicago "in," has since proclaimed her a Chicago "out."

Bonnie's rise in Chicago society has been something of a long haul in itself, but, despite a decade of local residence and good works, she hasn't gained all that much altitude. She was able to hook up with the Chicago Boys Club, but it took her a while to make the board of that. She did manage to become chairman of the American Needlepoint Guild's 1974 New York Needlepoint Festival, but that's hardly "super."

Da Mare took a liking to her, though, and made her cochairman of the Chicago Bicentennial Committee. Daley always was fondest of rich people who didn't start out that way.

There is a photograph floating around the newspaper files taken of Bonnie in the 1950's—Bonnie posing on a swing in a pair of tight, tight pedal pushers—which makes it clear how she might have caught a gentleman's eye. Nowadays, she dresses more sedately, in ruffles and shiny boots and things.

Now a maid of more than fifty summers, Bonnie still keeps in shape through constant exercise and by subjecting herself to brown rice diets when necessary. The other women Bonnie has around her always seem to be older, or less good-looking, but that may be just an optical illusion.

Whatever you might say of her, Bonnie's a game girl, with the panache to walk into a fancy reception with her nametag stuck on her rear and the courage to make it so handsomely through life, having been blind in one eye since the age of six. She is a crack shot and quite fond of shooting.

If Bonnie isn't at the top of everyone's list in society, the millions of Chicago people who aren't in society aren't aware of it. One newspaper reporter didn't even blink when Bonnie said: "Power? Me? Yes, I suppose I do have power." And it went that way into print. John Wayne called her "the queen bee of Chicago society" right in front of the mayor and everyone. Chicago society knows she's not the queen bee, but it shouldn't be bothered that everybody else in town thinks she is. Should it?

Honorable Mention: Heather Bilandic

Though the daughter of gypsum mogul Graham Morgan, Heather Morgan Bilandic was never what one would call a society queen, and achieved most of her prominence by marrying Michael. When the Morgans were looking for a place to hold the wedding reception, the Casino Club found it convenient to be "closed," even though under similar circumstances it found it convenient to be open for the wedding of Brooks McCormick's daughter Martha. But Heather is a classy lady, and during Bilandic's brief reign she gave both City Hall and high society the kind of good name neither much enjoyed before.

Heather's mother and sister died under tragic circumstances when she was only six and her father, now chairman of the U.S. Gypsum Company, sought to compensate for this trauma by devoting considerably more attention to her upbringing and happiness than most rich kids ever get.

And the Morgans are really rich. Though they've not been listed in the Social Register, they did get into 1500 North Lake Shore Drive. Heather had her own checking account at the age of twelve; was educated at the exclusive Roycemore School in Evanston, Smith College, and the Cordon Bleu in Paris; and was otherwise made to feel wanted.

The result was a very dutiful young woman, Gold Coast style. "I was having a dinner party for a very influential group of people," Mrs. Vernile Morgan, Heather's stepmother, once told an interviewer. "And I had hired a special cook to come in. The day before the party, the cook got sick. I was telling Heather that I'd have to take all thirty people out. Heather said: 'Momma, I'll cook your meal. Just don't tell anybody I'm in the kitchen.'" The result, including a bombe dessert with layers of ices, custard, and fresh strawberries, was a spectacular success.

Heather did not become a cook, but took up employment as a sort of Lake Shore Drive city patronage worker. Starting as a public relations aide for Mayor Daley's "Reach Out" summer youth program—for which she organized a "Frisbee Fling," among other things—Heather progressed up through the Department of Aviation to become executive director of the Chicago Arts Council. And all this without a letter from her ward committeeman!

It's not known how many votes Heather carried for the Democrats in her precinct, but she certainly helped Bilandic carry the city in his first mayoral primary.

Heather professes to absolutely adore the Bridgeport way of life, even though there's no longer a political reason for it, but, occasionally, class will out. "Having my in-laws next door has turned out to be a real godsend," she once said. "Most of my life I've lived in an apartment building with a janitor nearby. Having Nick [Bilandic's brother] who's very handy—he can fix anything—next door has been terrific." And when you can't get a cook, there's always the strawberry bombe.

6

Real Estate

There are three major characteristics to the real estate business in Chicago: the first is the Big Score, as in, "make no little bucks;" the second is race, as in "there goes the neighborhood," and the third is politics, as in "how come the county assessor received seventy-seven thousand dollars in campaign contributions from real estate dealers?"

Every real-estate developer wants to make the Big Score, but they just don't seem able to pull it off in other cities with the ease and fancy style of the Chicago boys. New York's William Zeckendorff, who borrowed big in the hopes of instantly filling his buildings with long-term tenants, had a string of Big Scores, but then went spectacularly floperoo. Other big New York names like Tishman and Uris had their New York troubles. According to *Fortune* magazine, New York developers took a bath to the tune of more than $1 billion in the Manhattan high-rise boom of the early 1970's.

That just doesn't happen in Chicago. In part because if you know the right people, complicated problems like zoning variances can become mere formalities. City Hall has always looked fondly on new construction (depending on who's doing it) and has created a labor and tax climate most conducive to it. If worse does come to worse, and you're hit with low occupancy in a new building during

105

a recession, or for whatever reason, it certainly wouldn't be the first time if a public agency were moved in as a tenant to help take up the slack. If it turns out to be one of those federally-funded city anti-poverty agencies, and you're hitting it with top dollar rents that you'd charge, say U.S. Steel, well, isn't that what the war on poverty and federal funds are for?

But the chief reason for the phenomenal success of Chicago's real estate wheeler-dealers goes far beyond such useful helping hands. Basically, it's because they're very conservative. They don't mind borrowing. They also go in for big, mammoth deals. Indeed, nobody ever tried anything like one of Harry Chaddick's one-hundred-acre Chicago shopping centers in New York. What makes the Chicago lads different is that they like to avoid taking risks. They always, or almost always, put their money on a sure thing.

Companies like the First National Bank's Real Estate Research Corporation combine scientific method and LaSalle Street street smarts to make accurate predictions of which way the property value wind is going to be blowing ten years hence. And, in keeping with the city's generous spirit, when something is in the wind, the word is often spread around. When something is revealed to be a sure thing, everybody tries to cash in.

This has led to a curious juxtaposition of overdevelopment and underdevelopment. The Mies van der Rohe office building box in the Loop was a sure thing that made a lot of people a lot of money. So they keep on building them in the Loop, a practice architect Harry Weese decries as "mining the city until it yields its last dollar." Yet there's been only the most marginal development in the Skid Row area across the river just west of the Loop, or in the warehouse and loft district across the river just to the north. Too risky.

Arthur Rubloff's vision of North Michigan Avenue's "Magnificent Mile" came to life so gloriously that everyone scampered to get in on the deal. But instead of spreading their developments to either side of the avenue, all the money men wanted to build right on the grand boulevard itself. The Greater North Michigan Avenue Association, among others, tried to keep this maniac greed in line, but the avenue still lost lovely old treasures like the Diana Courts and the Italian Court and gained grotesques like the Marriott Hotel and Water Tower Place—losing much of its boulevard character as a consequence. The most idiotic thing about the glut of huge ugly towers on the avenue is that, if you go just one block west of

Michigan on Grand Avenue or Ohio and Ontario Streets, there's an expanse of parking lots, tenements, warehouses, and other junk that might as well be downtown Indianapolis.

This tendency to build as close to the money as possible has also resulted in such unpleasantnesses as the high-rise glut along the narrow streets of the Gold Coast, and, of course, the High-Rise Wall along the lakeshore running north all the way from the Loop to Devon Avenue.

There's one great hope for Chicago, though. The renovation and rehabilitation of old buildings that was for so long just a Near North Side fad has caught on and is attracting thousands of couples back to the city. The profits have been such that many of the wheeler-dealers are jumping in. The city may be saved through rehabilitation simply because enough sharpies see it as yet another way to make the Big Score.

Chicago began as a big real estate score in itself, having been founded on the most key crossroads for land and water travel in the Midwest at the beginning of a fantastic population boom that lasted for more than sixty years. Ownership of a mere couple of hundred hitherto useless acres produced enormous fortunes almost overnight. Before Potter Palmer—who had the shrewdest eye for Chicago real estate in the nineteenth century—built his mansion there, the Gold Coast was a worthless marsh. After he built his mansion, the Gold Coast became a gold mine.

And, when the Chicago Fire burned much of the city down in 1871, there were enormous fortunes to be made all over again.

Today, making the Big Score is a little more complicated and takes more guesswork than just checking the timetables to see when the next boatload or trainload of immigrants will arrive. A classic example is Arthur Rubloff's $100 million Sandburg Village, a sprawling modern apartment development started a generation ago ostensibly to provide moderate income housing on the Near North Side in an area sandwiched between the Gold Coast on the east and an Italian-German slum on the west. The Village, with its high rises, townhouses, stores, and pubs, quickly became what it is today: luxury city living for professionals and as many airline stewardesses or secretaries as can be bunked into one dwelling unit without violating city health codes.

Rubloff's canny foresight produced the Big Score that was North Michigan Avenue. The elegant boulevard did not make it as the

"New Downtown" until Phil Klutznick and friends devised the eight-story atrium shopping center that is Water Tower Place.

The Hancock Center was a Big Score in that it successfully mixed office and residential space in one spectacularly high and centrally located building. More buildings that imitate the Hancock mix are going up closer and closer to the Loop.

Harry Chaddick's first Big Score was the massive Ford City shopping center on the Southwest Side built in the 1960's, which he's trying to create again with his plans for five more huge shopping centers in the city (plans which in some cases went monumentally awry).

But the Biggest Score in Chicago history is now on the drawing boards. If it ever comes to pass, the gargantuan "North Loop Plan" proposed by Arthur Rubloff would, for all practical purposes, redo the entire northern half of the Loop from Washington Street to the river. Conceived as a massive counterattack against the changes which have so dramatically altered the character and commerce of downtown Chicago in the last ten years, the proposal calls for the demolition of all but two of fifty buildings in the seven-block project area—a sort of civic-progress version of Hiroshima.

The two buildings initially allowed to stand are a couple of crusty old architectural landmarks, the Reliance Building at State and Washington, and the 222 North Dearborn Building—both so dear to the hearts of Lib Chicagoans. A third structure, the even crustier old Chicago Theater, is also expected to survive, presuming that the people who have made a Great Cause out of its salvation do not relent, and they never do.

On top of the cleared rubble, the planners envision huge new hotels, luxury high-rise apartment buildings, some more office boxes, brand-new theaters that would *not* play Kung Fu movies, and probably some big stores. A lot of little stores and small businesses would be wiped out, but, in Chicago, that's always their lookout.

Mayor Jane Byrne is not viewing the plan with quite the enthusiasm Bilandic's administration did, and Rubloff ultimately could get squeezed out. The plan may yet end up a pipe dream. But that's what they said when Rubloff proposed the North Michigan Avenue project.

Rubloff, who put it to the city that it was his plan or nothing, claims to have billions behind him in the demolition derby deal and is ready to drop some $250 million of his own petty cash into the pot. The city, but most especially the federal government, would be expected to make contributions toward this civic improvement as well. "Everybody tells me it's too big," Rubloff said. "Well, what's too big for some people is not too big for me. Sandburg Village was something they said I couldn't do, but there it is. . . . I don't need a crowning achievement. I've got enough. To me it's just another job. I'm just glad I had the imagination, the vision, and the guts to do this."

In most Chicago real estate deals, race is a silent partner. The ebb and flow of black settlement has more to do with the rise and fall of property values than any other factor. That is the chief reason Chicago so justly earned the title of the nation's most segregated city. That is why you find so many "racists" in the Chicago real-estate business. Nothing personal, mind you. It's strictly business.

Governor Thompson garnered the wrath of the Libs when he not only refused to use four of the Loop's crusty old architectural treasures for state offices but vetoed funds for a new city college building to be built at the south end of the Loop. When asked about this travesty, one of the city's most respected architects and developers—a man revered by Chicago's liberals—matter-of-factly sided with Thompson.

"The last thing the Loop needs is another black school," the architect said, carrying on like one of the Southwest Side's anti-busing mothers about the crime and blight such institutions supposedly breed. As for black people and the housing market in general, the liberal architect had this liberal comment: "If we could teach blacks how to take care of real estate property, we would revolutionize the business."

Nothing better illustrates the impact of race and racism on Chicago real estate than the calamity that recently befell—of all people —multimillionaire wheeler-dealer Harry Chaddick, the shopping-center king. In 1973, Chaddick came up with a master plan for urban redevelopment that centered on a network of fifteen elaborate city shopping centers. Ten were to be of the smaller, forty-store variety, but five were to be shopping whoppers on the order of his big Ford City success, each with one hundred stores or more, right in the middle of the city.

One of the great jewels in this crown was to have been the Stockyards Mall, a one-hundred-store extravaganza to have been built on all that unused stockyards land in the mayor's Bridgeport neighborhood on the Southwest Side. Chaddick had the deal wired. He had put up $500,000 for planning, had located the $50 million development capital, and had gotten everyone, including the city and then Mayor Bilandic, to agree. The project was announced in one of those elaborate City Hall press conferences that Daley always used to announce anything major. It was estimated that the Stockyards shopping center would generate $500 million in sales, $2 million in city sales-tax revenues, and four thousand new jobs. Everyone was overjoyed, especially Chaddick. He was, after all, one of the best politically-connected developers in town, and the relationship was working again. Nothing could go wrong.

It went wrong fast. No one had bothered to consult the good people of Bridgeport, and they did not take kindly to the idea. Anything that big, said the Bridgeport citizens, would bring in outsiders —meaning black people. Bilandic yanked the rug. Chaddick was aghast, but the mayor had no choice. Money has a very loud voice in Chicago, but votes always come first.

Rubloff was soundly scorned by high-minded types when his Sandburg Village went from a low- and moderate-income clientele to an affluent one, but the critics meekly fell silent when the slum to the west went from a German and Italian one to a black one. Were it not for Sandburg Village, the black ghetto might easily have flooded past the boundary of Wells Street, linked up with the Skid Row deterioration of Clark Street, and imperiled even the Gold Coast itself. Mercy!

There was something of a Great Cause stirred up in the late 1960's in a vain attempt to keep the historic Red Star Inn German restaurant from succumbing to Rubloff's expansion plans for Sandburg. And Rubloff is still trying to figure out some way to drive the Huns of the Germania Club out of their historic sanctuary on Clark Street so that he can erect yet another Sandburg high rise.

But the anchor of prosperity that Sandburg Village provided for the area has made Rubloff seem a hero and visionary to many people. He single-handedly saved the Near North Side, and made it safe for all those rich liberals to live near Lincoln Park.

Rubloff's North Loop plan, if it ever comes to pass, would have as dramatic an impact. The rapid expansion of the black ghetto in Chicago created the phenomenon of two downtowns (in some cities it created the phenomenon of no downtown). The Loop has a daytime and nighttime face. During the day, the Loop area has remained a relatively prosperous, racially-mixed bustle of executives, office workers, shoppers, and shop clerks. But, starting in the late 1960's, the Loop was taken over at nightfall by black kids commuting in from the ghetto. The Loop crime rate has remained one of the lowest in the city, but the sheer mass of all those young dudes scared the white folks out. What resulted was a "New Downtown" of restaurants, night clubs, movie theaters, and department stores across the river on and near North Michigan Avenue.

Whatever its original intentions, Rubloff's North Loop plan would drive those ghetto kids back where they came from, if only by depriving them of their main reason for coming—entertainment. Nearly all the big Loop movie houses would be removed in the plan, and with them their usual fare of Kung Fu flicks and violent "black man gets the honky" movies. The record stores, junk jewelry joints, and dude fashion shops would also go. All there'd be left for the kids to do would be to admire the architectural styles of the new high rises.

There's only one thing wrong with this massive, sweeping solution to what has been perceived at City Hall as a major urban problem: Mayor Daley didn't live to see it. Whether Daley liked it or not, and he didn't, Chicago in the 1970's became a predominantly black city, with the majority of the school population and nearly half the total city population black. This was the result of decades of migration up the Illinois Central railroad line from the South and at least three generations of welfare-induced population explosion.

For decades, Chicago's black ghetto had been traditionally confined to a long, perpendicular rectangle extending south from the Loop, with some scattered settlements on the West and Near North Sides. By the mid-1960's, it had grown into an inverted "T."—the perpendicular segment reached from the Loop all the way south to the city limits and the horizontal segment reached from the Loop west to Cicero Avenue. By the late 1970's, the southern perpendicular segment had swollen to take in most of the South Side and the vertical portion had pushed north to North Avenue and west to Austin Avenue, right across the street from Oak Park. The Near North Side ghetto—that which had made the Gold Coast ladies so nervous—had flung black people north along the Howard elevated line all the way to Howard Street itself.

Several all-white or predominantly white communities have held out against what a number of real estate developers (and panic peddlers) decried as a "black tide." Bridgeport, as we have seen, simply used its immense political clout. Alderman Eddie Vrdolyak's steel-mill-laden 10th Ward and surrounding Far South Side environs used what might be described as another kind of clout, the kind that dents hard hats. The World War II refugees from Lithuania who carved out a second Lithuania around Marquette Park vowed to fight to the death against an incursion. The University of Chicago's Hyde Park was of course more genteel, but its approach to the problem amounted to a quota system.

Census Bureau surveys now indicate that the migration of blacks to Chicago and other big cities has trailed off. The black ghetto populations in the city have more or less stabilized. The flow now is back to the prosperous "Sun Belt" South or out to the suburbs, where the jobs are. In the south suburbs, portions of Chicago Heights, Harvey, Robbins, etcetera, have become really nasty ghettos (even farther to the south, east of Kankakee, is a piece of some of the worst squalor in America called Pembrooke Township, which the Feds would do well to investigate).

In the western suburbs, Bellwood is becoming what Maywood has been for a long time, which isn't all that bad. Black people will probably never get to live in either Cicero or Berwyn (for the same reason they'll never get to live in Marquette Park), but lovely old Oak Park is becoming integrated, in the most sensible fashion. A system similar to that used in Hyde Park has proved workable, and the village has prevented the paranoia that panic peddlers are so good at generating by financially guaranteeing property values.

To the north, Evanston's big (fifteen thousand) black population has been kept in bounds (as they say) by the suburb's skyrocketing real estate prices. Farther up the North Shore, there has been a small black colony in Lake Forest that dates back to the nineteenth century. This has provided Lake Foresters with a sense of egalitarian pride—and numerous servants.

With little attention from the news media, some spectacularly successful integration has occurred on the North Side of Chicago. The great condominium boom of the early- and mid-1970's produced an incredible glut of new and converted condo units all along the Lincoln Park lakefront. All those developers were trying to make a Big Score out of a Sure Thing. Condominium developers have to sell their building units in a hurry, because their profit comes from the last units in a building to be sold. So, the developers did what they had to, which is also what the federal government said they were supposed to do—sell to anyone. In record numbers, they sold to middle-class black people, who are now living quite harmoniously in one of the better-balanced ethnic mixes to be found in any American city.

Black people aren't the only ghetto folk in Chicago. There's a white Appalachian slum in Uptown just west of the North Side lakefront and a rapidly growing Puerto Rican ghetto on the Near Northwest Side in what used to be Polish country. Both these ghettos are well-armed and considered dangerous, especially the Puerto Rican areas near Humboldt Park, where arson has become a neighborhood pastime.

In the mid-1960's, Commissioner Lew Hill's Stalinesque Urban Renewal Department was fond of bringing about racial stability by leveling whole blocks and thus creating rather effective neighborhood boundaries. In more recent years, this sort of urban renewal has been taken over by the ghetto residents themselves. The riots following the 1968 Martin Luther King assassination left a large part of the West Side looking like bombed-out Berlin, and it's been more or less left that way. Since then, other sections of the city have been reduced to rubble fields. The ghettos may end up as the least densely populated sections of the city, unless you count rats.

One group of ghetto residents the city's ward politicians have welcomed are the Mexicans, whose number may now exceed five hundred thousand. Remarkably similar to the European immigrants of the late nineteenth century, the Mexicans tend to be very religious, property conscious, family oriented, and imbued with the work ethic. In many Chicago Mexican families, you'll find the father with two or three jobs, the mother holding down a job, and the older children with jobs. They tend to bring stability wherever they settle. Their only real drawback is that so many of them neglect to become U.S. citizens, and therefore cannot vote. But the ward bosses will think of something.

Real estate dealers in Chicago enjoy a symbiotic relationship with the political apparat more cozy than any other. The real estate boys are a never-ending source of campaign funds and they control, as much as anyone does, the residential, and hence, political makeup of the city. City Hall, the zoning boards, and the party-run courts control the means to make life very happy, or very miserable, for real-estate developers.

The power of the assessor's office is so awesome in terms of being able to make or break a business that its occupants have been treated as sacred personages. Former Assessor P. J. "Parky" Cullerton could always count Arthur Rubloff as one of his great pals. Would the two have been so chummy if Cullerton were city aviation commissioner? Tom Tully came into the office after Parky as a reformer, but a private little thousand-dollar-a-plate campaign breakfast for young Tom Tully attracted the biggest names in Chicago real estate as guests. It also attracted some curious reporters, but they were turned away, not being able to come up with the price of the meal. Young Tom Hynes, the new guy, has the cleanest image in the Democratic machine after Neil Hartigan, but that didn't stop Hynes from accepting $77,000 in campaign funds from Harry Chaddick and assorted other real estate fellows.

City Hall likes to boast that its building code is one of the toughest in the nation. It's probably *the* toughest in the nation. But that hardly serves as a brake on commerce and industry for the simple reason that—as the Mirage tavern exposé and so many other scandals stirred up by the *Sun-Times* and the *Tribune* attest—the code is so often applied selectively. The fatted envelope can bring on the blurriest myopia when it comes to inspectors gazing at exposed wiring and crumbling walls. An attitude less generous than this—or worse, the wrong kind of political activity—can make an inspector as keen of eye as the hawk, seeing violations that sprang into being with the inspector's visit.

No one in his right mind would try to build anything, even a birdbath, without a building permit. To do so would invite a parade of fellows in gabardine overcoats, with open palms. But, once in a while, someone tries it. The First National Bank started its enormous Loop tower without benefit of permit. It dug the hole in the ground and then kept on building for months, without a permit. Magically, a permit finally appeared from City Hall.

"We tried time and again to get the permits," Gaylord Freeman, then the bank's chairman, told *Fortune* magazine, "but they were so fussy about this and that so I said, 'Let's go without them.' If we had less of a man as mayor [Daley], we wouldn't have had the courage to do that!" Or the clout. Even if they're just putting up a tree house for their kids, most Chicagoans wouldn't have the courage to try that.

Then there's the interesting matter of zoning—a matter of life, cost per square foot, and millions of dollars to developers. There are many examples that would illustrate how this sort of business is often transacted, but one fascinating case should say it all: In October of 1976, the City Council in rather cursory fashion voted to rezone some crummy land on the South Side from "restricted manufacturing" to "residential." Restricted manufacturing is about the least profitable classification there is, and the land was totally without streets, alleys, sewers, and other such niceties.

In May of the next year, the City Council voted to join with the state in a $3.1 million street improvement project in the area.

Then, the next month, according to the *Tribune*, none other than alderman and attorney-at-law extraordinaire Eddie Vrdolyak purchased twelve lots in the section, six of them fronting the improved street, from the four little old ladies who owned the land. He paid $2,666 a lot.

A year later, according to the *Tribune*, Vrdolyak sold the best six of the lots to a subsidiary of the First Savings and Loan Association of Hegewisch. He received ten thousand dollars a lot.

What would a savings and loan want with six lots zoned residential? Well, three months later, the savings and loan applied for permission to move its main office to the site.

Two months after that, a request to rezone the six lots from residential to "business service district" was referred to the City Council's Committee on Buildings and Zoning for approval. The chairman of the committee was Eddie Vrdolyak. The following month, the committee took less than one minute to approve the change unanimously. Vrdolyak did not object. And the next month, the change was just as quickly approved by the entire City Council, and everyone lived Happily Ever After.

Governor Thompson is not a totally negative fellow. When he rejected the idea of putting state offices in the Loop's four antique landmark buildings and vetoed money for that south Loop black college, he decided to do something positive. He approved a plan to have the state buy up the defunct, vacant Sherman House hotel at Clark and Randolph Streets and put up a $100 million shiny new state office building in its place. The new structure wouldn't be able to house as many state offices as the four landmark buildings, but it would be lots taller.

Thompson's opponent in the 1978 election, Michael Bakalis, raised some questions. The state was agreeing to buy up the old hotel for $15 million. The owners of the hotel needed the money in part to pay back a $5.25 million loan owed to the Teamsters. The Teamsters had just endorsed Thompson for reelection.

Bakalis cried deal, but he got it wrong. Such large sums of money involving major hunks of real estate don't get thrown around like that for a little quid pro quo endorsement. That's not how the city that works, works. Certainly the decision made the hotel owners and the Teamsters happy, but it also made Arthur Rubloff happy because the new state office tower would fit in with his great North Loop plan. The project would make a great many construction contractors and trades unions happy. It would make parking-lot owners in the area happy and it would make the lawyers who handled all those millions in bonds very happy.

The word soon got to Bakalis that he had been mistaken. He quieted down on the subject. He also lost the election. And it looks like everyone's going to live happily ever after.

The two terms most likely to send a Chicago real-estate developer up for a few laps around his ceiling are "rent controls" and "landmarks." Despite the condominium boom, there is a lot of real-estate money to be made from rent, especially in the sprawling vastness of six-flats and four-plus-ones west of the lakefront. Under pressure from the high-minded, a committee was assigned to look into the possibility of rent controls as a means of preventing gouging, but it responded as though it had been asked to look into a sour old garbage can. The general conclusion was that controls would stultify construction. Real-estate taxes in Chicago average 20 to 22 percent of gross income from rental properties, compared to only 12 to 15 percent in rent-control cities like New York and Washington. Controls thus would further restrict landlords' profits —a new Illinois law is already making them pay interest on tenant security deposits—and so deprive them of incentive. It is likely that Chicago will have a Republican mayor before it gets rent controls.

Landmarks are more of a problem for real-estate men in Chicago because the news media and the Feds are always sticking their oars in to save things old. Actually, except for Navy Pier, the Water

Tower, and Mayor Daley's Bridgeport bungalow, all the really meaningful landmarks in Chicago are already gone. Fort Dearborn is remembered only with a plaque in the sidewalk at Michigan and Wacker. Lew Hill steamrolled the St. Valentine's Day Massacre garage on Clark Street more than a decade ago, along with Nelson Algren's favorite saloon just up the street, and replaced both landmarks with ever-so-quiet housing for senior citizens. The Potter Palmer, Swift, and other Gold Coast mansions are gone, as is the famed Morrison Hotel, in the back rooms of which Da Mare first came to power.

If Europe had dealt as cavalierly and churlishly with its history, Westminster Abbey would doubtless now be a McDonald's. But efforts are being made to save what's left, which is almost guaranteed if you can get your favorite landmark approved by the Commission on Historical and Architectural Landmarks, the Illinois Department of Conservation's Division of Historic Sites, the National Register of Historic Places, and the Chicago City Council. Which is to say, nothing's guaranteed at all. As it stands, Chicago has fewer than fifty official landmarks.

One of these does include most of an entire street—Astor Street—a rather densely charming public way lined with trees, Victorian rich people's houses, ugly new high rises, and too many cars. Astor Street runs through the Gold Coast from Division Street to North Avenue and Lincoln Park. Declaring the "Astor Street District" an official landmark put a brake on high-rise construction as well as on property values (only rich people can afford rich people's houses, whereas a dozen stewardesses banding together can swing a high-rise efficiency).

Some people carry the landmark business a trifle too far. Architect Harry Weese and some others tried—in vain, it seems—to have the Loop's rattly old El tracks and trains preserved as a historic landmark, which some might liken to preserving the old municipal sewage-treatment plant.

Other of Weese's ideas have proved more popular with his more money-minded colleagues. Phil Klutznick, among others, had denounced "rehab," complaining that there was no money in it. But, now that Weese and his fellow visionaries have shown that the "back to the city" movement is turning rehabilitation into a Big Score, all sorts of wheeler-dealers are giving it a whirl.

A major problem with rehab is that so many of the lofts and

warehouses that people want to remodel into living quarters cannot legally be used as residences. Many of the old buildings are made of wood and brick, and exceed the legal height limit for such structures. Thousands of other code violations are being encountered. But, as we have seen, ways can always be found to cope with a building code. And, if rehab proves a big enough score, someone might even be moved to change the laws. Perhaps Eddie Vrdolyak might have some ideas about what to do.

Big national outfits like American Invesco, Century 21, and Homefinders have been moving onto the Chicago scene, rendering the hundreds of mom-and-pop realty firms that used to handle most of the city's residential business obsolete, if not extinct. But, around the big money, you still see a lot of old Chicago names: Rubloff, Wirtz, Baird & Warner, Sudler, and Whiston.

Real-estate firms are among the last of the major corporations in the city to remain family outfits. Real estate is ideally suited for families, because there are so many different aspects of it to be run independently. There are the political and legal aspects of it, the land acquisition, fund raising and promotion, property management aspects, and, of course, the visionary aspects.

Though they've come to use computers and other modern marvels, the old Chicago firms tend to remain conservative and, sometimes, anachronistic. Romanek and Golub, for example, have built three spanking new office boxes on North Michigan Avenue, two others in the Loop, and sixteen residential high rises along the lakeshore. They've got a glittering new Xerox Centre high rise going up at Monroe and Dearborn in the center of the Loop. All these buildings have one thing in common: No thirteenth floor. "When you come right down to it," said Marvin Romanek, "despite all the sophistication and hundreds of millions of dollars involved in this business, everyone is superstitious."

Superstitious, maybe, but often lucky. Romanek-Golub put up a high rise on Sheridan Road in the Belmont Harbor area. It was a beautiful building with balconies, but it suffered from the fact that there was a block's worth of other buildings between it and the lake. And, for a time, its units sold like coldcakes.

But the market swung the other way, and soon units in that building were going for a hundred grand or more. Between July 1977 and July 1978, real estate prices in Cook County increased an average of 105 percent, according to a survey made by First Federal Savings. What with rehab and reclamation and refurbishing and all that, the average price of a dwelling unit in the Lincoln Park-Lakeview area went from $36,000 in 1977 to $93,500 in 1978. As any alderman would agree, that beats even sirens in the night.

THE TOP TEN REAL ESTATE DEVELOPERS IN CHICAGO

1. Arthur Rubloff

Now in his late seventies, the king of Chicago real estate is more than half as old as Chicago. Six feet tall, with a pointy chin, pointy eyebrows, and rounded girth, he looks rather like the Joker character in the Batman and Robin adventures in comic books and on television. Extremely myopic, he wears thick glasses that, while stylishly crafted, seem to contain lenses lifted from some high-powered microscope. Always lavishly, expensively, and—though the effect never really seems to come off—elegantly dressed, Rubloff is the closest thing to a fop in the Chicago business establishment. By comparison, Potter Palmer dressed like a bum. Yet, as close as he comes to social splendor (he was probably Da Mare's favorite rich guy) he frequently ruins the image with his gravelly snarl of a voice and such malapropisms as "It came to me like a shot out of the bull." (No wonder he was Daley's favorite rich guy.)

Arthur Rubloff sure didn't start out rich. The winner of a Horatio Alger Award, and now director of the Horatio Alger Awards Committee, Rubloff was born in 1902 as one of five children of Solomon Rubloff, a traveling jewelry salesman. The Rubloffs lived in Duluth, Minnesota, at the time, but shortly afterward moved to the small town of Virginia, Minnesota, where Arthur's old man opened a store. They lived in a succession of tar-paper shacks, and did not prosper. Young Arthur worked selling newspapers, shining shoes, and setting pins in a bowling alley, sometimes earning as much as 50 cents a week. By the time he was thirteen years old, he had $100 saved—enough, he thought, for him to go out and make his way in the world.

He ran away from home, and took a job as a galley boy on a

Great Lakes freighter. A shipmate lifted $83 from him, but he had hidden the remaining $17, and when the ship landed at Buffalo, he used the money to make his way back west as far as Cincinnati. Flat broke, he took a job in a furniture factory, where he worked until he was fifteen. Learning that his family had moved to Chicago, he accepted a railroad ticket from his father and took a job in his father's ladies' wear factory—which burned down the day after his father had canceled the insurance for want of funds. His old man sent him down to get a job on the West Side's Market Street, and Arthur took one, with a real estate man.

By 1920, at the age of eighteen, he was earning $8,000 a year. By 1930, working for Robert White & Company, he was making $50,000 a year. Then he went into business for himself. It didn't go so well at first. By 1934, when he married Josephine Sheehan, he had only $700 in the bank. It was enough. He was able to find bankrolls for a few Big Scores, and was on his way.

For a man who later did so much to save all that glitters in Chicago, the onetime cabin boy at first confined himself to the most circumspect ambitions. Starting out in the wholesale district west of the Loop and specializing in leasing industrial and commercial properties, Rubloff never dabbled in anything east of the El tracks on Wells Street. Then, in 1944, he got an idea—the Magnificent Mile on Michigan Avenue. The plans were unveiled in 1947, to a response not unlike that currently greeting his North Loop plan.

"I'd spent fifty thousand dollars preparing the plans and I was called all sorts of names," he said. "Some people thought I was trying to steal the town."

Rubloff now owns property all over the world. He has opulent digs at 1040 Lake Shore Drive and 781 Fifth Avenue in New York. Though a kingpin of the Standard Club, and not the Casino, he's made it to the board of the Lyric Opera and life membership with the Art Institute, which is more than that sailor who swiped his $83 ever did.

Rubloff, whose name appears on thousands and thousands of buildings throughout the Chicago area, shows no interest in retiring. He will go to his grave still looking for the biggest of scores. As a friend put it almost thirty years ago: "He's like a cat watching a mousehole—when a mouse comes out, he's on it."

2. Arthur Wirtz

A contemporary of Rubloff and the fabled A. N. Pritzker, Arthur Wirtz is a man of whom both admirers and detractors have said: "He owns everything he ever bought."

Whether that is true is something only those knowledgeable about the intricacies of Chicago's land-trust and title business would know. But what is otherwise known is that Wirtz owns the Chicago Stadium—and with it, the Chicago Blackhawks and part of the Chicago Bulls—the Bismarck Hotel; the American Furniture Mart; the 333 North Michigan Avenue Building housing the prestigious Tavern Club; a $150-million-a-year national liquor distributorship; a Milwaukee radio station; the Ivanhoe Stables; no fewer than twenty luxury high rises on the lakefront; and the Lord only knows what else that makes up what *The Wall Street Journal* once described as "one of the nation's largest privately-held business empires."

A relentless worker, the septuagenarian Wirtz started in business as the son of a Chicago cop who farmed on the side. Among his first great real estate holdings was 120 acres of Illinois farmland his grandfather had bought in 1850 for something like one dollar an acre.

Like many Chicago real-estate men, Wirtz's fortune was in large part built up during the Depression—although, in his case, not solely from real estate. He and a Canadian wheeler-dealer managed to more or less corner the American grain market. He also scored big by discovering and financially advising a figure skater named Sonja Henie. As Wirtz told *Town & Country* magazine: "The Sonja Henie show made enough so that I acquired control of Madison Square Garden, acquired the St. Louis Stadium, and paid off the mortgage on the Chicago Stadium." The financial advisor to Miss Henie later performed a similar function regarding city real estate patterns for a less *zoftig* Mayor Daley.

An enormous fellow (six foot four inches tall and weighing nearly three hundred pounds) Wirtz likes big things. He keeps a Lake Michigan-sized 47-foot sailing yacht in Chicago, and a 123-footer with seven bathrooms in Fort Lauderdale. LBJ and Da Mare were among the many imperial poobahs whom Wirtz has entertained on his yachts. Wirtz entertained the King of Norway on his four-hundred-acre farm near Barrington.

In 1976, Wirtz had 500 of his friends out to the Chicago Stadium to dine and dance to the music of Peter Duchin in celebration of the Wirtzes' Golden Wedding anniversary. Surely a man with that much money has more friends than that.

3. Phil Klutznick

When Arthur Rubloff built suburban shopping centers, he built them, like Evergreen Plaza, right next to the city limits so that Chicago residents would not be encouraged to leave town. Phil Klutznick never thought that way. When Levitt of Long Island's Levittown was teaching postwar New Yorkers that there was more to life than a walk-up apartment in the Bronx, Klutznick was doing the same thing for Chicagoans with a brilliantly planned if somewhat modestly priced south suburban suburb called Park Forest.

As much as Rubloff has been trying to keep the city together, Klutznick has thought highly of the suburbs. After Park Forest, he cut into big suburban shopping-center deals such as River Oaks, Old Orchard, and the enormous Oak Brook behemoth. Having helped draw thousands and thousands of Chicagoans out of the city in this manner, he more recently put together the Water Tower Place that has drawn so many of them away from the Loop.

With the city really keen on developing the old railroad land and what-have-you south of the Loop into nifty housing for the affluent, Klutznick has come up with plans for what amounts to a big suburban development in the middle of the city, complete with outer walls and gates. Instead of a Rubloff Sandburg Village or one of Harry Weese's exciting designs, Klutznick would bring Hoffman Estates within walking distance of the Loop.

One of the very few Americans with a law degree at the beginning of the Depression, Klutznick was born in Kansas City and served as an assistant corporation counsel and later assistant U.S. attorney in Omaha in the early 1930's. By the middle 1930's, he was working for the federal government in a number of housing programs, and somewhere along the line got the idea that federal money could be used to finance some really Big Scores.

Klutznick said that, back in the late 1940's, he was several times on the brink of going broke—paying off $2.5 million in bills at the end of the month and having only $5,000 left to tide him over.

A tidy-looking septuagenarian who favors conservative vested suits, Klutznick is notable for actually residing in his own developments, or as he put it: "I believe in living over the store." That meant living in Park Forest in the early days, which meant that other Park Foresters knew where to find him when they were angry about something. Nowadays, Klutznick lives in his Water Tower Place, where there aren't nearly so many complaints.

4. Charles Swibel

Someone once wrote of *Washington Post* Editor Ben Bradlee that he looked like an international jewel thief, a remark that Bradlee probably found immensely flattering.

If you wrote that about Charlie Swibel, which you could, he probably wouldn't like it that much. This dark-haired, narrow-eyed gent who developed Marina City and scores of less notable properties cherishes his respectability.

In a business in which many of his colleagues had parents born in Eastern Europe, Swibel was himself born in Poland—born "Cwibel" in Wolbron, Poland, in 1926. As a young man in this country, he attended both the University of Illinois and Northwestern, and learned enough about local real estate to be able to begin putting together the Marina City deal in the late 1950's. Daley handpicked Swibel to run the Chicago Housing Authority, and never seemed to mind Swibel's many outside business interests. Swibel is a man of such consequence that he is still running the CHA even though his protector is long gone.

Swibel lives first class, with fancy clothes, a big home in Winnetka, and Don Reuben for an attorney. He has been the recipient of every rags-to-riches honor imaginable, including the Free Enterprise Association's "Success Story Award," a "Good American" award, an "Immigrant" award, and a JC "Young Man of the Year." He made it to the board of Israel Bonds and is a member of the Covenant Club, which isn't the Standard Club but beats the Bucktown Hotshots.

For all his ups, Swibel has had a few downs in life. There were some nasty questions about how the fellow who installed the burglar alarm in Charlie's house ended up with a CHA contract, and how a private-management firm Charlie was connected with got a contract from a bank holding CHA funds. But matters never progressed beyond the questions.

In 1976, an unthinkable thing for one so high placed happened to Charlie. A search of court records showed that Swibel was sole beneficiary of a land trust that owned a flophouse on Madison Street's Skid Row, and Charlie was fined seven hundred dollars for building code violations. But seven hundred dollars is the smallest of potatoes.

Much more tragic to him, no doubt, was his failure to get his big Skid Row Madison-Canal Street development project off the ground. It was supposed to have been a Big Score, but at the time didn't pass muster as a Sure Thing. For the time being, the only profit that seems to be coming from Swibel's west-of-the-Loop holdings is the kind that comes from people who pay one dollar a night.

5. Harry Chaddick

The very distinguished-looking Harry Chaddick has long been thought to be a man as closely wired to City Hall as Charlie Swibel. This multimillionaire developer more or less wrote the city zoning ordinance (his extensive holdings in the city notwithstanding) and served as chairman of the city's Zoning Board of Appeals. He was appointed to the Public Library Board and as cochairman of the Chicago Economic Development Commission. He was head of the mayor's committee studying rent controls—which decided the city didn't need any. The city has thoughtfully leased space in at least one of Chaddick's buildings and at least a couple of Chaddick's corporations have thoughtfully given people like Bilandic some four-figure campaign contributions.

But for all that closeness, things haven't been going so well lately for the genius developer of Ford City. Of the five major, one-hundred-store-plus shopping centers he proposed for Chicago in 1973, only one is doing well: the Brickyard, a fifty-acre site at Diversey and Narragansett on the Northwest Side that was formerly occupied by the old Carey Brick Company.

Of the others, Green Acres—to have been built on the grounds of the old city tuberculosis sanatorium, of all places—ran into opposition from neighbors who wanted the space for a park. The Stockyards projects ran into Bridgeport racism and the Humboldt Square deal was compromised by riots, arson, vandalism, and other antisocial behavior on the part of the local Puerto Rican community. Harbor Mall, down by Calumet Park on the South Side, had to be abandoned because of an awful stench perpetually emanating from a nearby landfill.

But somehow, millionaire Harry manages to get along. He spends a lot of time at his big lavish home in Palm Springs, an area he helped develop (without fear of landfill smells).

6. The Pritzkers

There is no point in trying to single out any one of the Pritzkers for this list. They are individuals, but they are Pritzkers. They are also rather well off, being the richest single family in Chicago. Their holdings must easily approach $1 billion, most of it held in trust. They founded and control the Hyatt hotel chain. They own or control steel companies, auto-parts maufacturing firms, farm-equipment manufacturing, musical-instrument concerns, coal mines, lumber companies, a publishing house, a bank, and amusement parks. And miles and miles of real estate. Their Centrex Industrial Park in Elk Grove Village is the world's largest.

The head of the clan is octogenarian Abram Nicholas Pritzker, whom everyone calls "A.N." "Those who don't," he told the *Chicago Daily News*, "call me a son of a bitch."

A.N.'s father came to the United States from Kiev, Russia, and was able to see to it that his son went to Northwestern University and the De Paul law school. As a lawyer, A.N. turned to real-estate deals during the Depression. And other kinds of deals, too. For example, he bought the Cory Company coffeepot-and-appliance firm in 1941 for $25,000 cash. He sold it in 1967 for $27 million.

A.N. sets the style for the Pritzkers, which is one family very big on privacy. They like to own or control their companies absolutely. They dislike stockholders, lawyers, and other outsiders. "You can't be public and be honest," A.N. once said.

A.N. is very close to the First National Bank, which helped him a great deal during the Depression. Each year, he makes a point of buying at least $500,000 in Israel bonds. Naturally, the Pritzkers are pillars of the Standard Club. They also mix with the society set at the University of Chicago. The University's Pritzker School of Medicine is so named because of a nice little gift of $12 million.

A.N. is considered the wizard of the clan. His younger brother

Jack, a lawyer, now in his middle seventies and recovering from a stroke, is the real-estate expert. He and his wife Rhoda are noted art collectors and she is one of the world's leading benefactors of wildlife.

A.N. also has two sons, now in their fifties. Jay is the financial brain and Robert the management genius. All told, there are twenty-seven Pritzkers in the immediate family, but there's more than enough money to go around.

7. John Baird

Born in Evanston in 1915, John Baird is Scottish, very establishment, rather straight-laced, and president of a firm that has been doing business in Chicago for a century and a quarter. Baird and Warner, which has had four generations of Bairds associated with it, is the most respected real estate sales, development, and management company in the city. Its checks never bounce, or even quiver.

Tough-minded, conservative in demeanor, and personally somewhat stingy, Baird is every bit as intelligent as the rags-to-riches boys who have piled up such enormous fortunes. But he evidences a quality they seldom do—sensitivity. As a developer, Baird has always shown a remarkable concern for the effect his projects will have on people, and not just bank balances. And, often, he doesn't seem to care about bank balances at all. Such is his penchant for doing good works just as good works that, according to his friend Harry Weese, many others in the business wonder if the well-mannered Scotsman isn't some sort of anti-capitalist subversive.

Asked to name his major accomplishments for this book, Baird pointed not to towering high rises, vast shopping centers, hundreds of millions of dollars, or a 123-foot yacht. He cited his happily integrated and hugely successful South Commons and Lake Park Manor residential developments on the South Side lakefront, the daring Campus Green and Lawndale Manor projects on the West Side, and the Printers' Row rehab project he and Harry Weese have going south of the Loop. Baird believes that Big Scores are measured best by their social usefulness.

An Eastern-educated fellow—Wesleyan University, Harvard Biz (he's a history scholar as well)—Baird served as an army captain in World War II, joining the family firm in 1946 and becoming its president in 1963.

He's a director of the Harris Bank and Carson Pirie Scott, a past president of the Metropolitan Housing and Planning Council, a trustee of the Chicago Architecture Foundation, a member of the Chicago Economic Development Commission and the Chicago Historical and Architectural Landmarks Commission, a former president of the Northeastern Illinois Planning Commission, and a former director of the Chicago Conference on Religion and Race, among a whole slew of other activities.

A member of the Chicago, Commercial, and University Clubs, along with the Indian Hill Country Club, Baird is a Winnetkan, though not a great neighborhood buddy of Charlie Swibel.

8. James C. Downs

Every so often, when he's not warming himself in Florida or cooling at Lake Geneva, an elderly fellow makes his way to an unpretentious office he keeps in the Loop's Bell Savings building. He's not terribly active. He comes around just to keep his hand in. It was way back in 1973 that he retired as head of the First National Bank's Real Estate Research Corporation. But, if knowledge is power, James Downs remains one of the most powerful men in Chicago real estate.

An extremely close friend of the late Mayor Daley, Downs and his son, Anthony, served as consultants to the assessor's office and masterminds of the reforms there that started in Cullerton's last days and continued throughout the Tully administration. Downs was sometimes known on the street as "the real assessor." Job seekers responding to ads for deputy assessor were sent to Downs's office.

Downs was president of the Chicago Central Area Committee, which brought about things like the State Street Mall. He was a big pusher and shover for the Regional Transportation Authority, president of the Chicago Dwelling Association, and on the board of the Chicago City Colleges. It was Downs who took on the job of predicting the direction of black expansion in the city for the Chicago Board of Education—very valuable stuff for a real estate man to know.

9. Nelson Forrest

Not all the movers and shakers of Chicago real estate are multi-millionaire moguls and executives of major corporations. Nelson Forrest, executive director of the Greater North Michigan Avenue Association, is a power simply by being Nelson Forrest. Except for a house in Barrington, he doesn't own that much of anything.

Forrest's association is supposed to be a local lobbying and civic-improvement outfit looking out for the interests of its well-heeled business members along Michigan Avenue's Magnificent Mile. But, under Forrest, it's stuck its nose into practically everything and turned the metropolitan area into a sort of Greater North Michigan Avenue Co-Prosperity Sphere.

The association has fought fare increases by airport limousines and the North Western Railway and opposed tighter fire and building codes (they would "end high-rise construction in Chicago"). It has fought proposed parking bans in the Loop and the alteration of the Lake Michigan shoreline with new peninsulas. It has even taken on the mighty Rubloff in trying to stop him from putting up a rather visible billboard.

Perhaps its most controversial stand was the association's opposition to extension of the Kennedy rapid-transit line to O'Hare Airport—at a point more than twenty miles from Michigan Avenue. This was against the public good, Forrest argued, because the rapid transit line would take airport passengers into the Loop, which would be "inconvenient." Inconvenient to what? To the hotels on Michigan Avenue.

More positively, the association has campaigned for tax incentives to encourage development west of Clark Street and north of the Chicago River, as well as for more high rises on LaSalle Street.

Forrest has been the chief spokesman and strategist for the association in these and hundreds of other matters. A big, bluff fellow, who looks like he should be wearing a straw boater, driving a 1924 touring car, and pulling up in front of Jay Gatsby's, Forrest may well be the most expert witness in the state. He can talk nonstop for hours, citing every conceivable fact and statistic to reinforce a point until members of zoning boards and legislative committees all but wither away and die.

10. Harry Weese

Harry Weese is merely an architect, and a dreaming, visionary one at that. Worshipped by the news media and the Lincoln Park cocktail party set as the conscience of Chicago and the modern era's Daniel Burnham, Harry has zillions and zillions of plans for the beautification of the city and the humanization of the city. The plans look great on his office drawing boards, but that's where most of them stay. Arthur Rubloff and Phil Klutznick spend more time attending to their shoeshines than caring about what Harry might have dreamed up recently.

Harry, the Chicago Press Club's 1978 "Man of the Year," belongs on this list, however, because all that's beginning to change. And it's not just that so many real-estate developers admire the design of Weese's unfortunate Marriott Hotel.

Harry expressed his theories of urban redevelopment thus: "When I first came back to Chicago after the war I thought the city was in really bad shape. I was of the slum-clearer mentality: Tear everything down and build anew. Then, over the years, I perceived that you can rebuild a city where it's falling down and leave the rest. Every building is a landmark until proven otherwise."

The wheeler-dealers for years dismissed this as idiocy, but now, with rehab and neighborhood reclamation so popular, with remodelled Victorian houses and new townhouses in Lincoln Park-Lakeview going for $250,000 and up, they're beginning to wonder if crazy Harry might not be right. If the trend continues, Weese might be proved a one-man Chicago enlightenment.

More significantly, Harry has learned to think like a wheeler-dealer himself. The way to affect development in Chicago is not to hold press conferences and wave artists' renderings about, but to get yourself cut in on the deal. He's learned to use government agencies as a means of obstructing wrongos like the Franklin Street subway because obstruction is the agencies' most effective function. He's learned to move quickly, because that's how the wheeler-dealers move. And he's learned to get into the real estate business himself.

Weese and John Baird have some really big and rather splendid plans for the residential development of the area south of the Loop.

They are implacable foes of Klutznick's "suburb in a city" idea. But, instead of just holding press conferences, they and a few partners bought up "Printers' Row" and some other strategically located land in the area. In the great wrangle that will ultimately decide the fate of this prime territory, Weese and his friends will have to be counted in and dealt with, not just ignored.

Weese has long gnashed his teeth at the misuse of land along the Chicago River. What will soon prove to be some of the most valuable river frontage in the central city is a strip along the west bank opposite Wolf Point, where the river divides into its north and south branches. The mind winces at what a "Big Score" developer might decide to put up, as Weese's mind might have winced.

But he moved fast—and first. He and Denver developer Jack Wogan bought up the land, to be improved with a forty-story highrise apartment building and an adjoining twenty-two-story terrace structure. The project is to have all those things Harry has dreamed about for so many years—a marina, riverfront shops, and a shoreline boardwalk. And, there's an old warehouse on the property. As must make Klutznick wince, Harry plans to convert it into apartments.

Weese would also love to get his hands on all that water frontage owned by the Chicago Dock and Canal Company along the river near Navy Pier and the Ogden Slip. He talks about sidewalk cafes and such things. Of course, not even the great Rubloff could get hold of that prime parcel, but, just because Harry's gotten into real estate doesn't mean he should give up dreaming.

7

Banking

Banking forms much of the base of the Chicago power pyramid. Banking means business—all businesses need money, and banks can decide to whom the money should go. Banks can tide corporations over in bad times, and help bring off major business coups in good times. The building boom that Chicago has witnessed in the past few years has been brought about in large part by friendly downtown banks. Banks have also funded minority enterprises and helped bring blacks into the Chicago establishment.

Banks also mean politics. Bankers and politicians have always been close in machine-dominated Chicago. Banks appreciate political stability of the kind that kept Daley in power and led to the ascendancy of Bilandic without bloodshed and revolution. And even the ascendancy of Jane Byrne without bloodshed, if not without pique.

The importance of the right kind of City Hall to the city bankers can be gauged by the fast action of the city's most powerful banker, A. Robert Abboud, after the death of Mayor Daley. The day after Daley died, Abboud volunteered to buy up all the city bonds at the previous day's prices in order to preserve Chicago's bond rating and confidence. Abboud also played a key role in bringing the city business establishment solidly behind Bilandic. Shortly after Byrne's victory was affirmed, she was talking on the phone with Abboud.

Abboud has a lot of leverage in City Hall, but there's another reason for the banker-pol symbiosis: the city needs to sell bonds to finance new projects. Banks buy bonds. Banks like having big money on deposit. The city likes to put its millions into the treasuries of a few safe banks. Until Congressman (then State Representative) Henry Hyde pushed through a bill requiring county treasurers to deposit funds in interest-bearing accounts, millions of dollars in public funds went to big Chicago banks without interest being paid. Former State Treasurer and now Secretary of State Alan Dixon, though a Democrat, helped Hyde get his bill through the legislature. Wisconsin Governor Patrick Lucey, also a Democrat, was told about the Illinois law that would make Illinois counties put their money in interest-bearing accounts. "You mean they don't?" Lucey asked, incredulously.

Banks and politics have all kinds of ties: former Lieutenant Governor and trusted Daley aide Neil Hartigan is now a vice-president of the First National Bank. A big Continental Bank executive (which has the motto, "We'll find a way"), Ed Rosewall, went on to become county treasurer.

Banking in Chicago has little to do with its universal reputation as a bloodless profession. But the old images of bankers and banking die hard. Even Abboud, now president of the First National and one of the city's supreme poobahs, used to disdain bankers. When recruiters from the First National Bank gave him an employment pitch while he was a student at the Harvard Business School, Abboud dismissed the idea as preposterous: "I told them that bankers were either stuffed shirts or poor, and I intended to be neither."

Abboud eventually proved everyone wrong, himself included. The world he reluctantly entered is at the core of Chicago power. And, as Abboud learned when he later met a man named Lance, Chicago banks serve as a liaison for the Chicago establishment with power centers like New York and Washington.

And Chicago is growing as a banking center. Two of its banks, Continental and the First National, are among the nation's fifteen biggest. Chicago is a leader in black banking: while New York and Detroit each have only one black-owned and operated bank, Chicago has six, and the Independent Bank of South Cottage Grove Avenue is the largest black-owned bank in the nation.

Chicago is also fast becoming a center of international finance. Since the law prohibiting foreign banks from having branches in Illinois was lifted in October 1973, more than thirty full-service foreign banks have opened shop in the Loop. Foreign branches have brought the world closer to the Midwest's agricultural and industrial power. It pays to be the world's No. 1 soybean exporter. The landscape of La Salle Street, that somber canyon enclosing some of the world's most austere architecture, has changed a bit too: now the crowds of lawyers, politicians, and bankers can check the time by the Bank Leumi Le-Israel clock at La Salle and Washington, a seven-foot-high timepiece marked in Hebrew characters.

Chicago banking is big, innovative, and growing, yet it's saddled with a ban against branch banking that severely limits it. West Virginia is the only other state in the nation that prohibits branch banking and only West Virginia ranks below Illinois in the number of banks per person.

Every year, State Senator Philip D. Rock, a high-ranking Chicago Democrat, introduces a bill to lift the ban. Every year, city bankers like Abboud and Continental's John H. Perkins evangelize on the need for branch banking in Illinois and attack the curious system under which Illinois banks now operate (a system that allows savings and loan associations to open branches). And every year the bill is defeated, in large part by downstate legislators who fear that Chicago operations would take over downstate banks. Opponents of branch banking echo Senator John Groteberg's famous 1977 summation, "I don't think that the people in my community give a damn about branch banking." The gap between what Chicago can do as a financial center and what it's confined to by the state legislature rankles.

But the ban makes one big, active group very happy: Chicago's myriad currency-exchange operators. Some people, including the members of a federal grand jury, have wondered whether currency exchanges haven't been a bit too zealous in their lobbying and in their campaign contributions to state and local candidates for public office. At any rate, currency exchanges are satisfied with the status quo.

All is not well along La Salle Street. Not only does the branch banking ban inhibit bank growth; bankers have been stricken by a far worse fate. They've become good reading. It used to be that Chicagoans relied upon the criminal class and politicians for entertainment. Now bankers are getting into the newspapers. People like to read about them, about deals that were cut, about bankers indicted for doing unspeakable things like "breach of fiduciary duty."

It's been a marvelous few years. Eight officials of local banks have been convicted and sued for elaborate schemes involving mail fraud, misappropriation of funds, and bad loans. Continental Bank sued for permission to hire a private detective to search for Helen Voorhees Brach, the missing candy heiress whom investigators suspect has encountered some foul play. Bert Lance received that generous $3.4 million loan from the First National Bank as he was moving to Washington and that desk in the Office of Management and Budget, a loan heavily publicized and heartily regretted. After the Lance fiasco, the First National suffered another blow: $1 million was spirited away from a money cart in the bank's subterranean vault.

Tribune reporter Michael Edgerton surveyed bankers on how they feel about the high jinks and high-finance trend in banking. John Perkins, president of Continental Illinois Bank and Trust Company and president of the American Bankers Association said, "Sure, six or seven people were caught and punished, but that's a sign the system is working to correct itself. I'm worried about potential overreaction, the saddling of a system that's working well with excessive rules and regulations. Sure, a couple of banks have been mismanaged, but most of us have extremely high standards. The big point is that nobody lost a nickel and that no bank stockholders lost money."

For all the sophistication of some deals cut in the past few years, Chicago banking has sort of a homey atmosphere. The First National Bank (from the outside at least) has sort of a fairground feeling. In summer the sunken plaza in front of the sixty-story skyscraper hosts jazz groups, dance troupes, and high-school drum and bugle outfits. People bring their lunches to the plaza, listen to concerts and the splash of plaza fountains and look at the gaily colored tiles of the Chagall *Four Seasons* mosaic—the stone wall that shows how things are done in Chicago: Mayor Daley commissioned it, society's William and Eleanor W. Prince had it shipped and assembled, and the First National accepted it. Graciously.

The First National also sponsors a plaza popcorn wagon that dispenses approximately one thousand cartons of popcorn a day at twenty-five cents a carton. The wagon reportedly averages a gross profit of 62 percent, making it, according to the percentages, the biggest moneymaker of all First National operations. "That's probably the widest gross margin of any of the bank's many investments," said Stan Golder, vice-president of First National's First Chicago investment corporation.

Continental Bank sponsors an annual venture that has nothing to do with profits of any kind. Every year, during the week before Thanksgiving, Chicago's biggest bank gives its seven thousand employees, on three separate shifts, a Thanksgiving dinner featuring roast turkey, cranberry sauce, celery, dressing, giblet gravy, peas, sweet potatoes, and mince or pumpkin pie. The cost is twenty-five cents, plus tax, per person. The 150 night-shift workers at the bank have their feast between 1 A.M. and 3:30 A.M.

Chicago banking has never been staid. The first bank to open in Illinois in 1821 printed and loaned its own paper currency. This convenient setup lasted for only fourteen years, after which the bank had to pack up its money-making equipment.

Both of Chicago's largest banks got their start during these freewheeling financial times. Continental Bank began as the Merchants Savings Loan and Trust Company in 1857. As Chicago's oldest bank, it has weathered the trials of Job. First came the Civil War. Then the Chicago Fire gutted the bank building, destroying all customer records. Bank business was carried on in the home of Solomon A. Smith (ancestor of the Smiths of the Northern Trust) at Wabash Avenue and Hubbard Street. Solomon came up with a unique solution to the fact that the bank now had no records: he gave customers credit for whatever bank balances they said they had before the Fire. In 1919, a Goodyear dirigible exploded over the Loop and crashed through the skylight of the bank's newly erected two-story building. Ten bank employees were killed, twenty-seven injured, and, for the second time, customer records were destroyed. The bank reverted to trust again, asking depositors for word-of-honor description of their bank balances. Then-president John J. Mitchell liked to boast, "We didn't lose one penny."

Chicago's second largest bank, and its most influential, the First National, weathered the same crises as Continental, but had a bit more luck. The First was founded in the middle of the Civil War in 1863, under the National Bank Act signed by President Lincoln. When the First opened, it had a staff of four and initial capital of $100,000. (Today the First has assets in the billions and it's run like a European principality. The bank has its own print shop and the fourth largest police force in Illinois, after Chicago, Peoria, and Evanston.) The Great Fire of 1871 gutted the First National Bank Building at State and Washington, but the bank safes and vaults were unscathed and, unlike the unfortunate forerunner of Continental Bank, no customer records were destroyed. The First didn't run into trouble with valuables missing from vaults until the Great Vault Robbery of 1977.

By the 1920's, Chicago was recognized as the second leading money center in the nation after New York. During the Depression, when bank ledges became popular jumping-off places for failed financiers, Chicago banks hung on. The Northern Trust Company, that imperturbable bastion known as "The Gray Lady of La Salle Street," showed it was made of stern stuff. From 1929 to 1934, as banks and bank officers folded around it, deposits at the Northern grew from $56 million to $256 million.

Today, Chicago banking, even hamstrung as it is by the branch-banking ban, is formidable. Besides local banks and savings and loan institutions, Chicago has been embraced by foreign banks, which no longer seem to view the city as a frontier outpost. Chicago is the entryway to the Midwest's rich crops and harvests. And Chicago bankers have long been cutting figures overseas: they dazzle the hometown folks with exotic doings like cutting off relations with the Arabs or banning South African Kruggerrands.

At home, Chicago banks are known for fiscally daring deals. Continental Bank has even bankrolled Straight Arrow Publishing Company, the outfit that produces *Rolling Stone*. Continental floated a "seven-digit loan" to Straight Arrow Publishing to help its *Outside* magazine from shutting down. (It was later sold.)

Financing publishing ventures is one area where Chicago banks surpass their New York counterparts. After the *Rolling Stone* deal, financial consultant James B. Kobak explained in an interview that the lack of branch banking in Chicago allows bankers to see the Big Picture: "The New York banks have become too branch-oriented. The branch nearest the business handles the loans and, as a result, the branches handle all kinds of loans and lack the expertise to understand and evaluate the economics of publishing.

"The Chicago banks—Continental and First National—have their lending departments organized on an individual basis and have the expertise to evaluate these kinds of loans. Publishing is an intangible business. Your inventory goes home at five o'clock. Banks feel more at ease with more standard investments. Not many people understand publishing economics and fewer bankers do."

Chicago bankers are much sought after. They appear on all the right speakers' platforms, boards, at negotiating tables, and society gatherings. Banker Bob Abboud may be Chicago's most photographed man. Each year, for instance, at the opening of the Lyric Opera, Abboud appears between acts with endless combinations of people: politicians, corporation heads, social lions—all of whom want to be photographed with the powerful fellow. It must be reassuring to hang a picture on the corporate wall of oneself smiling down upon the great Abboud.

Abboud is the banker Chicago banks on. Politicians, industrial magnates, commercial caper-makers, and art sponsors all seek out Abboud. He occupies a rarified atmosphere of influence all his own. Chicago has several other bankers who figure prominently in the city's substructure, but their position is roughly akin to Napoleon's generals: they may be brilliant planners themselves but they're dwarfed by the one preeminent strategist. Abboud is Chicago's top banker—the rest are merely highly qualified.

THE TOP FIVE BANKERS IN CHICAGO

1. A. Robert Abboud

Alfred Robert Abboud is chairman and chief executive officer of First Chicago Company and its major subsidiary, First National Bank of Chicago.

During the Depression, when Bob Abboud was a small child growing up in Boston, his father's heating and ventilating business was ruined when a Boston bank refused the senior Abboud a $5,000 loan. The Abboud firm folded, its employees went out on the street, and the family's Packard was repossessed by a finance company. Abboud's earliest experiences with banks were not ones calculated to inspire faith in finance; Abboud has stated in several interviews that "because of the bank, my father's business went bust."

The experience shaped Abboud. The Napoleon of La Salle Street, the commander of a financial empire that reaches to mayoral chambers, the White House, industrial confabs, and foreign policy, he has always appreciated the power of banks. But Abboud's command and political influence rest upon his conviction that banking is not an abstract science but a power that can make or break individuals.

Abboud described his philosophy to *The New York Times* in 1976, shortly after the First National was criticized for making "problem loans": "You lend money to people, not to companies. Integrity and character are what should be the criteria. We made some mistakes in lowering the criteria. Maybe we were mesmerized a little bit and looked too much at the glitter."

According to Abboud, Depression-era banks destroyed themselves by ignoring their small depositors: "The bankers forgot that their vitality was tied directly to their customers' vitality. They've learned since then that it does no one any good to foreclose on an individual or push him to the wall. You can and should make a good loan on just a good idea. We've never had a situation since the Depression where a depositor has lost a dime. We've never lost money to an honest poor man."

Abboud sees himself as the "Good Banker," the kind of heart-feeling fellow who would never refuse a man like his father a simple $5,000 loan. Abboud's lending policies, however, have branded him as a razzle-dazzle financial player who might sometimes make loans to people like Bert Lance. This one loan does distress Abboud. Not because there was anything illegal about the bank's $3.4 million loan to Lance, the checkbook balancer who bounced out of office, Abboud says. He is mostly distressed by the press he's gotten from the Lance deal, by the association still made between him and the glad-handing Georgian.

Mostly, Abboud is appreciated just for what he is: a powerhouse of Chicago politics, business, and finance. In 1977, the Associated Press conducted an interesting survey: it asked thirty-six Illinois leaders in business, government, labor, and education whom they considered the ten most powerful people in Illinois. Banker Abboud topped the list, winning out over recognized kingpins like Governor "Big Jim" Thompson and publisher Marshall Field.

A lot of Abboud's power comes from his ability to mix it up with other movers and shakers; he's the least retiring, least soft-spoken of bankers. The bouncy Lebanese comes on more like a police detective or Chicago labor leader than a banker.

Abboud likes being seen. It's said that Abboud has advised colleagues to travel, to talk to the press, and to get photographed with political leaders. In a speech before the University of Chicago's Graduate School of Business Administration, Abboud pushed for bankers to go public: "The insensitivity of corporate leaders to everyday bread-and-butter politics is often incredible. Even more damaging is the impression sometimes communicated by businessmen that the practice of politics represents a lower calling. Businessmen have got to become more actively involved in political decision-making or that decision-making will be adverse to business."

Abboud is nothing if not actively involved in political decision-making. He used to be a Daley insider and a Bilandic insider. He's as close to Jane Byrne as any Chicago banker. When Daley reigned, Abboud floated a $55-million loan to the city at a time when federal funds were withdrawn because of the controversy over police-department hiring practices. Abboud rode to Springfield with Daley when Daley addressed a joint session of the Illinois legislature on the merits of overriding Governor Walker's public school aid veto. He heartily endorsed Daley for another term in 1975. After Daley's death, Abboud went before the assembled powers of the Cook County Democratic Central Committee and pledged his support for non-charismatic Alderman Michael A. Bilandic. No one was surprised by his subsequent meetings with Jane Byrne.

Abboud is not the kind of banker who glides, silent and unseen, through the halls of influence. He gives it all he's got, whether it's a timely endorsement, a politically advantageous loan, or a key appointment. Abboud is seen in some of the best conference rooms around town, and frequently, in some of the best back corridors in City Hall.

Abboud's role goes beyond political wheeler-dealership. He's given the credit for transforming a staid, fiscally conservative regional bank into an international power. First Chicago, with assets comfortably established at around $20 billion, is the ninth-largest bank in the world. Since Abboud's training and interest centered on the world monetary system, he pushed to establish First Chicago's fifty-four offices in thirty-one countries.

"We'd get down on our knees to get a domestic portfolio as good as our foreign one," Abboud once told a reporter. "We've been very selective about which countries we've gone into and we decided beforehand that we'd lean to the same type of customers we started with here: the farm-implement makers, the food processors, the farmers, and the buyers of grain. The world's economy is now so tightly integrated that if you are going to be a part of it, you've got to be directly involved in it." As Abboud treats Chicago, so he treats the world.

The grandson of Lebanese immigrants who came to Boston at the turn of the century, Abboud believes that the current Mideast situation represents more opportunity than threat for the U.S. In interviews, he has poured oil on U.S. worries about Arab domination: "The importance of the Mideast was underemphasized in the past and it's overemphasized now. What's going to happen is that all the money is going to go into the financial stream of the world just as if Japan or Germany had it. They're never gonna have enough money to buy what we have to sell them. This is just an opportunity for America, not a problem."

Abboud's always been a team player. At the Roxbury Latin School, he played a double-wing quarterback on the football team. At Harvard, Abboud again played football, but confesses that he was too short to see over the linemen. He was a classics major at Harvard. What Abboud liked best about reading Greek historians was the way they described the Greek phalanx, an offense of tightly interlocking spears and shields. "I was really into the Greek phalanx," he has recalled, "I really was."

Abboud later created his own phalanx at First Chicago, with the top management trio: himself, Chauncey E. Schmidt, and Richard L. Thomas presenting a tightly united front that sweeps across fiscal fields. Abboud, ever a fighter, enlisted in the Marines after college and fought in Korea, earning a Bronze Star and Purple Heart. His ambition was to become a career officer; he even asked to be sent to Indochina as a liaison officer with the French, but the Corps turned him down. Abboud liked the Marines; he later said, "I enjoyed the discipline of the organization, and I saw what teamwork and esprit de corps could accomplish."

Abboud's next taste of esprit came after he had put himself through Harvard Law School by coaching frat-house football and training Marine recruits. While he was attending the Harvard School of Business Administration in the late fifties, he met the man he eventually replaced as chairman of the First National Bank, Gaylord Freeman. Gaylord did a great selling job on the son of a man whose business career was ruined by a bank. "He convinced me that there was one hell of a lot of excitement and challenge in banking, and particularly at his bank."

In 1958, Abboud started his rise in the corporate world by working as a clerk in the bank's mailroom for $5,600 a year (it's astounding how many eminent men started out in the mailroom or, at least, claim that they once stamped and sorted with the best of them).

Not for long did the wily Abboud work among the mailbags. After some brief drudgery in the teller's cage and a little grueling labor with securities, Gaylord Freeman's Harvard pick was sent to head the bank's branch in Frankfurt, Germany. From there, Abboud became head of the international section, then head of domestic and international bank activities. And then—the perfect fulfillment of any Horatio Alger story—Abboud aced out the competition (Harvard grad Chauncey E. Schmidt and Richard L. Thomas) when Gaylord Freeman stepped down as First Chicago poobah in 1975. Freeman made an interesting prediction about Abboud: "Too often, managers, by the time they reach the top, have lost much of their creative drive and youthful zeal. You won't see that in Bob Abboud."

2. Roger E. Anderson

Roger E. Anderson, chairman, Continental Illinois National Bank and Trust Company of Chicago, looks like a banker. He has the high brow of a thinker, a head that could hold trillions of actuarial tables and family secrets with ease. Anderson is quiet, reserved, discreet, dignified, and very, very smart.

Anderson has a banker's background. Growing up during the Depression taught him the value of a dollar; as Anderson told an interviewer: "The Depression, I guess, made a great impact on me. I went to college with the idea that I needed to make a living, and was going to have to work hard at it." And he did work hard. Anderson put himself through Northwestern University (where he majored in accounting) by working as a packing boy at R. R. Donnelly and Sons.

But Anderson, like Bob Abboud, came to banking reluctantly.

After serving in the Navy in World War II, Anderson cast around for a career; he considered General Motors, but joined Continental, still with some misgivings. "Banking wasn't the best money offer," Anderson once said. "I was still uncertain of what I wanted to do, but banking, I felt, would give me an inside look at a wide variety of businesses. It offered an interesting combination of sales and analytical work."

For someone who went into banking with the trepidation of a Republican running for mayor, Anderson has moved fast and done well. He opened up Continental's first international office branch in London in 1962. Anderson's work as head of the bank's metropolitan division assured Continental's position as Chicago's richest bank.

Continental is so big and so successful that its bank officers have to downplay its power for fear of turning away over-awed customers. And Continental Bank, a gray pile dominating La Salle Street, looks a bit too much like a bank. Anderson was instrumental in changing Continental's image: he long ago recognized that "this is a big bank with big pillars. It's cold and impersonal in appearance." The slogan of the nation's eighth-largest bank is "It's the big bank—with the little bank inside." The bank mascot is a kangaroo with a baby kangaroo in its pouch. While this doesn't make much sense, it does give the banking monolith a reassuring, homey touch.

Anderson is the archetypal banker—he's quiet, unassuming, even bland: a man to tell secrets to and a man canny enough to tap Chicago's hitherto unknown passion for kangaroos.

3. John H. Perkins

Like Bob Abboud, John Perkins, president of Continental Illinois Corporation and its subsidiary, Continental Bank, believes that a politician's best friend is his banker. Perkins was a close and trusted advisor to Daley; he got on well with Bilandic, he will probably get on well with Byrne.

Perkins even has a pet project to push in City Hall. He wants to redevelop most of the Loop (he was a past president of Chicago 21) and is especially enthusiastic about putting up housing complexes over the railroad land south of the Loop.

Perkins gets really fired up about the branch banking issue. Up until two years ago, Perkins evangelized with little reticence when branch-banking bills were reintroduced in the Illinois legislature.

Now, as president of the Association for Modern Banking in Illinois, and Chicago's top banking spokesman, Perkins has toned down his impassioned appeals, but the craggy-faced, silver-haired money man, who looks like a TV doctor, is still a presence in Chicago politics and planning.

"I never did have a burning desire to be in any one particular field," Perkins once told an interviewer, "I had some ideas of going into law school." Perkins majored in economics at Northwestern and, later, when he had joined Continental, picked up some night-school classes in finance.

He commanded a destroyer escort in the far Pacific during World War II. One of his jobs was running the "ping machine," the radar and sonar devices that searched out Japanese submarines. Now Perkins runs another kind of ping machine and he's very good at it.

4. Norman Staub

When the Harvard School of Business in 1936 told job-hunting "Bud" Staub that the Northern Trust of Chicago was looking for some office trainees, Staub hesitated. "I told them my only experience with banking was on the other side of the desk as a borrower, but they said that might not be all bad."

It hasn't been, either. In 1978, Staub succeeded to the top position at the Northern Trust, Chicago's fourth-largest bank, a bank founded and managed by three generations of the closest thing Chicago banking has to an aristocracy, the Smith family (Chairman and Chief Executive Officer Edward Byron Smith, whose name graces the best charity boards in town, has recently announced retirement).

The Smiths have always set the tone for the Northern. The fortress called "The Gray Lady of La Salle Street" has been singled out for its conservatism in a very conservative business. The Northern has never sought out customers, has never tried to lure them in with stuffed animals, plates, umbrellas, or rosebushes. The Northern's attitude is that the customer enters when he feels himself worthy. The traditional joke about the Northern is that once, when a customer wanted to open a savings account there with a mere $25,000, the bank clerk inquired politely, "Don't you think you might be happier somewhere else?"

Harvard-educated Chairman Staub fits the Northern's old money image. He doesn't look like the lean and hungry boys at Continental and First National; he has the rosy look of a beadle or barrister in Dickens. Staub belongs to the Chicago Council on Foreign Relations; he traveled to China last year "to see what they have in mind regarding exports and imports." Staub lives in conservative Winnetka. His hobby is growing orchids. And Staub is staunchly conservative; upon his succession he told a *Tribune* reporter: "The Northern Trust enjoys a great reputation in Chicago and the world for being a conservative bank. But I like to think that means a cautious and deliberate appraisal of new things—not that we don't move forward. The record of the bank indicates we haven't moved backward, either."

5. Michael E. Tobin

Before Tobin was elected president and chief executive officer of American National Bank, his element was the controlled pandemonium of the Midwest Stock Exchange. President of the Stock Exchange from 1968 on, Tobin has often described it as "fascinating, always changing, exciting, and sometimes a little too exciting." Now Tobin is in a somewhat more staid and settled world. For one thing, on the floor of the bank, he can actually be heard.

Tobin replaced the outspoken maverick banking magnate, Allen P. Stults. Stults was the Horatio Alger of Chicago banking—he never went to college and he started out as office boy with American National Bank the day the bank opened on December 4, 1933. His first assignment was to water the flowers sent for the bank's grand opening. Stults has always been a diehard perfectionist; he once confided, "If I ever found someone in the bank who was satisfied with the job he was doing, I'd get someone else to do that job." Stult's retirement at sixty-five took people aback.

The Tobin regime at Chicago's fifth-largest bank promises to stir things up. Tobin, in his early fifties, has seen all sides of the financial scene: his first job was as a forty-dollar-a-week management trainee in Philadelphia's Snellenberg department store. He analyzed the J. P. Morgan Company's personal trust department for Arthur Young and Company, an accounting firm. Arthur Young sent him to Chicago in 1959 to head its management consulting branch here. Tobin did some work for the Midwest Stock Exchange and saw that his futures lay in grain dealing and pork bellies. Tobin's role has always been to size things up. Now that Tobin has moved in on banking, Chicago finance may never be the same. It will certainly know that it's been sized up.

8

Street Gangs

Street gangs have always been part of Chicago's social fabric. Mayor Daley belonged to what amounted to a street gang, the famous Hamburgs. Street gangs give poor kids the same kind of advantages—namely, status and connections—that rich kids enjoy. Kids from moneyed backgrounds have traditionally gone to the Chicago Latin School, Eastern prep schools, and Ivy League colleges, where they meet the kind of people who could help them later on. It works the same way with street-gang members. School is very important for them too—the members of street gangs form some of their most valuable connections, the kind of people who will help them in later life, right in the neighborhood schoolyard.

The very first group of ruffians that Daley ever associated with were members of the Hamburgs, a neighborhood Bridgeport bunch. The late Mayor was not alone in this early urge to join a boys' club. From the turn of the century, Irish, Italians, Polish, and Jewish youths have joined street gangs. And, of course, some of the Italian and Irish street gangs of the 1920's ultimately became America's most successful corporation, the Chicago Mob.

Chicago street-gang members have a keen sense of the amenities. They're highly conscious of what just isn't done on the street. Members of street gangs can get killed, for instance, for being on the wrong turf at the wrong time, for swiping a rival gang member's sweater, or for flirting with another gang member's girl. Some of Chicago's goriest murders have stemmed from breaches of street-gang etiquette. For example, a leading light in the Outlaws motor-cycle gang allegedly once stuffed a rival in a sewer for looking at his girlfriend.

Street gangs also keep strict accounts. A few years ago, Emilio Perez, an eighteen-year-old member of the South Side gang called the Harrison Gents, was beaten to death by the Latin Kings behind the Cotillion Dance Hall at 23rd Street and Sawyer. One of the Kings proffered this explanation to the police: "We did it because the Harrison Gents beat the hell out of me at the beach."

Street-gang members believe that all courtesies should be extended toward their walls and their sweaters. According to a Gang Crimes investigator, graffiti on walls covers a multitude of purposes: "It maps out the gang's boundaries. It usually lists the entire hard-core membership, and when the initials 'C/S' appear, meaning 'Can't Say,' they're telling opposing gang members not to deface that wall." Should a rival gang member with inspired graffiti in his soul deface the wall, the offended gang will probably deface him.

Latino gangs on the city's North Side are especially conscious of sweater etiquette. Latin gangs use sweaters to show club member-ships: the Latin Kings wear sweaters with a yellow stripe, the Latin Disciples have sweaters featuring a light blue stripe, and the Junior Dragons sport gray sweaters with maroon stripes. Gang sweaters are somewhat like the school ties that members of the British upper classes wear throughout life—both fashions show where the wearer has been and where he's probably headed.

Sweaters can also conceal guns and knives. Therefore, gang members fit the fashion to the territory they're traveling through. As one gang investigator put it, "If I'm in your 'hood and I've got my sweater buttoned, I stand a chance of getting jumped because it means I might be packin'. If I'm going to walk through your 'hood, even if we're at peace, I'm going to open my sweater or put it over my arm. It's a sign of respect."

Gangs are a little compulsive about enforcing their rules: an aver-age of thirty street gang members a year are murdered for breaking gang traditions. The Chicago Police Department can't even put a

number on the cases of assaults and beatings that stem from violations of the gang code. People outside the gang are also victimized
and intimidated by the dictates of the neighborhood gang.

This is nothing new. Street gangs—which can range in size and
purpose from a few kids who hang out together on the corner, to a
group which regularly gets together for a friendly afternoon of
burglary, to the multitudes that once made up the "Mighty P Stone
Nation" in the late 1960's—have long figured in the Chicago scene.
As Commander Tom Hughes of the Gang Crimes Unit says,
"We've always had street gangs. We've always had violence with
street gangs. Always."

Experts point to immigration and racial or ethnic conflict as the
origin of both the gangs and gang warfare. As Frederick Thrasher
explained in his landmark 1927 study of the 1,313 street gangs then
operating in Chicago: "When nationalities and races become segregated into relatively homogeneous groups such as immigrant col-
onies, antagonisms are likely to develop. . . ."

Chicago used to be overrun, from the 1880's through the Depression, with Irish, Italian, and Polish gangs. These gangs were versatile—they went into everything, including athletics, athletic
bloodletting, beer hijacking, rum running, car stripping, and
burglary.

Old-time efforts to reform gangs seem to have been about as
successful as modern attempts. One social worker filed this report
in 1925 about an unregenerate gang called the Bandits: "The boys
in this gang seem to be mentally deficient. They are all Italian,
fifteen to eighteen-years-old, and are all a shiftless bunch. None
of these boys is at all athletic and we've been unable to get any of
them interested in the gym. They hang around street corners and
talk and get into all sorts of mix-ups; driving off automobiles, stealing, etc. . . . The whole group has been recently interested in a
Saturday afternoon dancing class where they do social and folk
dancing with girls."

In the early part of this century, some gang members went
straight, going into politics or the police or big business, and some
went on to better things, like organized crime.

Chicago's crime syndicate grew out of street gangs smart enough
to follow the first principle of American business: organization for
profit. Prohibition was simply too big a deal to waste on intra-street-

gang conflicts, so conglomerates formed: Dion O'Banion's Irish thugdom controlled the liquor flow on the North Side, while the Italians, led by Johnny Torrio and Al Capone, watched over operations on the South Side. This way, gangs rose about their petty conflicts and used all their abilities to concentrate on the second great principle of American business: wiping out the competition. The consolidation of street gangs into the Mob is a street-gang Cinderella story.

Even today, when organized crime has gone national and the profits from gambling alone average $50 billion a year, the Mob is still close to its roots. The Chicago Police Department's Acting Superintendent Joseph DiLeonardi, who served as head of the Gang Crimes Unit from 1969 to 1974, says that the Chicago syndicate still recruits would-be mobsters from street gangs. According to DiLeonardi: "The Mob may use street gangs in certain ethnic areas. If the Mob has a Latino gambling operation, they may recruit some older guys who are involved, say, with the Latin Kings, and use them as muscle. Or, with some black gangs, if the Mob wants to use some muscle in the policy rackets, which organized crime controls, they may solicit the aid of street gang members. And with white gangs, too—I'm sure that if there are white gangs out there with some knowledge about prostitution or gambling, the Mob would solicit the aid of a white gang member who had some smarts."

DiLeonardi says that recruitment from street gangs does happen, but not that often, because the Mob has to have "smart people hanging around" and street gang members don't quite make it to Mob IQ standards: "Generally, you'll find that these kids involved in street gangs lack academic intelligence, to say the least."

State's Attorney Bernard Carey has often remarked how little things change in Chicago crime. There seems to be something eternal about Chicago street gangs: "Half a century ago, gangs of young thugs used the same tactics and techniques being employed by present street gangs. Now as then, the tools are extortion, arson, dynamiting, terror, slugging, and murder."

Traditionally, street gangs have been fairly small, hard to categorize (Lieutenant Edward Pleines, head of Gang Crimes North, has defined gangs as everything from social clubs to extortionist groups) and very troublesome. Busting windows, taking lunch money from school kids, bullying old ladies, along with murder, robbery, rape, extortion, and narcotics dealing, are regular street-gang pastimes. Gangs have usually been splinter groups with no central organization, no regular chain of command, no large profits. Strictly small time.

In the one-hundred-plus years that Chicago gang members have been hanging around street corners, two wonderful and completely unexpected things happened that transformed them, for a time, from corner bums to Great Powers. The first thing, of course, was Prohibition. The second was the miracle of federal funding.

In the late 1960's, three Chicago street gangs—the Blackstone Rangers and the Devil's Disciples on the South Side and the West Side's Conservative Vice Lords—were flooded with money from foundation grants, philanthropists, and government agencies. The Rangers and Disciples split (the McClellan investigating committee might say, "split with") a $927,341 federal grant from the Office of Economic Opportunity for an ill-fated job-training program. The Rangers received a lot of other help. W. Clement Stone, head of the corporate mastodon Combined Insurance Company and the high priest of Positive Mental Attitude, loaned the Stones $60,000 to help them meet some "short-term business debts." Charles Merrill, Jr., the son of the founder of Merrill Lynch, Pierce, Fenner and Smith, gave $60,000 to Blackstone Rangers headquarters, which were then housed in the First Presbyterian Church of Woodlawn. Auto heir Charles F. Kettering II set up a $260,000 legal defense fund for the oft-misunderstood Rangers. Oscar Brown Jr. helped the Stones put on their very own musical comedy called "Opportunity Please Knock." Audiences loved the revue—it was whimsical, uplifting, a sort of "Gidget Joins the Street Gang." It gave Chicagoans a rare chance to see the fun side of the Blackstone Rangers.

The Conservative Vice Lords did pretty well for themselves too. With the help of professional organizers, including Bostonian social worker David Dawley, funds poured into the Lords' coffers. The Ford Foundation awarded the gang $300,000 to improve gang leaders' "executive skills;" the Field Foundation funded a Lords' cleanup of 16th Street with $16,000, and the U.S. Department of Labor gave $36,000 to the gang so the Lords could learn black history, business correspondence, and sales skills.

What were these Chicago street gangs doing that suddenly made them so likeable, lovable even, to the tune of millions of dollars? The gangs said they were reforming. Leader Jeff Fort said that the Blackstone Rangers were evolving into a "Nation" based on Stone Love. The Vice Lords claimed they were leaving gang crimes behind and going into business for themselves. It was the American dream played out with street gangs. David Dawley wrote: "If Horatio Alger had lived in the ghetto, he might have been a Vice Lord." Dawley went further: "Many have been sceptical about the ability of the Vice Lords to move beyond street fighting, but the qualities that make men company presidents and political leaders are also qualities that lead to success on the street."

Street gangs as community groups and businesses was a whole new idea. David Dawley described it this way in a 1978 interview: "The idea was to stop busting people on the head. The gang wanted to change the violence and the things that were getting the Vice Lords killed, while preserving the positive things about gangs: the group cohesion, the way a gang can be a family to people who have no family, and the way a gang can provide role models. The idea was not to be deviant, but to work through the law."

Chicago street gangs grew into "super gangs." The Blackstone Rangers took over smaller South Side gangs, like the Four Corner Hustlers, the Pythons, the Warlocks, and the Pharaohs, until they grew into a Nation, with a membership estimated at between 3,500 and 8,000. The Vice Lords swelled. Their peak membership in 1970 was 10,000, and they became incorporated.

Gangs became media stars. "Black Prince" Jeff Fort and Vice-President "Bull" Hairston of the Black P Stone Nation used to hold press conferences in the neighborhood First Presbyterian Church. Jeff Fort was invited to President Nixon's inauguration in 1969. He declined, but sent two representatives. One was Bobby Jennings, later tried for attempted murder, aggravated battery, and conspiracy. Fort's other representative at the inaugural festivities was the late Mickey Cogwell, known as the "Black Al Capone" for his labor-organizing tactics and narcotics peddling. DiLeonardi takes a dim view of the Stone presence at Nixon's bash: "Jeff Fort was invited to the President's inauguration. Isn't that something? Haven't we stepped up in the world? Fort wasn't invited because he was a charming person, but because he was a leader and he had some people believing he was going straight. I'm sure there are a lot of fine blacks who would have loved to have been there—but they chose Jeff Fort."

One erstwhile street gang leader ran for the City Council. José "Cha Cha" Jimenez, whose resumé included high-ranking membership in the Latin Eagles and the Young Lords, in 1975 ran against Alderman Chris Cohen of the 46th Ward. Jimenez was endorsed by the Independent Voters of Illinois and the Independent Precinct Organization, the two big lakefront Lib outfits. Cha Cha's campaign was based on opposition to "crime, inadequate housing, poor city services, and poor education." Cohen, who subsequently became the regional honcho for the Health, Education, and Welfare Department (his father is Wilbur Cohen, once *the* HEW honcho), based his campaign on "vote for me or you'll get Cha Cha." Cohen's victory margin was one of the more spectacular that election. Cha Cha was not heard from again until 1978, when he was charged with aggravated assault and battery.

Chicago's infatuation with street gangs soured suddenly. The $947,000 job-training program of 1967–1968, funded by the OEO and administered by The Woodlawn Organization (TWO) went awry. The idea was to have Stone gang leaders teach dropouts marketable skills. Some people felt that the Stone leaders probably weren't ideal teachers: none of them had completed fifth grade and Jeff Fort, whose education ended in fourth grade, has a recorded IQ of 48. But the gang leaders were nothing if not inventive. According to testimony delivered before a Senate investigating committee, the gang leaders forged names of "trainees" on class attendance sheets, collected salaries and trainees' checks for themselves, and demanded kickbacks from other gang members. The OEO grant wasn't renewed after 1968, and the festival of funding ended.

Somehow, after the McClellan investigation uncovered the ingenious way the Stones ran their job-training program, people no longer thought of gangs as "constructive social forces." When Charles F. Kettering II arrived in Cook County Jail on April 18, 1971 to talk to Jeff Fort, then Jail Warden Winston Moore chastised him severely. Moore told the Denver millionaire: "Are you the one who brought all that money to cause all that crime here? Don't you have any bad kids in Denver you can fund?"

David Dawley still feels that the gangs were victimized by

changing times. "In the late sixties and early seventies, a lot of social forces overwhelmed the gangs. There was Vietnam; the economy was falling apart; a lot of social agencies were in trouble, and the Beautiful People who had been giving money got scared and pulled out. All the gangs' support systems fell down."

Today, most of the 1960's gang leaders are dead, in jail, or, as Criminal Court Judge Earl E. Strayhorn says, "They got wiser as they got older." The Disciples' David Barksdale is dead; Mickey Cogwell was slain; and Bobby Gore, the Vice Lords' leader, has earned his B.S. degree in Social Justice in Stateville Penitentiary. The only 1960's leader still on the scene is Jeff Fort, back from probation in Milwaukee, and now billing himself as Minister Malik, the founder and prophet of a new religion.

The Mighty P Stone Nation has largely degenerated into splinter groups distinguishable from other South Side gangs only by their name and common greeting: "Stone to the bone and D to the knee." The Vice Lords are out of business. They lost their tax-exempt status in 1968 and now are reduced to a few small factions on the West Side.

Ten years ago, there were one thousand street gangs in Chicago, with membership in the tens of thousands, and there was all kinds of action. In 1967, when the Chicago Police Department reported 150 gang-related homicides, Chicago enjoyed the dubious distinction of having chalked up the highest number of street-gang killings ever recorded for an American city.

Today, the Gang Crimes Unit of the Chicago Police Department estimates that Chicago has about 150 to 200 street gangs, with a total membership of 3,000 to 5,000, depending on the time of year. Gang membership swells during the school year, according to Commander Hughes, because then it's both safer and wiser to belong to a street gang than to fight it.

Is it safe to walk the streets now? Gangs are no longer grabbing federal funds. They've collapsed from conglomerates to corner groups, and have settled into their old comfortable routine of scaring old ladies, beating up kids who don't want to join the gang, and killing members of rival gangs. A surge of this in the spring of 1979 made parts of the North Side seem like the Wild West.

Chicago has even had to take a back seat to New York in recent years. New York City has three hundred street gangs, while Chicago comes in second with its paltry two hundred (one more galling source of the Second City complex), but when it comes to street-gang enterprise, Chicago is second to none.

Chicago gangs learned from their brush with stardom. For one thing, Commander Hughes claims that "all that federal funding gave gang members some very expensive habits." So Chicago street gangs have had to step up their money-making schemes. They get their money from neighborhood storeowners (the gang calls this money "contributions"; police call it extortion), from people in the neighborhood who crave the gang's "protection" (the name that gangs give to refraining from busting windows or setting buildings on fire), and from school children who pay the gangs money so they can walk into school buildings unmolested, walk through the halls, go into classrooms, and use the cafeteria and gym. Paying tribute money to street gangs is just one part of the rising cost of education.

Gang members are no slouches when it comes to business, either. Joseph DiLeonardi holds that the greatest difference between the street gangs of the 1960's and today's smaller versions is sophistication. Sixties' gangs may have known how to get attention, but the gangs of the seventies know how to make money. DiLeonardi says there is less fighting and more profiteering in today's gangs: "The shootings in the street—gang-banging and the argument over turf— that has declined. Now street gangs are involved in the prosperous fields. They're into business, they're into unions, they're into the liquor business, they're in narcotics, the policy racket, prostitution, gambling, extortion. . . . They're into more sophisticated crimes. They sort of graduated up." The police look on the eternal presence of street gangs in Chicago philosophically. Commander Hughes put it this way: "If you've got gangs, you're going to have crime and you're going to have killings. The only way you can stop that is to eliminate the gang."

Most of the power in street gangs is psychological. It starts with brand-name advertising. Street gangs know the importance of labeling; they give their gangs fearsome names like Hell's Henchmen, The Outlaws, The Mad Black Souls, The Imperial Gangsters, The Supreme Gangsters, and Rising Up Angry. Even the Northwest Side gang called The Popes seems closer to the Spanish Inquisition than to saintliness. These are names to reckon with, nightmare names. They make people forget that street gangs are made up of young kids with low-level intelligence—that gang members are sometimes as young as six years old and rarely older than eighteen. The names also make people forget that each gang probably has no more than twenty hard-core members. Street gangs are highly effective public relations operatives.

Chicago cops don't fall for the power pitch, though. Gang Crimes investigators make a point of referring to street-gang terrorists as punks, bullies, and bums. Gang Crimes Commander Hughes, who talks about the gangs his unit studies with undisguised contempt, insists that gang members are no more than "a bunch of mental midgets who prey upon the young and the old."

How can these groups of youths terrorize entire communities, exacting tribute, taking over apartment buildings, holding absolute sway over schools, and destroying property at will? It seems ludicrous that a loosely organized group of ten or twenty punks can dictate terms to large neighborhoods. Yet they do hold sway throughout Chicago, and they do this through a combination of unsurpassed nastiness and street psychology.

Street gang members do not have the instincts of Boy Scouts. Frederick Thrasher said of one 1920's gang: "Their motto should be, 'Be blythe of heart for any adventure.'" Chicago street gangs just aren't blythe any more.

Commander Hughes says that terrorization is the modern street gang's way of killing time. "They intimidate people—they destroy whole areas—because the businessman can't afford to conduct his business in the area because they're stealing from him and wrecking his property and chasing his customers out, so the guy leaves. So now you've got a vacant store and when the gang has nothing to do some night, they throw a Molotov cocktail and burn the store down. For no other reason than: 'Let's burn so-and-so's store down. We don't like him.'"

Mike Royko turned over his *Daily News* column on June 17, 1976 to an apartment building owner in Humboldt Park who told how a neighborhood gang worked to get a clubhouse of their own: "They decided they wanted to use the basement—my basement— as their clubhouse. I mean, they don't even live in the building.

"They went in, moved in chairs and tables, wrote their names on the floors and walls, and started hanging out there.

"So I called the police and the police came and told them to get out.

"After they got out, I had workmen put in steel gates over the basement door to keep them out. They just ripped the gates off, and they smashed out the back windows and came in that way . . . . Then they dismantled the porch. I mean what I said—they dismantled it. They took off the railings, the posts, tore up the steps. By this time, about four families moved out. They were afraid. I can't blame them. So was I."

It's this kind of stick-to-it-iveness that may have made gang members look like promising corporate material in the late 1960's, but it now makes them distinctly unpopular. Chicagoans now view gang members' protests that they're saving the community as so much hood hype. Gang Crimes head Hughes has heard it all: "Any gang member you talk to, it's like playing a record. 'The police harass us. We don't do anything. We're just trying to protect our neighborhood. We don't want any of them dope people selling dope around here. We don't want anybody bothering our women.' But the only people causing problems in the community are them. They write graffiti all over the walls. They sell the dope, and they commit the crimes."

All power is based on a certain amount of ruthlessness, and street gangs just have inordinate amounts of it. The gangs also have psychology on their side. Many times, it's not what street gangs do so much as what they say they're going to do that makes people cower. Criminal Court Judge Earl Strayhorn has presided over hundreds of cases involving juveniles, the vast majority of whom belonged to some street gang, and he wonders at the psychological inventiveness of young hoods: "Street-gang terrorists are very good psychologists. They have an excellent understanding of psychological tactics which affect the mass of people. I don't know where they get it. Most of them are high-school dropouts. They've had no formal education in psychology or in methods of controlling people, but somehow they've got an innate sense as to the psychological methods that are useful."

Intimidation is the real power base of gangs. Like mobsters, street-gang members know the salutary effects that regular beatings, window breaking, arson sprees, gang killings, and a few well-publicized riots can have on the community at large. Terror is good for keeping people in line and for converting them into paying customers. Every function of street gangs—getting little kids to fork over their lunch money, getting little kids to join the gang, getting merchants to pay protection money, and exacting tribute from the neighborhood—is based on a sound management practice: Scared people are helpful people.

Recruitment is a showcase of gang intimidation. Street gangs are very interested in working with young people. Youths under seventeen are useful as lookouts, gun-runners, narcotics carriers, and hit men. Little kids are especially valued when a big-time crime is scheduled, like arson, burglary, or murder, because, under Illinois law, juveniles receive much lighter sentences than older punks.

Joining the neighborhood street gang isn't so much a voluntary act as it is a form of self-preservation. DiLeonardi says that it's impossible to survive in certain neighborhoods unless you join your local gang: "Kids are scared to go to school or to go to and from the grocery store. So to walk in certain gang turfs, they just join the gang. They just say, 'Okay, I'll be a Latin King so I can walk around without harm.'"

From time to time, horror stories surface in court reports and newspaper accounts about the fate of unwilling gang recruits. The most famous case of gang intimidation came to light in July, 1969, when Blackstone Rangers Jeff Fort, Charles Bey, and Andrew McChristian were charged with murderous assault upon Jackie Turner, a former Ranger and Vietnam veteran who criticized Ranger recruiting methods after his return from Vietnam in 1966. Turner testified in court against the Rangers, and castigated the whole notion of "Stone Love." Said Turner, "I was out here in it. I got shot by it." The case was dropped because of inconclusive evidence. Turner himself concluded that all Chicago was waiting for him to "become a martyr so they can bring roses to my grave." Turner was shot again on October 16, 1971. This time, he refused to testify.

Professor Walter Miller of the Center for Criminal Justice at Harvard has made an extensive study of street gangs. He holds that Chicago and New York have the highest percentages of gang victimization of children in the nation. Most of the gang violence goes into recruitment efforts. With good results, apparently: Chicago (along with Philadelphia) has the youngest gang members in the nation. Chicago street gang members range from eight years old to a very street-wise twenty-two.

Gangs get volunteers too. Gang members carry a lot of prestige.

They've got those snazzy club sweaters with great embroidery that not only spells out the club name, but also presents the names of murdered gang members. Street gangs have the street corners and schools to themselves. Often, they're the only people in the neighborhood with regular sources of income.

Lieutenant Fred O'Reilly of Gang Crimes South once told *Tribune* reporter Bill Griffin that joining a gang is a jump in status for most kids. "You take a kid in an inner-city neighborhood. He may not have a father, or his dad works in a factory or as a laborer. Along comes a gang leader with money, a fancy car, and clothes. Why wouldn't the kid join a gang?"

Kids join street gangs so they can retain the use of their limbs. It also brings them some status; a street gang is the slum dwellers' version of the Chicago Club. And once you're in, you're in. It's difficult to resign membership from the gang, though membership is largely a matter of enjoying property destruction and hell-raising.

Gangs make their members feel lucky to belong. Commander Hughes relates a typical gang gambit that keeps new members grateful: "They keep younger members under a constant state of siege. The Latin Kings tell kids, 'If you go anywhere out of this area, the Imperial Gangsters are going to get you. But as long as you stay right here with us, we won't let anything happen to you.' And they keep drilling this into these kids so the kids feel they're under constant attack. Some of the kids have never left the area for that reason. They've never even been to the beach. They're afraid to go to the beach because this nitwit is telling them: 'If you go to the beach, The Imperial Gangsters are going to get you.' The Imperial Gangsters don't even know who the hell the kid is. Now you take a kid who is ten to twelve years old and keep pounding that into his head until he's thirteen, fourteen, fifteen years old—now the gang is his family. 'They protect me. They give me money. They do everything my family is supposed to do.'"

Gangs control the younger set in their midst through what Professor Miller calls the "Fagin plan." The Fagin plan allows juveniles to commit major crimes for their elders. A very canny move, that. Juveniles in Illinois are not tried as adults, except after a long and complicated court process. Usually juveniles get off with a reprimand or are sent to a juvenile facility for a few months. Commander Hughes describes the process and what it does for street gangs: "See, it's very funny. No matter what the kid is found guilty of, he can't be charged as an adult, so he's handled as a juvenile offender. He's sent to juvenile court. The first thing they do is hold a hearing. If they judge him a delinquent, he can be held. Otherwise the kid's got to be returned within three days. You can imagine being held up by the kid who lives across the street and who's ready to put a gun to your head, and the most he can be held is three days. Maybe he's found guilty. Say he's really a bad kid and the court sends him to the Illinois Youth Commission or to one of the juvenile homes. The most he can stay incarcerated is nine months—the most. Even if he's committed murder. Now most of these kids hit their Diagnostic Centers, and they're back on the streets right away. These people at the Diagnostic Centers record the kid, and they say, 'Well, you know, he's here because he's from a broken home and he probably needs some psychiatric counseling. The next time around, we'll know how to handle him.' And the next time around, the kid knows how to beat the system."

Judge Strayhorn agrees that the juvenile justice system helps little punks became better punks: "There's a pattern with youth offenders. You'll find that almost all of them have substantial juvenile court histories. They start early—stealing, shoplifting, strong-arming their classmates in elementary school for nickels and dimes. Then they progress on up the ladder."

Gangs control neighborhoods virtually by royal edict. It's no accident that the West Side was ruled by the Vice Lords in the late sixties, or that the Blackstone Rangers' rallying cry was "All Power to the P Stones," or that today's Latin Kings have taken over North Side neighborhoods, and are rivaled by the Imperial Gangsters. Many neighborhoods are controlled by the Punkocracy, the ruling class that collects tribute, grants protection, and punishes the erring.

Take extortion. Gangs often advise merchants that giving the gang a little something, like a case of Coke a week, or a side of beef, can help grease the wheels of commerce. Both gang members and merchants know that the prompt payment of protection money can save businessmen some serious inconveniences. Paying merchants don't have to worry quite so much about having their fingers smashed, or their stores burned down, or their kids beaten up, or worse.

Worse is reserved for the people who live in the neighborhood.

At least merchants can feel they're appeasing the gangs by paying them off. Other people can't make protection payments. They passively watch as gangs deface buildings, puncture tires, beat up little kids, break windows, take over buildings, and perform all the perverse little acts that may occur to their tiny minds. Living in a gang-ruled neighborhood is like being in the courtroom during the Salem witch trials. You might be able to leave, but you'd better not criticize the proceedings.

People keep quiet about what gangs do to them. Commander Hughes relates a typical scenario of gang intimidation: "Say you've got a twelve-year-old kid and your twelve-year-old is robbed going to school. And the punks that robbed your kid are fifteen, sixteen years old. They live across the street from you. You call the police, and everybody goes into the station. These kids are juveniles, but they're very mean juveniles. The next day the kids come over and they beat the hell out of your twelve-year-old. And they tell you, 'If you call the police again, we're gonna come back and we might kill you.' What are you going to do?"

As DiLeonardi says, "Intimidation is their whole life. That's what they're all about, these bastards. They keep intimidating you until you say, 'Hey, what do I care? What's a broken window? I'll replace it.' Where does it stop? It stops when they kill somebody."

Police claim that the only way people can break out of the gangs' fear bag and cripple gang power is by refusing to be intimidated, by signing complaints against gangs, and by keeping their court appearances.

Residents who bucked gang power put a powerful North Side gang called the TJOs (for "Thorndale Jagoffs") out of commission a few years ago. The TJOs used to be so powerful that in 1973 they entered a $1 million civil-rights suit against the Chicago Police Department, claiming "excessive arrests without sufficient evidence." DiLeonardi, head of Gang Crimes North at the time and named the chief defendant in the street gang's suit, was keenly aware of the suit's irony: "Here are the leaders of this gang, Ganci and Kellass, who each had twenty-three arrests and who both ended up being arrested for murder, and they say they're being harassed." The TJOs became even more harassed; they were eventually driven out of the neighborhood because people faced up to them. DiLeonardi says, "The people in the Argyle-Ardmore area united together and just about destroyed the gang. The TJOs are no longer active. Thank God for that."

Citizen action is still the exception to gang rule. Gangs have lost their 1960's star status. They've lost their federal funding. They've been reduced to splinter groups. But they haven't vanished, and they haven't gotten any nicer. As Commander Hughes says, "The gangs are still there. They didn't go away."

Ranking Chicago's top antisocial clubs is based on total membership, territory controlled, and havoc wreaked. It's a little harder to rank gang leaders, since the control of gangs changes hands about as often as the management of major-league baseball teams. Gang leaders' reigns are often cut by short spells in juvenile homes or longer stints in Stateville. Sometimes leaders marry and quit the gang; sometimes they're murdered and their next appearance is made on the street gang's sweaters, with their names tastefully embroidered under "Deceased." Only a few gang leaders in the 1970's have gained notoriety. Most gangs exist in a state of continual siege where leadership changes from fight to fight.

THE TOP TEN STREET GANGS OR LEADERS IN CHICAGO

1. The Latin Kings (leadership being negotiated, noisily)

The city's largest gang has six separate factions and a constantly shifting leadership. Nevertheless, the Latin Kings make their presence felt. When a Latino is a King, he rules.

If you're on the North Side, between the lake and seedy, commercial Clark Street; and between Foster and Montrose, in a once solid residential but now crumbling neighborhood; or anywhere near Logan Square, Lakeview, or Uptown, you're in King country. It's hard to miss the street gang ads: school buildings, garages, grocery stores and the sides of El platforms sport the telling initials "L/Ks" floating above a crown. When you're looking at graffiti, the King presence is still somewhat removed. But when you start seeing adolescents who look like extras from *The Lords of Flatbush*, slight guys, mostly, who saunter under slicked-back hair, wear yellow-striped sweaters that look like something out of prep school but are really the outward symbols of inner Kinghood, and guys who give just that hint of concealed weaponry, you know you're in trouble.

The Kings even get to the usually unshockable Gang Crimes investigators. Says Lieutenant O'Brien of Gang Crimes West: "The Kings are vicious. Of course, all gangs are vicious in their own way, but members of the other gangs don't bother me so much. I've come across some Kings a couple of times, though, and they really made me think about what I was doing."

The Latin Kings, who now have an inner circle of about twenty hard-core members and hundreds of associates and hangers-on, are the fastest growing gang in the city. According to Gang Crimes specialists, Chicago has always had Latino gangs, but in the past ten years there has been a sharp increase in both Hispanic immigration (Chicago's Latino population has doubled since 1970 to more than 500,000) and Latin street gangs. The North Side teems with Latin gangs like the Spanish Cobras, the Latin Panthers, the H-Boys, the Imperial Gangsters, the Latin Disciples, the Junior Dragons, the Orchestra-Albany gang, and, most imperiously, the Latin Kings. Currently, more than 30 percent of Chicago street-gang members are Hispanic.

The Kings' nerve center is in the Chicago Police Department's 14th District, easily the most gang-ridden in Chicago, with twenty-nine gangs in its eight square miles avidly competing in drug traffic and the extortion business.

The Kings do the usual things such as attacking members of rival gangs, like the Spanish Cobras, the Imperial Gangsters, or the powerhouse white gang, the Gaylords, for real or imagined offences. Any self-respecting King would be murderously offended by someone swiping a gang sweater, throwing paint on a King wall of respect, or, worse, writing a rival gang's initials on a King wall. Kings strong-arm area merchants, and take money from kids. Latin Kings have police records for murder, armed robbery, rape, extortion, arson, and narcotics peddling.

The Latin Kings even have an annual event, the Humboldt Park riot. Every year, on June 4, Puerto Rican Day, families gather in Humboldt Park on the near Northwest Side for a day of picnicking, and gangs gather for some celebratory fighting and sometimes car-torching.

In 1977, a gang confrontation between the Latin Kings and the Spanish Cobras is thought to have touched off two days of rioting, arson, and looting in Humboldt Park that left three people dead, 147 injured, and countless stores along Division Street burned and vandalized. In the midst of the riot, former Police Superintendent James Rochford told reporters, "Mostly it's just young kids throwing rocks, having fun."

2. Jeff Fort

Jeff Fort, who looks like a very small Jesse Jackson, was the Moses of the Blackstone Rangers in the 1960's. He led them from small-time corner skirmishes to the land of media and money. It was great while it lasted. The Rangers became the Mighty P Stone Nation, a coalition of sixty South Side gangs with five thousand members and unlimited power on the streets. The P Stones were an active group. State's attorney's office records for 1970 showed that 80 percent of all indictments against street gangs involved members of the Stones.

The P Stones were also loaded with talent. The Stones' musical revue traveled all the way from Minister Fry's First Presbyterian Church to the Smothers Brothers Show.

The P Stones were reformers. They proved it by accepting five thousand dollars from the Woodlawn Organization in 1967 so they could be bused out of town on Bud Billiken Day and thus forego the usual festivities and street fighting with the Devil's Disciples.

Then things started to go wrong for the Stones. They couldn't get renewed federal funding. They couldn't get money from professional optimists like W. Clement Stone anymore. They couldn't even keep their musical revue afloat. Worst of all, Jeff Fort was sentenced for his crimes and became a minister on parole in Milwaukee.

So the Rangers returned to their original identity as a fairly large, very vicious street gang.

Now the Rangers are ready to make a comeback. Commander Hughes says they've been waiting for it all along: "There's a group of old Rangers, some of the original members of the 47th Street Stones, who never went to jail and have stayed together through the 1970's when Jeff Fort and everybody else went to jail. Now

these guys, along with the Blackstone Rangers who are getting out
of jail, are getting together again."

It should be quite a reunion. Fort's back in town. He has a new
religion to preach, a new name for the gang—El Rulkans—and,
police suspect, some new way to get federal funding. The Rangers
now bill themselves as "Moorish Americans"; they follow Islamic
teaching, and accept Jeff Fort (who has evolved into Minister
Malik) as their prophet. Gang Crimes feels that the latest Rangers
incarnation may be the weirdest and most powerful yet.

3. "Top Cat"

The darkly handsome "Top Cat" may not be a King, but he's the
next best thing: the slick champion of the Latin Kings' most hated
and most dangerous rivals, the Imperial Gangsters.

The Imperial Gangsters are bogeymen to all Latin King kids. The
members of this North Side gang are depicted by Kings as monsters
who lay in wait for the smaller fry of the city's largest street gang.

The Gangsters don't go out of their way to look appealing, either.
They're publicity hounds, and often pose for newspaper and magazine photographers wearing their club sweaters and sporting paper
bags over their heads. The paper bags are a nice terrifying touch,
according to Commander Hughes. The bags—reminiscent of KKK
sheets, and hit men's ski masks—carry a threat, well-calculated to
keep little kids and old ladies in line. The paper-bag pictures are
also effective recruitment posters. Says Hughes, "Imagine some
kid who's living on the edge. He lives around Division Street,
maybe. He's not doing too well in his marks at Clemente. He's
right on the edge. So he's either going to quit school and hang with
the bums or he's going to turn around and make something out of
his life. And he sees this article about the mighty Imperial Gangsters—all these guys looking threatening with paper bags over their
heads. Here's a thirteen-year-old kid who's not too sharp to begin
with, right? He's not getting any direction from his mother and
father because they're first generation and they're too busy working
anyway. What do you think he's going to do? He's going to quit
school and he's going to fall in with these bums. It's as simple as
that."

The Imperial Gangsters are the second-largest Latino gang in
the city. The Gangsters are divided into two factions: the Palmer

and Drake Imperial Gangsters and the Cameron School Imperial Gangsters. The latter group carries the elementary school's name, not as a badge of school spirit, but because the Imperial Gangsters have reportedly taken over the school, inside and out. The Cameron School might be called "Imperial Gangster Grade School."

It's difficult to put a number on gang membership for either the Imperial Gangsters or the Latin Kings, because virtually everyone in the neighborhood feels compelled to belong to one of the gangs. Sergeant Mingey of Gang Crimes North says, "It's a survival thing. Everybody—young kids, mothers, fathers, old people—allies himself with the gang in some way so that they won't be harassed by the neighborhood gang or by any other gang that happens to drop in."

4. The Magoon and Resa Brothers

Street gang coalitions have a way of not working out. It's the kind of feudal arrangement where a bunch of serfs feel comfortable with one lord. The street gang doesn't lend itself to power sharing.

That may be one of the reasons that the North Side Gaylords are reputed to be one of the toughest gang ventures in town. Two sets of brothers reportedly control the Gaylords: the Magoon boys, and the Resa brothers. They exercise joint rule over the two factions of the Gaylords, the LA Gaylords (not named after Hollywood types but after the lads who live in the Lawndale-Altgeld area) and the Palmer Street Gaylords. The Magoons and Resas have reportedly achieved an uneasy working coalition. The cohesion that the LA Gaylords and the Palmer Street Gaylords enjoy appears to be built upon a hatred of everything nonwhite.

The Gaylords, Chicago's largest white street gang, are considered a violently bigoted outfit. Gaylords are always ready to take on any Latino or black gang (they don't seem to have discovered the Chinese gangs yet). The Gaylords have one of the fullest fighting schedules of any city gang; their gang engagement book must be crammed with upcoming Imperial Gangster, Spanish Cobra, Latin Panthers, and Latin King bouts.

Police describe the Gaylords as a "very active gang." When police attach the "active" tag to a gang, it usually means that their little hands are not only busied with switchblades and chains, but with high profit ventures.

5. Monroe Banks

The dapper Monroe Banks represents the new breed of black street-gang leader: he's not a scrambler, like Latino and white gang leaders who look upon gang membership as one long battle, nor is he a revolutionary or media type like Jeff Fort or Bobby Gore. Monroe is a businessman; he views gang leadership as a money-making opportunity.

As Lieutenant Mingey of Gang Crimes West puts it, the Four-Corner Hustlers gang is active in "all money-making ventures."

The Four-Corner Hustlers got their start in 1971 as the "Pulaski Fours," and are now centered around Laramie and Lake Streets.

6. The Spanish Cobras (leadership in question)

Lieutenant O'Brien of Gang Crimes West describes this Near North Side gang as "just an average street gang" but as very active in street fighting. According to O'Brien, the Cobras are a radical group: "They hate blacks and whites." They're also reportedly much given to Molotov-cocktail parties.

The Cobras are prime street mixers. They like to fight with the Imperial Gangsters; they're sworn enemies of the Latin Kings, and, for a year or so, there's been a war on between the Cobras and the Spanish Lords.

O'Brien characterizes the Cobras this way: "They'll fight at the drop of a hat. They'll kill if somebody steals one of their club sweaters. They're always jumping interlopers on their turf."

Cobras' headquarters is a Chicken-Burger stand at Maplewood and Division. Investigator O'Brien had some trouble remembering the stand as a Chicken-Burger franchise because the Cobras had long ago destroyed its sign.

7. The Black Ghosts, The Ghost Shadows, The Gray Shadows (leadership presently inscrutable)

Chicago's Chinese gangs are centered in Chinatown around 22nd Street and in the "New Chinatown" near Argyle and Broadway. The Chinese gangs, which are mostly comprised of émigrés from Hong

Kong, are new to Chicago, but have long plagued Chinese communities in San Francisco and New York. According to Belmont Robbery Lieutenant Augusto Locallo, the Chinese terrorist gangs wield enormous influence in Chinese neighborhoods because "the Chinese are reluctant to report a crime." This is also the reason that little is known about the leadership of Chinese gangs.

The existence of Chinese robbery and extortion gangs first came to public attention a couple of years ago when Chinese restaurateurs in Chicago were victimized by groups of youths who came into their restaurants, ordered elaborate meals, instructed the waiters to "charge it to the Black Ghost," and returned to the restaurant later, offering lucky restaurant owners "protection"—for a price, of course.

On February 29, 1977, fifty Chinese-Americans were seeing in New Year 4675 at the Hip-Sing Association on West Argyle, when eight reputed members of the Black Shadow Ghosts broke up the party and cleaned the revelers out of thirteen thousand dollars in cash and jewels.

Jimmy Wong, Chicago's famous restaurateur and sage, was one of the victims of the Hip-Sing heist. He expressed shock to a reporter over the new generation's ideas of how to get ahead in the world: "These were not Chicago boys. They were outsiders, this bunch. They are misfits. They want things easy. They don't want to start from the bottom and work up in the laundry or restaurant business."

8. The Orchestra-Albany Gang

In the early 1970's, Carl Schurz High School on the North Side had a really fine marching band. One day, a member of the band was slain by an unknown gang for unknown reasons. The band instantly disbanded and its vengeance-minded members organized a street gang. The gang's name is a link to its once tuneful past: the Orchestra-Albany gang.

The Orchestra-Albany boys no longer harmonize. They're known as a wantonly vicious and extremely disruptive Latino gang. Their leader, "Sugar Bear," is a skilled street fighter and is definitely not one of the sweeter types that Gang Crimes investigators have dealt with. "Sugar Bear" belongs to the traditional type of gang leader: he seeks out fighting engagements for his boys and scrambles at the front to give his boys inspiration.

9. The Royal Family (leadership presently inaccessible)

Gang leaders, if they don't die, are just jailed away. They then use their keen organizational skills and sense of espirit de corps to form gangs within prisons. The gangs are all there in Stateville and Joliet: Vice Lords, Rangers, Disciples, Kings, Imperial Gangsters. Gangs transfer their loyalties and pet hates to the pen. The result is a pure gang, undiluted by marriage or Mob recruitment, and preserved by prison routine and discipline. When the gangs are in jail, gang fights become prison riots. When they come out, they put to use on the streets all the skills they've picked up from cannier cons.

The Royal Family didn't start on the streets; all the members of this South Side gang were recruited while they were doing time in Stateville. These 26 ex-cons are now highly successful. Their usual MO, according to police, is to seek out dope peddlers who may feel a bit under the influence, put the arm on store and tavern owners, and hit well-stocked homes for heists.

Gang proceeds go toward high living. The Royal Family is known for fancy clothes, fancy cars, and for running up huge bills in Rush Street nightclubs.

But the Royal Family plans for the future, too. According to police, much of the gang's stickup money is socked away into a special jail-bond fund.

10. The Outlaws (leadership in motion)

Those who know the Outlaws claim that Chicago's top motorcycle gang is unequaled in cruelty. The Outlaws even give hard-bitten cop Hughes pause. Hughes concedes: "If I were to be scared of anybody, I would be scared of those people. They're nuts. Those guys are really nuts." Hughes supports his claim by describing Outlaw customs. Like all cycle clubs, the Outlaws conduct initiation rites designed to eliminate any infiltrators or normal people. Gang members' jackets (called their "colors") play a key role in initiation ceremonies. According to Hughes, "They urinate on one another and defecate on one another, and, afterwards, never wash their colors."

The Outlaws are offensive in many other ways. Hughes says they beat up and murder recalcitrant gang members and anyone else who happens to get in their way. One Outlaw leader is considered a horror story in himself. Two years ago, the police got a statement under hypnosis from one of his girlfriends. According to Hughes, "She remembered going down into the Florida swamps with Tony seven or eight times. The police went there and found the bodies he had buried."

The Outlaws began as a cycle gang in Ohio and rolled into Chicago in 1962. Gang Crimes treat bike clubs as street gangs because, as Lieutenant Mingey explains, "They're into the same things." The Outlaws and other Chicago cycle gangs, like Hell's Henchmen, The Born Losers, The D.C. Eagles, and The Galloping Gooses, reportedly earn a great deal of money smuggling narcotics and transporting stolen cars and motorcycles across state lines. Gang members have also been involved in white slavery, mass rapes, shoot-outs, and beatings.

Most of the Outlaws shun the city, and live in Chicago suburbs. In the winter, they go to Florida.

9

Fine Arts

Joseph Shapiro, founding father and retired president of the Museum of Contemporary Art, was never optimistic about getting Chicagoans involved with art. He used to recount the following story. During the Depression, Shapiro had a job at the Chicago Public Library. He once took some reproductions of famous paintings that he had clipped out of magazines and hung them along a library corridor. Said Shapiro: "I learned how most people look at art. I had noticed that many library users passing through that exhibit corridor didn't even look up to see the pictures. Well, that was an insult not to be endured, so I put a little box with slips of paper at one end of the corridor, with a sign that said, 'Vote for your favorite picture.'

"And do you know what picture won, hands down? *Gone with the Wind*, with Clark Gable and Vivien Leigh. They thought I meant a motion picture, and they *still* hadn't looked at those paintings."

Shapiro's "Best Picture" fiasco could have happened anywhere. It's too bad that he staged it in Chicago. Things like that might convince people—especially New Yorkers who are already convinced—that Chicagoans are cultural rubes, newly emerged from the ooze of the primordial soybean fields.

Chicago does not come off as having a lot of culture. People know it's got an Art Institute, a concert hall, and an opera house. Everyone knows that it even booted the books out of the Public Library and stored them in a warehouse next to the Chicago River until a new library could be built (complete with a McDonalds on the first floor). The old library was transformed into a genuine "Cultural Center," with costume exhibits and dances from many lands and Heather Bilandic demonstrating how to whip up some French cuisine at low prices. Chicago has culture, all right. But no one seems to think so.

Especially New York. That's what really rankles. Chicago should have a place on any listing of oppressed nations for the treatment it suffers at the hands of the Overbearing Apple. New Yorkers portray the average Chicagoan as a cross between a truck farmer and a hit man. They worry about Chicagoans' wearing leisure suits to the opera and tracking mud all over the museum floors. The Chicago arts scene, in the view of New York, is a lot of farmers overturning chairs and setting mud-encrusted boots on the furniture. To New York, Chicago is one long reenactment of the inaguration of Andrew Jackson.

According to New Yorkers, Chicago is a good place for artists to be *from*. Chicago is where artists suffer; New York is where they succeed. New York's scorn for the unshorn peaked in a *New Yorker* profile printed two decades ago. In the piece, critic A. J. Liebling examined Chicago, holding it, as it were, carefully between gloved thumb and forefinger, and pronounced it "the Second City."

And Chicago bought it. Chicago has become the City that Beats Its Breast. It's sorry it's not New York. It's sorry it has flat Midwestern accents; it's sorry it says "cultch-er." It's sorry it's got migrating talent.

But Chicago tries to make amends. It has a thriving cultural import-export trade. It will send New York all its David Mamets, Nelson Algrens, Geraldine Pages, and John Belushis for the promise of one constantly returning Barbara Rush. It likes it when New York likes Chicago. It even uses blurbs from the New York critics to advertise its own Chicago Symphony Orchestra.

"We wonder why the Sam Hill we're the Second City," says Bill DuVall, chairman of the Illinois Arts Council, "We've made ourselves a Second City in the arts because we believe it and we don't even mind too much being Second City. The syndrome feeds on itself. We're like a small town where the town educates its kids and then the kids leave. We encourage our artists to go someplace else—and when they do go, we lose.

"And then we take the usual Chicago path. We assume that anything that comes out of New York or has a big name is terrific. The city sits back and says, 'We'll be consumers. We'll import from New York. We'll believe that seeing Tony Randall in "The Music Man" is the greatest. And God, if we can get an actor from England over here, or better yet, one from Wales. . . .' That's a terrible indictment of the Chicago cultural community."

DuVall points to the fate of young Chicago artists ignored here and discovered elsewhere. Art Institute School graduate James Sessions had his first national show in New York; Richard Hunt, born and bred in Chicago and another Art Institute product, was first brought to critical attention at the Metropolitan Museum of Art. Says DuVall, "If things like that don't discourage artists and give them a strong message that you can't make it in Chicago, it would be a miracle. We don't allow our own art to flourish here. Unless something is done to offset this trend, Chicago will become a wasteland of culture consumers."

Why does Chicago always take second balcony to New York? According to several critics of Chicago culture, neither Chicago artists nor the general public are to blame. After all, some of the finest talent in the country has come out of (and moved away from) Chicago.

The Goodman School of Drama alums include Geraldine Page, Karl Malden, Shelley Berman, and Sam Wanamaker. The School of the Art Institute has graduated fully ten percent of the artists listed in *Who's Who in American Art*, people like Georgia O'Keefe, Thomas Hart Benton, Robert Indiana. The Art Institute also produced the Beautiful People's designer Halston. Claes Oldenburg came out of the Art Institute. Claes later repaid the city by giving it its own permanent brickbat—the Batcolumn sculpture on Madison Street captures precisely what a one-hundred-foot-high baseball bat with holes in it should look like. Second City, the improvisational comedy troupe housed in the Old Garrick Theatre on Old Town's Wells Street, has virtually populated NBC-TV's Saturday Night Live with veterans like Gilda Radner, Dan Ackroyd, Bill Murray, and John Belushi. And Chicago once had Nelson Algren until he decided he liked it better in Passaic, New Jersey, of all places.

It's not lack of talent, then, that gives Chicago the reputation of being artless. The blame rests on the people who run the show and who eventually run it out of town: the society people who cherish the Symphony and the Lyric Opera as grand settings for grand entrances, the financial supporters of the arts who use financial backing to gain political and social status, and the personalities that dominate and suffocate the companies they run like country clubs.

Chicago has an Arts Mafia. It's a structure so inbred and so difficult for outsiders to crack, that the crime syndicate, by comparison, seems a model of egalitarianism and openness. Looking at annual reports and committee listings for Chicago's main cultural establishments (the Art Institute, the Chicago Symphony, and the Lyric Opera) can give the least psychic person the eerie experience of déjà vu. Not only do the same names keep cropping up on the arts rosters, names like Blair, McCormick, Armour, Swift, and Field, but the same names have been cropping up for more than a century.

The Art Institute is a case in point. The Art Institute was founded in 1879 by the meat-packing mogul, George Armour. The museum was stocked with French Impressionist paintings at the behest of the late and never-surpassed Mrs. Potter Palmer. The Art Institute also has one of the world's finest collections of Japanese prints because Clarence Buckingham took a fancy to Japanese art at the 1893 World's Columbian Exposition; Buckingham later shared his taste with the city through a massive bequest of Oriental art. Mrs. Stanley McCormick gave the Institute the two gardens that face Michigan Avenue. The twin bronze lions that guard the entrance to the Art Institute, each weighing three tons, were a gift made by Mrs. Henry Field in 1896. The Fields, Armours, and McCormicks have been guarding the arts establishment ever since.

The nineteenth-century merchant princes in Chicago established a corporate monopoly on culture. They also established the down-on-our-knees syndrome, the habit Chicago has of importing rather than developing art. One close observer of the arts scene describes how the Chicago arts inferiority complex evolved: "These people— the Armours and McCormicks and Fields—have made up the boards of the cultural institutions for as long as the institutions have been around. The original Armours and McCormicks spent all their time working. They sent their kids to Eastern schools and these kids came back and were trend setters. I guess if you're educated at Harvard or Yale, you probably wouldn't think of buying a Chicago painting. You'd buy things from the East or from Europe."

So now we're stuck with the descendants of the sausage makers and retail wizards and the like. They crowd the memberships of the arts boards, filling vacancies with friends and making sure that Chicago culture, with a few notable exceptions, remains WASPish, and that the arts scene is ruled virtually by the "elite."

But these people love art. They look so good standing next to it at openings. They love getting close to art. For example, the Lyric Opera Board holds its annual meeting on the stage of the Opera House where the board members can eat and drink surrounded by a lavish opera set: in 1977, the board members dined in the midst of the *Lorenzaccio* opera set; in 1978, the set from *The Barber of Seville* framed them. And no one can say that these people don't know how to have fun. When the artifacts and statues from the buried city of Pompeii came for an exhibit at the Art Institute in 1978, the junior members of the Art Institute Auxiliary decided to hold a "Toga Ball." Auxiliary President Dave Hilliard was enthusiastic about the junior members' commemoration of the wreckage of Pompeii: "Sometime during the evening," proclaimed Hilliard, "we'll stroll through Pompeii in our togas."

These arts people sure know how to do things. The "old money" in Chicago has even gotten involved in the newest art form, film. When Robert Altman was hunting around the country for a suitable setting for *A Wedding* (suitable meaning a wooded estate equipped with riding stables, tennis courts, guardhouses, and set by a body of water) who should come through but the widow of Lester E. Armour? The Armour estate was surrendered for the making of the Altman extravaganza, on condition that some of the film proceeds go to Mrs. Armour's favorite charity.

The real power in the Chicago arts scene does not reside with local artists, authors, musicians, playwrights, or performers, but with the people who sit on arts boards, especially those who repose in glory on the boards of the Art Institute, the Chicago Symphony, and the Lyric Opera Board.

Getting on the right board is the name of the Chicago arts game. Some are born to boards; some gain membership through persistent proferrings of money (as did at least one socially prominent non-

WASP couple who managed to buy into the WASPS' nest), and some make herculean efforts to join the board, but fail. One Chicago beauty, who married well but wasn't born well, is continually excluded from the best boards. There's a prominent executive who has persuaded his company to pour millions into the arts because his second wife forlornly craves the social acceptance that counts most in Chicago, a seat on the Lyric Opera Board, a chance to sit annually among opera sets.

Actual artists have only a token representation on the boards that direct and control Chicago's cultural institutions. Blacks, Latinos, and Jews (except for a few like the Leigh Blocks and some Museum of Contemporary Art trustees) are also inadequately represented. One corporation head, commenting upon the fact that the Art Institute has only one black and no Latinos on its board, said, "If that were a corporation, the government would shut it down." The reigning philosophy seems to be that you don't have to know what's good as long as you know who's good to know.

The trouble with the way the arts are run in Chicago is that two groups are largely excluded: the performers and the public. One observer of both the New York and Chicago arts scenes put it this way: "The problem with Chicago is that people here use the arts as a social existence. In New York, presidents of companies and chief executive officers usually don't give a damn about the arts. In Chicago, most corporations and banks are heavily involved for the sake of the social exposure and business clout it brings. There's a lot of pressure in Chicago in terms of society; most of the people involved wouldn't give a damn about the arts otherwise. People here want status. They want to be on the class boards; they especially want to be on the Lyric Board. This kind of system doesn't serve the city and it sure doesn't serve the arts."

Except for the most prestigious Chicago cultural institutions, the rest of the arts go begging. Society people don't want to serve on "low class" or "high risk" boards, like the boards for the other 131 professional performing companies in Chicago, boards for small theater companies, fledgling music groups, alternative art galleries. Corporations don't make many contributions to experimental or unproven art forms. Fiscal conservatives see that form of contribution—and competition—as dangerous. One executive explained, "Take any corporation. The guy who's in charge of contributions knows that he'll never get in any trouble giving money to the

Lyric, the Symphony, or the Art Institute. But with these other groups—every once in a while they might take off their clothes or use some dirty words—so it's safer just to give to the Big Three. Then there's no risk."

Smaller arts groups, especially theater groups, have a tough time in Chicago. One problem is funding. Small theaters are shoestring operations; as Illinois Arts Council head DuVall said, "They're just hanging on by their fingernails."

Small theaters are also beset by Chicago's building codes. These places have a choice: they can try to meet the high cost of constructing a new building, or they can refurbish an existing one. Many times, the Chicago building codes as they affect small theater companies are ridiculous. DuVall gives this example: "A porno theater can operate downtown from 9 A.M. to 2 A.M. and no parking spaces are required. But with the legitimate theater, for a box that seats maybe 149 people, you've got to provide parking spaces."

Despite their privileged position at the head of every corporate giver's and social headhunter's list, the Chicago arts triumvirate also suffers from an economic crunch. The socialites and the top money-makers are there, but enough money isn't.

Even the descendants of Fields, Armours, and McCormicks don't have it like they used to. Taxes doth make peasants of us all. The really huge fortunes, the kind that Armour used to build the Art Institute; that Morton, the salt king, used to build an entire wing on the Art Institute, or the money Samuel Insull sunk into the magnificent Civic Opera House, just don't exist on that scale anymore.

Wacky business practices, more than anything else, cripple Chicago arts. Cultural institutions expect to run in the red. For example, the Lyric Opera loses thirty dollars on every ticket sold. The Lyric is in continual financial trouble. Lyric Opera publicist Danny Newman takes it all philosophically; he once said in an interview, "We're in deficit all of the time; yet we're solvent. We have a symphony orchestra; we have principal singers; we have a ninety-voice chorus, an army of stagehands, a physical production, a ballet company. What individual performing arts have singly, we have it all. . . . All of them are in deficit, without having to have all the additional things we must have.

"We are the sport of kings . . . but without the kings to pay the bills any longer. Royal treasuries used to provide the subsidies for grand opera, and in the earlier American era, the great tycoons like the McCormicks and the Insulls supported the opera. But that time is past."

Corporate backing for the arts still lags. According to DuVall, a survey of 158 Chicago companies revealed that 25 percent gave no support at all to the arts.

We've entered the age of the Arts Marathon. Now society scions sell the arts by offering the public the chance to get a virtuous tug at the heart for contributing—along with a genuine Chicago Symphony Orchestra T-shirt. Since 1976, Ray Nordstrand's classical music radio station, WFMT, has hosted four sixty-hour pledge-drive marathons in which symphony lovers can win valuable premiums, wonderful things like a Chicago Symphony key ring, a replica of Sir Georg Solti's baton, live performances in one's home by the Chicago Symphony Chamber group, a catered Italian feast for one hundred, or a corn-fed steer.

For the 1979 season, Lyric Opera Board chairman T. M. Thompson announced that lovers of the Lyric could buy, for sixty-five dollars, a Gucci scarf bearing a reproduction of the famed Jules Guerin painting on the Opera House fire curtain. And the Art Institute's gift shop does a flourishing trade, with cardboard models of the Water Tower and the Field Museum, and Pompeii book bags.

But not even these *Amazing Offers* can rescue the Chicago arts scene. The Lyric Opera, Chicago Symphony, and Art Institute continue to survive, but not every arts endeavor is so lucky. In 1978, the Chicago Ballet fell flat on its face. It wasn't just that the two-year-old troupe was terrible, that the corps de ballet looked like the Dallas defense, or that the spooky enchanted maidens in *Giselle*, called the Willis, gave audiences the willies. Chicago's foray into ballet was a financial disaster. Renowned artistic manager Ben Stevenson quit, dancers were forever quitting, but the Chicago Ballet kept growing as more and more society ladies were awarded positions on the sinking enterprise. After a flurry of dark hints about how the ballet company was hamstrung and rumors of backstage plots that would make *Romeo and Juliet* seem straightforward, Mrs. Geraldine Freund, the ballet's mentor, announced there would be no more seasons. Football enthusiasts were saddened. There are plans afloat to resurrect the ballet, but no one is holding his breath.

Money has gotten so tight on the arts market that the prestigious boards (unseemly as this may sound) have actually gotten into nasty quarrels over it. In 1976, a prominent Chicago investment banker and longtime supporter of the arts, James Hemphill, died. His will revealed that the old banker must have had a sense of humor. Hemphill had pledged $500,000 each to the Lyric Opera and the Rehabilitation Institute before he died. His will, however, left $3 million to be divided equally among the four organizations he had served so long as a board member: the Lyric Opera, the Rehabilitation Institute, the Chicago Symphony Orchestra, and the New York Metropolitan Opera Company. The legal battle that ensued was heir-raising. Hemphill's estate was tied up in a four-way suit. Attorneys for the Lyric and Rehabilitation Institute held that the money should not be split until the Hemphill pledges had been paid to them. Chicago Symphony Orchestra and New York Met attorneys felt that the entire $3 million should be distributed equally to the needy boards. Ultimately, lawyers Lee Freeman for the Lyric and Edward Bryant for the Rehabilitation Institute prevailed.

The arts cannot live on the well-bred alone. They need a broader base of support from the government and the general public. Steps have already been taken. In 1975, the Chicago Arts Council was founded, headed by Heather Morgan, who wowed City Hall types with her cultch-er. Heather started the Culture Bus on its rounds around the city's artistic hot spots. Since then, the Chicago Arts Council has sponsored theater, dance, folk art, and music in a series of imaginative and sometimes daring programs. State-wide funding by the Illinois Arts Council has increased by 70 percent annually; grants go to 342 cultural programs, 170 of which are in Cook County. Illinois Arts Council chairman DuVall thinks funding can keep artists down in the soybean fields: "I'm tired of the assumption our town makes that nothing in Chicago is first class. A lot of people think that if you want opera, you've got to go to Italy; if you want dance, you've got to go to New York; if you want art, you see it in New York or Europe. But if we could encourage artists to live and work here and produce the right kind of climate, this city could really take over the No. 1 spot nationally. It's all here. Don't forget, people in places like DeKalb, Decatur, and Omaha think this is the big city."

Until that day when Chicago can support a large number of

theaters, dance companies, art museums, and symphonies, and can rely on resident performers rather than New York and Vegas imports, attention and funds will center on what's worked, socially, if no other way: the Chicago Arts Triumvirate—the Art Institute, the Symphony, and the Lyric Opera.

The Art Institute, which celebrated its 100th anniversary in 1979 with the return of three of its priceless Cezanne's that had been stolen in 1978, is built on business; its architecture reflects its need for financiers. The old trading room of the Chicago Stock Exchange, a magnificent rococo explosion of columns with gold capitals, stenciled ceiling ornaments, and four hundred cast-iron-framed skylights, is now part of the Art Institute. This last surviving commercial work of Sullivan and Adler was rescued from the clutches of the Three Oaks Wrecking Company in 1973 and then painstakingly reassembled as the core of the Art Institute's new wing. At the dedication ceremonies in April, 1977, the talk was more of business than of art. William McCormick Blair, president of the Art Institute from 1956 through 1966, admitted that "my first seventy years in the investment business has had its ups and downs." Trustee Stanley Freehling commented that "The elegance of this room reflects the elegance of our business before negotiated rates."

The Art Institute is still a businessman's club. Manufacturing magnate James W. Alsdorf has been chairman of the board since 1975. The formidable Edward Byron Smith of the Northern Trust is treasurer of the Art Institute's Auxiliary Board. Marshall Field, Payson S. Wild, Bowen Blair, Brooks McCormick, the old Chicago guard, are there. William W. Prince also serves.

Despite the corporate heft of the Art Institute board, the museum is just now pulling out of a dismal period of administrative chaos and financial brinkmanship. The late director of exhibitions and collections, John Maxon, was apparently hard to take. The Art Institute still hasn't recovered from Maxon's reportedly imperious management and the bad feelings it created.

Art Institute annual reports for the past few years have read like domestic tragedies: the bad news is prefaced by gloomy explanations rare in the usual upbeat hype of annual reports. The directors note sadly "the disturbing trend of increasing operating deficits," the deficit reaching a cool $1.5 million a year.

The Art Institute even had to sacrifice the famed Goodman School of Drama in 1977 because it could no longer pick up the

Goodman's deficits. This loss was a severe blow to Art Institute prestige. The Goodman had long given Chicago its own serious theater-in-residence where experimental dramatists like David Mamet could train. The Goodman had a tragic and romantic origin. The school and theater are named after U.S. Navy Lieutenant Kenneth Sawyer Goodman, the son of a millionaire Chicago lumber dealer, who died in the 1918 influenza epidemic. His parents commemorated his death by giving the Art Institute a building directly behind the museum, spookily designed as a replica of the Goodman family mausoleum in Graceland Cemetery. In 1977, DePaul University adopted the Goodman School of Drama. The school is now housed in that red brick monument to Positive Mental Attitude, the W. Clement and Jessie V. Stone Building on the DePaul campus. The Goodman Theater is still in the mausoleum behind the Art Institute. It's shakily independent, but helped out by Stanley Freehling's Chicago Theater Group and by the fact that David Mamet (the chronicler of *Sexual Perversity in Chicago*) is playwright-in-residence.

The Art Institute may have lost a Goodman, but it's gaining a paperweight collection. Arthur Rubloff, the real-estate king whose really favorite art objects seem to be wrecking balls, grandly announced in the summer of 1978 that he planned to donate his entire paperweight collection to the museum.

Besides the Art Institute, Chicago has a great symphonic orchestra, generally acclaimed as "the world's greatest." Chicagoans even get to hear it. For thirty-seven weeks a year, Sir Georg Solti and his merry band plug away in Orchestra Hall. Since the grand hall is not air-conditioned, the Symphony summers at Ravinia Park, the wooded setting for outdoor concerts and posh picnics twenty miles north and several income levels beyond Chicago. For the rest of the year, Solti and the Symphony send the folks back home news about how they're doing in the East and in Europe. In Chicago, people don't hear the Symphony as much as they hear about it.

Maybe it's the weather that keeps Solti out of Chicago so much. Solti once remarked that Chicago winters take a toll on musicians: "I work for days on the most exquisite pianissimo. Eventually, the orchestra is playing like an angel's whisper. Then comes the concert, and perhaps it's been a typical Chicago week: the temperature around twenty below. The pianissimo comes, and all I hear is a hall full of coughs and sneezes."

Or it could be the challenge of Carnegie Hall that lures the orchestra out of the farmlands. Solti has noticed that ingrained Chicago desire to please New York: "The orchestra still suffers quite a lot from the 'Second City' complex. Carnegie Hall is still the magic name, and so we're very obsessed with conquering Carnegie. I have to tell the players, 'Don't look at the crowds. Try to relax; it's just another concert.' But it never works. In New York, the orchestra plays with a tension that surprises even me."

Solti has been with the Chicago Symphony for eleven years. In that time, Chicago has clinched the title conferred upon it by Leopold Stokowski: "the greatest orchestra in the world."

Even the city's mayors have been Symphony buffs. When the Chicago Symphony returned from its first European tour in 1971, Colonel Jack Reilly, director of special events under Mayor Daley, sent out a directive to all city employees, urging them to turn out on State Street and cheer the return of the orchestra. Reilly laid it out: "The Cubs, the Sox, the Bears, the Bulls—they can't win, but the Chicago Symphony did—they brought home the title 'World Champion of Orchestras.'"

The Chicago Symphony Board is run with Teutonic precision and Chicago exclusivity. The trustee meetings for both the Symphony and the Lyric Opera are closed to the public. The actual budget for the Chicago Symphony, according to music critic Robert C. Marsh, is known only to its trustees. The Chicago Symphony is frequently criticized for its patronizing treatment of subscribers; for example, the order folders for the 1978 subscription series listed dates of performances and names of conductors, but no mention was made of what the audience would hear. The Chicago Symphony Orchestra's general manager, John Edwards, explained to *Tribune* critic Thomas Willis: "Nobody cares about programs but you critics."

Powers on the Symphony board include Louis Sudler, John Swearingen, husband of Bonnie and chairman of the board of Standard Oil of Indiana; and Paul Judy, who succeeded Joseph A. Burnham as head of the Symphony board. Social tone is given the board by the presence of the grand descendants of early Chicagoans: Mrs. Vernon Armour, A. Dean Swift, and George B. Young.

The third part of the Chicago Arts Triumvirate is the Lyric Opera. The Lyric is different. Donald R. Britten, business manager for the opera company, said it: "We aren't your typical corporation." The twenty-three-year-old grand-opera company is always impoverished; the Lyric is a $6-million annual business with a $3.4-million annual deficit. Even with a mammoth subscribership of 23,000, the Lyric is financially quaky. Former Lyric Opera Company President J. W. Van Gorkom blames it on Chicago: "The Lyric is as good as any opera company in the world, but you can't convince Chicagoans of that. People think it must be better if it's in Italy or Vienna." Publicist Danny Newman claims the Lyric's financial distress is just part of being an opera company when there are no more kings around to finance lavish productions. According to Newman, "It costs us ninety-three thousand dollars to raise the curtain every night."

If they raise the curtain. The past few years have witnessed frequent labor disputes between the Lyric management and the orchestra. In 1967, the entire season was canceled. The 1974 season came to the brink of cancellation, but then Da Mare, with his appointed labor negotiator William A. Lee, bailed it out. Daley made peace between the Lyric and its orchestra in 1974; in 1975, the City of Chicago gave the Lyric a $100,000 grant that landed the Lyric a $1-million bundle from the Ford Foundation. When Daley died, Danny Newman sent the *Sun-Times* a letter in which he grieved: "No institution of this city mourns the late Mayor Richard J. Daley more than does the Lyric Opera of Chicago."

Despite the fact that the Lyric is forced to stage grand opera with one eye on the cash flow and the other on the labor force, it is a magnificent opera company, ranked in the U.S. after the New York Metropolitan Opera and the San Francisco Opera Company. Maria Callas made her American debut at the Lyric Opera in 1954. The famed tenor Luciano Pavarotti (known across the nation for his discussion of diets on *The Tonight Show*) has signed to perform Lyric roles from 1979 through 1983. Maria Tallchief is in charge of the Lyric's ballet company. Carol Fox, the opera's founder and general manager, cuts costs by producing a small number of operas each season.

The Lyric Opera Board is packed with the cream of Chicago board-sitters: William O. Beers, Blake Blair, Mrs. Leigh Block, Mrs. John L. Kellogg, Arthur Rubloff, John Ward Seaburg, and W. Clement Stone all grace it. These people have their priorities straight. At the last annual conclave, as the board ate and drank in the midst of the set from *Lorenzaccio*, the Lyric backers were galvanized by the philosophy of Tom Mulroy, chairman of the Lyric Opera nominating committee: "The Chicago Bears want experienced backs. We want greenbacks." Treasurer Sam Di Giovanni left board members with a hopeful note: "The most notable achievement is that we survived—again."

Positions on the three Big Boards are sought after by people who want to do their bit for culture, social standing, and corporate power. Beyond the Big Three are a host of other arts organizations, all more or less in states of chronic fiscal starvation, all carrying a bit less social prestige. Two years ago, a seat on the board of the Chicago Ballet carried some weight—Geraldine Freund even invited Heather Bilandic's mother to the board—but now that the Ballet has stumbled, admitting that you used to belong to it is like admitting that you were on the steering committee for H.M.S. Titanic. But it is good to be connected with the new, ragingly successful North American International Dance Festival, the dance gala that served up thirty-seven—count them—big ballet stars from everywhere in the world except Chicago (the Chicago Ballet troupe got to run across the stage a few times when the ballets called for crowd scenes). And it's nice to be part of Michael Kutza's International Film Festival. Or to help Lucy Salenger of the Illinois Film Office find a mansion suitable for a Hollywood production.

Beyond that, there really isn't very much that a self-respecting socialite can help with in Chicago. So many groups, like the Organic Theater or Second City or the myriad small, experimental theaters jammed into converted warehouses, aren't established enough or respectable enough for corporate heads and social lions to bother with. Maybe that's why they survive.

THE TOP FIFTEEN ARTS PEOPLE IN CHICAGO

1. Sir Georg Solti

Sir Georg, conductor of the Chicago Symphony, is Chicago's reigning cultural symbol. Without him, the world would still view Chicago as Frontier Land. With him, it's got certified class. Solti is perfect. He's not only British; he's titled. Solti can also wear the Great Cross of the German Republic, or shine forth in the decorations of the French Legion of Honor. Solti's second wife, the former

Anne Valerie Pitts, has stricken local ladies with somewhat terrified awe.

Unlike some European conductors whose audiences may entertain some niggling doubts about what they may have done during World War II (Solti's greatest rival, Herbert von Karajan of the Berlin Philharmonic, enjoyed the support of Hermann Goering), Solti is stain-free. His early career as conductor for the Budapest Opera House from 1934–1939 was interrupted by the war; Solti fled to Switzerland where he worked as a pianist for six years. He then went to Munich in 1946, where he prospered as general musical director for thirteen years.

Before Solti emigrated to the American prairie, he conducted music fests in Salzburg, Aix-en-Provence, Edinburgh, and Glyndebourne, and was engaged as musical director for the Royal Opera House in Covent Garden. When Solti assumed the conductorship of the Chicago Symphony in 1969, he good-naturedly described it as "the greatest provincial orchestra in the world."

Chicago has always recognized what an asset it has in Sir Georg. On October 29, 1977, Solti hurried out of an elevator on the thirtieth floor of the Ritz-Carlton Hotel and fell on his conducting arm, thus rendering it inoperable for an upcoming bout with Mahler's Eighth. The press gave Solti's arm the kind of coverage it usually reserves for Chicago Cubs pitcher Bruce Sutter.

Solti rules his orchestra with an iron baton. Though in his late sixties, he puts in fifteen-hour days—as do his musicians. Solti believes that constant attention to detail is necessary to keep the Chicago Symphony from becoming a bunch of symphonic slobs: "This orchestra, like any other, can go downhill rapidly. That's why it is essential to maintain standards. The working discipline is very high. Not every orchestra has it, and I am very proud of it," Solti once told an interviewer. The great conductor even issues annual directives to the Women's Association of the Chicago Symphony Orchestra. His instructions always include the order to "hush people who talk during concerts, and if somebody's bracelets are jangling, tell them to stop it!"

The Solti style of discipline extends to Chicago Symphony breaks. Once, during a break from a recording session in Medinah Temple, a soloist asked Solti if he could borrow his reclining chair. Solti dictated: "I want it understood that the chair is to be used strictly for resting. I shall examine it minutely when I return. I'm not worried about your morals. I just don't want too much vibrato in the Tchaikovsky."

2. Carol Fox

Carol Fox, general manager of the Lyric Opera, studied opera under Italian singing masters in her youth and has an opera star's build. She also entertains great dreams, ambitions of sustaining grand opera in the center of the Midwest. As Carol Fox once told a reporter who questioned her about the wisdom of lavishing money on opera stars and opera sets in an inflation plagued era: "The words are 'grand opera.' My ambition was to form a great opera company. This was not to be a little shack of an opera company."

Chicago has had a succession of twelve opera companies since the end of the last century. Opera operations here came and went with the speed of traveling circuses until Carol Fox entered with determination. In 1954, she and two co-conspirators, Lawrence Kelly and Nicola Rescigno, established the Lyric Theatre of Chicago. The Lyric's first season was blessed with the American debut of Maria Callas, who stalked about the stage in *Norma*. By 1956, Kelly and Rescigno had backed off from the Lyric, leaving Fox in command.

Fox embodies the old adage, "If you can't sing, you'll just have to manage." Carol Fox always wanted to be an opera singer. As a girl, she underwent private voice lessons by the score from teachers like Giovanni Martinelli, Vittorio Trevisa, Virgilio Lazzari. She studied in Italy. All to no avail. In 1947, at the age of twenty-one, Carol realized that her voice was nothing to sing about. She developed other talents. By the time she was thirty, the wily Fox was general manager of the Lyric. By the time she was thirty-two, she had earned a law degree from Rosary College. Carol Fox has what every opera company needs: a sound appreciation for voice and music and the ability to negotiate labor disputes.

She is criticized by some for her relying almost exclusively on Italian singers; she herself has described her modus operandi in the beginning years of the Lyric as going to Italy and trying to "grab the ten best Italians I could find and bring them here." One arts commentator said, "She ought to get an award from the Italian government." Carol Fox did. In 1956, she was decorated *Cavaliere al Merito della Repubblica Italiana*.

3. James W. Alsdorf

The chairman of the board of trustees for the Art Institute is the corporate prince of the Chicago art world. Alsdorf attended the Wharton School of Finance and Commerce at the University of Pennsylvania from 1932 to 1934, and then went on to conquer the world of coffee services, steel products, duplexes, and machine products. Alsdorf directed the far-flung empire of Cory Food Services, Inc. for many years. He brought the Cory Coffee Service Plan to Toronto, Zurich, Stockholm, Oslo, and Helsinki. Now he directs the entiry Cory operation from Chicago as its chairman and director. The tireless manufacturing executive also heads the A. J. Alsdorf Corporation, exporters and international machinists.

When Alsdorf is not overseeing his business interests, he sits on a host of Chicago arts boards. His most important association is with the Art Institute, whose chairman he became in 1975, succeeding the powerful but not terribly popular Leigh Block. Alsdorf has felt one keen stab of embarrassment as chairman. His first task was to find a replacement for the late choleric director John Maxon. The board hit upon Alan Shestack, director of the Yale Museum Art Gallery. Shestack accepted, came to Chicago, met the board and the Art Institute staff, and promptly begged off. It was Alsdorf's distasteful task to announce that Shestack didn't want to work in Chicago (rumors circulated that Shestack couldn't abide the ingrown nature of the Art Institute board). But those connected with art, as so many corporation heads have learned, must suffer.

Alsdorf and his second wife, Marilyn, are avid art collectors. In addition to the Art Institute, they've acquired an extensive range of handcrafted objects from the Near and Far East. Because she has the same initials as Marie Antoinette, Marilyn Alsdorf loses her head over anything that once belonged to the ill-fated French queen. Marilyn's collection now boasts a large number of beautiful trinkets Marie Antoinette left—somewhat hastily—behind.

4. John Edwards

As general manager of the Chicago Symphony, John Edwards is the organizational mastermind who arranges 211 concerts a year, sets up recording and taping sessions in Medinah Temple (the

Chicago Symphony has seven albums among the all-time top forty sellers in classical records), soothes the temperaments of the orchestra's 110 musicians, its trustees, and the public.

Edwards runs the Symphony with an authority that makes Solti seem almost lamblike. When Solti fell on his conducting arm in 1977, Edwards vowed to the press: "Solti will make amends!" Edwards then introduced the Chicago Symphony's elaborate cover system for those occasions when Solti is unavailable. The chief cover for Solti, Henry Mazer, is a madcap conductor who has brought the orchestra to Woodfield Mall and to White Sox Park. The latter conducting caper was truly memorable. Mazer assumed the podium at the ball park for the seventh-inning stretch, leading sixteen thousand fans through *Take Me Out to the Ball Game* played on kazoos.

Edwards is often sharp with the press. This surprises some critics since Edwards himself started out as music reviewer for the St. Louis *Globe-Democrat.*

5. Ruth Page

When Ruth Page was a fifteen-year-old girl in Indianapolis, Anna Pavlova came to tea at her family's home and changed the young Page's life. Pavlova felt that Ruth Page was meant to dance. In 1916, Ruth left her Indianapolis home, studied ballet, assumed the stage name Natasha Stepanova, and enjoyed tremendous success, especially for someone from Indianapolis. Ruth Page toured South America with Pavlova, appeared as premiere danseuse with the Municipal Opera Company, and was the only Westerner invited to dance at the Emperor Hirohito's coronation ceremonies.

What's a dancer like Ruth Page doing in Chicago? Part of it is accident. In 1925, Page married the wealthy Chicago lawyer Thomas Hart Fisher. And as Page grandly allowed, "I decided I should stay and try to give Chicago a ballet. If I don't do it, nobody will. So I'll sacrifice myself."

Ruth Page has been the driving force in Chicago ballet for the past fifty years. She was the Lyric Opera's first ballet director, a post she filled from 1954 until 1969. She formed her own ballet companies here, the Ruth Page Chicago Opera Ballet and Ruth Page's International Ballet. The first folded in 1966; the second went down in 1969. Page has choreographed scores of ballets; her

most memorable is the annual Nutcracker Suite. Page founded
the Chicago Ballet. She gave $750,000 from the Ruth Page Founda-
tion to support it, and found space for the company in an old
Moose Lodge at 1016 North Dearborn Street.

Now a widow, Ruth Page has an apartment on East Lake Shore
Drive between the Roger Bensingers and the Len O'Connors, a
home in Montparnasse, and two villas in St. Tropez near Bridget
Bardot's hideaway.

She feels that dancers are mistreated in America, and holds that
"it's tough in America. We don't have the government to support
institutions. In Russia, they're taken care of from the time they're
eight until they die. Here, dancers wait on tables. To me, it wouldn't
matter if the whole world goes Communistic; which it probably
will anyway, because the dancers will be taken care of."

6. Geraldine Freund

Geraldine Freund is associated with one great artistic failure
and one great success. Since 1976, Freund has served as president
of the Chicago Ballet board, a clumsy ballet clumsily managed.
But Mrs. Freund conceived and brought into being the North
American International Dance Festival, a three-day Opera House
world event featuring Mikhail Baryshnikov, Judith Jamison of the
Alvin Ailey American Dance Theater, Ghislaine Thesmar of the Paris
Opera, Merle Park of the Royal Ballet—and as little of the Chicago
Ballet troupe as possible.

The fest was meant to shore up the Chicago Ballet. Geraldine
Freund described her motives to critic Richard Christiansen: "I
will tell you a story. Michelangelo was once asked how he created
his statue of the young David. He replied, 'I took a block of stone
and carved away until there was David.' That's what we are doing.
We are carving away to create a beautiful dance company. That's
all I care about; I don't want any credit for myself."

Somehow the carving didn't take. Some critics feel that Mrs.
Freund hacked away at the company, its artistic directors, and the
board. Ramon Segarra, one of a stream of Chicago Ballet masters,
told the press upon quitting, "Mrs. Freund is using the Chicago
Ballet for her own whims and purposes. It could be a good company, but it's too unsteady when you have artistic policy being

set by a fund raiser and, unfortunately, she is the last word around here."

It's true that Geraldine has done a lot of fund raising in her time. She and her husband, psychiatrist Dr. J. Dennis Freund, are guarantors (people who contribute one thousand dollars or more annually) to the Lyric Opera. Mrs. Freund is a governing member of the Orchestral Association. She helped raise money to refurbish the Executive Mansion in Springfield when James R. Thompson moved in.

Mrs. Freund has been a successful fund raiser in her own life, too. The Freunds once owned the Fairview Hospital, a center for the treatment of the mentally and emotionally disturbed. Freund even took a turn at gold digging. In the 1960's, she was president of United Placer Industries, a group that established placer gold mining in Arizona.

Geraldine Freund objects to the widespread belief that she's rolling in dough: "Some people think I'm filthy rich, but I'm not. I'm just rich in giving."

7. Eleanor W. Prince

Eleanor W. Prince, wife of William W. Prince, industrialist and cousin and adopted son of Frederick Henry Prince, is the closest thing Chicago has to a royal benefactress.

The Chagall mosaic depicting the Four Seasons that glitters in the plaza in front of the First National Bank is there because of the W. Princes. They prevailed upon Marc Chagall to accept the commission (Chagall has been known to be a guest in the W. Prince apartment duplex overlooking Lincoln Park). Then the industrious W. Princes paid the costs of transporting and setting up the seventy-foot long, fourteen-foot high, one-inch thick mosaic. They also worked to bring Chagall's six stained-glass panels, the *American Windows,* to the Art Institute. In one of the W. Prince bathrooms is a framed portion of tablecloth that a tipsy Chagall once doodled upon.

Eleanor also gives considerable support to ballet companies. She was credited with being the chief financial backer of the Chicago Ballet. Her generosity even earned her a cameo role by proxy in the film "Turning Point." Rumor has it that Eleanor was once considering endowing the American Ballet Theater. In the film, ABT co-director Lucia Chase spies a matronly woman entering an elevator and murmurs to a companion, "She's worth at least twenty-five thousand dollars." In real life, it's reported that Eleanor overheard the appraisal of what she might give. In any event, she quietly withdrew her support.

8. Heather Morgan Bilandic

Until socialite Heather Morgan met and married Michael Bilandic, she was known as the beautiful and chic head of the Chicago Council on Fine Arts. Heather was an art history graduate from Smith College (former classmates of Heather's remember the matching nightgowns and peignoirs she wore down to breakfast each morning), had traveled and studied in Europe, and knew which fork to pick up at banquets.

As the first executive director of the Arts Council, Heather published a guidebook to Loop sculpture, worked on a monthly fine-arts calendar, established a career guide for the arts, organized the free noontime summer shows staged in the Daley (Civic) Center before the Picasso, and started the Culture Bus rolling.

Heather wears clothes by Chicago designers like Gino Rossi and Noriko; she drags the former mayor along to gallery openings, and makes nice little speeches about the importance of art in a place like Chicago. Mrs. Bilandic has it in perspective; as she has remarked: "The arts will survive long after scandals, wars, and oil shortages [And snows?]. They will be a reminder of a time, a place, and a spirit."

9. Lucy Salenger

Lucy Salenger, director of the State of Illinois Film Office, always carries with her a portfolio crammed with pictures of the more photogenic spots in Illinois: Stateville Penitentiary, the Chicago El, the Armour estate in Lake Bluff, Starved Rock State Park, Lincoln's log cabin near Springfield, the Sears Tower. Like a proud parent, Lucy waits for someone to ask her about her babies. Salenger speaks about Illinois as virtually undiscovered territory: "It's really time for people to see what this marvelous state looks like. I am constantly amazed at the number of sophisticated, well-traveled movie producers and directors who, when they come into Chicago, say to me, 'Well, I never knew it looked like this!'—because they only know Chicago from O'Hare."

For four years, since the Illinois Film Office was created as part of the Business and Economic Development agency, with a staff of four and an annual operating budget of less than $100,000, Salenger has been an aggressive seeker after moviemakers. She landed the old Armour estate for Robert Altman's *A Wedding*. She convinced the producers of *Looking for Mr. Goodbar* that the BBC disco and Sweetwater on the Near North Side had the right kind of slave-market atmosphere. She even got Governor Thompson to make a phone call to the producers of *The Omen* when they were threatening to move the whole ghastly production to Kentucky. Thompson reportedly told the *Omen* makers: "Look, we want you in Illinois." *Omen* producer Harvey Bernhart was finally convinced: "Chicago is a fantastic city. It has a pulse and beat like London and San Francisco. And it has areas with, oh God, just the right look of entrenched wealth."

Thompson, who is fond of celebrities, pushed to bring *The Omen* to Illinois ostensibly because the business of film production fills state coffers. "For a relatively few dollars, a state can bring in millions of dollars," claims Miss Salenger. She estimates that with fourteen films made in Illinois in the past two years, the state has gotten around $8 million in extra revenue. And when movies are filmed in Chicago, storekeepers, restaurant owners, and the Chicago Park District—which collects tiny sums from its permit fees ($6,290 in 1977)—grow fat and happy.

Salenger is just right for the job of collaring Hollywood producers. She's aggressive, attractive, and, according to a few Salenger detractors, compulsive. She is also loaded with expertise. She has produced documentaries for *Eyewitness News* on ABC-TV in Chicago, and worked as a researcher and field producer for *Sixty Minutes*.

Lucy has put Illinois and Chicago back in the film business. Before 1918, when the Midwest winters finally got to actors and crews, Chicago was the nation's silent-movie capitol, with Essanay Studios on West Argyle churning out Charlie Chaplin, Gloria Swanson, and Wallace Beery classics.

10. Michael Kutza

The director of the Chicago International Film Festival is multi-talented. Kutza has been a freelance motion-picture cameraman for WGN-TV in Chicago; an art director and graphics designer for a host of film companies and agencies; film editor for the Lerner Newspaper chain, and for the big time in film criticism, *Il Tempo* in Rome. Kutza has chaired film festivals in Venice, Tehran, Lima, and Delhi.

Kutza will go down in the record books, though, for putting together the Chicago International Film Festival, the only competitive film festival in the United States. The Film Fest has been held since 1965. It's a three-week affair that averages about thirty films and operates on a $325,000 annual budget. All the films are selected by Kutza himself; the festival is strictly his show. The only thing wrong with this arrangement is Kutza's taste. Kutza, of Hungarian background and strong East European preferences, seems always to be showing films that highlight the daily grind of Bulgarian potato harvesters. Film critic Gene Siskel has long howled against the Kutza method: "He regularly prefers dreary, somber films of confused politics and sexuality." But this very strangeness and incomprehensibility give the Chicago Film Festival its air of élan, its convincing stand that if you can't understand it, it must be good.

11. Maria Tallchief

Maria Tallchief, artistic director for the Lyric Opera Ballet and one of America's most celebrated ballerinas, was born in 1925 on an Osage Indian reservation in Fairfax, Oklahoma, the daughter of an Osage tribesman, Alex Joseph Tallchief, and a determined Scotch-Irish mother, Ruth Mary Porter. Tallchief struck oil with the rest of the tribe, and Ruth began training Maria for the demanding role of rich reservationist. Maria Tallchief says she owes it all to her Spartan upbringing: "My life was one of complete study—two hours of piano a day and much of the rest of dance, and fulfilling a demand by my mother that I receive the highest possible grades in school. It sounds as if it was dreadful, but I'm glad I did it."

Tallchief, who took ballet lessons from the age of three, danced with the Ballet Royale of Monte Carlo when she was seventeen. At twenty-two, she married choreographer George Balanchine and danced until 1965 as the prima ballerina of his New York City Ballet Company. When Nureyev defected, Maria was his first dancing partner in the U.S. Tallchief rocked dance circles in 1965 when she suddenly quit the New York City Ballet. Her reason: "I don't mind being listed alphabetically, but I do mind being treated alphabetically."

The marriage to Balanchine was annulled long ago, and Tallchief has been married since 1957 to a rich Chicago contractor, Henry D. Paschen. Tallchief has coached the Lyric Opera dancers since 1972; sometimes Balanchine choreographs for them.

Tallchief now leads the life of a Chicago socialite, but is a somewhat aloof one. A commentator on the Chicago arts scene remarked, "Maria is very independent; she keeps away from all the infighting." Tallchief does hold an exclusive early-morning exercise class that friends Bonnie Swearingen and Ruth Edelman faithfully attend.

12. Gregory Mosher

Ever since 1928, when the Goodman's first director, Thomas Wood Stevens, grandly announced, "We have made Shakespeare pay," the sixty-one-year-old acting company has tried to make legitimate theater turn a profit.

The Goodman's new director, thirty-year-old Gregory Mosher, is the youngest artistic director of any major American theater. He's done a lot to shake up the company that turned pro in 1969. And he's turned a good profit in the process.

Mosher originally didn't want to get to where he is today. He was a drum major in his high-school band; he always wanted to conduct a symphony orchestra when he grew up. Mosher eventually faced reality: "When it became clear that I was not going to be Reiner or Bernstein and when I realized there were other raging musical prodigies around the place, I reconsidered."

Mosher became an acting and directing major at Oberlin and Ithaca Colleges; he studied under John Housman at the Juilliard School of Drama. Mosher's great passion is experimental theater —he directed the Goodman's Stage 2 series, a spin-off of the regular company where you can have your disbelief stretched, from its inception in 1974. Mosher backed the world premieres of David Mamet's *American Buffalo* and *A Life in the Theater*. Now, he has Goodman playwright-in-residence Mamet hard at work on a musical called *Lone Canoe*. According to Mamet, his new work will bring back the jolly frontier days on the plains: "It's about Indians and whites in early Waukegan. There will be lots of English, French, and Indians, all singing and dancing."

Mosher sees the Goodman as having a major role to play: "The Goodman must influence the aesthetic of theater in America. We must not settle for clichés. As theatrical artists, we must prick the protective layer of noninvolvement."

13. E. Laurence Chalmers, Jr.

Though president of the Art Institute, Larry Chalmers doesn't claim to know a lot about art. Chalmers confesses that he has only a "layman's" knowledge.

His real forte is in psychology (Chalmers holds a Ph.D. in psychology from Princeton). His other strength is administration—he served as the assistant dean of faculties at Florida State University from 1962 to 1964, dean of the College of Arts and Sciences there from 1966 to 1969, and finally capped his administrative career as chancellor of the University of Kansas from 1969 to 1972 before he accepted the Art Institute presidency in 1972. Chalmers once told critic Richard Christiansen that he didn't believe the director of the museum had to be a curator or arts historian: "I didn't have to be a neurosurgeon to run a department of medicine at the University of Kansas."

The genial Chalmers, easily identifiable by his bow tie and pipe, has done well in the presidency. He hasn't run afoul of the really big power, Chairman of the Board James Alsdorf, yet (his predecessor, Charles G. Cunningham, was heartily disliked by Alsdorf's predecessor, the mighty Leigh Block, and Cunningham resigned). Chalmers brought the ruins of Pompeii to Chicago in 1978. He expects to have the Art Institute budget balanced by 1981. He's working on finding a replacement for the unpopular but capable art director John Maxon. Chalmers may not know much about art, but he seems to know how to run an art institute.

14. Danny Newman

Lyric Opera publicist Danny Newman looks like a theatrical manager out of a 1930's musical. He sweeps around in capes, sets off his remaining fringe of hair with velvet hats, and talks at an average speed of 78 r.p.m. His press releases are renowned for their verbosity: Newman describes any soprano on tour from Torino as if she heralded the Second Coming. Danny believes his own publicity: "Any attraction I represent is the greatest and any employer I work for is beyond criticism."

Newman has been working for the Lyric Opera as head of its PR department since Carol Fox began operations in 1954. He's given credit for boosting subscription sales for the opera season and with getting ordinary Joes to try a night at the opera. *Variety* has called Newman the "St. Paul of subscription theater tickets sales, a combination of messianic zeal and manic energy." Now in his sixties, Danny Newman still keeps a whirlwind pace. "I don't think there is any question that I travel more than any U.S. Secretary of State," he said.

Before Newman started selling the Lyric Opera, he represented a variety of clients: his first job was doing publicity for the Chicago Board of Education; after he dropped out of Wright Junior College, he wrote all the newspaper ads for Essaness' thirty-one movie theaters in Chicago, represented circuses and vaudeville acts, and wrote ads for Minsky's Burlesque. Danny gave stripper Dardy Orlando the title, "Anatomy Award Winner of 1950."

In all his endeavors, Danny Newman has gone after just one goal: "What I hope for when someone reads my publicity is one response: 'Martha, where's my checkbook?'"

15. John Hallmark Neff

John Hallmark Neff, director of the Museum of Contemporary Art, is an enfant terrible of the Chicago arts world. In a museum that cultivates the offbeat (the Museum of Contemporary Art once called in artist Christo Javacheft to wrap its entire outer facade in canvas and manila ropes), Neff is seen as really daring. When Neff was curator of the Detroit Institute of Arts, he used to issue manifestos like this one: "It's about time we took a serious look at the soda can. The twenty-first century certainly will be curious about our advertising, the expensive way we package things. It is something museums ought to start looking at now. I believe, in fact, that a museum of contemporary art should take a look at everything."

Neff has done his bit. In Detroit, he mounted an exhibition featuring the T-shirt as art and kept pressing for an automobile exhibit. Since he succeeded real-estate developer Lewis Manilow to the directorship of the Chicago Museum of Contemporary Art in the fall of 1977, Neff has been pushing for an airplane exhibit. The MCA may come to resemble an auto showroom or airplane hangar.

It's not that Neff doesn't care about art. He does, after all, hold an art history Ph.D. from Harvard, and he wrote his dissertation on Matisse decoration. Neff just feels that many things can be considered art: "I would happily show the works of a sixteenth-century Bavarian glass painter if I thought it would illuminate some aspect of the modern sensibility; but at Detroit we had some rewarding sessions with vanguardists, too. . . . I am also fascinated by a show someone is doing in Texas on the phonograph record as a kind of conceptual medium."

While Neff is being conceptual, the rest of the museum crew is hard-nosed about the problems of keeping alive the museum that has largely been passed over by the Chicago arts establishment. The Museum of Contemporary Art, sometimes nastily called the YMCA, or "Yiddish Museum of Contemporary Art," is a product of the Art Institute board's apparent long-term inability to find any artistic-minded Jews in Chicago. Many Jews who thought they were artistically minded found a home.

Founder Joseph Shapiro summed up the ingredients of the MCA's survival at a museum birthday celebration in 1978. Shapiro's words apply to all the arts in Chicago. According to Shapiro, the museum is still around because of its backers' "vision, energy, money, and the capacity to part with it."

10

Commodities

People who devote their lives to the study of how much decibel shock the human ear can withstand before the peace of partial deafness sets in, often test noise levels on El platforms, in subways, or in the midst of rush-hour traffic. All this is well and good. It goes a long way toward showing how much it takes to deafen and madden the poor urban dweller —but the noise experts are missing out on one of their best bets.

If the noise boys want to sample the ultimate, the world's only planned pandemonium, they should visit the block at the foot of La Salle Street. There, in a somber structure crowned by a statue of Ceres, the Roman goddess of grain, nearly five hundred people assemble every day to stand crammed into seventeen octagonal wooden pits and shout out orders at each other while making exotic hand signals in each other's faces. The people shouting on the floor are surrounded by phone banks, electronic quotation boards, and teletype machines. The noise begins and ends with the striking of a large gong. This is the Chicago Board of Trade—world's largest and the nation's oldest commodities trading market, a holdover from the days of open auction, the triumph of chaos over computers, and a monument to noise.

The Chicago Board of Trade could have many other uses: head-

197

ache commercials could be filmed there; expressionistic filmmakers could use the trading floor as a symbol for modern communications; psychiatrists could send anxiety-ridden patients there to get a glimpse of what it's like to really live in the throes of tension; people could pick up tips on life by listening to trading floor maxims: "Never add to a losing position," "Cut your losses," "Don't lose so much that you can't come back," "Let your profits run."

As it is, the Chicago Board of Trade houses an incredible amount of daily transactions. This is the land of live hogs and pork bellies trading, where soybeans, soybean oil, and soybean meal are king, where corn, wheat, oats, iced broilers, Winnipeg rapeseed, and Chicago stud lumber come to market.

Ex-Mayor Bilandic used to go there to get inspired. He told traders at the 130th anniversary of the Chicago Board of Trade in 1978: "What's nice about this place is that it gives a lot of people opportunity. You have MBAs from Harvard and you have people who walked in off the street, all competing in a free and open marketplace. That's what's so great about this place. That's why, every time I come here I once again get my confidence restored in this great country and in the free enterprise system. Everybody should come here periodically and get a recharge of free enterprise."

Ninety percent of the nation's commodity trading is conducted in the Chicago Board of Trade and the Chicago Mercantile Exchange pits. Commodity trading has risen above inflation. The Board of Trade and the other commodity exchanges have price fluctuations licked. For example, the Board of Trade has broken its own volume records every year since 1970. The Board of Trade annually trades in futures contracts worth over $400 billion, while the annual value of stocks and bonds traded at the New York Stock Exchange is estimated at about $250 billion. The future, it would seem, belongs to pork bellies and soybeans.

Commodities trading had a simple enough beginning. It grew out of the disgust and frustration nineteenth-century farmers felt when they hauled their goods all the way into Chicago every year after harvest, only to have their goods bought cheap because of the available glut, or to watch their grain slowly rot because storage bins couldn't be found. There was nowhere to store grain, no standard way of measuring it, and no central marketplace to buy and sell it. Trading was haphazard. The whole process was conducted like a medieval open market.

So on April 3, 1848, eighty-two Chicago merchants got together in a flour store located at what is now Wacker and Clark and put together the Chicago Board of Trade: a central, year-round marketplace, where trading was to be conducted according to uniform practices, where farmers and merchants could contract for future delivery dates of goods, and where huge fortunes could be quickly made—and lost. The eighty-two merchants established grain gambling and laid the foundations for making Chicago's commodities markets "Las Vegas North."

The Chicago Board of Trade still looks sort of primitive. It's conducted according to the open auction system, but it's an auction without an auctioneer. Each of the board's 1,402 members, whether they represent outside individuals or businesses or themselves, acts as his or her own buyer or seller: the upshot is that a seller is surrounded by pushing, shoving, shouting, competing buyers.

The system is primitive, too. The Chicago Board of Trade uses "open outcry" (screaming one's willingness to buy or sell and for how much) and a set of hand signals: if you stand, or try to stand, in the middle of the pit with your palm facing yourself, you're indicating you want to buy; if you stand with palm outstretched, Roman orator style, you've got something to sell. Then there are a number of interesting things you can do with your fingers that ultimately could lead to a career with the Muppet Show: for grain contracts, each finger held in a vertical position indicates 5,000 bushels, or one contract. A clenched fist indicates a full cent; an open hand with four fingers poetically and horizontally extended indicates a half cent.

All this is fairly straightforward. But commodities traders don't just stand around flinging their hands and fingers about like automatons. These people are *artistes*. They bring baroque refinements to signaling. They execute leaps across the pits that would shame Baryshnikov. They arrange intricate pit-encounter groups —ten red-faced buyers advancing on one seller. Their hands are finely tuned instruments. Traders even assume interesting positions in repose: they stand with their arms bent and crossed over their heads, ready to shoot forth again at the drop of a bid. The most amazing feature of life in the pits is how traders print up their trading cards. In the midst of the fury, with competing buyers jostling all around, the broker who has completed his transaction bends his head as he fills in his card—unscathed, unruffled, an island of serenity unto himself.

The broker has much to be serene about. People can make embarrassingly large amounts of money by screaming and signaling in the trading pits. Good commodity traders pull down hundreds of thousands from soybeans and pork bellies every day. The worth of a seat on the Chicago Board of Trade is reflected in the going price. Seats usually sell for from $60,000 to as high as $215,000.

One Chicagoan has even found a way to play Beach Blanket Broker. Richard Deal works the commodities exchange in the summer by taking his telephone, television, and video terminal to the lakefront park near his North Side home. His lakefront exchange flourishes and Deal himself is happy with the arrangement: "It's just like operating on the exchange floor in the pit," Deal gloated to a reporter, "only I'm in the park on Eastlake Terrace."

Commodities trading is the traditional way to make a good killing in live hogs, pork bellies, and soybeans. It's also the seventies' answer to inflation. Commodity futures contracts are commitments to buy or sell a specific quantity and kind of a commodity at a specific price at a future date. The Board of Trade members who take their positions near "May Wheat" aren't being poetic, but are signaling the month they want to deliver or receive the wheat. The differences between the stock market and the commodities market show why many traders believe the future is in futures. When you buy a stock, you're buying a share in a corporation. When you deal in commodities, you gain a contract. The stock market provides capital for industries. The commodities market gives price protection to producers, distributors, and users. People like farmers, flour millers, grain-elevator operators, plywood warehousers, processors, and exporters can breathe a little easier because of the futures market.

The commodities market isn't just a place for nervous grain-elevator operators to get a chance to conquer price fluctuations, however. The market—like the stock exchange, politics, and life—is made up of both people who shun risk and people who thrive on the surge of adrenalin that winning or losing fortunes can give. Our language has taken an expression from cautious commodities traders—it's called "hedging your bets." The hedger lives to minimize risk; his hope is that futures trading will give him price insurance. This kind of insurance is necessary. Droughts, floods, plant diseases, ill-considered federal programs, and even foreign wars keep commodities prices fluctuating. But the hedger couldn't exist without the speculator, who assumes the risk for Br'er Hedger.

The speculator is a thinker, and, in order to survive, he's got to be a very fast thinker. Pity the adventuresome speculator who has to instantly decide whether to "sell short" if he thinks prices will drop, or "go long" if he thinks he can sell to contract at a higher price later. The speculator can't withdraw to the side to ponder his moves, either. None of this Hamlet "sicklied o'er with the pale cast of thought" stuff succeeds in the trading pits. All the speculator's decision making is done in the midst of Bedlam, while rivals push past and gesticulate all around him. This is the kind of activity that brings apopletic roses to the cheeks, that sets grown men screaming and flailing about.

It's also the kind of activity that can reap enormous profits. If a speculator is smart, knows the market, and isn't a pathological gambler, he can earn the kind of money enjoyed by Arab oil sheiks and some Chicago aldermen.

Mid-America trader Chuck Fanaro once explained it this way: "If you hang around here long enough, you realize that the American dream is not an illusion. A person can come here—male or female, black or white—long on ambition and integrity and short on funds, and find out if he has what it takes. If he has it, well, the rewards are fantastic. I know of no other business in modern times where a guy can change his standard of living radically on a little amount of capital and with the application of self-discipline."

One Board of Trade legend has it that a few years ago, a psychologist with $5,000 to venture ordered his broker to buy wheat futures and to use any profits gained to keep buying wheat futures. The psychologist was too nervous to stay in Chicago and watch his money melt, so he took off for Trinidad. When the shrink returned five months later, he discovered that his $5,000 venture had swollen into a $200,000 profit.

A secretary for one commodities broker—dabbling in the market in her spare time—pulled in nearly $100,000 one year, buying herself a mink coat and her policeman husband just about the most expensive motorcycle there is. Her boss told her not to say anything; not all the firm's clients did so well.

Trader Fanaro qualified his rosy profit picture by saying that he who loses at life will lose in commodities trading. "The market is like life. Only it's like one hundred years of life in a week. Many people go through life rationalizing, or kidding themselves, but the consequences of their rationalizations are dragging so far behind them in time, it's difficult to learn a lesson. In the market, however, if you rationalize and if you're wrong, you know pretty quickly. People who constantly rationalize never make it as commodities traders."

Success stories are actually relatively rare. A few years ago, the Commodity Exchange Authority published findings that showed that only 25 percent of speculators make a net profit. According to the CEA, the chief problem was that speculators didn't know when to cut their losses. According to Chicago writer and commodities expert Edgar Shook, commodities traders have a favorite saying: "The speculator who dies rich dies before his time."

Commodity speculating is still very attractive. The commodity speculator enjoys more leverage (the ability to control a lot of value with a little capital) than does the stock-market player. You can start speculating with relatively little venture capital; for example, putting up 5 to 15 percent of the total value of the contract will generally give the trader the benefit of the price movement on the full contract. The speculator can control a $9,000 soybean oil account for $750—if the price of soybean oil increases by 5 percent, the speculator will have realized a 60 percent profit. This leverage, the leverage that can move soybean contracts and huge profits, makes commodities trading an easy game to get into and a hard one to get out of.

Commodities markets are great places to visit (the public can view the action in the pits during trading hours at Chicago's exchanges). Depending on the individual's outlook, what transpires below may seem the crowning glory of capitalism or a foretaste of hell. They're great places for flour millers and grain-elevator operators to protect their money and they're great places to gamble.

Commodities trading reaches beyond the trading room floor, however, and affects all consumers in subtle and sometimes dramatic ways. The deals reached in the pits put a price tag on next year's loaf of bread, determine how much breakfast lovers will fork over for their bacon (pork bellies is the preferred commodities term), and how much the consumer will get plucked for a frozen chicken (iced broilers to the commodities boys). Pit pacts affect the prices the Soviet Union will pay for U.S. grain, the world-wide importation of Illinois soybean products, the reception of Midwest agricultural products abroad. Beyond that, commodities trading protects producers and, ultimately, consumers, from wild price swings resulting from changes in supply and demand. If a farmer's crop is wiped out by insects, he's covered. If his herd of cattle drops dead on the way to market, he's covered. Commodities trading helps stabilize a rocky and vulnerable economy. Those hyperactive people in the pits—each one looking like a candidate for early cardiac arrest—are cutting deals that affect everything from the price of bread to U.S.-Soviet relations.

Commodities trading does not begin and end with the Chicago Board of Trade. Chicago has three other thriving commodities marketplaces: The Chicago Mercantile Exchange, the nation's second-largest commodities trading center, the MidAmerica Commodity Exchange, and the young exchange that has driven Wall Street up the wall, the Chicago Board Options Exchange.

The new structure that houses the Chicago Mercantile Exchange, a shiny black glass box at Jackson and Canal, was designed with coronary victims in mind. The Merc has its own emergency room for traders who might suffer heart attacks on the floor. The emergency room is also equipped with a hotline to the Fire Department ambulance dispatcher.

The Mercantile Exchange has other amenities for its hard-driven denizens. The floor is made of skid-proof black rubber and the trading pits are considered "stumble-proof." The pits have exhaust vents to help absorb the body heat generated in the pitch of bidding; the Merc has no windows (who would want to look outside when he could watch his own futures brighten or dim in one room?). Rather than shackle commodities traders with a superfluous view, the designers of the Merc, architects Perkins and Will, covered the thirty-four-foot-high walls with quotation boards. The ceiling is sound-absorbent. The chairs in the Merc have been screwed to the floor so they won't be constantly toppled over by profit-rushers. Even the coatracks' design makes allowances for the traders' notable lack of patience—they're all motor-driven, just like commodities traders.

The Merc is Chicago's second largest commodities exchange. The star at the fifty-three-year-old exchange has always been pork bellies, but it also does a hefty business with live cattle, turkeys, Idaho potatoes (the Merc board codes potatoes as "POT"), ham and eggs.

The Merc has never been shy about drumming up business. In 1976, Merc traders, anxious to get into live cattle trading, trotted out a grand champion steer onto the trading floor. A few years ago, the exchange shocked more conservative outfits like the Chicago Board of Trade with a series of goofy ads that explained commodities to potential traders. One ad captioned a portrait of Sir Francis Bacon with "Sir Francis Pork Belly." Another ad assured people that "If you've got a little risk capital, we've got the risk." Still another Chicago Mercantile pitch intoned: "Say to yourself, 'I am not afraid to trade cattle futures. I am not afraid to trade cattle futures. I am not afraid to trade cattle futures.'"

The Merc has enjoyed an astounding growth rate. In the past decade, its volume has quadrupled. Thirty years ago, a seat on the Merc could be had for around $3,000. Now seats sell for as much as $200,000. In 1978, trader Richard Nertz paid $100,000 for a seat; he explained in an interview the wisdom of this purchase: "The seat is your investment. It's your gas station."

Many traders feel that the most exciting aspect of the Merc is its International Monetary Market. The IMM, which began in 1972, is the world's first currency futures market. At the IMM, futures in gold and in eight foreign currencies are traded. Chicago had the only currency futures market until last year when New York (Second Commodities City) got into the act.

The MidAmerica Commodity Exchange, Chicago's third-largest futures market, is where small traders can become big ones. It's considered a training ground for traders who eventually make it to the big time at the Chicago Board of Trade or the Merc. Seats at MidAmerica sell for a mere fraction of the going rate at the other exchanges. The MidAmerica's smaller contracts allow neophyte traders to make bad contracts and learn from mistakes that would wipe them out if they were playing with the big boys. MidAmerica has always been a kind of nursery for commodities traders. Once you've mastered the rudiments of screaming and flailing around with thirty other bidders, you're ready to move into the body language Olympics at the Chicago Board of Trade.

MidAmerica's image has been changing of late. It's not only viewed as Commodity Row's dollhouse, but as a very attractive and vital alternative to mammoth trading. Within the past few years, three of the country's largest securities firms have bought seats on the MidAmerica. Merrill Lynch, Pierce, Fenner and Smith; Shearson Hayden Stone; and E. F. Hutton and Company now grace MidAmerica with their grand presences.

It's those "mini-contracts" that lure the paying customers every time. The MidAmerica is the only exchange in the United States that offers "mini-contracts" for grain futures in minimum units of one thousand bushels.

MidAmerica has futures contracts on all the hot commodities: soybeans, silver, corn, wheat, oats, and live hogs. But MidAmerica's contracts on these commodities are just one half to one fifth the size of contracts traded at the Board of Trade or the Chicago Mercantile Exchange.

The advantages to this system are more than you can shake an outstretched palm at. For one thing, investors can get in the game at MidAmerica with a smaller amount of risk money. Speculators can make trades in several commodities. At the MidAmerica, they're not hog-tied to one contract. Even hedgers can profit from the Lilliputian trading at MidAmerica. Small farmers can indulge in a practice called "scaling up," whereby they can make a series of small futures sales at progressively higher prices.

The MidAmerica Commodity Exchange began life in 1868 as Pudd's Exchange, an open-air market at the corner of Washington and LaSalle Streets where farmers and merchants got together to haggle over wheat and hogs. Old Pudd's became incorporated in 1880 as the Chicago Open Board of Trade. The Chicago Open Board of Trade had some fancy rules: speaking was forbidden on the trading-room floor; traders were discouraged from standing on chairs and desktops to watch the trading fray.

MidAmerica in the twentieth century was fairly quiet, until two explosive events shook up the traders. The first was the Soviet grain purchases, which catapulted the MidAmerica, along with all other commodities exchanges, into the Big Money. Between 1971 and its grandest year to date, 1974, MidAmerica's volume increased by twenty times to 2.6 million contracts.

The second shocker was the 1978 dress code set down for MidAmerica traders, which forbade "nonbusiness" attire like blue jeans, sneakers, and T-shirts on the trading floor, and also placed smoking, eating, and drinking under interdict. All this fits in with MidAmerica's rise in the commodities world. Traders are supposed to look prosperous, or at least look as if they might have enough venture capital to take the bus home at night. But one clause in the Mid-America code could seriously hamper some traders. The trading floor is not the place, states the Exchange's code, for profanity, vulgarity, or "speech which intimidates others."

Chicago's newest and most daring exchange, the place that weds trading stocks with trading in commodities futures, is the Chicago Board Options Exchange. In 1973, leaders at the Board of Trade hit upon a blockbuster concept: trading in stock-market futures. The Board of Trade set up the CBOE to organize the trading. Ever since, the Chicago Board Options Exchange has been busily supervising trades in call options to buy or sell a major listed stock at a fixed price at some future date.

Former Board of Trade chairman Paul F. McGuire knew all along that they had struck gold; he told *Business Week* that "the creation of the CBOE dwarfs any single thing ever done in commodities or securities." McGuire added a personal note of satisfaction: "I never fail to realize one hundred thousand dollars a year in the options market."

Six years of buying and selling stock options have proven McGuire right. The volume on the Chicago Board Options Exchange is estimated at more than a third of total New York Stock Exchange volume, a feat all the more remarkable because the CBOE trades options in about eighty-five stocks, while the Big Board trades in eighteen hundred issues.

Chicago hedgers and speculators have taken to stock-option trading as naturally as they used to handle pork bellies and iced broilers. It's all done by good old-fashioned pushing and shoving and through the newfagled putting and calling. "Puts" are options to sell a widely traded stock at a prearranged price before a certain date. "Calls" are options to buy a major listed stock at a prearranged price before a certain date. Puts are bets that the price of the stock will fall; calls are bets that the price will rise. Options trading is based on the futures theory, but the action at the Chicago Board Options Exchange is more like what happens in a casino than at an auction.

Options action takes place on the CBOE's twenty-thousand-square-foot trading floor, a floor that is half the size of a football field, a floor that weighs three hundred tons and hangs above the frantic Chicago Board of Trade pits, a floor that was constructed entirely at night and on weekends so that the Board of Traders would not be disturbed. (The question arises: What could disturb commodities traders? Wouldn't it be more likely that the roar from the pits would disturb the solderers and welders at work?)

Some of the transactions that the five hundred traders at the CBOE engage in are a bit too swift for the Securities and Exchange Commission. One trading tactic that really worries the SEC and the CBOE itself is the way that some traders "go naked" on the floor. Going naked refers to some call traders' practice of selling options for stocks they don't own. This practice can force the entire stock market up or down through pure speculation.

The Chicago Board Options Exchange has had some scandals in its short history. Brokers have been suspended for trading customers' options without bothering to get customers' permission, for dealing with insufficient margins, for making payoffs to other traders, and for profiting from trading errors. Former CBOE president Joseph Sullivan once said that the new exchange has been conscious of protecting against flimflam artists from its inception: "We've done a lot from the beginning to guard against the miscreant out there, who would do God knows what—run the price of the underlying security up, drive it down, what have you." Sullivan took heart from the fact that the CBOE only trades in major listed stocks, "Some Palooka is just not going to manipulate General Motors."

There was a fascinating scandal in February of 1979 when federal drug agents raided the CBOE and found a very interesting commodity being traded, though quite discreetly: cocaine.

However disreputable CBOE may have seemed at the outset, and however volatile its trading continues to be, the CBOE brand of stock trading has definitely caught on. The American Stock Exchange (AMEX) and the PBW (Philadelphia-Baltimore-Washington) Exchange have already followed CBOE's lead in establishing stock-options trading. New York is following suit. The other stock exchanges are paying the pioneer Chicago board the ultimate compliment—trying to obliterate it.

No matter what trading wars the next few years bring, Chicago will always retain a unique spot. Old-time Chicago farmers and merchants began commodities trading; they developed the peculiar but effective system of trading through oral outcry and hand signals; they made it a roaring success.

The men who run Chicago's commodity exchanges are all financial wizards, most of them came up from the pits, and several have had real live experience with real live hogs. These men are hot commodities.

THE TOP FIVE COMMODITIES MEN IN CHICAGO

1. Robert K. Wilmouth

Robert Wilmouth, president of the Chicago Board of Trade, was a one-time contender for A. Robert Abboud's job. Wilmouth is banker to the bone. He had been with the First National Bank ever since he graduated from Notre Dame in 1950 and was steadily climbing those banking rungs, moving all the way from trainee-gopher to chief of the First's skyscraper plans in the 1960's and to executive vice-president in 1972. In 1973, the management deck at the First was reshuffled, Abboud and his team came out on top, and Wilmouth's hopes of heading the bank crumbled.

Wilmouth became a powerful bank president anyway. In 1974, he was named president of Crocker National Corporation and its subsidiary, Crocker National Bank, in San Francisco. And then Wilmouth was offered the top spot at the Chicago Board of Trade, a position that ranks third in the financial world after Abboud and J. P. Morgan's ghost. Besides power, Wilmouth's new position provides some generous profit-sharing and investment-fund income that surpassed his $172,000 Crocker Bank salary.

Most important, Wilmouth landed a job that rates with whale harpooning and leech gathering as one of the most difficult and peculiar occupations ever created. After his appointment was announced, Wilmouth said pridefully: "I don't think there is another job like it in the U.S. I'll have 1,402 bosses (the members of the Board of Trade) and not all of them think the same way."

Wilmouth is in charge of a pretty unruly group, all right. Commodities traders are supreme individualists. They don't make good team players. But Wilmouth, with his solid banking background, wants to improve the image of the Board of Trade scrappers, at least with the Commodity Futures Trading Commission, which has taken a dim view of the Chicago boys of late. Wilmouth has repeatedly fought against the popular image of commodity traders as profit-mad; as he's said, "Too many people think of us as a bunch of speculators who only serve to drive up food prices. We've got to do a better public-relations job and change that impression."

2. Ronald F. Young

R. F. Young, chairman of the Chicago Board of Trade, looks like he's more highly evolved than the rest of us. His forehead is not only high, but jutting, indicating an awesome cranial capacity. Young's gaze has that sharp, direct look seen only in geniuses, madmen, and commodities traders. A young Young (barely forty), he moves fast and acts fast—here is not the man in power who looks like he's about to topple from chronic three-hour lunches.

Young came up fast. He went to Harvard Business School, where future business tycoons do not earn MBAs so much as they earn the privilege of saying they went to Harvard Business School. Then Young went out into the field. Literally. His first job, with Continental Grain Company, involved running a grain elevator at harvest time. Young also got to trade some grain at Continental. His organizing talents were early recognized. In 1970, Young became president of Conti-Commodities, a brokerage firm that specialized in commodity futures. Then he helped out the flagging commodities segment of E. I. Du Pont and Co.

Young always wanted to trade for himself, so he finally bought himself a seat on the Chicago Board of Trade for thirty thousand dollars. He later said, "There's a tremendous kick to being a trader. The rewards are tremendous—which they should be because the risks are great."

Since he succeeded William D. Haferty, Jr. as Board of Trade chairman in January 1978, Young has been in the more muffled world of upstairs management. But the action is still intensive and ulcer-producing. Young has to fight for better relations with the Commodity Futures Trading Commission. He regards the CFTS as a necessary spoilsport; Young told the *Tribune* after his election: "The Board of Trade is one hundred thirty years old, and for only three of those years has there been the existence of a large regulatory body watching over us. We hope we will be able to somewhat change the direction of the CFTC, although obviously we don't expect miracles and we don't expect them (the CFTC) to go away."

Like Wilmouth, Young is annoyed that farmers and food buyers don't think better of the Board of Trade. Young has lamented, "We know we represent something good and valuable, but how do we make other people appreciate that fact?"

3. Clayton F. Yeutter

The Merc has been fortunate in its leaders. The exchange grew into a power during the twenty-five-year leadership of Everette B. Harris. Harris knew commodities trading inside and out, but never ventured onto the trading floor himself. He once admitted, "If I were a trader, I'd be broke." And Harris' standard advice about how to get and stay rich in the market was, "Get far, far ahead and quit."

When Harris did quit in 1977, the Merc mantle fell to Clayton Yeutter, now president of the Chicago Mercantile Exhange. Yeutter is the Leonardo da Vinci of commodities trading. He's done everything. He holds a Ph.D. in agricultural economics and a doctorate in law. Nixon appointed him Assistant Secretary of Agriculture for marketing and consumer services. Ford tapped him to serve as deputy special-trade negotiator. Yeutter went into law, and when the Merc chose him as Harris' successor, he was running his own farm in Eustic, Nebraska, where he raised wheat, corn, and cattle.

The Merc was jubilant about its find. Chairman Lawrence M. Rosenberg knew they had somebody who could argue the pits' point of view in Washington: "It was a big thing to me personally to find someone who knew his way around Washington. We needed a man who knows where the doors are in Washington and who's not afraid to knock on them."

Yeutter hasn't just knocked on doors; he's opened them. Last year, the first six months of trading at the Merc outshone 1977 trading by 79 percent. The Merc's International Monetary Market keeps expanding. Yeutter is after more growth, both from Washington and from the guys working on the expansion of the Merc's trading floor. The Merc has already sunk $6 million into getting 40 percent more floor space by the fall of 1979. But Yeutter remarked in July 1978: "If the volume of trading continues as it has so far this year, we'll probably discover the trading floor is too small just about the day the expansion is finished."

4. Lawrence Rosenberg

Larry Rosenberg, chairman of the Chicago Mercantile Exchange, has spent nearly half of his four decades in the pits. He grew up on the North Shore, the son of a scrap-iron dealer, and majored in economics at Lake Forest College. After Rosenberg was discharged from the army, he got a job as a runner at the Chicago Board of Trade. Running is the commodities exchanges' "keep fit" job—sometimes the runners who scurry around the trading floor, bearing buy or sell instructions, wear pedometers and find that they average about five to eight miles a day. Running is also an ideal way to see a lot of trading action.

Rosenberg was a runner for a year, and then made the big leap. He borrowed $5,800 from his mother so he could buy a $7,000 Board of Trade seat. The gamble paid off—Rosenberg broke even his first year of trading and has never had a losing year since. In 1965, Rosenberg traded in one hyperactive world for another when he bought a Merc seat for $8,000 (now a seat on the Merc can set a young runner back $160,000).

Larry Rosenberg has always been an independent trader. As Rosenberg puts it, "I just like making my own money and my own mistakes."

But Rosenberg is ever respectful of the ultimate craziness of commodity trading. As he said after his election at the Merc: "I've been trading here sixteen years, and I haven't seen a sure thing yet. The market has a way of giving you a good kick in the rear end at times."

Rosenberg is bullish when it comes to the fortunes and future of the Merc. He has hinted that the three-year-old Commodity Futures Trading Commission would be well advised not to meddle with a good thing: "I just don't believe that there's a better way to take care of supply and demand than the free market. It has proved itself over and over again. The only time things go wrong is when somebody tries to tamper with it." Rosenberg also sees Chicago as the center of the trading universe: "When I started, the New York Stock Exchange was the Mecca, the place to be. I think Chicago is now the place to be. The International Monetary Market, options, interest-rate futures are all being copied elsewhere." Rosenberg the Runner can be counted on to keep the Merc on its hysterically successful course.

5. Joseph M. Sullivan

When Joseph Sullivan was named president of the Chicago Board Options Exchange in 1973, no one held out much hope for him or for the new exchange.

At thirty-four, Sullivan was the youngest head of an exchange in the nation. Sullivan was the protégé of Henry H. Wilson, the former administrative assistant to President Lyndon B. Johnson. Wilson became president of the Chicago Board of Trade in 1969. Many Chicago traders resented Wilson; as one Board of Trade director confessed to *The New York Times*: "We found ourselves with a president who had absolutely no credit with the new Nixon regime, who didn't know wheat from soybeans."

Sullivan himself was often described as "painfully shy." His background wasn't in pork bellies, but in journalism. Sullivan came to the Board of Trade after Princeton, the Columbia University Graduate School of Journalism, and *The Wall Street Journal's* Washington bureau, where he covered Congressional news.

The most telling sign of the original status Sullivan and the CBOE held is that the exchange's first headquarters were in the former members' restroom and lounge off the Board of Trade's main trading floor.

People have since changed their minds about Sullivan and the CBOE. The pioneer stock-options exchange is the greatest thing in trading since wampum, and Sullivan (now with Paine Webber) is the man responsible for its growing from an odd idea to a powerhouse.

Sullivan may appear shy, and he may not have been the suavest spokesman around. (He stunned the Financial Analysts Federation at a meeting in the Palmer House last year when he joked about the State Street mall construction going on outside, which was making the room's chandeliers shake. Quipped Sullivan: "This is quite a day in Chicago. The plumbing is out and now the gods are tinkling.") But Sullivan took on the SEC, Wall Street, and disbelieving Chicago traders to get acceptance for the CBOE. Sul-

livan is now rightly considered a financial mastermind and negotiating whiz.

Sullivan's 1978 announcement that "I'm not the guy for the long-
term hitch here" shocked LaSalle Street. Sullivan later told *Sun-
Times* reporter Alan D. Mutter: "Five years before the mast of any
membership organization produces a lot of wear and tear. And who-
ever is on the firing line takes its toll." The shy, soft-spoken reporter
who threw the trading world for a loop with a gutsy new concept
will be hard to replace.

11

Architects

Visitors to Chicago always know they're in Chicago—even if they've never watched *The Bob Newhart Show*. You might confuse Houston for Minneapolis or Cleveland for Buffalo, but Chicago's skyline and landmarks are instantly recognizable. Its bold, vigorous, and sometimes outrageous architecture is a marvel to tourists from all over the world and a much greater asset to the city than its snooty symphony or its reputation as a place where machine politics makes the trains run on time.

Chicago's famed if malodorous stockyards have closed down. Its steel mills are wearying. Much of its other industry has moved with the white folks out to the suburbs. Chicago's erstwhile husky, brawling image is imparted mostly now by its powerful skyline.

Architect Harry Weese says that all architecture is masculine. Chicago's is not merely masculine but macho. In fact, one of the city's more notable architects is famous for designing houses that resemble male genitalia.

Few Chicago architects are functioning components of the city's power structure, but it is an inherently powerful profession nevertheless. It affects so many people. Chicago architects have changed the horizons of the world. Twice in the last 100 years, a "Chicago

214

school" of architecture has totally dominated the profession. A Chicago architect named William LeBaron Jenney invented the structural steel skyscraper in the building boom that followed the Great Chicago Fire of 1871. A Berliner turned Chicagoan, Ludwig Mies van der Rohe, invented the stark high-rise boxes that since World War II have found their way into every major city on the planet. Chicago's Oak Park gave Frank Lloyd Wright to the ages, and that suburb today treasures the many homes he designed there as holy relics. In recent years, Chicago architects like Weese, Helmut Jahn, and Bertrand Goldberg have had entire magazines devoted to them in such faraway countries as Japan.

Chicago is not a very reverent sort of town, but it is reverential toward its architecture. Mayor Daley loved the new big buildings and would carry on as happily at "topping-out" ceremonies as he did at his own election victories. Jerome Butler, Chicago's city architect, became so important a figure at City Hall that he was made director of public works.

The *Tribune's* Pulitzer-Prize winning Paul Gapp is one of only three full-time newspaper architecture critics in the country. Judy Kiriazis' *Inland Architect* magazine is read and valued throughout the Midwest. Books on local architecture appear as regularly in Chicago as political books do in Washington. Architectural walks and tours are as commonplace as tours of stars' homes are in Hollywood—and probably more interesting.

With its long lakeshore and flat, open spaces, Chicago is one of the few major cities in the country where the high rise really works. New York is an oppressive jumble of high rises. The Manhattan skyline, once so splendidly dominated by the Art Deco pinnacles of the Empire State and Chrysler Buildings, now resembles a crowded patch of tall weeds. It may be breathtaking to look upon, as they say, but you have to live on Roosevelt Island or in New Jersey to see it.

San Francisco has been disfigured by high rises. Its once rolling Romanesque profile has been so obliterated by ugly towers that, from the distance, it's hard to tell there are hills. If it weren't for San Francisco Bay and the uniquely grotesque TransAmerica Pyramid—easily the world's most hideous building—it would be easy to mistake San Francisco for Minneapolis.

But the high rise has made Chicago architecture. Rising from the flat line of lake and prairie to such awesome and improbable heights, they seem almost the works of gods, which may be why Daley was so fond of them.

Three of these giants—the Sears Tower, the Standard Oil Building, and the Hancock Center—stand out from all the others the way basketball players do from ordinary folk. They're visible from suburbs as far as twenty-five and thirty miles away.

Chicago has twice beaten New York to the world's tallest building title. Its defending champion at the moment is the Sears Tower, complete with flashing strobe lights at the top to warn off meandering jetliners. That top is 1,454 feet and 110 stories high, reaching from the southwest corner of the Loop almost into the O'Hare approach pattern.

With its sixteen thousand bronze-tinted windows and black aluminum skin, the Sears would look striking even without its stratospheric height. Designed by the gargantuan architectural firm of Skidmore, Owings, and Merrill (otherwise known as SOM), the building has a number of step-backs occurring at different and unexpected levels, giving it a dramatically different appearance when seen from different angles. Its lobby corridors are much too narrow and the base of the building *is* beastly looking, but who cares about that when you can wave at airline stewardesses from your office?

Rising 1,136 feet and eighty stories from the north end of Grant Park on the city's lakefront, the Standard Oil Building is a stretched white tower that looks as though it might have eaten one of Alice in Wonderland's "eat me" cookies. Loved by tourists but hated by some local architects, the Big Stan is largely the work of the late Edward Durell Stone, who did Washington's Kennedy Center and apparently had a considerable thing for white marble. The huge lobby resembles something from an Alexander Korda movie.

Despite its great height, the views from the Big Stan are confined and less than inspiring. The windows are so narrow you'd think they were leftovers from Harry Weese's famous downtown federal jail. At the base of the Big Stan is an outdoor wind sculpture, which you can't really hear because they put it near a ninety-foot waterfall.

The first of Chicago's superbuildings to have been built—and the most interesting architecturally—is North Michigan Avenue's one-hundred-story Hancock Center, another SOM creation. With its twin television towers on the roof and X-shaped cross braces along its sides, the Hancock looks as though it might be some gigantic transistor radio. It was originally supposed to be two buildings—one for offices and one for apartments—but there wasn't enough room on the block. According to legend, one of the geniuses at SOM simply stuck one of the model buildings on top of the other and said "Eureka!" or something.

A major reason there wasn't enough room on the block is the nearby and haughtily one-storied Casino Club, whose many rich and powerful members would certainly not have been budged. The Hancock occasionally gets its revenge by dropping large pieces of ice through the Casino's roof. On one exciting morning, a naked blonde lady came plummeting down from one of the Hancock's supposedly unbreakable windows, but she missed the Casino. The Casino is seldom crashed by blonde ladies, especially naked ones.

A doorman at the Continental Plaza Hotel across the street was compelled to wear a hardhat during the Hancock's construction. He managed to collect an entire set of wrenches that fell from above.

Despite its bold design, the Hancock has fared rather poorly in architectural award competition, a circumstance which the *Tribune*'s Paul Gapp attributes to the silly concrete trim that SOM put around the base of the building so that the major ground-floor tenant—Bonwit Teller—would have neat rectangular windows to display its finery in.

There is an overpriced restaurant at the top of the Hancock, the name of which was happily not inspired by New York's Top of the Rock.

Another notable Chicago building is the sixty-story First National Bank, which thrusts out of the ground in two sweeping curves. Some architects complain about all the heavy concrete that's hung on the First's sides, but all those high-priced bank executives and lawyers up there probably need to feel secure. The chief flaw of the First National is that it's plunked right in the middle of the Loop, making its dramatic lines impossible to see from afar.

One of the easiest and most pleasing Chicago buildings to see is the graceful, curving, seventy-story Lake Point Tower, by far the prettiest high rise on the lakefront and one of only three east of Lake Shore Drive. Inspired by an idea the great Mies van der Rohe had back in 1921, Lake Point Tower was designed by some of Mies' protégés. It contains 600 apartments, yet hasn't a single straight edge to its lines.

The twin beehive towers of Marina City, located on the Chicago River just north of the Loop, were an extraordinary feature of the city's skyline in the 1960's, but now they're just sort of lost in the jumble—the jumble now including the hulking dark IBM building next door.

Up on North Michigan Avenue is Water Tower Place, which is the most obtrusive building in town. Shaped like an erect "L" and covered with marble and concrete slabs, Water Tower Place has the paw of its base crouching over the avenue, while an ungainly sixty-two-story concrete tower rises from the rear, ruining the Hancock's view. This tower portion is chock full of interior decorators and other rich apartment dwellers, and also contains the Ritz-Carlton Hotel, which despite its astronomic prices has been in financial trouble. The paw—a twelve-story-high hulk that would cause riots in Paris if they put it up on the Champs-Élysées—harbors a glitzy atrium shopping mall and such respectable names as Dunhill's, F.A.O. Schwartz, Lord & Taylor, and Marshall Field & Company.

For sheer, huge mass, there's old Joe Kennedy's four-million-square-foot Merchandise Mart on the river just north of the Loop, and the lakefront's McCormick Place exposition hall, which looks something like a beached aircraft carrier.

The gargoylesque Tribune Tower on Michigan Avenue, which might be called Charles Addams' idea of an office building, is one of the city's more cherished structures, as is the splendidly white Wrigley Building opposite—which, except during the occasional hysteria of an energy crisis, is kept brightly illuminated by spotlights at night.

Three prewar Art Deco buildings have been obscured by towering new neighbors, but remain classics. Samuel Insull's majestic, forty-five-story Civic Opera House on the western edge of the Loop, put up in 1929 at the then-extravagant cost of $20 million, was designed as a gigantic throne facing west toward the prairies and the sunset. It now bears the Kemper name, as do some of the more celebrated people attending the Opera.

At the north end of Michigan Avenue, facing the Oak Street Beach and the Drive, is the very chic and elegant Drake Hotel. And a block to the south is the marvelous old Palmolive Building,

whose beacon used to guide early mail-plane pilots like Charles
Lindbergh but now mostly irritates people in the nearby Hancock.
The Palmolive has been disfigured by a huge "PLAYBOY" sign
on top. When Palmolive owned it, there was never a huge "PALM-
OLIVE" sign.

Most of the Frank Lloyd Wright creations in the Chicago area
are in Oak Park or River Forest, but the eleven-room Charnley
(not Charnal) House on Astor Street was designed by the Great
One when he was a young architect starting out with the famed
Dankmar Adler and Louis Sullivan. Other late nineteenth-century
mansions of more classic design survive here and there in the Gold
Coast, where one can also observe some actual rich people, although not many nineteenth-century ones.

Adler and Sullivan did not write comic opera, though some of
their buildings might indicate otherwise. A few are still to be seen
in the Loop. Though majestic in their day, they now seem just so
many grimy old ghosts, housing stationery stores and coffee shops
in their ground floors. The High-Minded landmarks people have
gone gaga over them, forgetting that the late Victorian era was
probably the most architecturally awful in history, redeemed only
by the fact that it didn't produce anything at all like the Trans-
America Pyramid.

In the beginning, Chicago architecture was the usual ramshackle
frontier boom-town stuff, unique only in that many of the buildings
ended up with entrances below ground level when the city decided
to raise a lot of the streets one story to escape the perpetual mud.

After the 1871 fire, however, architects from all over the country
swarmed to Chicago to get in on the lucrative rebuilding boom.
Redoing the center of the city almost from scratch, they struck
bold new concepts, reached for new architectural horizons, and
filled their pockets. One of them, the sainted Daniel Burnham,
devised an elaborate plan for the city and its lakefront, which,
if it had been carried out, would have made Chicago one of the
great classic cities of the world, ranking right along with Paris
and London. As Burnham put it: "Make no little plans."

But the motto of too many other Chicago architects and developers was: "Make no little bucks." And so little of the Burnham
plan was ever realized. Mayor Daley never liked sidewalk cafés
that much, anyway.

Burnham, Adler, Sullivan, Jenney, William Holabird, and the

others became known as the "Chicago school"—their notion of architecture and urban development dominated the rest of the country until almost World War I.

After that, in the 1920's, Chicago fell into the romantic Art Deco period, which saw its architects doing what architects everywhere were doing—creating the Palmolive, Board of Trade, and Civic Opera Buildings as their New York counterparts were putting up the Empire State and Chrysler Buildings and Rockefeller Center.

The Depression put an end to Art Deco, most building construction in Chicago, and, consequently, its architectural development. But something else occurred in the 1930's that was to ultimately make Chicago the focal point of not merely a renaissance in world architecture but a revolution.

Adolph Hitler, content to have his stadiums, concentration camps, and what have you designed by the amiable likes of Albert Speer, kicked nearly all of Germany's architectural geniuses out of the country in the 1930's. Among them was Ludwig Mies van der Rohe of the Berlin Bauhaus, whom Gapp, among thousands of others, has called the single most-important architect in the world in his time.

Mies came to Chicago in 1938. World War II saw most of the nation's architects either designing quonset huts or sleeping in them, but after the war Mies was able to bring forth his "less is more" revolutionary theories as a revealed religion—an intensely Chicago religion, initially, but one that spread swiftly and universally.

Mies took over Chicago's old Armour Institute trade school, renamed the Illinois Institute of Technology, and transformed it into a globally renowned institution that produced not students but disciples.

Bertrand Goldberg, now one of Chicago's leading architects, worked with Mies in Berlin in the 1930's. In a recent article in *Horizon* magazine, he described the master-boy relationship: "I asked Mies," he said, " 'am I to look forward to copying you all my life?' " Mies' answer: "Isn't that enough?"

Chicago's army of Miesians grew and grew and the stark, Miesian glass-and-skeleton box became an urban fixture. It was the product of his genius, of the postwar hunger for new buildings, and the rapidly expanding western economies that could afford such structures. But mostly the Miesian high-rise box was made possible by the incredible technological advances made during the war.

Light and strong building materials; high-speed elevators; sophisticated heating, ventilating, and air conditioning systems; and improved, war-plane-perfected glass were all products of the war and basic to the Mies high rise. Lake Point Tower could not have been built in 1921, unless its residents would have been willing to spend most of their time in their apartments, fanning themselves to keep cool and waiting for the daily elevator.

This, then, was the second Chicago school—a one-man show that has taken some thirty years to go from revolutionary to reactionary. Chicago now has more Miesian buildings than any other city in the world. It seems to have more Miesian buildings than any other kind. Because Mies produced so many followers, and because Chicago is so fond of being reactionary, the city is still building Miesian boxes.

But Chicago architects are turning to different things. With Mies gone, the Illinois Institute of Technology has lapsed into just another good trade school. Even Mies hard-core disciples are experimenting with such heresies as rounded corners.

According to Gapp, the new design styles are not at all unique to Chicago. The "greenhouse" look and the atrium came to places like Madison, Wisconsin, before they did to Water Tower Place. "Slick"—the mirrored-glass outer membrane—was big in Manhattan long before it amounted to anything in Chicago. The "high-tech" look—with pipes, beams, and other functional building parts and guts exposed—is wonderfully represented by a Notre Dame gym in South Bend, Indiana, but hardly at all in Chicago. One does see a bit of "post-modernism"—doric columns slapped onto a high-rise box for a bank, for example—in Chicago, but one saw it in Minneapolis first.

If the second Chicago school is no more, Chicago's ever-xenophobic architects are hoping desperately for a third one. No New York school has yet emerged, nor, thank heavens, a San Francisco one. Perhaps the continuing energy crisis will goad someone into a revolutionary new concept. Mighty SOM has hundreds of people at the drawing boards in their Chicago offices. Like the proverbial infinite number of monkeys, maybe they'll come up with something.

No one really runs Chicago architecture, certainly not since

Mies died and certainly never in the sense that people have run the city's political machine or its arts. Considering the immense effect architecture has on people's lives, and the really big bucks to be made from it, this seems remarkable, but it is true. Chicago's architects are not quite the free spirits that painters and writers are, but they tend to be talented and fiercely independent fellows— which is to say, many of them are raving egomaniacs.

They are subject to some strong Chicago "influences." The political establishment has shown a fondness for a few of what Judy Kiriazas calls "palace" architects, and the business establishment has to some degree followed suit. To compete with such favored firms successfully, it is necessary even for such individualists as Harry Weese to maintain some political connections—and go to the right cocktail parties.

Architects are also subject to the infinite vagaries and tyrannies of the city's nit-picking building department and money-mad real estate developers. Even within their own firms, design architects often find their work subservient to that of "mere" engineers.

They must also contend with "tradition"—which in Chicago frequently means having to repeat whatever design last made the most money.

In the post-Miesian era, how Chicago's top architects have reacted to these influences has tended to divide them into three groups. The biggest—or, at least, richest—is the Establishment Group, consisting most notably of such giants as SOM, Charles F. Murphy and Associates, Perkins and Will, and other firms large enough to be considered major corporations in themselves. They're believers in the "make no little bucks" credo, and have adhered to the Miesian ethic because it's been so profitable, but they've also produced some wonderful buildings, such as the Hancock Center, Sears Tower, and First National Bank.

FCL, otherwise known as Fujikawa, Conterato, and Lohan, should be included in the Establishment Group as well, if only because it is the firm most directly descended from Mies and, as such, is the principal keeper of The Truth.

The second group, naturally enough, is the Anti-establishment Group—an odd assortment of Young Turks, Old Turks, Enfants Terrible, enfants who have grown up and are now merely terrible, some unaffiliated absolute wild men, and the "Chicago 7," a gang of architectural provacateurs who took their name from the 1968

Chicago convention-riot conspiracy trial and who now, according to Miss Kiriazas, probably number a dozen.

The third group consists of one man: Harry Weese.

THE TOP FIFTEEN ARCHITECTS IN CHICAGO

1. Harry Weese

If there is anyone in Chicago at all like the Howard O'Rourke character played by Gary Cooper in Ayn Rand's *The Fountainhead*, it is Harry Weese, except that he's much less a zealot than a dreamer.

The 1978 Chicago Press Club's "Chicagoan of the Year," Weese is a happy-go-lucky sort of visionary, a man as amused and bemused by his grand, sweeping plans for the city as he is enthralled by them. He is the closest thing Chicago has to an architectural conscience (Chicago real-estate developers do not value architectural consciences all that highly). He is certainly the best known Chicago architect outside of the city—winner of the 1978 AIA Outstanding Firm award, and the only living heir to Daniel Burnham. And, while Weese would "make no little plans," he knows very well that, in Chicago, the successful dreamer must also be a bit of a schemer.

Now about sixty, Weese in person seems ill-suited for an iconoclastic role. Courtly, patrician, and with impeccable manners, he looks to be more comfortable in a three-piece pinstriped suit than in the tweeds and corduroys he often wears. Born in Evanston, he grew up in Kenilworth when it was really elite. He went on to Yale and MIT, and served as a naval officer during World War II. A clubman (the Arts, University), he has been a trustee of the prestigious Latin School and the almighty Art Institute.

Still quite well-off despite his many adventures and costly crusades, he includes as his residences a townhouse in the Lincoln Park area, an apartment on Lake Shore Drive, a country estate in Barrington, and a mountain place in Aspen. He travels to Europe almost as much as Da Mare did to Grand Beach, Michigan.

Even without his crusades and conscience, Weese could take first place on the list on the strength of his architecture alone. His modernistic U.S. Court House Annex downtown, better known as the federal jail, has been described as a three-dimensional IBM card but, more approvingly, as the most humane prison in the world. His golden-glassed Time-Life Building near the lake and his tree-lined LaSalle Plaza going up in the Loop are major architectural attractions, as is his semicircular Seventeenth Church of Christ, which fits so neatly and dramatically onto the wedge-shaped piece of real estate at Wacker Drive and South Water Street.

Harry's twin apartment towers at 345 Fullerton Parkway opposite Lincoln Park are among the really fine residential high rises on the lakefront—testament not only to his designing skill but also to the developer's willingness to lay out a little extra cash to build two smaller but more graceful towers than one great big ugly one.

He is responsible for the resurrection of the Auditorium Theater and other memorable fixtures. Weese has also designed Washington's new Metro subway system (the best in the country), the U.S. embassy in Ghana, Milwaukee's Performing Arts Center, and what amounts to an entire city in Saudi Arabia.

Harry's forte is his humanity. He thinks of cities as places in which people live rather than as pedestals for corporate monuments. He worries about such small details as how a hot-dog kiosk should look and function, how many doors an elevator really needs, and what people should be able to see from their buildings. Instead of designing apartments uniformly when only one side of a building has a good view, he compensates those on the opposite side with more living space, or wider balconies. He thinks of cities as fun places, and not the kind of fun New York's former Mayor Lindsay suggested. Weese would cover parking lots and alleys with grass. He'd like to build a Mount Fuji in Chinatown—although very few of the residents there speak Japanese.

Instead of combating urban decay with massive, Stalinesque urban-renewal demolition, Weese is a prophet of building rehabilitation—bolstering failed neighborhoods with new townhouses, warehouses converted to apartments, old storefronts made into boutiques, cafés, and restaurants. Harry has even been trying to get the Loop's rusty old elevated structure refurbished, quieted, and preserved as a historic landmark. In the scrummy old warehouse and dock area along the Ogden Slip, he'd put sidewalk cafés (the bums there now use the area as a sidewalk café, but they don't have any tables or chairs).

Weese's most grandiose plan calls for rearranging the lakeshore with islands and peninsulas to make the waterscape less flatly dull. He'd also like to put an athletic stadium and race track on an island in the lake adjoining downtown, and put Navy Pier into the same fun shape it was at the turn of the century. He'd like the city to host a World's Fair in Chicago in 1992.

The city has not responded to Weese's plans with boundless enthusiasm. His proposal to convert the slip between Navy pier and the Filtration Plant into a badly needed, not-for-profit marina was greeted quite coldly. The new marina would be more convenient, cheaper, and better (privately) managed than any of the city's park-district harbors, which are run as a monopoly. But Park District officials—especially those convicted of shaking down boat owners for bribes in return for moorings—seem to like the present system.

There will never be a Weesian school of architecture the way there was a Miesian one because Harry does not believe in doing things the same way over and over. This is fortunate if only for one reason. There is a building on Michigan Avenue that people hope Harry will never repeat anywhere, even at Miami Beach. That is the beastly looking twelve-hundred-room Marriott Hotel at Michigan Avenue and Ohio Street.

Built on the site of the much-missed Art Deco masterpiece known as Diana Courts, the Marriott is big, hulking, monotonous, and painted an icky khaki color reminiscent of the Afrika Korps. The hotel's lobby is even uglier, ablaze with so many violently clashing colors that you'd think it was sprayed with what might result from putting tropical birds into a food processor.

Weese's defenders argue that the Marriott folk fought and defeated his ideas all the way down the line. It's noted that the flaming hues of the lobby were selected by an interior decorator, not Weese, and that otherwise the lobby is brilliantly designed. They also sigh and point out that, if Weese didn't take on this stuff once in a while, he wouldn't have the financial wherewithal for his great ideas and crusades. Maybe so, but that huge, cash-register-like hotel will always stand as a monument.

Harry says his firm is now in such good shape that he does only what he wants to do. It is to be hoped. Michelangelo didn't do Christmas cards.

2. Fazlur Kahn

Faz Kahn is a quiet, soft-spoken, low-key, and terribly serious little fellow whom you'd scarcely notice on a bus or street corner. But, as SOM's chief structural engineer, he has writ his signature on the city skyline larger than anyone else's. Without Faz Kahn, there would be no Hancock Center or Sears Tower as they appear today.

The primary function of a building is to stand up, and The Faz's buildings stand up magnificently. "If he isn't the world's most brilliant structural engineer," said Paul Gapp, "then he's certainly in the top three."

With the Hancock, The Faz hit upon the concept of "the trussed tube." The building is supported, not merely by its foundation, but by those giant "X" cross braces, providing lateral stability and absorbing the strains and stresses caused by the action of Chicago's fierce winds. As it is, the top of the building sways from between ten to fifteen inches, though not so's you'd notice from the restaurant on the ninety-fifth floor—where you're distracted by the prices anyway.

Because of the "X" braces, a toppling Hancock would not fall over like a felled tree but would probably twist and spin on its foundation, strewing debris and, with any luck, knocking out that silly "PLAYBOY" sign on the top of the Palmolive.

For the Sears Tower, Kahn used not one but nine trussed tubes, bundling them together and breaking them off at different levels to achieve the setback effect.

As is often the case with The Faz, when he finished laying out the structural plans for the Hancock and the Sears, there really wasn't much more for the design fellows to do except pick out some colors and decide where the door handles should go.

3. Helmut Jahn

According to Paul Gapp, one of the secrets of the success of Charles F. Murphy and Associates is that they have always had at least one certifiable genius on the staff at all times. Helmut Jahn, CFMA's head of design, is the genius now in residence.

Some have tried to dismiss Jahn as "exquisite" or "a Skrebneski person," (after the famous Chicago photographer who made both Michael and Heather Bilandic look chic and glamorous). But the German-born and Munich-educated young man (he's barely forty) is responsible for some internationally acclaimed masterpieces, including the Kemper Arena in Kansas City (even though its roof collapsed in a recent thunderstorm), that strange high-tech gym at Notre Dame, and the prize-winning Auraria Library in Denver. Jahn is also hard at work on a curved tower, to be put in the middle of the Loop boxes.

Jahn studied briefly at Mies' IIT, but dropped out in something approaching disgust after three months. It is Jahn who is chiefly responsible for leading CFMA out of the box mold—not only into new styles but into smaller buildings. Though associated with the best politically connected establishment firm in the city, Jahn is also an active and outspoken member of the nonconformist Chicago 7, even to the point of participating in the 7's madcap and macabre "The Exquisite Corpse" exhibit. With Jahn, so many things are exquisite. Except thunderstorms.

4. Walter Netsch

One of the ranking partners and powers at SOM, the extremely kempt Walter Netsch is the quintessence of the Chicago palace architect—the sort you meet at all the right parties and just the sort you need if you want a monumental building that looks like it was designed by an architect and not an engineer. Although you may not immediately be able to find the door to it.

Very distinguished looking, Netsch has the *longest* hands, and seems rather what a Skrebneski person might look like if a Skrebneski person went to MIT.

Netsch does a lot of work for higher-education institutions, having established his reputation as a genius with his inspiring Air Force Academy Chapel. He also did the University of Illinois Chicago Circle Campus, where even Alice in Wonderland might have trouble finding some of the doors, and assorted things for Northwestern University and Grinnell College.

He is a member of the Gargoyle Society, though he'd doubtless shoot the first one he saw clinging to one of his buildings.

Netsch is married to the famous lady lawyer Dawn Clark Netsch of Illinois State Senate and Lakefront Liberal fame. They live in a Lincoln Park townhouse designed by Netsch himself—one of those places in which you never know whether the platform you're standing on is the floor, a stair landing, a bookshelf, or a bed.

They keep it filled with expensive Persian rugs and extremely contemporary art. "The "right" parties in Chicago often include the ones that the Netsches throw.

5. Charles F. Murphy Jr.

Charlie Murphy is a society architect only in the sense that he runs with that high-toned crowd while earning his living as an architect—or if you will, running the city's No. 2 architectural firm. Murphy is not a society architect in the sense of the late Benjamin Marshall, who designed the Drake Hotel and all those mansions. No one is that anymore.

Under Murphy, CFMA has been one of the city's foremost "house" architectural outfits, in that it's received such lovely little projects to do such as O'Hare Airport, McCormick Place, and the Chicago Civic (now Daley) Center. Murphy is always described as one of Chicago's best-connected architects, but mostly in the sense that he and his father were very, very close to Da Mare.

It also helps to have gone to Notre Dame.

Of CFMA's many achievements, Murphy likes to boast of Helmut Jahn's Kemper Arena, which shows his good taste, and of CFMA's job on the beastly F.B.I. Building in Washington, which shows his bad. CFMA also had a hand in Water Tower Place, the rotters.

One of the richest architects in the city, Murphy is very much a part of the upper strata. He belongs to the Chicago, Racquet, and Saddle and Cycle Clubs, and was made a trustee of the Field Museum.

Murphy was once photographed by Skrebneski for *Town & Country* magazine, but didn't come out looking like a Skrebneski person. His chic, sleek second wife Patricia looks very much like one, however. She is constantly bicycling, running, tennissing, and squashing to stay that way. Murphy runs and cycles, too, but it doesn't have quite the same effect.

6. Larry Booth

Now in his forties, the brilliant Larry Booth of Booth and Nagle
is probably the most likely candidate to succeed Harry Weese as
the "important" Chicago architect on that distant day when Harry's
ready to hang up his aura. Like Weese, Booth is one of the very
best residential architects in Chicago, known particularly for his
award-winning townhouses in the Lincoln Park area, along with
some less famous ones in the western suburbs.

Booth also won a major award for what may be the world's
most perfect gas station. Its many design advantages include the
capability—if business becomes slow at a location—of being quickly
dismantled and set up again on a busier corner. It is also one of
the least obtrusive gas-station designs ever.

A leader of the Chicago 7 rebels, Booth is increasingly becoming
a major influence in the city—not because his tiny little firm has
that much clout but because he is looked up to for his exceptional
intelligence. If brain power ever comes to be valued in Chicago
architecture as much as financial or political power, Booth will be
on top in a hurry.

7. Dirk Lohan

The youngish, very German Dirk Lohan of FCL is the best
Miesian left in Chicago, and his firm is *the* place to go for those
who still like that sort of thing. Now in his forties, Lohan was one
of Mies' closest disciples. In an era when Miesians are pretending
to do something else, or trifling with rounded corners, Lohan still
does Mies by the book. FCL's offices are in Mies' grim Illinois
Center east of Michigan Avenue over the IC railroad tracks. A
handsome, low-key, very serious fellow, Lohan even looks like
someone who would do a Mies building. Even the most passionate
haters of the Miesian box have this to say about Lohan: "Awfully
good."

8. Bruce Graham

The other big whizbang at SOM, Bruce Graham is an old Holabird, Root, and Burgee boy who went to SOM as a chief designer in

1951 and became a full partner in 1960. Now in his fifties, he is more a decision-maker than a grubber at the drawing board—in the sense that the president of General Motors is more of a decision-maker than an assembler of automobiles.

Graham has been identified with such lesser but admirable SOM works as the Loop's nineteen-story Inland Steel Building, which went up in 1957 and was one of the first high rises in America to use external steel for support. He's also had a hand in the Brunswick Building, the Connecticut Mutual Life Insurance Company Building, and the Equitable Building. After Faz Kahn had worked the structure out, Graham was one of those pondering what colors to use for the Hancock and Sears Towers.

Born in Bogotá, Colombia, of American parents, Graham attended the University of Dayton and then the University of Pennsylvania. Like colleague Netsch, he lives in his own Lincoln Park townhouse. Also like Netsch, he's a fiend for modern art, having served as president of the Society of Contemporary American Art. Married to a charming Latin-American lady, Graham travels in rather select circles and is not above dropping names like Kennedy. And, of course, his own.

9. Bertrand Goldberg

A somewhat strange and brooding genius, Bert Goldberg is the former Bauhaus Mies student who couldn't stand merely to be another Mies, and so turned to something completely different. Hence the beehive Marina City towers, which are about as completely different from the Miesian box as anything with windows can be.

If different from Mies', Goldberg's more notable works aren't terribly different from each other. The Hilliard Homes for the Elderly and the Prentice Women's Hospital Maternity Center of Goldberg's are cylindrical and look, if not like beehives, at least like hair curlers.

A Harvard chap who came to Chicago during the Depression, Goldberg feels very strongly that architecture should have a profound social function. He does not find this in big-money Chicago. As he told *Horizon* magazine, this has made him feel alone and isolated: "The discrepancy between rich and poor, black and white, is getting wider. Harry (Weese) talks about architecture that is fun, eclectic. I think Harry and I must eat different food. The failure of the city has given us an architectural mandate."

A man with a shaggy English sheepdog haircut, melancholy eyes, and a tweedy taste in clothes, Goldberg is now in his sixties. He lives on Astor Street, which has certainly done its share in contributing to the discrepancy between rich and poor.

Goldberg has won shelves of awards, has been named to the board of the American Society of Contemporary Music, and is kind of clubby, belonging to the Arts, the Tavern, and the Harvard.

10. Jerome Butler

In a city that has seen too many judges' nephews and vote-hustling sanitation workers rise to high government office, City Architect and now Public Works Director Jerome Butler stands out as a man eminently qualified for his job.

A Far North Sider who came out of the University of Illinois and the University of Wisconsin, Butler spent a brief time with a couple of local architectural firms and then joined the city's Department of Public Works in 1960. He was made city architect in 1966, made director in 1979, and is likely to hold onto the job for as long as he likes, even if he doesn't deliver any votes.

With so many new fire stations, garages, and what-have-you, the city is into architecture in a big way, and, under Butler, no longer in the old humdrum who'll-get-the-concrete-contract way. Butler has won a number of prizes, especially for his two best works—the restoration of Navy Pier (they now have gala parties out there) and the new Police Training Center.

Paul Gapp called Butler "the best city architect anybody ever had"—although Bathhouse John Coughlin and Hinky Dink McKenna might not have agreed.

11. William Hartmann

A major and senior power at SOM—and, like Murphy, one of the most socially-prominent architects around—William Hartmann may end up being remembered as the man who helped convince Pablo Picasso to make a gift to Chicago of that huge thing in the Daley (Civic) Center Plaza. If you like that huge thing, or at least Picasso, that ain't bad.

Now past sixty, Hartmann hasn't put his name down as chief designer of a building for some time, but is honored as the dean of the big office-building architects in the city and, like Faz Kahn, has his signature on the skyline, too. Not the one that says "PLAY-BOY."

Very, very clubby, the former World War II colonel hangs out in the Chicago, Casino, Tavern, and Saddle and Cycle clubs and is an Exalted One with the Art Institute.

12. Carter Manney

Carter Manney is what you might call the William Hartmann of CFMA, an august presence in Chicago architecture, and in City Hall. Like Hartmann, he served as an unofficial advisor to the late Daley, and then to Bilandic, offering advice on such matters as which famed sculptor should be honored with the glorious task of creating a public memorial to the late Great One. Jane Byrne will doubtless have need for him.

Manney also played an important role in such CFMA undertakings as the original design for O'Hare Airport and the beastly F.B.I. Building.

A onetime Michigan City, Indiana, lad who is now very much Lake Shore Drive, Manney drips with prestige. He graduated magna cum laude from Harvard and was a Taliesin Fellow. Taliesin is that peculiar place out in the Arizona desert where worshipers of Frank Lloyd Wright go to think and move rocks around.

A Tavern and Arts Club man and director of the Citizens Bank of Michigan City, Manney was named to the board of the Graham Foundation for Advanced Studies in Fine Arts and was president of the Chicago chapter of the American Institute of Architects.

In his sixties, Manney has a home on the Michigan City lakeshore, which must make him feel close to his roots, or at least to his bank.

13. William Brubaker

Winnetka's Bill Brubaker could be called the establishment's answer to Harry Weese. A ruling partner in Chicago's big Perkins and Will—which went in with CFMA on the First National Bank Building—Brubaker is a great dreamer and planner.

Brubaker talks with a sketch pad and felt pen the way some people talk with their hands, constantly setting forth new concepts like building new linear neighborhoods along elevated tracks.

He sits on the board of the Metropolitan Housing and Planning Council and has some really good connections (not everyone gets cut into deals like the First National with outfits like CFMA), but Brubaker's visions often don't succeed any better than Weese's, and sometimes not even as well.

Where Weese has a WASPish sort of chutzpah and the nervy instincts of a riverboat gambler, Brubaker is a trifle laid back. He is regarded as a fine architect, and his firm is one of the biggest and best in the country. Maybe it's just that he lacks that raging ego.

A Purdue graduate, Brubaker is one of Chicago's notable yachtsmen, of whom there are very few in his hometown of South Bend.

14. The Epstein Brothers

To list Ralph and Raymond Epstein among Chicago's top fifteen architects might draw a gasp or two out of Taliesin way, but Chicago architecture is not all Harry Weese or Helmut Jahn any more than the city is all First National Bank Buildings and Lake Point Towers.

There are thousands of big brawling factories, warehouses, and processing plants out there, and many of them have been designed by the Epsteins.

If "form follows function," as Louis Sullivan said, there is no one keener on function than the Epsteins. Geniuses at making the most workable use of space, the two brothers have built aircraft plants in California and what seems like every Polish sausage plant in Poland.

And, just to show they can go uptown once in a while, the Epsteins are doing the annex to the Regency Hyatt Hotel on the Chicago River east of Michigan Avenue. They have also done a number of county jails—though none that any Chicago alderman of note has ever stayed in.

It would be impossible to list one brother without the other. Both live in the same building on the South Side's Chicago Beach Drive. Both are members of the Standard Club and both are very, very active in Jewish charities. Raymond is the chairman of the firm and the president is Ralph. Or is it Raymond?

15. *Stanley Tigerman*

The most terrifying of the "enfants terribles" and wildest of the wild men is Stanley Tigerman, who is also the most iconoclastic member of the Chicago 7. Stanley makes Harry Weese seem stodgy and the Epstein Brothers seem, well, Skrebneski persons.

Though an MIT and Yale man, Tigerman knows no bounds. He has designed a widely acclaimed library for the blind and handicapped, an extraordinarily well-organized industrial park in the suburbs, and a sleekly handsome lakefront-area high rise. But he has also gone in for some Piper's Alley Old Town tourist glitz and far-out sexual symbolism. He's the chap who did the house designed as a phallic symbol out in the Dunes.

Tigerman is very clever, and a standout engineer. He won a big award for an Arby's fast-food stand at Michigan and Chicago Avenues. He can be quite morbid. His contribution to the Chicago 7's "The Exquisite Corpse" exhibition was a house full of stairs going nowhere ascended by people cut in two.

But Tigerman seems to rejoice in being an anti, and it may be his most valuable contribution to Chicago architecture. He has called Mies' IIT a Jesuit seminary and described Goldberg to *Horizon* magazine as "Orwellian in the round." He called New York architects "closet queens of ideas."

Though many regard Stanley as a wildman, he's won a slew of awards, including one from the prestigious Graham Foundation. He's served as a professor at the University of Illinois's Chicago Circle Campus and has lectured at Yale, Cornell, and New York's prestigious Cooper Union.

If Stanley calmed down and stopped doing genitals and the like, he could be at the absolute top of any list. But, nearing fifty, he shows no sign of calming down, and he may not think of that genitalia and stuff as junk. Were he to be commissioned to do a domed stadium for Chicago, it might well come out looking like one of the two reasons for the Mae West legend. In fact, Stanley might insist that there be two domed stadiums.

12

Unions

During his last mayoral campaign, Richard Daley was criticized by his opponent because Chicago was the only place in the known universe where it took four men to work a garbage truck. In his characteristic style, the mayor turned flaming red, stammered through a torrent of incoherent phrases. and finally decided to defend the practice on the basis that the "fourth guy can watch out for little kids playing in the alley. How would you feel if a little kid got run over by a garbage truck?"

Thousands of obedient Democratic Party workers cheered so loudly that Daley playfully went one step further. "Maybe," he twinkled, "we ought to put five men on the trucks."

This philosophy has served in Chicago for decades to soothe restive labor leaders. It has resulted in a closely tied labor-political coalition that exists nowhere else in America. But Chicago is not a "union town." It is merely a city where the unions are assured their place in the line, where the most powerful segments of the union leadership have joined with the governmental and business establishments in an arrangement that assures full-time employment at maximum wages for the unions' rank-and-file members.

In exchange, they are content to follow the dictates of the political power structure and contribute to its well-being, both physically and financially. That's not how union towns like Pittsburgh or Akron are run.

With few exceptions, the most successful and influential labor chiefs in Chicago are the leaders of the trade and service unions. Their workers are directly linked to the great Chicago tradition of tearing down and putting up, and making things run smoothly until it's tearing-down time again.

Not since the bloody days of the 1930's have the leaders of these unions had to scrape for jobs and wages in Chicago. City Hall hands them out. They go to carpenters, electricians, plumbers, and iron workers; to clerks, janitors, building engineers, bricklayers, garbage collectors, laborers, and elevator operators. "There has never been a big secret about keeping labor happy in Chicago," one key union boss said. "Whenever a politician asks what he should say before a labor audience, I tell him two words: 'prevailing rate.'"

The prevailing rate is not always the highest paid in the nation, but that's what Chicago has always paid. The money that saves here and there is good for government, and the security of the jobs City Hall controls is good for the unions. This handshake arrangement also compels private industry to match the wage rates, which makes negotiations much simpler for labor chiefs here than in other areas of the country.

This cozy system comes from City Hall, and it comes with strings. There are no contractual obligations between city government and its employees. Public employee unions as they are known and feared in New York don't even exist in Chicago, let alone hold power. No city workers except teachers have union recognition or collective bargaining rights. As far as municipal workers are concerned, they might as well be working for Czar Nicholas.

But the trade unionists are noticed, especially at election time, for they often double as precinct captains. "All of the unions are integrated into politics in this town," a veteran labor organizer said. "They get jobs to do precinct work."

Chicago's tradition of treating its municipal employees as political minions extends even to police and firemen, who have been granted collective bargaining contracts in almost every other major American city, but not Chicago.

George Meany, the Great Poobah of American Labor, griped about this every time he visited Chicago. And every time, he was politely ignored—although it's believed that Daley may have privately expressed his thoughts to Meany on the subject.

During the bitter bargaining fight between Mayor Bilandic and the firemen in 1978, most local labor leaders made certain they didn't sound too supportive of the fire fighters' efforts to win a contract. The firemen found themselves about as popular as Republicans.

What never seems to surface in these annual battles by police and firemen for contracts is that the first item on any negotiating schedule is always the elimination of the requirement that they must reside within the city limits of Chicago to hold their jobs. The dollars and cents involved in the disputes, whether in wages or benefits, are not as important. The issue is whether the removal of the residency requirement would result in an immediate flight of about twenty-five thousand white families to the suburbs.

Such sudden demographic changes can be upsetting for people who are investing millions of dollars in city development. They can be traumatic for the labor leaders whose union workers are to get the construction and trades jobs. They can be injurious indeed to the machine that's supposed to be controlling everything.

Building unions figure strongly in Chicago's power structure. Nearly all construction in Chicago is handled by union employees, while, nationwide, only an average of 50 percent of construction workers are union. Again, the job security provided by the Chicago setup fulfills a major requirement of union leadership and results in an amazing longevity for union bosses. William Lee, head of the Chicago Federation of Labor, which embraces all the AFL-CIO outfits, recently won a ninth four-year term despite the fact that he is in his eighties.

If the building trades unions have a larger degree of influence in City Hall than any other union group, that influence doesn't extend too terribly far. Much of the time spent by Chicago labor leaders in the company of government officials and businessmen is dedicated to listening, not talking. The chief function of labor leaders sometimes seems to be that of cheerleaders—especially when the city announces some mammoth new building project.

The quid pro quo is extremely simple. Union leaders get the jobs to employ their membership, which ensures their continuing as union leaders, which ensures that the politicians who provide the projects will continue to receive labor endorsements and campaign contributions, which ensures that they will be in office when the bankers and builders come up with another big project. This self-nurturing cycle is one reason why Chicago is unique. But there are others.

Chicago has never been a town dominated by a single industry—a town where a few corporate executives could become so powerful as to dictate public policy, which would inevitably lead to the creation of strong unions as a balancing force. It's not like Detroit, where the auto makers are the colossus of the local economic picture; or like Akron, where rubber is king; or like Pittsburgh and Youngstown, Ohio, where big steel dominates everything.

Union leaders are feared in other cities because of their power to call strikes. In Chicago, it would be difficult to cause much damage with a single-industry strike. In Chicago, labor leaders are in part so influential because they rarely call strikes of any magnitude. Their reliability is what gives them their clout.

Chicago has a large union population, but it has never rallied to a Great Crusade, even during the first major violence in the city growing out of a labor dispute: the famous Haymarket Square riot. That occurred on the city's West Side on May 4, 1886. What began as a demonstration for the eight-hour workday drew a crowd of fifteen hundred persons. Police tried to disperse them and a bomb was thrown.

The ensuing rioting left eleven persons dead and more than one hundred wounded. Eight individuals labeled as anarchists were convicted and four were subsequently hanged. The site of the riot was marked for years by a statue of a nineteenth-century era policeman. It became a favorite target for protesters in the turbulent 1960's. Toppled by a bomb, it was later rebuilt and moved to the safe confines of the Chicago Police Academy.

The last labor violence of significance in Chicago occurred May 30, 1937, when ten men were killed by police during a walkout of steelworkers at three plants in South Chicago. Labor nationally commemorates the event as the "Memorial Day Massacre." Chicago remembers it as just another riot.

The steelworkers are the only union with any real potential for economic impact on the city—and that potential is regional. They are generally isolated from the rest of Chicago in a Far South Side section along the shore of Lake Michigan. A strike might have great effect upon this sooty, working-class pocket of the city, but would be barely noticed on Michigan Avenue, where North Siders and suburbanites would cheerfully continue to stimulate the Chicago economy. Even the occasional, morale-building trade-union walkout has little impact on the city because union members are spread out all over the county and City Hall Democrats don't worry much about sample ballots in Arlington Heights.

Union campaign dollars, however, are one of the major sources of financial support for the Chicago Democrats and help make the City Hall welcome so warm. In this area, big unions like the Teamsters and United Auto Workers particularly shine.

As city and state attitudes and laws have generally been favorable to labor, the dollars that go to candidates are intended to maintain rather than expand union gains. "We don't want much except to be left alone," one labor leader said.

And, labor bosses and unions don't get much involved in other people's conflicts. They don't say much about inferior or segregated housing, and they aren't often heard denouncing the poor quality of education (although it has compelled some of them to initiate training programs for their own employees to raise their reading and arithmetic skills). The only time labor has sat down to worry over the shortage of minorities in the building trades has been when the Feds told them to.

Dabbling in social ills has not paid dividends for unions in other cities, labor leaders argue. They also fear they used up too many IOUs in pushing through programs like Medicare, resulting in a later string of defeats for union causes like common situs picketing.

The violence attendant to labor organizing in the Depression in Chicago was in keeping with the city's tradition. The Capone mob began drooling over the prospect of fortunes in union dues almost the minute Prohibition ended. The mob's attempts to infiltrate unions over the years has led to all manner of nasty slayings. A number of the city's labor chiefs have been burned, beaten, and threatened by hoodlums during their careers.

In the 1950's, rival union groups fought it out to dominate the Chicago taxi industry. As a result, several cabs were parked on the bottom of the Chicago River. The restaurant business has always been caught up in mob intrigues and seldom does a year go by without some labor-related café bombing.

Perhaps this is why Chicago is the only city in the country with a labor detail on its police department. But not entirely. The police labor detail is there to watch labor, not necessarily to protect it.

In the suspicious view of Chicago's political bosses, labor organizers who tended to question the way things were done could be considered subversive. One labor leader recalled asking Daley many years ago why the city had a police labor detail, since it did not have a "business detail" or "banking detail." "Isn't it better that the police know who you are?" Daley replied.

The power of Chicago's labor leaders is not always determined by the number of workers they represent or the size of their pension funds or their long tenure. Many of those high-ranking officials with powerful voices in international union circles are not as influential as local subordinates who have established and maintained close connections to the Chicago political establishment.

Except for the many commissions and committees they have to join, or the downtown luncheons and Lucy Nunes' parties they have to attend, Chicago labor leaders like to shun the limelight and the news media. Though many of them lead affluent lives, they do so quite privately. They seldom go in for sleek limousines or big entourages. They don't need to. In Chicago labor, there's no doubt as to who's important.

THE TOP TEN LABOR LEADERS IN CHICAGO

1. Edward Brabec

Ask a dozen people to describe Edward Brabec, honcho of Chicago Journeyman Plumbers Union Local 130, and they'll all say pretty much the same thing: "He's a son of a bitch and a great guy." That's a bit too brief, but it helps explain why Brabec is the No. 1 labor leader in Chicago, even ahead of the Chicago Federation of Labor's Bill Lee.

A handsome if rough-edged fellow in his forties, and known best to Chicagoans as chairman of the St. Patrick's Day parade, Brabec's power and influence crosses the usual union, political, and business lines.

His rise in the labor ranks was forecast by his ancestry much the same way that Nelson Rockefeller's future was predictable. Brabec's uncle was Stephen Bailey, head of the Plumbers Local 130 from 1935 until his death in 1966. Bailey came from Bridgeport and grew up with Dick Daley. They were such close friends that he was the first labor boss to endorse Daley's then-uncertain mayoral candidacy in 1955. The plumbers automatically became the pre-eminent labor group during Daley's reign and the chairmanship of the St. Patrick's parade served to symbolize that fact. But the Daley connection really has nothing to do with Brabec's power. Daley's record shows he did better at thwarting ambitious careers than at nourishing them.

Having started out as an apprentice plumber, Brabec became the first union leader ever invited to help shape the nation's fiscal policies as a member of the Federal Reserve Board. When he talks about discount rates, tariffs, federal pension regulations, and interest rates, he sounds much more like a Harvard Biz grad than a wrench wielder.

As a vice-president of the International Plumbers Union, Brabec has already been labeled one of the new breed of union leaders. He is the public relations chief for his eleven-state Midwest region, and travels extensively.

He has been close to George Meany and there is speculation he might someday take over George's job, or Bill Lee's. He wants labor leaders to show concern for the welfare of American business because so many union pension funds are heavily invested in business.

An unassuming fellow, Brabec still lives on the South Side in the Garfield Ridge neighborhood and drives his own car. Famous for his candor, he devotes every Thursday night to dealing with the individual problems of the members of his eight-thousand-man local at its headquarters at 1340 West Washington Street. A lot of politicians have made speeches in that union hall. A lot of politicians like to be wherever Ed Brabec is.

2. William Lee

Every day, two Chicago policemen escort an elderly white-haired gent from his apartment building on Lake Shore Drive to his downtown office. They have not always been the same policemen, but it has been going on for twenty-eight years, ever since William Lee was accosted by several thugs who wanted a word with him. They didn't get it because Lee slammed his office door in their faces and went about his business of being Chicago's senior, if not the most powerful, labor leader.

As head of the Chicago Federation of Labor, Lee has maintained the unions' conduit to City Hall for more than thirty years. He represents some 450,000 workers in the city, many of them in the profitable and influential buildings trades.

But Lee has also managed to be as active behind the scenes as he is in front of them. He is probably more responsible than any other labor boss for insuring that the Democratic Party's candidates had the right opinions about unions, and he also stamped many of City Hall's decisions with labor's imprimatur, and all the campaign cash that implies.

Lee became a union man with the Bakery Drivers in 1915 and moved up to that union's presidency in 1926. Despite his other labor posts, he retained the bakery local's presidency until 1960. In 1957, he thought he might go after the international presidency of the Teamsters, but was beaten out of that by a Detroit labor boss named James R. Hoffa.

As head of the CFL, Lee found himself serving on every kind of civic committee and commission imaginable as Daley developed his theory of bringing labor and business neatly together to agree on what he deemed important for Chicago. Lee has probably served on more committees than any living Chicagoan, and his clipped, high-pitched, and always brief remarks have blessed every idea conceived in City Hall in the past thirty years.

But it isn't a one-way street. When one union chief was asked if he could remember a single instance where labor didn't go along with the mayor, he paused, and finally said, "No. But I can't think of one where he didn't go with us, either."

When the Illinois AFL-CIO threatened to withhold its traditional Democratic endorsement from Michael Bakalis, the party's candidate for governor in 1978, it was Lee who led the counteroffensive that secured the endorsement after all.

Lee knows as well as any ward boss where labor's best interests lie in Chicago government. He led a delegation of twenty key union chiefs to the conclave of Democratic party leaders who were choosing a successor to the fallen Richard Daley. When the Democratic Central Committee members voted to endorse Bilandic, Lee led his delegation out of the room for deliberations. They were gone exactly the length of time it required to step out the door, turn around in the hallway, and troop back in again and add their cheers to Bilandic's selections. After Jane Byrne won, she and Lee had a friendly telephone chat. But her inclination to bounce him from the Park District Board indicates they may not be friendly for long.

3. Louis Peick

Louie Peick is the one Chicago union boss whose power stretches throughout the state and beyond the borders. He is head of the Teamsters Joint Council 25, which makes him the boss of all the truckers in Northern Illinois, and is a vice-president of the international union, which has more than two million members.

In his mid-sixties, Peick looks like a movie version of a labor boss —rumpled, craggy, and brusque, with a flair for the vivid and well-aimed obscenity.

Like many of his peers, Louie started in the labor movement in the 1930's, joining Teamster Local 705. He moved steadily if slowly through the ranks until he became the head in 1956. Peick clarified his own power in the 1960's by successfully resisting Jimmy Hoffa's efforts to forge all the local Teamsters into a single unit for bargaining purposes. Peick has always negotiated his own contracts and his settlements usually set wage patterns for Teamsters elsewhere in the country.

His conduct around City Hall is by no means as servile as so many of the others because Teamsters financial support during political seasons is especially plentiful and the pols avoid any conflicts that would shut off the flow of campaign money. He does have strong ties to the Democratic hierarchy, and is a member of the Police Board, which supposedly oversees police-department administration and activities but usually just applauds the mayor's decisions.

But Peick is not irrevocably tied to the Democrats. In 1976, while Daley was still alive, Peick's Teamsters gave ten thousand dollars to Jim Thompson—the first union support he got on his way to the governor's mansion. More money and support went to Thompson in 1978.

This independent political streak reinforces Peick's reputation as a hard, open negotiator whose pension funds are sound and free from the aroma of so many Teamster financial dealings.

His early days in labor were devoted largely to keeping racketeers out of his union. In 1947, he was kidnapped and tortured by four men who forced him to open a union safe, which they then emptied of twenty thousand dollars in cash and checks. In 1950, he was confronted outside of his Park Ridge home by two men who smashed both his hands with a baseball bat, then shot him in one hand and a thigh.

Peick rose to national union power in the train of Ray Schoessling, his predecessor as chief of Joint Council 25, who is now secretary-treasurer of the national union and was a close ally of Da Mare.

Peick is paid $154,000 a year for his various union chores, which beats what you get driving a rig.

4. Eugene Moats

For Gene Moats, honcho of the Service Employees International Union Local 25, it's members and results. His union represents some ninety thousand workers in the Chicago area. When he speaks in the councils of the state AFL-CIO, he speaks for about 10 percent of the total membership, and when he speaks, many listen.

Moats is in many ways like Brabec, a new breed unionist who realizes that the old bombast and heavy-handed ways won't keep labor in a pivotal role. Moats has more international experience than any Chicago union chief, having spent many years in high-level national staff positions, including several as an assistant to George Meany.

He lacks any close personal link to the main men in the city's power structure, and, to many labor leaders who respect him, he's still an outsider. But he's smart enough to have learned how the city works.

A typical Moats' touch was his noting of the high rate of ethnicity among the janitors and building-service employees he represents. He had his contract agreements reprinted in Polish. He, too, has learned that unions cannot afford to be synonymous with Democrats. He was a backer of Thompson, even though the state AFL-CIO declined to go along.

5. Thomas Nayder

Thomas Nayder is not that important a union leader, but he represents an important group—the Chicago and Cook County Building Trades Council.

Not really strong enough to override the various trade-union leaders who operate under his council's umbrella, he functions as a consensus leader and conduit, rather like Bill Lee.

With twelve thousand building-trade jobs on the city and county payrolls, though, he has found ways to stay in close touch with City Hall. He was put on the Board of Education, where civic high-minded types complain he has served City Hall's interests more than chlidren's. But what do they know, as Da Mare would have said.

Nayder lost the presidency of his own bricklayers local a few years ago, but if he's lost some power, he still has friends in the right places.

6. Robert Johnston

Bob Johnston, head of the area's United Auto Workers, is the only Chicago labor leader of consequence whose search for jobs doesn't lead him to City Hall. But he's also the only state-wide labor chief who has managed to achieve any influence in Chicago affairs.

He's been particularly effective in selectively doling out campaign funds, especially in state legislative races. He represents forty-six thousand UAW workers in Chicago, who with their families constitute a rather sizable voting bloc that the machine dare not ignore.

Johnston made an effort to get involved in city problems, frequently serving as a mediator who was always true to his word. While he never became a member of the Daley inner circle, the big machine pols have always respected him. In the meantime, he is a dominant figure in Springfield, where he has supported Republicans.

7. Alphonse Soudan

Alphonse Soudan is one of the most envied labor leaders in town. Since 1965, he has headed the International Brotherhood of Electrical Workers Local 134, which has been described as the world's richest union local. It holds more than $100 million in pension funds for fifteen thousand electricians, who are not exactly members of the food-stamp set.

Soudan's big advantage locally is that most of the electrical contractors in Cook County belong to the National Electrical Contractors Association. Once Soudan gets an agreement out of this outfit, all the other contractors usually fall in line.

Not in the best of health in recent years, Soudan generally likes to stay in the background, though he has accepted a few token civic appointments from time to time.

8. George Vest

George Vest, Jr. fits into a triumvirate with Brabec the plumber and Soudan of the electricians. Vest heads the Chicago District Council of Carpenters, an umbrella outfit representing thirty thousand well-paid hammer-and-saw men.

With this setup, Vest doesn't have all that much unilateral control over the union. Or, as one peer put it: "Vest has everyone biting at his ass all the time." Some also say he's a little wishy-washy, but you have to be careful with all those snapping teeth around.

Vest manages some $100 million in pension funds. He and Soudan probably have more direct impact on the average Chicago-area resident than most labor leaders, because the wages they obtain for their workers are immediately reflected in the cost of housing, which in Chicago is costly indeed. Yet, the remarkable absence of contract disputes involving their unions has brought stability to the Chicago building industry, and has been a big factor in the city's relatively healthy economy. Tell yourself that next time you make a mortgage payment.

9. Robert Gibson

There aren't many people who hold secondary positions in an organization who can be ranked as "powerful"—except when Ford was President and Don Rumsfeld was running the country—but Robert Gibson, as secretary-treasurer of the state AFL-CIO, did very well.

Gibson developed into a key coordinator between various unions and various government offices, and has now succeeded Stanley Johnson as head of the one-million member organization. He is Illinois labor's top strategist for legislative affairs (meaning lobbying) and is a keen-minded political strategist.

Although the state AFL-CIO organization doesn't have much direct effect on Chicago, its statewide activities and influence are regarded as very useful by City Hall. Gibson counts.

10. Angelo Fosco

The Laborers International Union, more affectionately remembered as the hod carriers, is classic Chicago old-time unionism. It was headed for years by Peter Fosco, an Italian immigrant whose associations with Capone-era hoodlums did not prevent him from winning public office and once earning an Italian-American award at a dinner addressed by Richard Nixon. This huge international union is now run by his son, Angelo, and watched by the Justice Department.

The union was built on the strength of thousands of immigrants who needed unskilled jobs and were easy conversions to machine politics. Many of these sweat laborers were able to move up into such trades as bricklaying and carpentry. The Laborers Union has always had a healthy treasury, kept brimming with hard-working workers' dues.

Lawyers

To fully understand the relationship of lawyers to the scheme of things in Chicago, one need only ponder the following statistic: There are about eleven thousand doctors in Illinois, some five thousand of them practicing in the city of Chicago. There are twenty thousand lawyers in Chicago. One out of every twenty-three lawyers in the United States practices in Chicago.

Mayor Daley was a lawyer. Former Mayor Bilandic is a lawyer. The late, great Adlai Stevenson started out on his world-saving crusade as nothing more than a LaSalle Street bond lawyer. Jim Thompson and all Illinois governors in recent memory have been lawyers.

Lawyers are among the very first families of Chicago society. Some are also close to the first families of Chicago's Mafia. The Chicago radio actor who played "Jack Armstrong, the All-American Boy" abandoned show biz to become a lawyer. Lawyers fill the dark canyon of LaSalle Street and the adjoining public ways as thickly as pigeons. They roost in the First National Bank Building and the Standard Oil Building. They inhabit little one-flight-up offices on the edge of the Loop and out in the neighborhoods.

When Pablo Picasso completed his weird five-story sculpture

that was his gift to Chicago, he told no one what it was supposed to represent. For more than a decade, passersby at the Daley (Civic) Center Plaza have peered up at its cold, steely eyes, its ribbed, winglike shoulders, and its long, sharp proboscis. They've wondered what Picasso was at. What is that thing? A bird? A woman? A dog? If you've looked into those cold steely eyes long enough, and spent any time in the Circuit or Federal courts, you know precisely what Picasso must have had in mind. He made a sculpture of a Chicago lawyer.

The law is so popular in Chicago for a very simple reason. Chicago is a big-money town, and its lawyers get their share. How else but through the law could so many Bridgeport Irish lads become millionaires without work?

A recent survey of the top law firms around the country showed their partners drawing a mean income of $85,000 a year. In Chicago, that figure is in excess of $100,000 a year. The top partners in the big firms draw as much as $350,000 or $400,000 a year. In contrast, Hugh Hefner of *Playboy* makes just over $265,000. Of course, he gets to mess with the broads.

If Chicago lawyers don't have to work hard, they do have to take risks. In one recent case, a group of 260 stewardesses who had been fired by American Airlines for pregnancy won their jobs back, plus $2.7 million in back salaries and compensation. The lawyers took $992,881 of that money in fees. "When you handle a case on a contingency basis, you get nothing if you lose," said one of the esteemed counsels involved. "If you win, you get some extra because you're taking a risk. They wouldn't have gotten a dime except for our efforts."

The Cook County courts are noted for awarding some of the most generous personal-injury verdicts in the country. Such masterful personal-injury practitioners as Philip Corboy and John J. Kennelly routinely win damage awards of $1 million or more. The late Judge Jim Dooley of the Illinois Supreme Court amassed a $10-million fortune from his personal-injury work as a lawyer. He could probably have run that up to $100 million if he were starting all over again today.

If you have a greedy wife and a failing marriage, you'd be best advised to get the hell out of Cook County as soon as possible. The rejected spouse and her crafty lawyer have traditionally been the object of oceans of judicial sympathy in this jurisdiction.

The wife of Duane Swimley, a well-to-do Air Force colonel living in the suburbs, was convicted of trying to hire a hit man to murder him. Yet it was a couple of years before the Circuit Court saw fit to grant him a divorce. When he finally received one (she was on her way to jail), he was still ordered to pay her a cash settlement of $147,000.

When famed Chicago author Saul Bellow was granted a divorce from his third wife, Susan, in 1968, the settlement called for a lump sum alimony award of $165,000—based on his estimate that his future income would not exceed $30,000 a year. In 1977, after he had won the Nobel Prize for literature, her Chicago lawyers went to court to get her settlement resettled. The court then ordered him to pay her another $500,000, plus $800 a month and private schooling for their son, plus $200,000 to cover her legal fees.

Billy Lynch, a Bridgeport boy who hardly spoke the same language as Oliver Wendell Holmes and Charles Evans Hughes (and probably didn't know who they were) became a wealthy lawyer handling cases for such city-connected business as the Chicago Transit Authority. He was subsequently appointed to the august federal bench. His law partner, interestingly enough, was named Richard J. Daley.

Another Irish lad, former Alderman Thomas E. Keane, became a multimillionaire through his law practice. He had the most uncanny ability for a lawyer to guess which interesting transaction involving city property might be approved by the City Council's Finance Committee. He also happened to be chairman of the committee. Keane also went to the federal bench, but as a defendant. Off on a long holiday at the expense of the federal prison system, he saw his law practice continue to prosper. Some law practices are like that.

But a good number of Chicago lawyers are paid a lot of money simply because they are good. There is nothing of more moment to the American Telephone and Telegraph Company than antitrust. Its antitrust work is not handled by a New York or Washington firm but by Chicago's Sidley and Austin.

If J. J. Kennelly has become airline-crash personal-injury lawyer to the world (the survivors of the Entebbe hijacking are among his clients), it's because he has proved himself a genius at such work. For all practical purposes, the major Hollywood studios and producers need only one lawyer in the Midwest (unless they're suing each other)—the Union League Club's Robert Bergstrom.

Chicago's John Paul Stevens now sits on the United States Supreme Court, and he does know who Oliver Wendell Holmes was. Someday, Federal Judge Prentice Marshall may sit there. Justin Stanley, until recently the guiding hand at Chicago's Mayer, Brown, and Platt, served as president of the American Bar Association. His successor at Mayer, Brown—Edmund Stephan—has turned away offers of federal judgeships the way the rest of us do panhandlers.

In Chicago as elsewhere, lawyers are not a powerful bloc in their own right, like, say, bankers or politicians. Lawyers get power only by serving those who are major components of the power structure. In this sense, they are as mortar is to bricks—or, more appropriately, as oil is to a machine.

Lawyers are on the boards of most of the major Chicago corporations and often function as company officers. They mingle and ingratiate themselves with "old-money" Chicago families by serving on the boards of favored charities. They tie themselves to the city's political apparat with nice little gestures like putting together fund-raising committees and functions. Winston and Strawn's Tom Reynolds arranged that tidy little thousand-dollar-a-plate fund-raising breakfast for Democratic County Assessor Tom Tully in 1974. Not long after that, he was performing similar favors for his new, close Republican friend, Jim Thompson.

As things are neatly arranged in Chicago, through lawyers, one can reach anywhere—into the legislature, the City Council, the local and federal bureaucracies, the corporate boardrooms, union halls, and even Lake Forest garden clubs.

Should a society lady wish to talk to, say, a leader of the Black P Stone Nation, as used to occur in the radical chic of the 1960's (they were so marvelous at parties), she need only contact her lawyer, who would need only contact the gang leader's lawyer. Recently, a steel-company executive heading up a civic improvement project sought out the advice of a politically influential newspaper executive on how to handle the mayor on a touchy question. He did so at a little dinner at the home of a mutual friend—a lawyer.

A few years ago, a Chicago crime syndicate chap decided a quick trip abroad would be highly advantageous to his health. To acquire the money he needed for expenses, he thought he might inquire of a prominent Republican he had once worked with under interesting circumstances. The Mafioso contacted a well-connected lawyer who knew them both. The lawyer contacted an associate of the prominent Republican, who sent the Republican's own lawyer back with an envelope "for our friend." It contained only half the money but that often happens when you deal with Chicago lawyers. The trip didn't do the Mafioso much good. Someone blew his head off not long after.

Lawyers always try to make themselves indispensable. With clients who like to keep things in the family, they just become part of the family. Probably the most indispensable lawyer in Chicago is the celebrated Don Reuben. When the big and prestigious Kirkland and Ellis law firm gave Reuben the boot because of the unseemliness of his peripheral involvement in Jane Byrne's "greased taxi-deal" saga, Reuben did not walk out of those paneled offices alone. He took with him to his newly formed firm of Reuben and Proctor such longtime Kirkland clients as the *Chicago Tribune*, the Lake Shore National Bank, *Time*, Panax Publications, NBC Radio and Television in Chicago, the CNA Corporation, the Olin Corporation, the Chicago Bears, and the Catholic Archdiocese of Chicago. The *Tribune*'s Colonel McCormick had founded Kirkland and Ellis.

A uniquely challenging aspect of practicing law in Chicago is the squirrelly nature of the local courts. This is not to mean the local federal courts. Although Da Mare was able to deposit on the federal bench such cronies as Billy Lynch and Abraham Lincoln Marowitz—and the Republicans made possible Judge Julius Hoffman and his Alice in Wonderland Conspiracy 7 trial—Senators Percy and Stevenson have of late been responsible for some fairly brilliant federal appointments. The afore-mentioned Prentice Marshall is one. Republican Joel Flaum and Democrat Stanley Rozkowski are others.

And, in the federal courts, cases are assigned to judges on a rotation basis. Lawyers have to prepare their cases according to their merits, without any help from connections or clout.

In the county courts, it's different. Everything is different. The county judges are elected, just like aldermen. As the Democratic machine dominates the political jurisdiction, being nominated for a judgeship is virtually the same as being elected. And the nominations are controlled by the party slate makers, who almost always are controlled by The Boss, or at least, A Boss.

In this kind of setup, the crummiest law degree from the sleaziest one-flight-up law school will do. What really counts in the way of qualifications are things like high-placed relatives, years of loyal vote production in the ward, and nearness to the mayoral throne.

A recent study by the blue ribbon Committee on Courts and Justice found that, of 162 full circuit judges in the county, 139 of them were Democrats and all but nineteen of them had been active in the party machine as precinct captains, ward or township officials, candidates, or government prosecutors and the like. Of twenty Appellate Court judges in Chicago, nineteen were machine Democrats and all but eight had been active in politics before putting on their black nightshirts.

Frank Greenberg, former president of the Chicago Bar Association, observed that legal ability is "purely or mostly accidental" in a judge's selection. "What really counts," he said, "are credits won as precinct captains or in other partisan political service, and political connections, political friendships, and relationships with what might be called successful political families." Indeed. The judges surveyed included Mayor Daley's cousin, his former personal lawyer, one of his law partners, and the sons of three of his best friends.

The cases in the county courts are not assigned to judges at random on a rotation basis but at the administrative whim and fiat of the presiding judge. The image this sort of thing has produced in recent years helped lead to Cook County voters booting out the presiding judge of the Criminal Court and of the Circuit Court when they came up on the retention ballot. Both examples are considered miracles, and quite rare ones at that.

There are attorneys in Chicago who manage to prosper without going near a courtroom, either because they are August Personages high up in prestigious law firms or because they find it easier to work by telephone, like the way Tom Keane has done from a pay phone in the federal pen.

Others, like the star personal-injury lawyers, seem to spend every waking hour in court, and some non-waking ones. If they're not in court, it's because they're in some other court. When they do end up with several cases going to trial at once, lawyers often resort to something for which the Cook County courts are notorious: continuances. Want to handle a dozen juicy personal-injury or divorce cases at one time? Just deal with the conflicts that arise by asking the judges involved to postpone some of the cases to a future date. Or have your secretary do it. They'll keep it up almost as long as you want. Which is why many cases drag on for seven years or more.

The backlog of personal-injury cases involving judgment demands of fifteen thousand dollars or more was in excess of forty-six thousand cases in 1978. And that was four thousand more cases than the 1977 backlog.

A judge from downstate Green County was transferred up to Cook County one summer to work as vacation relief. Aghast at having lawyers come before him not prepared to go to trial and asking for continuances, the judge began fining them for contempt of court. He soon heard from upstairs.

Cook County is a place where an extraordinary number of defendants demand bench trials instead of jury trials. It is a place where verdicts are often amazingly predictable. An alderman was tried recently in the county courts on state corruption charges. A bench trial, not a jury one. No one had the slightest idea as to what the verdict would be, of course, but his friends made a lucky guess and rented a hotel banquet room for his acquittal party hours before the verdict was rendered. A jolly time was had by all.

Any decision is possible in the Cook County courts. One Daley loyalist in the state legislature labored for years trying to outlaw some of the predominantly Republican suburban-township offices, but with little success. Then he became a judge, and simply declared them unconstitutional.

Some lawyers thrive in this system. Others constantly rail and fight against it. All in Chicago must cope with it.

P. Sveinbjorn Johnson, Icelandic consul and a prominent local attorney who likes to take on interesting cases in the criminal courts on occasion, once sued the city on behalf of the family of a boy who had been shot to death during a search by a policeman. The response from the Chicago Corporation Counsel's office was so sluggish it took Johnson weeks of badgering to get them to even send him a written communication. It was a form he was to fill out. It was for traffic accidents.

Now really.

THE TOP FIFTEEN LAWYERS IN CHICAGO

1. Edmund Stephan

Ed Stephan's great forte is advice, the best possible advice. Mayor Daley often got it for free but Stephan's clients have to pay a little something for it. They include General Electric, Continental Bank, Northern Illinois Gas Company, and a list of others long enough to fill *Fortune* magazine.

In his late sixties, Stephan is chairman and senior partner of Mayer, Brown, and Platt—if not the biggest, possibly the city's best law firm. A quiet-spoken family man, Stephan is as respected outside his profession as he is within it. He's the fellow the legal community in Chicago turns to as a leader or spokesman when it has a serious problem. Unlike most in his high station, Stephan actually spends a great deal of time working at the law, drafting briefs and reading statutes, settling disputes between partners, and assembling and directing his firm's famous multi-partner tag teams.

A devout Irish-German Catholic, whose father came out of the lead-mine country around Galena, Stephan and his wife filled their big Evanston house with eight children. He also performs in a fatherly fashion for Notre Dame University, where he has been chairman of the board of trustees since 1967, the first lay person to hold that position. He's famous for having tightened up on the exuberant lifestyles of male students while presiding over the merger of Notre Dame with St. Mary's College for women.

He is a director of a string of companies and has turned down numerous offers of the Bar Association presidency, federal judgeships, and similar honors. A confidante of the late Adlai Stevenson and a good friend of his senatorial son, Stephan is the lawyer other lawyers like Newton Minnow contacted if they wanted an audience with Mayor Daley. Stephan also occasionally led proceedings at Bilandic's prayer breakfasts (what do they pray for at those things, anyway?). Jane Byrne is fond of Notre Dame people.

One of his more junior partners described Stephan by saying "there's not an ounce of meanness in him." There are very few people at the top of the lists in Chicago of whom that can be said.

2. Howard Trienens

Glencoe's Howard Trienens is No. 1 man at a little shop called Sidley and Austin, the city's biggest law firm and one of its oldest. Newton Minnow is among its some two hundred partners, and its clients include A.T.&T., the Arthur Anderson accounting empire, and Carson Pirie Scott.

A fellow in the American College of Trial Lawyers, Trienens has been involved in such famous cases as the 1965 federal court decision redrawing all the state's legislative district boundaries. Under Trienens, Sidley and Austin has maintained a variety of political friendships and interests, but discreetly. If someone wanted to raise a lot of money, or call a meeting of the most important lawyers in town, Trienens would be the man to see to put such a gathering together.

Now in his fifties, Trienens came out of Wilmette and went into nearby Northwestern University, which he now serves as a trustee. He is also a director of R. R. Donnelley and Sons and the G. D. Searle drug company, which mingles him with Chicago's Old Money and interesting chaps like Don Rumsfeld.

When the great Don Reuben needed a lawyer to secure a comfortable severance from Kirkland and Ellis, he hired Trienens. What Trienens came up with was $375,000, which certainly helped tide Reuben over.

3. Hammond Chaffetz

Though now in his seventies, Hammond Chaffetz is still the man to see around Kirkland and Ellis—certainly now that Reuben isn't. The firm, which counts Standard Oil, International Harvester, and Westinghouse among its remaining clients, was described by Ralph Nader as "the most influential firm in any American city of significant size." Had it not been for the departure of Reuben and clients like the *Tribune*, Kirkland and Ellis would still be that and Chaffetz would be at the head of this list.

Chaffetz has stepped down from direct rule in favor of a four-man junta, but he remains the ultimate power, as he indicated in the showdown with Reuben, which reportedly featured an extraordinary shouting match between the two.

A Harvard man, and onetime Washington representative for those rich Annenbergs, Chaffetz has been attorney for Dean Foods, Standard Oil, and other really big corporations. He's a director of some major companies and banks, and is on the board of Ravinia.

4. Bert Jenner

For much of the 1960's and 1970's, the rest of the country must have thought that Albert Jenner was the only lawyer Chicago had. As counsel for the Warren Commission, a member of the President's Commission on the Causes and Prevention of Violence, and minority counsel to the House Judiciary Committee during those fun Watergate impeachment proceedings, Jenner, with his bow tie, seemed a sort of Republican version of Archibald Cox.

In fact, the Republicans thought he was so much like Democrat Cox that they tried to fire him from the committee. At the last minute, Chairman Peter Rodino rescued poor old Bert by putting him to work for the rest of Watergate with the Democratic staff.

Now Jenner doesn't mind Democrats at all. When former Governor Ogilvie decided to teach the local GOP a lesson for not slating his pal Lou Kasper for sheriff, he made Jenner a major participant in his successful plot to reelect Democrat Richard Elrod.

The firm Jenner and Block remains one of the most powerful and prestigious law outfits in Chicago. J & B's young superstar Tom Sullivan was made U.S. Attorney, but he'll be back. Among Jenner's biggest clients and closest connections is the very, very powerful Crown family of General Dynamics and Material Service Corporation fame.

One of the Crowns got caught up in a bribery-scheme case, but, with Jenner representing him, got out of it clean with a grant of immunity from then U.S. Attorney Jim Thompson. Jenner's firm later gave Thompson a twelve-hundred-dollar campaign contribution.

Named "Chicagoan of the Year" in 1975 by the Chicago Press Club, Bert loves to champion the underdog. When two Chicago Transit Authority public-relations aides got the sack for speaking to the press about something a CTA poobah would rather have taken the credit for, Jenner successfully won six thousand dollars in compensation for them. He has been a vigorous and successful foe of the many interesting kinds of police spying practiced in Chicago.

A sprightly septuagenarian, Jenner disdains lounging around his posh Kenilworth digs and keeps busy, busy, busy. A director of General Dynamics and the United of America Bank, he's also on the American Bar Association board of governors.

At times, Bert is perhaps a little too busy. An IRS investigation in 1978 showed that Bert had somehow failed to file federal-income-tax returns for 1973, 1974, and 1975—years in which he reportedly earned more than three hundred thousand dollars. Bert apologized profusely, claiming he had overlooked his taxes because of the "press of outside activities." The investigation was then dropped without any charges being filed. Which was nice.

5. Don H. Reuben

There are people who may not like Don Reuben, but his entrance can command silence in courtrooms and boardrooms alike. As Ralph Nader (who probably never realized what an enormous compliment he was uttering) put it: "No lawyer in any other city is as powerful or feared as Don Reuben is in Chicago."

A small, somewhat frail-looking man in his fifties, who is almost always to be seen in a gray pinstriped suit, Reuben has the coldest gray eyes in the business. He sports Gucci shoes and briefcase, attends all the glittery events, and rips about town in a canary-yellow Mercedez roadster, but you seldom see him smile.

Reuben grew up on the West Side when that was a middle-class Irish and Jewish section and not the unfortunate slum it is today. He went to Northwestern, where he won a reputation as a brilliant student and somewhat abrasive loner. He joined the Kirkland firm when it was still called McCormick, Kirkland, Patterson, and Fleming, and impressed his superiors so favorably they put him on the sacred *Tribune* account when he was only twenty-seven.

He is perhaps the finest libel lawyer in the country, and has pulled off masterful coups in other legal areas, such as persuading the State of Illinois to give $30 million to the thirteen thousand poor souls defrauded by the bankrupt City Savings and Loan.

Jane Byrne's "greased taxi-deal" charges are what is reported to have made Hammond Chaffetz so shouting mad, but Byrne's charges came to nothing and Reuben may end up much better off for it all. He plans to make Reuben and Proctor a one-hundred-partner firm one soon day, and with the kind of class accounts he carried off with him, it's certainly possible.

Reuben and his first wife divorced some years ago and he has since married an attractive blonde society lady named Jeanette Hurley. His own fortune is estimated at $5 million or better.

The Reubens live in a penthouse on Lakeview Avenue overlooking the park and the lake, which on stormy days matches the color of those cold gray eyes.

6. Tom Sullivan

No one messes with Tom Sullivan. His boss, Bert Jenner, once called him "this skinny, little Irish kid," but Sullivan is now the toughest kid on the legal block. A quiet, taciturn fellow now nearing fifty, Sullivan has a cold, steely mind like Reuben's, yet boundless quantities of raging moral indignation. Among the many foes he's vanquished is the House Un-American Activities Committee.

Before he was made U.S. Attorney, Sullivan for the defense used to eat federal prosecutors for breakfast, sometimes winning eight cases in a row. After that, it was defense attorneys who discovered that (as someone once said of Abraham Lincoln) anyone who underestimated this man is likely to find his back against the bottom of a ditch.

Sullivan came to Jenner and Block straight from Loyola University Law School in 1954, having paused for only a brief stint in the army. He had become a $200,000-a-year senior partner by the time Senator Stevenson invited him to succeed that long list of Republicans in the U.S. Attorney's office. His income returning to private practice should easily be twice that. If Reuben has a rival for ultimately ending up No. 1 on the list, it is Tom Sullivan.

Some of Sullivan's past clients are what you'd expect of a corporate law partner living in Kenilworth: American Express, Eastern Airlines, Material Service and the Crowns, and the American Broadcasting Company. Neither was it surprising that he represented former State Revenue Director Ted Isaacs in the Kerner bribery trial, some officials of the Teamsters' pension fund, or twelve of the fourteen policemen involved in the notorious Black Panther Raid case.

But much of the luster of Sullivan's legal reputation has come from his willingness in private practice to take up causes and clients on the outs with the establishment. He defended accused subversive Dr. Jeremiah Stamler before HUAC, "Chicago 7" attorney William Kuntsler on contempt charges, and *Playboy* magazine's ill-fated Bobbie Arnstein on drug charges.

He's represented the NORML marijuana people, the black Contract Buyers' League, and even ex-Governor Daniel Walker in a libel case. Tom Sullivan would have been a much likelier candidate for counsel in that case involving the Devil and Daniel Webster.

As U.S. Attorney, Sullivan did not go charging after corrupt politicians with the zeal and single-mindedness of Jim Thompson, although he did take up that nasty matter involving Bill Scott's peculiar finances and went after the city's sweetheart deal with the Airline Canteen Service at O'Hare Airport.

Thompson wanted to be governor, if not President. If Sullivan wants to be something, no one knows. Unlike Thompson, he doesn't talk about himself very much. Or about much of anything.

7. *Philip Corboy*

Phil Corboy is fond of money. The son of a cop, he used to deliver gin for a liquor store as a kid and went through Notre Dame on the G.I. Bill. Now he owns a magnificent house in Evanston, has had as many as thirty pairs of shoes, and ten watches. At one time.

He is in precisely the right profession for a man of his tastes. He is the top personal-injury lawyer in Chicago and possibly the best jury-trial lawyer in town. He is one of only six Chicagoans to be admitted to the select if rather materialistic Inner Circle of Advocates, a small but growing society of lawyers who have won $1 million or more in damages for a single client in a single case. Three of the other five Chicagoans who have made it are protégés of Corby's.

A past president of the Chicago Bar Association, Corboy has

staged dramatic performances in courtrooms that make Perry
Mason seem dull. Not content to describe the terrifying menace of
a faulty transmission, he will have the offending device hauled into
court. Rather than talk about such unpleasant things as how a
client has a catheter stuck in him, he will produce said catheter and
show the jury just how and where.

Through such methods, Corboy has judgements of $500,000 to
$1 million rolling in all the time. He won $750,000 from the Chicago Transit Authority for a single bus crash and $1.14 million
from Beatrice Foods for a truck accident.

There is no one Corboy won't sue. He even took on *Playboy*
magazine for lampooning an M & M candy "melt in your mouth"
advertisement in "an erotic manner."

The snowy-haired Corboy is a generous fellow. His name has
appeared on lists of contributors to politicians like Da Mare—in
amounts like one thousand dollars. He declined a seat on the
Illinois Judicial Inquiry Board (the outfit that investigates judges)
but was fond enough of Springfield to lobby there against legislation to limit malpractice suit damages.

In 1976, Corboy's twelve-year-old son was killed in a tragic
automobile accident. The driver had no insurance.

8. George Cotsirilos

Before Tom Sullivan leaped the fence to become a prosecutor,
it was arguable whether he or George Cotsirilos was the best defense attorney in Chicago. The dapper little man is still contesting
for the title, and remains one of the better-known heroes of Chicago's Greek community.

A former assistant to the now-retired Judge John S. Boyle when
that great Irish jurist was Cook County state's attorney, Cotsirilos has since defended an assortment of accused swindlers; a
Young Republican official charged with draft evasion; Black Panther raiders; the convicted crooked cop, Clarence Braasch; and
Eugene Hairston, the Blackstone Rangers leader who got off with
only five to fifteen for using underage juveniles as hit men.

Not terribly fond of Jim Thompson and his extravagant use of
the immunity doctrine in political-corruption cases, Cotsirilos denounced the practice as a "rampant and limitless refuge to scoun-

drels." He also attacked Thompson's interim successor, Sam Skinner, for "vilifying defendants by use of insulting and inflammatory epithets." So there.

Much involved in Bar Association work on procedural reforms, he isn't quite so zealous about other kinds, such as merit selection instead of patronage selection of judges. A wealthy Winnetkan, Cotsirilos occasionally ends up on things like the Executive Committee of the Lawyers Committee to Retain George Dunne. He has friends there.

9. George Burditt

Tall, lean, brilliant, fiftyish, terribly suburban, and kind of gee-whizzy, George Burditt is regarded as the best food-and-drug lawyer in the United States. His prosperous practice shows it.

A former Northwestern University law teacher, Burditt is such a straight-arrow Boy Scout he almost seems an embarrassment to his profession. Despite this Mr. Clean stuff, he became fascinated with Illinois politics. Elected to the state legislature from west suburban La Grange, he ran for speaker of the Illinois House in 1970 and lost, disastrously. In 1974, as a favor to a Republican Party that couldn't get anyone else to run, he took on Adlai Stevenson for the United States Senate, and lost, disastrously. Illinois politics and Boy Scouts don't often mix.

10. Tom Foran

Tom Foran has always been as close to politics as one can get. Looking and sounding uncannily like the gruff "Mr. District Attorney" of ancient television days, Foran was Jim Thompson's Democratic predecessor as U.S. Attorney.

With the help of his bright first assistant (and now law partner) Richard Schultz, Foran put together a superior conviction record, though certainly not very superior as regards Cook County political-corruption convictions.

Foran was kept on in the federal prosecutor's job for a while to play ringmaster at the "Chicago 7" circus for President Nixon. He briefly ran for governor in 1972, abruptly and mysteriously halted his campaign just as it got going, and has been enjoying a prosperous private practice ever since.

Work seems to come his way. Foran has been special counsel to the Chicago Park District, the Chicago Election Board (which has often needed one), and the Cook County Health and Hospital Commission. His wife, who hosted charming little gatherings for Mayors Daley and Bilandic, was appointed to the Park District board, although Jane Byrne doesn't seem quite so pleased with her.

The impression should not be left that Tom was disinterested in political corruption cases. He skillfully defended County Clerk Eddie Barrett and County Commissioner Charlie Bonk when Thompson had them in the dock. The poor doddering Barrett was convicted (serving his sentence under a sort of house-arrest), but Bonk was not.

11. John J. Kennelly

If an airline stewardess should spill hot coffee down your neck, run quick to J. J. Kennelly. He might get you $100,000 in damages. That's something of an exaggeration, but not much.

Kennelly is without question the world's best aviation-disaster lawyer, which is why eighty-one survivors of the 1976 Entebbe hijacking chose him as their attorney in their $195-million lawsuit against Air France.

He likes numbers like that. On one occasion, he won a $2.4-million settlement for the families of four United Air Lines pilots who were killed when a generator failed—and $4 million for seven Nebraskans killed in a United crash at Chicago's Midway. In 1965, he raked in $2 million for a single death in a Northwest Orient crash in the Everglades. His counsel was sought in the horrible O'Hare DC-10 disaster.

A judge once related Kennelly's secret: He's a careful, methodical lawyer who goes after findings of fact without the theatrics of a Phil Corboy. But the findings of fact are relatively easy for him to come by because the National Transportation Safety Board investigates every accident and makes full and exhaustive reports. A pilot himself, Kennelly understands every word of the NTSB aviation jargon and can make it crystal clear to judges and juries.

As attorney for the Entebbe victims, Kennelly flew to London and Bahrein and all over to gather evidence. But when it came to seeking venue, guess where he filed his suit. That's right. The Cook County Circuit Court. "There's nowhere else," he said.

To be sure, there's nothing like it in the world. No wonder the Illinois Trial Lawyers made Kennelly their president.

12. Bob Bergstrom

A gaunt Norseman with piercing gray eyes, Robert Bergstrom is one of the Democratic machine's least favorite lawyers in Chicago. Along with George Ranney and Frank Greenberg, he has been a prime mover in the Committee on Courts and Justice's crusade to replace judicial patronage with a merit system of judicial selection. The machine has become so paranoid on the question that it's been trying to come up with some sort of passable merit system of its own. It has also started nominating some fairly well qualified and occasionally highly qualified candidates for judge.

On another front, Bergstrom has enlisted the League of Women Voters, the *Chicago Tribune*, the Junior Chamber of Commerce, and others in a crusade to reduce the size of the Illinois House by one third of its noisy, bickering, ineffective 177 members—and do away with the "cumulative-voting" system of electing state representatives that has put people in office who received only 8 percent of the vote in their district.

A wartime staff officer to Admiral Chester Nimitz, Bergstrom is an extraordinarily effective behind-the-scenes man, and—in front of the scenes—was one of the influences that helped keep the 1970 Illinois Constitutional Convention on the straight and narrow, if not out of the saloons.

Bergstrom has served as counsel to a legislative commission investigating scandal in the Sanitary District (which is rather like investigating coal in a coal mine) and is a frequent spokesman for the Bar Association on legislative and constitutional matters.

Another reason the machine has not adored him is that he is a Republican—and not the cooperative kind like Thompson or Ogilvie. Bergstrom was president of the traditionally Republican Union League Club. He was also president of the village of Glenview.

As a lawyer, he has been the motion-picture industry's No. 1 man in the Midwest, and has undertaken such challenges as having to prove exactly where those demon voices came from in *The Exorcist.*

13. Charles Davis

Charles Davis is a quiet, very dignified fellow with something of a high-pitched voice and no great zest for the limelight.

Except for indulgences like the Chicago World Federalists and the Winnetka Human Relations Committee (they do have human relations in Winnetka), a thrilling pursuit for him would be something like his work on the planning committee of the University of Chicago Law School's annual Federal Tax Conference.

Davis belongs on this list for a very simple reason: He is the very best tax lawyer in the United States. A senior partner with Hopkins, Sutter, Mulroy, Davis, and Cromartie, he learned to figure out the Feds from the inside out. In the 1940's, he was a tax legislation counsel for the U.S. Treasury Department and then served on the staff of the House Ways and Means Committee. In the 1950's, he was chief counsel for the Bureau of Internal Revenue, the forerunner of the I.R.S. He knows whereof they take.

14. Patrick Tuite

Our criteria for putting people onto these lists is basically that they excel in prestige, ability, power, or influence (if not all four). Patrick Tuite is a man of influence. A young, bespectacled Irishman, he is not quite the sort you'd expect to find on the U.S. Supreme Court one day, or even lunching at the Casino Club. But, as one lawyer said admiringly of him, "He knows his way through every back door in the city," and that counts for a lot in Chicago.

Chief of the criminal division in the state's attorney's office when the raging Edward Hanrahan was running that show, Tuite's clients in private practice have included an assortment of crooked cops, a cop who shot two women without apparent provocation, three of Sam Giancana's daughters, a reputed con man, and Mario DeStefano.

One of Tuite's more spectacularly successful cases involved a fire-department lieutenant who was videotaped by a local television station in the act of shaking down the owner of an auto-paint shop for a bribe. The lieutenant meekly pleaded guilty (called "copping

a plea" in courthouse vernacular), receiving a misdemeanor conviction instead of a felony. A short while later, Tuite quietly filed
a motion to have the sentence vacated. When the state's attorney's
office failed to object to the motion (if they had even noticed it),
the sentence was vacated. Tuite then argued that this was the
technical equivalent of an acquittal, and had the lieutenant re-
instated on the force. The television station still has the videotape.

Tuite and his wife, Cornelia, a former *Tribune* reporter, live in
a posh, luxurious condominium overlooking Lincoln Park and are
famous for their annual St. Patrick's Day bash for one hundred.
Tuite can afford big parties, for he doesn't depend on erring fire-
department lieutenants for all of his income.

In the early 1970's, he represented some movie-theater owners
who had been hit with obscenity charges for presenting such
cinematic *oeuvres* as *Deep Throat*. The case proved inspiring.
Sometime later *Tribune* columnist Bob Wiedrich disclosed that he
had become a part-owner in two movie theaters that specialize in
"all-male cast" porn flicks and function as trysting places for grop-
ing gays. Tuite responded simply by saying it was "a good investment." Chicagoans always admire the good investment.

15. Richard Ogilvie

As a young attorney, Richard Ogilvie wanted to go to the White
House. Now, as a former governor and an older attorney, he sits
in a rather smallish law office, his desk flanked by standing state
and American flags, with a few other political trappings sitting
on bookshelves or hanging on the wall. It is a far cry from the
White House.

The office is in the First National Bank Building, a prestigious
legal address, and Ogilvie is a partner with Isham, Lincoln, and
Beale. Though fallen from grace politically, he remains the best-
connected Republican lawyer in the state—a man who knows who
everyone is and where everything is. Isham, Lincoln, and Beale
do not find this insignificant.

As a mere lawyer, Ogilvie seems able to instantly inspire public
officials like young Dan Baldino of the Regional Transportation
Authority Board, who thought it a wonderful idea for Ogilvie's
longtime aid, Jeremiah Marsh, to become RTA attorney. Tom

Drennan, who played kitchen cabinet to Ogilvie's Andrew Jackson, has received some generous contracts from the RTA.

In addition to practicing law, helping out his friends, and civic good works like serving on Bilandic's stadium study committee, Ogilvie sits on the boards of some big corporations and is a member of the U.S. Railway Association (a functioning federal bureaucracy, not a bunch of train nuts).

His prestige as governor and friendships with people like Hope and Brooks McCormick eased his way into such prominence as residence in the exclusive 1500 North Lake Shore Drive building, as well as membership in the Casino. He's also on the board of Northwestern Memorial Hospital. Not bad for a Kansas City boy.

Despite all this high toned stuff, Ogilvie's been seen golfing with the likes of Alderman Eddie Burke and Alderman Eddie Vrdolyak. But you can't spend all your time talking about needlepoint with the ladies of the Casino Club.

14

Clergy

In a city where Mayor Daley is still revered as a god, more conventional religions have had to take a back pew. Ward committeemen and precinct captains count for much more as community leaders than do parish priests, rabbis, or Protestant ministers, except perhaps in Chicago's black community, where a substantial number of professional politicians are also ministers.

This is not to say Chicago is irreligious. The town that Billy Sunday could not shut down has still been the home of Mother Cabrini, the nun whose work among neglected Italian immigrants in Chicago and elsewhere resulted in her becoming the first American citizen to be made a saint. The late Paul Johannes Tillich, a giant in the field of theology, was a Chicagoan—or at least, a University of Chicagoan, which is almost as good.

Whether they are Bridgeport Irish, Humboldt Park Poles, Lake Shore Drive Jews, South Side blacks, or Gold Coast WASPs, Chicagoans flock religiously to their places of worship—in enormous numbers. Mayor Daley, in fact, used to attend mass every day.

But unless they hold political office, religious leaders in the city don't have much clout. They have to take their place in line with everyone else. There is not, for example, the close alliance that has for so long existed between cardinals and mayors in Boston. In Chicago, control over the masses belongs to the pols, and men of the cloth are supposed to stay out of the way. Ayatollah Khomeinis are not welcome.

The religious group that comes the closest to holding any real power in the city is, of course, the Catholics. Chicago is a Catholic town, even though Catholics are just 40 percent of the population. Moreover, Chicago is an Irish-Catholic town, despite the fact that only about one third of the Catholics are Irish, and are overwhelmingly outnumbered by Catholic Poles.

The reason for this is no more mysterious than the reason for the fact that the Irish, with just 15 percent of the city's population, hold 90 percent of its top municipal jobs. The Irish are top dogs in City Hall, and in the Cathedral.

As his name attests, John Patrick Cardinal Cody is not Armenian. The cardinal's chief assistants are Irish. Even his chief critics within the archdiocese are Irish. St. Patrick's Day is the high holiday in Chicago. The city does not dye the Chicago River a different color in honor of Italian or Polish saints—and, if the river occasionally gets a little orange in spots, that has nothing to do with the faith of Scotch-Irish Protestants. In terms of the people who run Chicago, the city's three most important educational institutions are De La Salle High School, DePaul University, and Loyola University, where names like Daley, Byrne, and Dunne are as common as blackboard erasers.

Cardinal Cody may have lost Illinois license plate "1" to the wife of Governor Ogilvie, but his mansion—nestled in among all those WASPs on Astor Street—is at more than $1 million the most valuable "single-family" dwelling in the city.

The cardinal has had little but spiritual influence upon the city's mayors, but he seems to have been greatly influenced himself by their style of government—notably by Daley's. His rule of the Chicago archdiocese has been so autocratic at times as to produce open revolt. According to some published reports, the last three popes have tried to persuade him to ease off, if not step down—including Pope John Paul I, with whom the cardinal was closely associated as a young priest in Rome. The 572-member Association of Chicago Priests has continued to press for his removal, charging the cardinal with not answering letters, closing schools without consultation, "ignoring the process of consultation in most decisions," and "an underlying disregard for the human dignity of priests and people."

But this is Chicago, where people are much used to that sort of thing, and His Eminence has hung on, and in.

Some would say there is no other way the Chicago archdiocese can be run. Occupying much of the metropolitan area, it is the nation's largest archdiocese, with about 2.5 million parishioners, compared to Boston's 1.9 million. Nearly a century and a half old, the archdiocese oversees twenty-three hospitals, one of the largest closed-circuit television operations in the world, a huge charity program, the Catholic Youth Organization, and an assortment of seminaries and cemeteries.

Its parochial schools, with an enrollment of more than 250,000, constitute the world's largest Catholic school system. Protestant politicians like former Governor Ogilvie fought valiantly to provide state aid to the archdiocese's schools—in large part because they kept so much pressure off the state's enormously costly public schools. With the considerable help of clerics like Bishop William McManus (another non-Armenian), Cody has been able to run his school system with something like one percent of the administrative staff required for Chicago's public schools.

But the state aid was not forthcoming, and Cody has been closing down unsupportable inner-city schools, in particular those largely attended by non-Catholic black kids. This and other controversies—aggravated by the fact that his 2,500 priests and 10,000 nuns range in ideology from right-wing zealot to left-wing zealot (there are also some moderate types who just want to get married) —have placed His Eminence in his pickle.

Some think the fact that the new pope is Polish, and an adroit, reform-minded politician, will have some serious bearing on the Cardinal's future. But Chicago is Chicago, where the Irish have always kept the Poles in their place, and the mayor is not named Jane Byrneski.

The most important Catholic church in Chicago is, of course, the Cardinal's flagship Holy Name Cathedral, notable for the highest of masses and such ecumenical events as Senator Adlai Stevenson standing on its steps and saying with a straight face that there was no such thing as political patronage in Chicago. The cathedral is also distinguished as one of the last relics of the Capone gangland era, in that a high-ranking mobster was shot down outside it. His name, alas, was Hymie Weiss, but he was a member of Dion O'Banion's gang.

There are Protestants in Chicago, more than a million of them. But they are such a disparate assemblage—ranging from hoity-toity Episcopalians at the Gold Coast's St. Chrysostom's to East 47th Street storefront Baptists to New Town "Jesus freaks"—that they hardly constitute an institution. In terms of power and influence, they fall into two distinct groups: the lakefront WASP elite and the South Side and West Side non-WASP not-so-elite—meaning, blacks. As churchgoers, it's the latter who have the most power and influence.

The WASP elite includes all manner of powerful corporate chairmen, society leaders, and charity heads, many of whom attend church dutifully, if not religiously. Many of them are at the level where they can reach the mayor or any other establishment leader with a single phone call. But this access and power seldom transfers to the WASP elite clergy, and the WASP elite clergy has little power over its flocks, especially where church attendance is considered a social necessity and not a spiritual one. Should the WASP elite clergy urge its congregations to kiss the feet of the poor or take in winos, blank stares and mutterings would be the only response. Along with a drop in the offerings and maybe a terse note from on high.

This is definitely not the case in the black community. Because the church was for so long the only profession the white man allowed the black man, the church has been the logical place for the black community to look for leadership. From the homicidal Nat Turner to the saintly Martin Luther King, the most compelling and effective black leaders have been clergymen. This continues in Chicago today—from the highly public Reverend Jesse Jackson and his Operation Push to the enormous Baptist empire of the Reverend Joseph Jackson to the lowliest 47th Street storefront preacher who works full-time as a garbageman. He may not have the social standing of a Gold Coast rector, but he knows whom to call at the ward hall, and he knows that his followers will follow. And vote—the way they voted in ousting Croatian Mike in the 1979 mayoral primary.

The political black army Bill Dawson led from the Republican

Party to a position of some consequence in the Democratic machine was substantially officered by preachers. Typical was the Reverend Corneal Davis, who went to Springfield in the 1940's, when black men were not allowed hotel rooms there, and survived nearly thirty years of political strife to become dean of the Illinois House. The great Mahalia Jackson started out working in a laundry and singing in only two public places: church, and—as she noted at Dawson's funeral—ward halls where she performed for Dawson's precinct captains.

The most notable Protestant churches in the city naturally include St. Chrysostom's on North Dearborn Parkway, serving the Gold Coast and Episcopalian high society with venerable aplomb. It is a favorite for bash weddings, located just a couple of convenient blocks from the Ambassador East Hotel, a favorite for bash receptions. During the annual North Dearborn-Astor Street Garden Walk, it is also one of the few available places around where you can go to the john.

Perhaps the prettiest church in Chicago, as well as one of the most prestigious, is the stone and ivy Fourth Presbyterian on North Michigan Avenue. Its cloistered courtyard is an island of peace in the big-city chaos, and has even been used as the setting for fashion photographs and ads. It is much favored by captains of industry, and by young fortune hunters looking to meet rich girls. At the Christmas Eve service in 1976, one of its younger ministers discussed the Three Wise Men as looking "tacky."

The Rockefeller Chapel at the University of Chicago—Baptist because John D. was—is a striking institution. The South Side headquarters of Jesse Jackson's Operation Push, as much a religious movement as anything, must be the most photographed, or at least televised, place of worship in the country.

Jews in Chicago suffer from a circumstance that their counterparts in New York certainly do not: There aren't very many of them, only about 250,000, compared to 2 million in the Big Apple. Concentrated along the lakefront from Hyde Park on the south to Rogers Park on the north, Chicago's Jews are a tightly-knit community, devout in their religious practices and highly organized and effective in their religious causes. Well aware of the Jewish community's financial power and unity of purpose, Mayor Daley was quite sensitive to their concerns about the survival of the state of Israel and the plight of Soviet Jewry, as when he let Jewish protesters demolish that state visit by French President Georges Pompidou in 1970 because Pompidou had withheld jet fighters from Israel.

But few rabbis ever get to bless Democratic machine dinners or share a dais with His Eminence John Cardinal Cody, just as Jewish political holdings in Chicago are mostly confined to a few aldermanic and legislative seats, the sheriff's office, and some judgeships. Daley may have admired the Jews for their close family life and the intensity of their religion, but he disliked their liberal independent politics. In his scheme of things, they ranked well below his fellow Catholic Poles and probably only just above the predominantly Republican Norwegians.

The Jewish synagogue is of course Temple Shalom on North Lake Shore Drive, at least in terms of social prestige. But the most significant in Chicago religious and historical terms is the nearby Anshe Emet Synagogue on Pine Grove Avenue. Either of them might easily serve as the Israeli embassy in the United States and are to Chicago Jewish charities what John D. Rockefeller was to the Baptists.

The Census Bureau lists a number of faiths under "other." Chicago has a large number of "others," and not just the kind who hawk books or stick flowers in your lapel at O'Hare Airport.

Elijah Muhammed's highly capital intensive and once highly racist Black Muslims have long been a significant force in the black community. Elijah used to regularly rail against "blue-eyed devils," but saw nothing wrong with trying (unsuccessfully) to foist a one-thousand-dollar "gift" on one of the city's most respected white reporters after he wrote a story about the Muslims that dealt with them fairly and objectively. Since Elijah's death, the Black Muslims have dropped antiwhite racism entirely from their cant and have been endorsed and embraced by the Muslem faith internationally.

Buddhism and other Asian religions flourish in Chicago, increasingly so as its North Side becomes a haven for Vietnamese refugees.

The "other" for which Chicagoans may be most grateful, if only in aesthetic terms, is the somewhat ecumenical if Persian faith of Baha'i, which produced what must be the Midwest's most serenely beautiful man-made structure—the extraordinary Baha'i Temple on

Wilmette's grassy lakeshore. Though Persian, Baha'i has nothing to do with the Ayatollah Khomeini, for which anyone who has ever walked the temple's serenely beautiful circumference may be glad. Machine guns are so noisy.

An irony of the Chicago clergy's lack of political power is the intensity of its political activism. This has diminished considerably since the riotous 1960's, but in its time it was extraordinary. It was almost as though, unable to communicate with their congregations from the pulpit, they took to the streets to try to communicate with them through the newspapers and television.

One Presbyterian minister turned his church over to a street gang for use as a weapons arsenal, while the Presbyterian Church nationally raised money for Angela Davis' legal defense fund. Methodist ministers in the Chicago area gave refuge to rampaging Weathermen during the violent and extremely obnoxious "Days of Rage." Baptists led drives to legalize abortion.

Except for occasionally winking at Irish-American financial support of Irish Republican Army terrorists and murderers, the Catholic hierarchy in Chicago tried to stay out of things. Even so, there were activists like Father Carl Lezak, who abandoned the Roman collar for a tweed sportscoat to ring doorbells for Billy Singer's campaign. And there were fellows like the South Side's and Right Wing's Father Francis Lawlor. He got himself elected a delegate to the 1970 Illinois Constitutional Convention, where he distinguished himself by running around with a jar containing a pickled fetus in an effort to constitutionally forbid abortion. He also got himself elected an actual alderman in the Chicago City Council, where he distinguished himself by not running around with a pickled fetus and by knowing absolutely nothing about patronage.

Chicago Jews have been active in every imaginable political cause, but their rabbis, not so. Perhaps they take matters like Israel's survival and Soviet Jewry too seriously to want to risk antagonizing the general Chicago public.

In any event, very little of all that political activism came to anything. Billy Singer did not become mayor and abortion was not constitutionally forbidden. All the Weathermen accomplished was breaking a few Cadillac windshields and electing Richard Elrod sheriff. The street gangs have their own arsenals now, thank you, and Angela Davis no longer needs defending. If Chicago clergymen had any effect at all, it was the black ones on Bill Dawson's old turf who kept rebel Ralph Metcalfe in the Congress, elected Bernie Carey state's attorney, and unelected Mayor Michael Bilandic.

If only Chicago Irish-Catholics would stop giving gun money to the I.R.A.

THE TOP FIVE CLERGYMEN IN CHICAGO

1. John Patrick Cardinal Cody

Plump, jowly, surprisingly jovial, and decidedly Irish in countenance, John Patrick Cody looks like the sort of cardinal Mayor Daley might have invented—or demanded that the Holy See produce. Indeed, he looks like he might have come out of Bridgeport—with one brother a cop, another a fireman, and another an alderman, and at least one sister a nun.

But there is an aspect to the cardinal that one seldom finds among the Chicago Irish (excepting the likes of Loyola University's Professor Lawrence McCaffrey and Father Eugene Kennedy): he is a learned scholar. Worse, he isn't even a native Chicagoan.

He was born in St. Louis, of all places, but escaped to become ordained a priest in Rome at the age of twenty-three in 1931. Two years later, he became an aide to Eugenio Cardinal Pacelli, the papal secretary of state who later gained fame as Pope Pius XII.

After earning two doctorates in philosophy, one in theology, and another in canon law, Cody returned from Rome to St. Louis in 1939, and became secretary to Archbishop John Glennon. Afterward, Cody was made an auxiliary bishop in St. Louis; labored in such vineyards as St. Joseph, Kansas City, and New Orleans; and in 1965—upon the death of Albert Cardinal Meyer—was moved into Chicago and made an archbishop.

A no-nonsense sort of fellow—he excommunicated Louisiana's formidable Leander Perez for obstructing the integration of New Orleans' parochial schools—Cody has liked to keep his eye, and thumb, on everything, just like Daley. As he put it: "I'm tough when I'm right." But right is in the eye of the beholder, and his stances often have offended both sides of issues, irritating liberals and conservatives alike.

"I've been in a good many tough spots. I've been in the thick of a lot of fights," the cardinal once said. (In one, he was robbed at gunpoint of two hundred dollars by two holdup men outside Holy Name Cathedral.) "There's something happening out there. It is not just the clergy. There's a tension in the air today—an impatience, a hatred of leaders, of everything that represents authority."

Nearly fifty years a priest, the cardinal is past seventy, has suffered a heart attack, and undergone gallbladder surgery. Some have suggested he might want to retire for reasons of health. The same was suggested about Richard J. Daley before he ran for reelection for the umpteenth time in 1975, the year before his death. He ran because it would have been such an awful thing to be alive and not be mayor.

It would be such an awful thing not to be cardinal.

2. The Reverend Joseph H. Jackson

The most powerful black clergyman in Chicago is named Jackson, all right, but his first name ain't Jesse. The Reverend J. H. Jackson, as he prefers to be called, is not only pastor for life of the South Side's venerable Olivet Baptist Church, he has been since 1953 the president of the National Baptist Convention of the USA, Inc. With 6.5 million members, it is the largest single organization of black Americans in the nation.

The Reverend Jesse Jackson has a flair for show biz and the ability to attract the maximum possible media attention to himself and his causes. Dr. J. H. Jackson, who is happy to be ignored by the news media and says "I am not seeking popularity," has millions of followers.

Dr. J. H. Jackson said, in one of his rare interviews: "I do not work on any white folks' secret agendas. I am not supported in whole or in part by white folks' money, as some civil-rights workers are. I am not employed by white people."

A minister's son who grew up in Mississippi, Dr. Jackson was described by *Chicago Daily News* religion writer Walter Morrison as having "the look of African kings." Certainly, Dr. Jackson has the conservatism of a king. He has long disdained the term "black," preferring "Negro." He supported America's role in the Vietnam War, and opposed Dr. Martin Luther King's campaign of civil disobedience. "You cannot have civil disobedience in a country such as this," he told Morrison, "without having violence."

An imposing figure of a man and given to conservative dark-blue suits, Dr. Jackson preaches a doctrine that the black man will prevail not through protest but through productivity. When black tenant farmers in Tennessee were evicted for trying to register to vote during the early 1960's, the response of Dr. Jackson's National Baptist Convention was to set them up on an enormous farm of their own—the National Baptist Freedom Farm. "We thought if Negroes wanted to vote in Fayette County, they should own some of Fayette County," he said.

Dr. Jackson's organization owns thousands of acres of land in the United States and in Africa, and contributes large sums to a variety of black, er, Negro, causes. A friend and advisor to Presidents Kennedy, Johnson, and Nixon, Jackson says that "cooperation will take you farther than confrontation."

"We were very poor," he once told *Tribune* writer Clarence Page. "I saw my father lead his mules away and come back with just the bridles. They had to be sold to pay our debts. I saw the lynching parties of white folks looking for Negro victims. Our father taught us not to be bitter children; yet, we were.

"We worked with our hands in the cotton fields. When the white landowner would ride through, we children would stop working. We wouldn't hit a lick. We stopped out of resentment for his presence.

"I had to gradually outgrow that. When I went to college I saw many fine upstanding Negro teachers; stately people who were not bitter. "I found many white fellows failing in college and I began to feel sympathy for some of them. I found they were not the superior creatures they told us they were. I decided to play life by the rules and I accepted the Constitution as the rules of the game."

Some wonder why there was not more racial violence and bloodshed in the 1960's. Those who know about Dr. Jackson and his huge organization do not.

3. Dr. Preston Bradley

Dr. Preston Bradley traditionally ends his radio religious commentaries with the advice: "keep looking up." Chicago's most indefatigable optimist, who finds truth and poetry in the most humdrum aspects of the city's life, Dr. Bradley has been looking up for all of his more than ninety years.

Something of a populist, Dr. Bradley was a champion of the women's right to vote and an ardent foe of Mayor William "Big Bill" Thompson. He first came to Chicago in 1911 and was assigned to a small Presbyterian church on the North Side.

"I got into trouble right away, because I said in a sermon that I couldn't believe God would damn a little child to eternal hell because it had died without being baptized. I said that if there was such a God, I should fight him all my life. And, since that was the accepted philosophy in that church at that time, I was encouraged to leave. I did."

In 1912, Dr. Bradley founded the People's (Unitarian) Church on West Lawrence Avenue in Uptown, where he still preaches— if not with his old vigor, at least with his same optimism. That same year, he began his radio talks, the oldest continuing religious broadcast in the country.

Dr. Bradley has served as a member of the Chicago Public Library Board for more than half a century, was founder and past president of the Izaac Walton League of America, and is a charter member of the Commission on Human Relations. He has served as a member of the Prison Investigation Commission of Illinois and the Citizen Schools Committee. He has written eleven books, been married twice, traveled around the world twice, and crossed the Atlantic some seventy times. The list goes on and on, as does Dr. Bradley.

Slowing down some (he and his wife, June, increasingly abandoned travels in recent years for retreats to their hideaway at Black Duck Island, Minnesota) Dr. Bradley still remains the most consequential white Protestant clergyman in the city. In the eyes of some, he's the most consequential clergyman, period.

And he keeps looking up. "The anthropomorphic God, created by man as a fellow who sits on a cloud with a harp, is dead," he told an interviewer not too long ago. "But the God of beauty and truth and goodness and love never dies, and never shall as long as man functions."

4. Rabbi Seymour Cohen

Nobel Prize-winning author Saul Bellow, actor Nehemiah Persoff, and columnist Irv Kupcinet do not often grace the same platform, but it was no problem for Rabbi Seymour Cohen to attract them to the ceremonies celebrating the one hundredth anniversary of the Anshe Emet Synagogue when they were held several years ago. Established in 1873, Anshe Emet is a continuing symbol of the struggle of Jewish immigrants to make a safe place for their culture in their new country.

It was started in the home of Louis Sax, one of the few places a group of English, German, and Russian Jews could find to hold religious services. The group then met in a series of other private homes on the Near North Side, moved to Phoenix Hall on Division Street in 1876, and in 1878 moved to the top floor of a Division Street grocery. In 1893, the congregation built its first house of worship on North Sedgwick Street—opposite what is now Old Town Gardens—and engaged its first rabbi, Solomon Bauer. In 1922, it moved to a spot near Broadway, and, in 1928, to its present location on North Pine Grove Avenue, where it serves some three thousand families.

Rabbi Cohen has led Anshe Emet since 1960. Despite his synagogue's long and colorful history, Rabbi Cohen is a forward-looking fellow. "An old saying says an anniversary can be either a couch or a springboard," he said on the occasion of the one hundredth anniversary. "We are viewing this as a springboard as we look forward to another century of challenge." An early (1963) champion of American involvement on behalf of Soviet Jewry, Rabbi Cohen now foresees the day when a woman rabbi will lead his synagogue, despite its conservatism.

Born in New York in 1922, Rabbi Cohen studied at the City College of New York, the Jewish Theological Seminary, and Jerusalem's Hebrew University. A former president of the Chicago Board of Rabbis, he has served as chairman of the American Jewish Conference on Soviet Jewry, and as cochairman of the

Interreligious Committee Against Poverty. A Phi Beta Kappa man and the author of several books, Rabbi Cohen lives on Lake Shore Drive.

5. Father Andrew Greeley

However long, or short, no list of ranking clergy in Catholic-dominated Chicago could be complete without Andrew Greeley. Indeed, the Catholic Church in Chicago would be incomplete without Father Greeley.

One of the most vociferous critics of the autocratic Cardinal Cody, he was one of the most ardent supporters of the autocratic Mayor Daley. He has denounced the Roman Catholic hierarchy as "morally, intellectually, and religiously bankrupt," yet railed at Eastern Establishment liberals for being anti-Catholic. He was an outspoken champion of the ethnics in the back neighborhoods of Chicago against the liberal elitists on the lakefront, while himself living in one of the lakefront's more expensive luxury high rises and savoring his own national reputation as a liberal intellectual.

He is a maze of contradictions. "There are two Greeleys," said a professorial colleague at the University of Chicago. "The one who writes scholarly works and the one who writes 'pop' pieces." Said Dan Herr of Thomas More Press: "I used to think there were four Greeleys. I was wrong. There are more than that."

The longtime director of the University of Chicago's Center for the Study of American Pluralism, Father Greeley is a nationally syndicated newspaper columnist and the author of more than fifty books. He appeared locally, and not too successfully, as a television commentator on Chicago's WTTW-Channel 11, but was an enormous hit nationally as a network television explainer of the machinations involved in the selection of Popes John Paul I and John Paul II.

A brilliant theologian and expert on canon law and the papacy, he remains tragically uninformed (as a wincing Irish government will attest) on such matters as the strife in Northern Ireland.

A defender of the Democratic machine—"A bit of corruption is the price of good government. The organization is no more corrupt than Lake Shore Drive limousine liberals"—he nevertheless delights in the intellectual acceptance he has attained as a frequent contributor to magazines like *The Nation*. "I deliberately set out to be a bridge between the church and the university and I ended up being unacceptable to both," he told magazine writer Jack Star. "The cardinal wants me out of teaching, out of the university, and out of writing. I feel great loyalty both to my archbishop and to my university. I don't enjoy being an outcast. I'd like to be accepted by both. But I'm not about to change."

Now in his early fifties, Greeley still has much of his youthful lean and hungry look, the burning look of Eisenstein's *Ivan the Terrible*. A woman admirer called his blazing blue eyes "the eyes of a poet, a saint, a fanatic, or an Irishman." Or all four.

In national terms, he is the best known Catholic clergyman in Chicago, although no one will argue that he is the best liked.

15

Advertising

Modern advertising began in a Chicago saloon. One afternoon in the spring of 1904, Albert D. Lasker was working away in the stuffy Lord and Thomas advertising agency at Randolph and Wabash, where Marshall Field's department store now stands, and he was handed a note. The note read: "I am downstairs in the saloon. I am in the saloon downstairs, and I can tell you what advertising is. I know that you don't know. It will mean much to me to have you know what it is and it will mean much to you. If you wish to know what advertising is, send the word 'Yes' down by messenger. Signed—John E. Kennedy."

Lasker went down to the first-floor saloon and met Kennedy, a former Canadian Mountie. After several drinks, Kennedy revealed: "I can tell you what advertising is in three words: 'salesmanship in print.'" Later in the session, Kennedy unlocked his mind a little more and told Lasker how to make advertising work: "You have to give them a reason why." Lasker knew genius when he saw it: he immediately hired the ex-Mountie as a copywriter at $28,000 a year, breaking a hallowed Lord and Thomas policy of never paying writers more than thirty dollars a week.

Kennedy's advice seems pallid today, but in 1904 the idea of "salesmanship in print" was revolutionary. According to Howard

Shank, recently retired president of Chicago's biggest ad agency, Leo Burnett: "Advertising had always been around, but it was mostly brand-name publicity. For instance, you might take a ride down a country road in your horse and buggy and see a sign for somebody's plug tobacco on the side of a barn. And nobody ever, apparently, thought in terms of using advertising to sell people things. The idea was just to make your name known and hope good things would happen."

The other form advertising took in those old days was fantasy— the churning out of patently absurd claims for patent medicines. Perry Davis's Pain Killer was a particularly popular panacea in the late nineteenth century. A typical Pain Killer notice exclaimed: "As the ships come in, they are liable to bring Cholera—which attacks people suddenly and without warning. In such cases no medicine is equal to Perry Davis's Pain Killer. In India, where the Cholera is so terrible, the natives worship Perry Davis's Pain Killer and call it Medicine of the Gods."

The Lord and Thomas agency changed all that. These ad pioneers firmly believed in giving customers a "reason why" they should buy a particular product; it might not be the best reason, but the customers got a reason nonetheless. For example, the star copywriter for Lord and Thomas, Claude Hopkins, sold Americans on eating breakfasts that were "SHOT FROM GUNS!" In 1913, Hopkins was assigned the flagging Quaker Oats account. He visited the Quaker Oats factory, noticed that the wheat and rice were heated to the exploding point in a big cylinder, and came up with this effusion: "All the inner moisture of the grains is changed into steam; then the guns are shot. A hundred million steam explosions occur in every kernel. Every food cell is exploded, so digestion can instantly act." Quaker Oats sales rocketed.

Hopkins did the same thing for Schlitz beer. He toured the Schlitz brewery in Milwaukee and seized on the fact that the beer bottles were steam-cleaned. A series of ads ran, comparing the "Poor Beer" of competitors to the "Pure Beer" of Schlitz— leaving customers to choose between risking diphtheria or drinking from a steam-cleaned bottle of Schlitz. What Hopkins' ads somehow failed to mention was that all breweries at the time steam-cleaned their bottles.

One of the most appealing reasons Lord and Thomas ever offered for buying a product was in an ad for Pears' Soap. The ad was a testimonial from a Skid Row bum, and read, "I used your soap two years ago; since when I have used no other."

Albert Lasker, who became a partner at Lord and Thomas in 1903, supervised the new art of copywriting and is thought by many to have invented advertising. Lasker is also responsible for the American habit of drinking orange juice. After World War I, the California Growers Exchange was so glutted with oranges that the growers were cutting down the trees. Lasker ran ads saying, "Drink an orange," and the country's orange surplus turned into liquid assets. Lasker fostered another habit—cigarette smoking. Between 1926 and 1931, Lasker's slogan, "Reach for a Lucky instead of a Sweet" brought huge amounts of women who had no desire to be huge into the cigarette market.

Lasker was the prototype of the very, very nervous advertising executive. He suffered three nervous breakdowns. At one time during the 1930's, Lasker was compelled to leave Johns Hopkins where he was receiving medical attention to attend an urgent meeting with the officers of the American Tobacco Company in New York. When the meeting was over, Lasker announced, "Gentlemen, I have done all I can for you. Good day. I must return to Johns Hopkins now and continue my nervous breakdown." Lasker survived until 1952. Lord and Thomas survived until 1943, when the agency became Foote, Cone, and Belding.

The late Leo Burnett was another great shaper of Chicago advertising. The Leo Burnett agency is Chicago's largest, the fifth largest in the world and the fourth in the U.S. Leo Burnett handles accounts like Marlboro, Virginia Slims, and United Airlines, and is the only one of the country's top ten agencies whose headquarters are not in New York. It houses fifteen hundred people on six floors of the Prudential Building. On the receptionist's desk is a bowl of red apples. The Leo Burnett agency spends about forty thousand dollars a year laying in a daily supply of apples. It is at once a gesture of hospitality and defiance. When Burnett set up shop on August 5, 1935, a critic told him he'd soon be out on the street selling apples. Burnett retorted, "I'm not gonna sell apples. I'm gonna give them away."

Burnett started with three Midwestern clients: the Green Giant Co. of LeSueur, Minnesota, whose fortune was to be made through the invention of the Jolly Green Giant (New York ad man Jerry della Femina called the Green Giant, somewhat jealously, "that gigantic green eunuch"), the Hoover Company, and the Realsilk Hosiery Company. Even today, Leo Burnett is unique among big agencies for the small number of clients it handles: while J. Walter Thompson and Foote, Cone, and Belding represent hundreds of accounts each, Leo Burnett never takes on more than thirty-five.

Burnett specializes in a canny use of corn. The Burnett agency created the Jolly Green Giant, to preside over all Green Giant products. Marlboro cigarettes were a woman's cigarette in the 1950's until Leo Burnett put them in a red-topped package and introduced the "Marlboro Men"—tattooed, macho types who looked like cigarette smoking was the least of their habits. And in 1969, Leo Burnett triumphed over regulations forbidding cigarette advertising on TV with the creation of the "You've Come a Long Way, Baby" Virginia Slims campaign.

The success of the Leo Burnett ad agency has astounded New York. Says a former Burnett employee, Don Tennant: "New York feels they have a corner on everything. But suddenly in the fifties here were Foote, Cone, and Belding and Leo Burnett, two agencies which had never been anywhere but Chicago and they were growing like weeds. Leo Burnett made himself sound like a farmer, like he had mud and manure on his shoes, just a country boy. And he looked like a janitor dressed up in a rumpled suit. But the fact was that Leo was much more sophisticated than people realized. He had the ability to communicate to the broad mainstream of Americans. The New York group created advertising for what they thought these people were like. But out here in Chicago, in the middle of those people, advertising was created that really did reach the people. And even New York was impressed."

Leo Burnett himself thought his Midwestern roots helped his advertising. His speeches before New York advertising clubs usually began with a joke about "how we appleknockers do things out there at home among the hayricks and silos of Michigan Avenue." Leo Burnett was dead serious, however, about the worth of Chicago advertising. In a 1961 speech called "Ad-makin' Town," Burnett asserted, "Chicago *is* the Midwest—the heart, soul, brains, and bowels of it. Its ad-making ranks are filled with folks whose heads are stocked with prairie-town views and values. Now I don't intend to argue that Chicago is in any way a worthier city than, say, New York. But I am suggesting that our sod-busting delivery, our loose-limbed stance, and our wide-eyed perspective make it easier for us to create ads that talk turkey to the majority of Americans—that's all!"

The motto of the Leo Burnett agency is a monument to Midwestern corn—an outstretched hand surrounded by six stars is captioned: "When you reach for the stars, you may not quite get one, but you won't come up with a handful of mud, either." According to Howard Gully, PR director for Leo Burnett, "We use it on all kinds of things. When you get your fifteen-year watch, the hand and stars appear on the band. The hand and stars also appear on our cuff links. And the Leo Burnett softball team has 'Reach for the Stars' T-shirts."

Burnett, who died in 1971 at the age of seventy-nine, epitomized the Chicago school of advertising. Don Tennant claims that advertising during Burnett's heyday in the 1950's and 1960's was best defined as "not phony, not pretentious, not slick, not sophisticated, not patronizing."

Even today, there's still a distinctive flavor to Chicago ads. Part of it is in how ads are made and how accounts are won in Chicago. Part of it is in what Chicago ads look like. Bill Peltier, who has worked for the Leo Burnett and Meyerhoff agencies and who once headed his own firm, Biddle Advertising, says: "Chicago advertising is basically nuts and bolts—bread and butter, we call it. It's the heartland of America and it's much more solid sell. Chicago is not at all 'show-biz advertising' where you might watch thirty seconds of a commercial done by a New York operation and have a really hard time finding out what the product is—you just have no idea what they're selling. You don't find this in the Chicago school—the idea is to get the facts out there and show your product is better than the competitive market. There's just more meat and potatoes coming out of Midwestern advertising."

According to Peltier, Chicago ad people are more involved with communicating with people than with producing artsy ads: "With Chicago advertising, the people get down on the street—they know what the people are thinking—they're talking to people rather than creating advertising without ever knowing what the consumer is all about."

Traditionally, Chicago advertising makes the product the star of the ad or commercial and relies very little on "borrowed interest," like using gorgeous models, beefy athletes, or background riots to spark interest in the product. Don Tennant, who now heads one of Chicago's top creative shops, cites the moonshot as a "classic example" of borrowed interest: "Everybody in the business world was trying to send a widget to the moon—whether it was powdered orange juice or whatever. It was strictly borrowed interest—their little widget had absolutely no interest by itself, but by God it went to the moon!"

Bill Ross, a native New Yorker who heads the mammoth J. Walter Thompson operation in Chicago, feels that New York talks to the sophisticate, while Chicago talks to more homespun types. "I think the city of Chicago is closer to the American norm than the city of New York. You could say that the Midwest is different from the East in that it's simpler, more direct, more straightforward. The country opens up a little more as you move West—it loses some of its subtlety. For example, there would be less of a culture shock if somebody from Indianapolis or Kansas City or Platte, North Dakota came to Chicago and spent two days. So, even if I did go out and talk to the people in New York, they might not be as typical as the ones I'd meet in Chicago."

Some recent Chicago ad campaigns show this "let's talk to the heartland" approach. Foote, Cone, and Belding dramatized the war between householders and bugs in their Raid commercials. Raid became not just an amorphous spray but a killer force. The Raid slogan suits the city so well acquainted with violence: "Raid Kills Them Dead."

The J. Walter Thompson agency put Sears paint in the public mind through their Great American Homes campaign. According to Bill Ross, the idea was that people would think that what was good enough to slap on a national shrine would be good enough to slap on their own homes. Of course, added Ross, "We went and offered to paint those national shrines."

Leo Burnett's "Fly the Friendly Skies" campaign for United Airlines has been playing since 1965. Don Tennant, who was with Leo Burnett at the time, claims that the ad extolling the airline's friendliness helped create the reality. "When Burnett came up with 'Fly the Friendly Skies,' the company was not friendly. It was cold and big and dependable, but nobody liked it very much. The campaign deliberately turned the airline's image around. And the company's management went out and told all their employees: 'Hey, folks, you're gonna be friendly because now we're saying that you're friendly. So now we're friendly.' "

Needham, Harper, and Steers in Chicago sells McDonald's hamburgers nationally in what many Chicago ad people describe as brilliant ads, ads that somehow manage to make a fast-food, fast-profit conglomerate seem homey, wholesome, filled with the essence of Mom and apple pie.

Leo Burnett characters frequently mirror people's frustrations. Charley the Tuna, the heart and soul of every social climber, has been trying to get some class since 1968. The lonely Maytag repairman, first created in 1967, is still waiting, Godot-like, for an appliance to break down.

Chicago advertising is distinctive, successful, and big—a $1-billion-a-year business in an industry that chalks up $24 billion annually nationwide. Of the cities with major ad agencies—New York, Los Angeles, Detroit, Chicago, Atlanta, Baltimore—Chicago ranks second. It has around seven hundred ad agencies that employ approximately three thousand people. Leo Burnett alone is a small city of fifteen hundred workers in the Prudential Building, and, with more than $800 million in billings a year, it's the fifth-largest ad agency in the U.S. Chicago advertising has some enormous accounts: Kraft Foods, Quaker Oats, Clairol, Hallmark Cards, Gillette, Schlitz, 7-Up, General Mills, Ford, Oscar Mayer, Sunbeam, Kellogg's, Pillsbury, Philip Morris, McDonald's, Nestlé's, and Campbell Soups all look to Chicago expertise for their campaigns.

And Chicago is the only town whose cardinal uses an old advertising haunt. John Cardinal Cody now presides over his archdiocese in the former Superior Street office of the late Fairfax Cone, the tough-minded heir to Albert Lasker, who transformed the old Lord and Thomas agency into Foote, Cone, and Belding Communications.

But the Chicago ad community still suffers from the Second City Syndrome. Those nasty New York ad people just won't stop condescending to Chicago. Perhaps the nastiest New York adman is Jerry della Femina, who wrote a book about advertising, *From Those Wonderful Folks Who Gave You Pearl Harbor*, and who obviously feels that ending up in Chicago is just one cut above getting fired: "When you go to Chicago, it's like being optioned to Newark if you're playing for the Yankees when the Yankees were the only team going in baseball. It's still Chicago, the minors. When you talk about the major leagues, you're talking about New York, with L.A. coming up fast. In between New York and Los Angeles you have very little except for Leo Burnett in Chicago."

People in Chicago advertising are pretty good-natured about the Second City slam—they pass it off as a fascinating bit of pathology, a peculiarly New York aberration. Bill Peltier dismisses the New York superiority stance as part bluff and part blindness: "They've fostered that for years and years and they've done it so well that Chicagoans and Midwesterners have started to take that Second City attitude, which is nonsense. Every month somebody from New York tries to break Chicago—some New York agent comes here and tries to buy somebody or open a Chicago office and it's become legion that they fail. They don't understand the people—it's a whole syndrome. All those old jokes about the people of New York not knowing there's a country west of the Hudson have a lot of truth. Chicago's different—we've got a city that works. We're not on a public payroll. We're the Midwest, basically."

Bill Ross of J. Walter Thompson understands the origins of the New York syndrome—he once suffered from it himself: "There's no question that New York has had a disproportionate influence on the rest of the country—it's the center of book publishing, the center of live theater, it's the center of many of the arts, and it has first call on European culture. But the unfortunate part is the insular attitude of the New Yorker who thinks that because New York is dynamic, it is superior to the rest of the country. That's just a peculiar kind of egotism."

Chicago's answer to Madison Avenue is North Michigan Avenue, that choice bit of mile-long real estate so sought after by store and hotel keepers, magazine publishers, and ad execs. All the big agencies are on or just off the Avenue—in the Wrigley Building, the Equitable Building, or the Hancock.

It's vital to have a Michigan Avenue address. According to one Chicago account supervisor, "Location is very important in this business—to be on Michigan Avenue in the glamor, show-biz part of the city. You've gotta have a place that's down along the Magnificent Mile. You've gotta have a nice office—it gives the client a sense of security because they're always worried about whether the company is going out of business."

The top three Chicago ad agencies: Leo Burnett; Foote, Cone, and Belding; and J. Walter Thompson, all dominate the Magnificent Mile. Clients must feel like they've come to the right place when they hit these offices. At Leo Burnett, in the Prudential Building just off Michigan Avenue, the visitor waits in a red and green waiting room and is comforted with Leo Burnett apples. At Foote, Cone, and Belding in the Equitable Building, the walls flanking the elevators are festooned with framed, back-lit pictures of client products and famous campaigns. J. Walter Thompson's reception room has the understatement of an agency that doesn't have to advertise itself, except for the ice-shard chandelier that hangs over the receptionist's desk, making hers one of the most precarious jobs in a precarious business.

The power in Chicago advertising belongs mostly to the three big agencies, "full service" agencies that are able to carry an account from the preliminary wining and dining to the congratulatory wining and dining. These agencies can research public opinion and public response to ads, create the campaign, see that the ad or commercial gets placed in the media so that the right people see it at the right time, and deliver the packaging and promotion for the product that will get it firmly lodged in the public mind.

The Leo Burnett campaign for Virginia Slims shows what a full service agency can do: the Burnett people researched how receptive women would be to having "their own" cigarette (Leo Burnett has a Public Opinion Center and exclusive rights to research at Woodfield Mall), created the campaign, and launched one of the greatest promotional showcases of all time, the Virginia Slims Tennis Tournament. And, according to Howard Shank, a new buzz word has entered the ad language. Ever since the Slims campaign, Leo Burnetters praise any good idea by saying, "It's got top spin."

The big ad agencies have the right stuff to stay in a murderously competitive business: they've built reputations, they have a stable of talent, and they have enough money so they don't panic over late payments or a lost account.

Ad agencies have to either make a lot of money or look like they make a lot of money. Many small and medium-sized agencies go quietly bankrupt because the alternative—pressing the client to pay up—just isn't done. Advertising in the big leagues is a gentleman's game. If the client isn't gentlemanly enough to pay, the ad agency is supposed to be gentlemanly enough not to mention that small oversight. Bill Peltier explains this odd business practice: "What often happens is that these agencies are working on a shoestring anyway, and then they get a major client who's slow paying them and it gets to the point where the guy is ninety or one hundred and twenty days overdue, and he's your biggest client. And what can you do? You can't resign him and throw him out because then you're up the creek. It's a constant problem.

"Sometimes the smaller agencies have a better deal than the medium-sized ones. They have maybe two or three people making enough to have a good living and they're doing a good job for smaller accounts. But when your business is worth eight million to twenty-five million dollars, and you've got sixty to seventy people working for you and you're handling a lot of accounts, it's just constant turmoil. Once you get corporate or real big you can lose a big piece of business and not be affected too much."

The talent pool is another key factor in agency success. As Peltier says, "Advertisers have to decide where they'll get the most service, and that's mostly what they're looking for, service—who's gonna be working on the account, what kind of experience they've got, and what kind of media placement and marketing the shop has got."

The big agencies have the stars, like Rudi Perz at Leo Burnett, who created the Pillsbury Doughboy, or J. Walter Thompson's Bill Ross, who dreamed up 7-Up's Uncola campaign when 7-Up was still with Thompson. The star system attracts business. The problem for an advertiser, especially a medium-sized one, comes down to whether they'll go with a big agency, where, as one ad exec puts it, "If they're not major accounts, the big bell-ringers, they'll get very junior people working on the account because they're not as important as the big accounts and don't bring in as much money," or whether they'll select a smaller agency where the talent will fall all over itself proving they can do a top job.

An agency's biggest drawing card is its reputation. Bill Peltier feels that status seeking has a lot to do with the agencies that clients are drawn to: "A lot of times it goes back to the chairman of the board or the president of the company wanting his neighbors or his golf partners to know who his agency is—there's a certain amount of ego gratification in having a known agency." Peltier also says that trust between client and ad agency is vital in such a volatile business: "If you don't believe in a client or that client's product, or they don't believe in you and your operation, then you're doomed from the start. It's not like buying a piece of machinery guaranteed to turn out so many screws a minute—this is very definitely a people business."

According to Don Tennant, who left Leo Burnett in 1970 to found his own agency, the way small agencies can survive in Chicago is by establishing an impressive record: "As you grow, you become more attractive. People want to find out about you. It's still tough to get into the business but if you have a spectacular growth, you get people's attention. It's like anything. People are attracted to winners. They want to be with winners. They don't want to be with some sleepy-time little agency that has grown from three million to three point one million dollars in billings and then, years later, their billings are three and a half million dollars. What the hell? That's nothing. If I were a client looking at these guys, it would bore me silly."

The firm of Weber, Cohn, and Riley shows how far connections can carry an ad agency. Jim Weber is a big, genial Irishman who was a great pal of Mayor Daley's and is a leading light in the city's Irish society. The agency traditionally lands politically connected and city accounts like Chicago 21, the Chicago Transit Authority, and the Regional Transportation Authority. Weber, Cohn, and Riley is responsible for the RTA ads that show Bears running back Walter Payton making great yardage as he charges aboard a series of buses, subway cars, and El platforms. It's not O.J. and airports, but it's close.

For all the things that have stayed the same in Chicago ad land—the importance of connections and reputation, the need for top talent, and a financial base strong enough to survive the slings and arrows of account turnovers—today's Michigan Avenue is a far cry from the old advertising days. Chicago advertising has gone corporate. It's dominated by a few giants. The days of the one-man agency like Leo Burnett once ran are gone, and the day of the "creative factory," as Burnett called the giant New York agencies, has arrived. There are no dominant personalities in advertising anymore, no one like Leo Burnett or Fairfax Cone. Chicago advertising today mostly shuns the star system and stresses teamwork. According to Howard Shank of Leo Burnett: "The one-man shop has disappeared."

What keeps even the corporate ad-making powers from getting comatose, however, is competition. An ad agency is only as good as its current campaign—no history of past successes can satisfy a client whose product is slipping. And ad agencies have nothing to offer but the brains of the people who work for them. As Fairfax Cone once said, "Advertising is the only business where the inventory goes down in the elevators at night."

THE TOP TEN AD PEOPLE IN CHICAGO

1. C. R. "Jack" Kopp

It has become part of the Chicago adman's ritual to say, "Things sure have changed since Leo died. It's all gone corporate," or better, "Oh yeah, I knew Leo," or, better yet, "Sure, I worked with Leo." It's like claiming you worked on the famous 7-Up Uncola campaign. Easy to say, hard to prove.

Jack Kopp, now chairman of the board and chief executive officer of Leo Burnett, really did know and work closely with Leo Burnett. Kopp came to the Burnett agency in 1955 and worked as an account executive. He still has the reputation along Michigan Avenue of being a whiz at company-client relations. Kopp, who is pushing sixty, is only the third chief executive officer that the forty-four-year-old agency has had: the other two were Burnett himself and Philip H. Schaff, Jr., the powerhouse financial and administrative executive who now serves as vice-chairman and chairman of the executive committee.

Detroit-born Kopp brought an unusual background to the *bonhomie* of account executive: he attended the Illinois Institute of Technology from 1945 to 1947, and then studied management techniques at the Harvard School of Business Administration. Kopp rose quickly through Burnett ranks, moving from account executive to account supervisor in 1959, to vice-president in charge of client services in 1963, and to management director in 1967. He directed Leo Burnett's domestic operations as president of Leo Burnett USA from 1970 on.

In 1975, Kopp copped the No. 2 spot at Burnett, when Schaff ascended into the heavens of chairmanship. Kopp was made president and chief operating officer of the parent organization, Leo Burnett Company—the one that directs all domestic and international advertising operations and shells out forty thousand dollars a year to keep every reception room around the world stocked with a daily supply of red apples. Phil Schaff sent a memo to Leo Burnett employees describing Kopp's rise that made top management at Burnett seem as cautious and ordered as the succession to the British throne: "You can consider these moves for Jack Kopp and me to be a slow turning of the wheel of management succession. This is part of a continuing plan so that the transfer of top management responsibilities will continue to be smooth, gradual, and harmonious over the years."

The wheel at Burnett turned again in January, 1978, making Kopp the top man in Chicago's top agency, with Phil Schaff overseeing management from on high.

Genial Jack has always been an organization man. He belongs to several clubs: the Harvard, the Racquet, and the Tavern. He serves on the Chicago Crime Commission. During World War II, he was commissioned a first lieutenant in the army, winning both a Bronze Star and Purple Heart. And, as a youth, Chicago advertising's most powerful exec was a Boy Scout.

2. Arthur W. Schultz

Arthur Warren Schultz, chairman of the board of Foote, Cone, and Belding Communications, is Albert Lasker reincarnated. It's almost spooky. The visitor to Chicago's second largest ad agency sits in Schultz's office in the Equitable Building, and looks at a gallery of pictures on the wall that all feature an iron-haired, stern-browed man, shaking hands and thumping backs of dignitaries. In the midst of this Schultz shrine, there is one picture of advertising pioneer Albert Lasker (PR head Jean Boutyette explains that "Lasker was more interested in making money than in having his picture taken"). Lasker frowns down from the wall, looking like Arthur Schultz in a grim mood.

Schultz looks and sounds like a patriarch. He has a gift for making the simplest comments seem like Pronouncements From On High. Schultz describes the line of succession at Foote, Cone, and Belding in almost Biblical terms: "Foote, Cone, and Belding is 106 years old and it's had only four managements: Lord and Thomas, Albert Lasker, Fairfax Cone, and me. I learned advertising from Fairfax Cone, and he learned advertising from Albert Lasker. And Albert Lasker invented advertising. That's a pretty straight line, right here in old Chicago town."

Arthur Schultz was born in New York City on January 13, 1922. He's a year younger than Burnett's Howard Shank, but looks like an Old Testament prophet. Schultz served as first lieutenant in the air force during World War II; after the war he attended the University of Chicago. Schultz has been with Foote, Cone, and Belding since 1948; he joined as a copywriter, served as vice-president from 1957 to 1963, and became chairman of the board in 1970.

Schultz is also a power in Chicago society. He's been a trustee on the Art Institute board since 1975, and a member of the board of directors for the Lyric Opera since 1967. He belongs to the Racquet Club, the Economic Club, the Commercial Club, and the Barrington Hills Country Club near his home in Barrington.

From 1965 to 1971, Schultz held an unusual position for an advertising executive and arts associate. He was director of the Chicago Crime Commission, the citizen's group formed in 1919 to combat organized crime in Chicago.

Arthur Schultz's first loyalty is to his ad agency. He likes to talk about the triumph of Shirley Polykoff, the Foote, Cone, and Belding creative staffer who invented the tag line, "Does She or Doesn't She?" for Clairol hair dyes. Schultz points to Shirley Polykoff's autobiography, called *Does She or Doesn't She and How She Did It* as a grand example of the Foote, Cone, and Belding spirit: "I have her book here, because she says something in it which is so wonderful. Her husband was dying. And his last words to Shirley were, 'Never leave Foote, Cone, and Belding.'"

3. William F. Ross

Bill Ross' claim to fame in advertising creative circles is the classic "Uncola" campaign he devised for the 7-Up Company in 1968—a concept that turned 7-Up's image around from something you pour into Seagram's Seven to the perfect counterculture carbonation, and that upped the corporation's sales by 50 percent within one year. (Of course, now that 7-Up has fired J. Walter Thompson, the largest ad agency in the world acts like 7-Up is the Uncompany.)

Ross, president of J. Walter Thompson, Western Division, represents a Chicago advertising tradition: he's a creative guy (he began at J. Walter Thompson in the 1950's as a copywriter) who has made it into top management. Since he rose to president, Western Division, in 1977, Ross has managed J. Walter Thompson's Chicago office—an assemblage of some four hundred great minds who plot campaigns and land clients from their base on five floors of the Hancock Building. Ross is also responsible for J. Walter Thompson operations in San Francisco, Los Angeles, and Honolulu.

Ross, who's reached the half-century mark, has lived in Chicago for years, but he was born in New York. He still remembers what it was like to discover life west of the Hudson: "I grew up thinking that New York was the center of the universe. One of the biggest shocks I had when I left New York was finding out that what was in New York wasn't necessarily in the rest of the country. I thought all cities were like New York. The first time I went to Baltimore, I kept waiting for Baltimore. It didn't occur to me that you could have a city without skyscrapers."

Bill Ross still oozes New York. The slim, black-haired, elegantly dressed boss of J. Walter Thompson-Chicago could have been the model for every Tony Randall movie ever made. Ross speaks softly and phrases his opinions with the care you'd expect of an ad executive making a pitch to the staff of the Oxford English Dictionary. One of Ross's convictions is that advertising is art: "To us, good advertising not only sells, but has added aesthetic values. It's like architecture. Good architecture doesn't just make the doors big enough, but it adds something for the soul."

Ross also philosophizes about what makes advertisers tick: "I consider us advertisers professional dilettantes. We like to know a little bit about everything, but not a whole hell of a lot about any one thing. We're a curious people."

4. Norman Muse

Muse, executive vice president of U.S. creative services at Leo Burnett, is as Midwestern as they come. He's handsome, square-jawed, with a direct gaze and that peculiar Leo Burnett trait of looking uncomfortable in a suit.

Muse, now in his mid-forties, spent his youth in Iowa. He graduated from Iowa State, with a B.A. in Journalism and Psychology. Before coming to Chicago, Muse worked in Cedar Rapids: first as a copywriter for the W. D. Lyons Company and later as assistant promotion manager for KCRG-TV.

Muse's career took him all the way from the Midwest farmlands to Paris—after joining Leo Burnett in 1960 as a copywriter, he moved quickly through the ranks: copysupervisor gave way to associate creative director, which led to membership on the Board of Directors, a seat on the corporate financial committee, creative review chairman, executive creative director, and ultimately, to the position of managing director for Europe and the United Kingdom for Leo Burnett Inc., headquartered in Paris.

Muse was summoned back to the farmlands abruptly in April of 1979 after he had headed the European connection for one year. A seismic shake-up of the Leo Burnett top management had Howard Shank retiring from his post as president and creative chief. Muse was called upon to assume the U.S. creative services mantle vacated by Shank—Muse denied any interest in assuming the presidency of Leo Burnett.

The creative Muse's return to Chicago is heralded by many Leo Burnetters as the beginning of an advertising Renaissance at Burnett. Many ad people have criticized Leo Burnett for going the way of the big account management dominated agencies; Muse's leadership is a victory for the creative powers over the account moguls. As one former Burnett worker told *Advertising Age*: "The people in creative (at Burnett) are probably overjoyed. Muse has been one of the creative stalwarts, big on Leo Burnett being a creative agency. Muse was their great white hope. And they were so depressed because account had taken over the agency."

5. *Ralph Rydholm and Keith Reinhard*

A few decades ago, creative men made the fortunes of ad agencies, pulled down the kind of money only seen by movie stars or ward heelers, and were treated royally. Today, when one-man shops have been replaced by gigantic advertising corporations, the directors of the big ad agencies like to downplay the notion that they might be dependent on a few creative people with a steady supply of bright ideas.

"We've got a ton of creative people here, just a ton," insists the head of a top Chicago agency, "I can't begin to single out any one person. We just don't have that old star system anymore."

But two names do keep recurring: Ralph Rydholm, senior vice-president and executive director at J. Walter Thompson, and

Keith Reinhard, executive director in charge of creative services at Needham, Harper, and Steers. We list them together because we simply don't know which to put ahead of the other.

Reinhard is credited with solidifying the spectacular growth of Needham, Harper, and Steers. The Michigan Avenue consensus is that, with the help of Reinhard, Needham has been coming up with the finest creative work in the business: Needham's commercials for McDonald's are already considered classics. Reinhard also has helped devise winning campaigns for creme rinses, shaving creams, and rug cleaners. Reinhard's wife, Rose-Lee Reinhard, serves as senior vice-president and management representative of Needham. In 1977, *Chicago Tribune* columnist George Lazarus put both the Reinhard stars in his list of ad men and ad women of the year.

Ralph Rydholm, the creative mastermind of J. Walter Thompson-Chicago, is a favorite subject of Michigan Avenue's tirelessly played game, the game of "How Much Do You Think He Makes?" Rydholm's a legend already, and he's only in his early forties. He's got expertise; *Who's Who in Advertising* listed his areas of special competence as "copy, marketing, toiletries, cosmetics, food, and beer." And Rydholm's got an independent streak. Instead of just ensconcing himself in the city's swankier clubs, Rydholm is a member of the Chicago Council on Foreign Relations and the Independent Voters of Illinois.

6. Barbara Gardner Proctor

In 1970, Barbara Proctor, president and creative director, Proctor and Gardner Advertising, founded one of Chicago's hottest black consumer-market shops. Today, Proctor and Gardner handles a hefty $6.6 million in annual billings and is ranked with two other notable black ad agencies: Burrell Advertising and Vince Cullers Advertising, Inc.

Proctor made the move to running her own agency because, as she once told *Daily News* interviewer Patricia Moore, she couldn't stand working for the "corporate bitch" that inhabited every agency she every worked in. Proctor decided to "be my own corporate bitch."

Proctor was the first black woman in the U.S. to own and operate an ad agency. She's been listed by *Business Week* as one of the one hundred top corporation women in the country and by *Ebony* in a grouping of one thousand highly successful blacks. According to Proctor, the ad game doesn't welcome blacks. She once told the *Chicago Defender* that, "As large as the major firms are, they engage in petty and underhanded things to keep black firms from getting contracts."

Proctor has a jazzy background. After coming to Chicago from Black Mountain, North Carolina, she took an inventory job in a record store owned by late-night deejay Sid McCoy just so she could meet him. Proctor found jazz as well as McCoy and became a music critic for *Downbeat* magazine, where she profiled people like Cannonball Adderley, Ray Charles, and Nancy Wilson. She then worked for VeeJay Records and landed the first U.S. record contract with the Beatles.

Barbara left the music business and entered advertising because it was uncomfortable being in the same business as her ex-husband and also because she wanted a new challenge: "I can say anything in three thousand five hundred words, but can I do it in eighty?"

Proctor-Gardner is one of the few one-person creative shops left in Chicago. Proctor has won big, so big that architect Bertrand Goldberg, who designed elaborate enterprises like Marina City, has taken on a tiny little project for Barbara: he's converting Proctor's twenty-two-room duplex penthouse on the South Shore to a simple seven rooms.

7. *Charlotte Beers*

Next to Jack Kopp, account executive emeritus at Leo Burnett, Charlotte Beers is the hottest account lander and handler in the city. J. Walter Thompson has a reputation for treating each client as if it occupies the center of the cosmos. Beers, senior vice-president and director of client services for JWT, deserves a lot of credit for this.

Even in a fast business, Beers had a fast rise at J. Walter Thompson. She started there as an account representative in 1969, was made a vice-president and account supervisor one year later, and in 1973 became the first woman accorded the status of senior vice-president in J. Walter Thompson history.

Much of Charlotte Beers's success stems from her peacemaking skills. In a business where every ego has elephantiasis, this kind of ability can save whole departments. When Charlotte accepted the title of Woman of the Year from the Woman's Advertising Club of Chicago in 1975, she told the group, "I hit this agency when the account people were in turmoil. Some account people didn't want to dirty their hands with the creative side and I thought that was pointless."

Charlotte Beers is account executive to the core. When she was asked to what she owed her success, upon receiving the 1975 Advertising Woman of the Year award, Charlotte promptly responded, "I've been lucky because I haven't had any crummy products to sell."

8. Carol H. Williams

Carol Williams, vice-president and creative director of Leo Burnett, is one of the brightest and most forceful personalities in Chicago advertising. She came up through the ranks at Burnett to her present position as the first woman and first black vice-president at Burnett (an outstanding accomplishment in itself; blacks are notoriously underrepresented in Chicago ad agencies). She holds a Ph.D. in psychology from Northwestern University, and she's won a clutch of awards, including the title Chicago Ad Woman of the Year.

Ms. Williams grew up in a housing development on the South Side and has written several scripts for *Good Times*, the national TV show that brought comedy to the Chicago ghetto. Her first job after college was working on entries for the massive Sears, Roebuck catalog. Now, Williams directs a crew of ten copywriters and takes charge of accounts like Pillsbury Foods and Procter and Gamble deodorants.

Carol Williams claims she made it so far in Chicago's biggest agency by ignoring the advice of others. In a *Sun-Times* interview, Ms. Williams reported, "I've been told what I could not do, being black, being a woman. When I came into this business, I was told I could not make it. Having been told since Day One what I cannot do since I'm black, I'm doing what I can do."

9. Don Tennant

Don Tennant, chairman and creative director of Don Tennant Co., Inc., is an old Leo Burnetter. He was director of creative services at Burnett from 1950 to 1970. From 1964 on, as executive vice-president for creative services, Tennant was second in command to Burnett in things creative. Tennant has that Leo Burnett style—he's open, friendly, has a non-slick surface, and likes to wear open-necked, short-sleeved checkered shirts.

Tennant is succeeding at the near-impossible in modern advertising: keep afloat a small creative shop. A couple years after Burnett died, Tennant left the agency and formed his own. Don Tennant Company is less than huge; it has $12 million in billings, five clients, and a staff of twenty-five. But Tennant believes his shop's smallness is a plus. He has fewer people working on accounts, a departure from the hordes that handle a single account in big agencies, and Tennant is a diehard critic of corporate advertising. "I felt there was a place for me to start, even though I started late. There's a vacuum, especially in this town, of hot creative shops. Advertising has gotten too corporate and top-heavy."

Tennant, now in his late fifties, likes to immerse himself in all aspects of advertising. He produced shows for NBC-TV from 1947 to 1949 and headed the TV-commercial department at Burnett. He has written and produced TV dramas and is a community theater buff (he's directed, produced, done set designs for, and acted in plays put on by a Chicago Heights drama group).

But Tennant also runs his own agency to spite the corporate stranglehold on Chicago advertising. Tennant talks freely about how Burnett hated slickness of all kinds. Tennant feels Burnett would feel at a loss on today's Michigan Avenue: "In the old days Leo Burnett disliked places like J. Walter Thompson and McCann Erickson. He felt they were just big factories. I think Leo might be distressed today if he could come back and take a look at Burnett, for instance, because Burnett has become very big and very professional and very client-service and financially oriented. They still turn out very good work, but now they're more closely akin to J. Walter Thompson than to what they once were."

10. Lee Flaherty

In Chicago, it always pays to run with the right people. Lee Flaherty, chairman of the board and president of Flair Merchandising Agency, runs along the lakefront every morning, often with ex-Mayor Bilandic. Since 1977, Flaherty has hosted the

Mayor Daley Marathon—a twenty-six mile run that has attracted ten thousand runners and lots of media attention, all done in the name of the globular, non-running man who used to run Chicago. For some reason, Flaherty and Mayor Byrne have announced a new name for the event: America's Marathon/Chicago.

Flaherty heads the largest merchandising operation in the world. Flair Merchandising specializes in putting the right packages and promotions around products, in setting up point-of-purchase displays, or, as one Flair observer puts it, "They sell cardboard."

The home base for the company is a renovated turn-of-the-century mansion on Erie Street, a three-story brick structure built by millionaire milk merchant Marcus Devine. Flair Merchandising is the only ad agency in the city that has stained-glass windows, Baccarat-glass chandeliers, a sixteenth-century monk's cabinet in the conference room, and an art department paneled with solid oak lockerroom doors from an 1890 Catholic girls' school.

Flaherty is a self-made millionaire. He lives in a Gold Coast apartment, is chauffeured about in a chocolate-brown Rolls-Royce, often wears velvet suits, sends his daughter to the Latin School, and pals around with people like Bilandic, the Daley boys, and Bonnie and John Swearingen.

Flaherty bills the Marathon as the "People's Race." Some people wonder if Flaherty may be considering running for something himself.

16

Bureaucracy

I f Chicago is the city that works, and it works most of the time, then the bureaucrats in that city must be different than the ones in New York or Cleveland or countless other places that do not work. They are. If nothing else, they're always watching each other. They know that, whatever they do, the mayor will know about it.

There are forty-two thousand city workers in Chicago. Their primary chores are to spend the $1.3-billion annual budget, be loyal and productive precinct workers, and not get caught at anything.

Interestingly, the cozy political relationship of the bureaucracy to the Democratic Party begins at the lowest levels and dissipates as it moves toward the top. The department heads, with few exceptions, are professional administrators who may have got their start as a result of some committeeman getting them a job but otherwise maintain low political profiles. The majority of them worked their way up the ladder, staying as neutral as possible and taking care not to offend anyone in political power. They became department heads because of their nonpolitical posture rather than in spite of it. Daley was always careful to make sure that cabinet-level officials held no political strength. The danger of a committeeman running a massive city department and unilaterally filling jobs to enhance his own political power was too great. Witness the trouble Jane Byrne is having with Park Superintendent Ed Kelly.

It is startling, especially in Chicago, to note that most of the appointments made by Daley, Bilandic, and Jane have been laudable. In the middle of the nation's biggest, most dictatorial political machine is a group of apolitical people who keep the streets clean, the garbage collected, the alleys lit, and the water safe. That is immensely important to the machine since it helps convince that large segment of the public whose vote is not controlled to keep reelecting the Democratic slate.

But there are other factors that have helped make Chicago the city that works. One of them was the Great Fire of 1871. Another was the typhoid epidemics of the 1890's.

The fire was a primitive but handy form of urban renewal that allowed Chicago to dispose quickly of massive areas of dilapidated buildings and haphazardly conceived street plans. The problems with typhoid and other diseases relating to poor water treatment led to the creation of the Sanitary District, which crept out early one morning in 1900 before federal authorities could do anything to stop it and reversed the flow of the Chicago River, sending the city's sewage away from Lake Michigan and toward such places as Joliet, Iowa, and Missouri, where the vote didn't count.

Reversing the river's flow was regarded as one of the century's great engineering feats. It has also allowed the city to pour green dye into the river on St. Patrick's Day. Instead of emptying into Lake Michigan, the green water blends nicely with the oil slicks and yellow crud downstream.

Keeping the sewage out of the lake and preserving the lakefront combined to give Chicago a unique asset. No other city has the expanse of waterfront parks and recreation areas that Chicago offers to its residents. And the green, uncluttered lakefront provides an aesthetic setting for the gleaming skyscrapers and luxury high-rise apartments. It is to the credit of every Chicago boss from "Big Bill' Thompson to Daley that the lakefront wasn't jammed with warehouses and commercial buildings. They must have been advised by real-estate associates that lake-view apartments would bring higher rentals.

The Sanitary District's historic association with refuse continues to the present day. A number of its elected board members have been sent off to federal jails for pocketing envelopes full of money waved about by gravel-and-sand peddlers and the like.

Daley's long reign, however, was by far the most important factor in the formation of the well-functioning bureaucracy. Until a recent change in the city's personnel code, no one ever held a job permanently. People could be booted out of extremely cushy jobs for a variety of reasons. The most flagrant was failing to deliver the vote, but incompetency in a key position was also frowned upon, and any conduct that might embarrass the mayor was grounds for immediate dismissal.

Of course, some jobs require no competence at all. City Hall has always kept a force of elderly fellows on the first floor whose sole duty is to watch which elevators are going up. Then, they solemnly point toward the empty door or the white lights above the door and proclaim, "Going up." They often miss a lot of the doors but it seems most people manage to get on the elevator anyway.

These are among the most prestigious of patronage jobs since the elevator pointers are certain to see the mayor every day. This magnifies their importance back at ward and precinct gatherings when they are casually asked, "How are things in the Hall?"

"Pretty good, da mare was in a fine mood today." Or, "Something must be up, da mare seemed a little concerned when she talked to me this morning." What da mare probably said was "Hi," but in Chicago, that's important.

If they kept to the straight and narrow, Daley provided great security for the people he placed in jobs. His continual reelections stabilized the bureaucracy and insured continuity in all city departments. When death or retirement removed a key department head or assistant, none of the fears of upheaval that often occur in other cities and in private industry were in evidence at City Hall, because no one goes into any office or agency with a broom except the mayor.

The new personnel code prohibits firing without cause and a federal order prohibits firing employees because they failed to contribute twenty-five dollars to their committeeman's annual golf outing. But the threat of transfer or being blocked from further promotions still motivates precinct workers.

While Daley insulated the bureaucratic hierarchy from the committeemen, he left enough job openings to ensure the committeeman autonomy in his own ward. One example is the system of ward superintendent, which enables the committeeman to care for his constituents in that special manner that ensures big pluralities.

Each ward has a superintendent who theoretically works for the Department of Streets and Sanitation. He is supplied workers, equipment, and services by that department, but he maintains an office in the ward and in reality works for the committeeman who appointed him. Byrne launched a purge of some ward superintendents almost immediately after taking office.

In the midst of a snowstorm, the Department of Streets and Sanitation can provide as many snow plows and salting trucks as it has available on an equitable basis. But it doesn't, as it didn't in the 1979 blizzards. Some wards are more equal than others and anyone who can add votes on the day after election can usually name these wards. Those ward superintendents are more likely to have snow-removal equipment on a priority basis, and it is up to the ward superintendent to make some discerning decisions about deployment. Namely, which precincts are more equal than others, and which streets are the preferred ones. The committeeman's house is usually the most preferred of all.

Only one committeeman holds a major bureaucratic post in Chicago. Ed Kelly, general superintendent of the Park District, had been working his way up in the district when he got the idea to run for committeeman of the 47th Ward on the Northwest Side where Republicans had one of their few strongholds. Daley gave Kelly his blessing because he recognized that Kelly, with the strength of his Park District post, might somehow be able to take over the ward from the GOP. He did. Spectacularly.

Other committeemen hold slightly less important bureaucratic posts, such as West Side boss Ed Quigley, who heads the Bureau of Sewers, but Kelly is the only one at the top of a major department. Committeemen do have certain areas of influence but the standard rule is that a committeeman can personally control only 15 percent of the jobs that he has direct authority over. This means someone like Kelly could have nearly four hundred Park District employees from his own ward. Others, like Vito Marzullo and Matthew Bieszczat, who have been entrenched in power for years, have had as many as six hundred.

The spheres of influence were decided decades ago based on immigration patterns. The Irish were in Chicago first and they had priority on the police and fire departments. But their basic employment was, in Chicago jargon, "on the cars." The Irish were the conductors and drivers for the Chicago Transit Authority, which meant the trolley cars, buses, and elevated rapid-transit lines. Many of them graduated from "the cars" to the police and fire departments, but they zealously guarded their CTA priorities and it wasn't until after World War II that Italian or Polish could drive a bus.

The small but influential German-American community had the post office, which in earlier years was a pleasant and secure place to work. The Italians had first dibs on Streets and Sanitation, where there were good paying masonry and inspector positions. Eastern Europeans who arrived last wound up with laborer spots in all the departments.

As more and more blacks began to move into the bureaucracy in the 1950's and 1960's, they preempted health and social-services agencies and the corrections jobs at the county jail. As the Irish abandoned "the cars," the jobs were taken over by blacks, who also replaced the Germans in the postal positions.

Unlike the major components of the establishment in Chicago, various agencies of the bureaucracy tend to operate independently, bound only by the political thread connecting all city personnel.

The biggest agencies are the Police and Fire Departments, the Park District, the Board of Education, and the CTA. They are the most highly visible and therefore often troublesome segments of the bureaucracy.

The service departments, such as Streets and Sanitation, Public Works, and the various bureaus of sewers, water, and buildings tend to be powerful because they spend so much of the city's money.

There are also offices which serve in advisory capacities to the mayor, such as the budget director, corporation counsel, and the heads of purchasing, revenue, and personnel. These positions always have the potential to be powerful and influential because of their proximity to the mayor, but they have no base of power outside of the mayor.

All the bureaucrats have traditionally played an interesting money game with City Hall that provided the basis for Daley's reputation as a financial wizard and builder. Each department head was expected to turn back 10 percent of his annual budget, which the mayor could use for some new and wonderful civic purpose without ever seeming to be spending too much. Each department is also budgeted for more positions than are ever filled. This helps to provide the 10 percent surplus and also makes it convenient to quickly pop some deserving person into a job slot, or to promote someone without causing raised eyebrows.

The latter practice has been especially helpful in the police department, where promotions are based on written tests, efficiency ratings, and oral testing. If some heavy politician wanted a relative promoted to sergeant and that relative missed qualifying by a few positions, the list could always be expanded. For instance, if the original plan called for promoting twelve persons to sergeant, and someone's favorite was ranked fourteenth, the promotion list would be delayed until fifteen or perhaps sixteen sergeants were needed. The list never seems to end with someone whose political connections would make his promotion suspicious. That's why policemen joke that they are always happy to be the guy ranked after the guy who has the clout.

Few of the top-ranking bureaucrats ever attain public recognition or real political importance. Typical is Ted Dubiel, who works in Streets and Sanitation and captains one of the Northwest Side precincts that turn out Democratic pluralities like 350 to 6. Dubiel is the supervisor of "bulk trucks," which one Democrat explained "is not a very glamorous job unless your garage is full of shit."

Each ward has two or three bulk trucks—big dump trucks that haul away debris, bedsprings, or the remnants of a church bazaar or Democratic Party picnic. But two and three trucks are never enough for the committeemen to provide all the special services that make Chicago work. So when someone really needs to help out a contributor or a voter or a relative, Ted Dubiel is the guy who gets the call.

Jack Reedy, a honcho in the Department of Water and Sewers, is popular among politicians who need a favor for a local voter. Each winter, and especially since the energy crisis began, newspapers write stories about families who have their electricity or gas turned off because they couldn't pay the bills. Rarely does anyone ever have his water turned off, partly because the cost of water is relatively cheap in comparison to energy fuels.

But Jack Reedy hears about those people because he's the guy the committeeman or precinct captain calls to prevent someone having his water turned off. "There's no greater favor," one precinct captain said, "that you can do for somebody. You can live without lights and you can pile on a lot of blankets if the heat's off for a little while, but without water you can't even flush the toilet."

In other places, when someone unexpectedly finds he has no water, he calls a plumber. In Chicago, they call the ward headquarters.

"Even if it's Christmas Day, someone will show up and check what they call the buffalo box, which is the feed from the main water line to houses. If there's no problem, they'll tell the guy it's a break somewhere in his line. Then they'll let the committeeman know and if he's on the ball a plumber will magically appear at the house, and he won't gouge anybody," the precinct captain explained.

That's what makes Chicago work, or at least makes people think it does, which amounts to the same thing on Election Day.

THE TOP TEN BUREAUCRATS IN CHICAGO

1. Joe DiLeonardi

For Chicagoans, there is no more important service than police protection. For a number of Chicago mayors, no city department has been more of a political migraine headache than the police force as Mayor Byrne learned going through the early months of her administration with a virtually leaderless one.

She ousted Bilandic's police superintendent, James O'Grady (actually, he nimbly resigned before she could get to him) and purged some ranking officials, but was compelled to accept O'Grady's deputy, Samuel Nolan, as an interim acting superintendent when the City Council balked at her choice of a replacement: outsider Patrick Murphy, who bossed departments in New York, Detroit, and Washington, D.C. After kicking Nolan upstairs to head the new Office of Public Safety, she came up with a more popular choice for the top spot—the legendary "Joey D."

Throughout her campaign, when people were paying attention, Byrne swore to bounce O'Grady if she was elected because he had "politicized" the department. Yet by demanding that his replacement be absolutely her own choice, she strongly implied that the superintendent's first loyalty should be to the mayor, and so contradicted her own position. Some critics attribute her opposition to O'Grady as revenge, noting the long string of parking tickets she received during her visits to Jay McMullen's high-rise following her dismissal from City Hall.

The now 14,000-member Chicago police department has had a past as checkered as its patrolman's caps. The police corruption of the "Levee" era ruined Carter H. Harrison's mayoral reputation and Big Bill Thompson was scorned by the voters after they learned that many of the city's cops were on two payrolls: the city's, and Capone's.

It even happened to Daley, who suffered one of the worst crises of his career when it was disclosed in 1960 that a group of policemen from the Summerdale District on the North Side had been moonlighting as burglars. It was many months before a Chicago squad car could stop at a traffic light without someone snickering, "Got any good prices on televisions?"

The 1968 convention riots and the subsequent tavern shakedown scandals didn't help either. But these, too, did pass.

DiLeonardi is probably the most respected cop—by his fellow cops—in Chicago. The press and public think so, too. A streetsmart cop not unlike television's famed Kojak (as a homicide dick on Rush Street, he used to sport purple suits and shoes), DiLeonardi is highly regarded for his humanity and compassion. With him, the victim always comes first. As politically adept as he is popular, he is a good bet to keep the job a long time.

O'Grady was respected, but not necessarily liked by his men. Some of the grizzled veterans thought him a bit overzealous, pointing to such incidents as his taking a bullet once while chasing a purse-snatcher in his off-duty hours. Some of the rank-and-file were privately pleased with his ouster, feeling it would signal an end to Irish domination of the department's upper echelons. Yet, sure and begorah, even the ranking black on the force has the name Nolan.

2. Donald Haider

If Jane Byrne somehow succeeds in keeping her promises to rebuild the city's neighborhoods and hold down taxes, Donald

Haider could be the single most important member of her cabinet. Under Daley and Bilandic, the city budget director wielded considerable political influence in the inner circle. Haider's academic credentials would seem to bely any sort of political background, but some people pick things up fast and, for the first years of the Byrne regime, he will be the moneyman.

A native of Wilmette, Haider is in his late thirties, an unusually cultured man for such prominence in the Chicago apparat, and a reputed genius at grappling with federal funding, of which Chicago continues to need a great deal. His record at Stanford University was impressive.

When Edward Bedore, an 11th Warder, ran the budget department, the job included taking charge of the regular organization's vote tabulating apparatus on election nights in the crowded basement Greenbriar Room of the Bismarck Hotel. He was also responsible for supervising city workers, employing two-way radios and lightning raids to make sure they weren't lounging in saloons or playing cards all day.

Haider does not seem bound for such a grubby role. However, while academically discoursing on New York's fiscal problems, he noted that the Big Apple's congressmen were much more interested in world affairs than in bringing home the goodies. That's philosophy to endear him to Jane and the boys.

3. Ed Kelly

Until Jane Byrne got into City Hall, Ed Kelly, the only party committeeman with a major bureaucratic post, was the most powerful bureaucrat in the city. By the time she leaves, he could be out on the street himself. Time will tell.

Kelly has 3,000 jobs in the Park District under his supervision and his patronage clout has given him the overt respect of all his party peers. He certainly has entree to all the established power cliques in the city. But Mayor Byrne decided upon him as her No. 1 political target after her inauguration. She demanded that he turn over all his patronage to George Dunne and, when he refused, announced (at a Washington cocktail party of all places) that she would fire him.

Kelly's lawyer, the ubiquitous Don Reuben, noted that Kelly

had a statutory term of office running until 1981 and that he could not be so cavalierly fired. Also, the federal courts frown on words like patronage these days. So, the two are at a stand-off. Whether Kelly decides to challenge Dunne, now a Byrne favorite, for the party chairmanship in 1980 may ultimately decide his fate.

Byrne did manage to oust two of the five Park District board members who had appointed Kelly, and threatened to deal similarly with board president Patrick O'Malley, another Kelly supporter. But O'Malley may have too much clout for her to get away with it. Despite all this, Byrne did agree to Kelly's plan for a thirty million dollar refurbishing of Soldier Field, an inexpensive alternative to the new sports stadium proposal that Bilandic was so excited about.

Kelly is a professional in the field of sports recreation and has won praise for Park District programs ranging from pinochle tournaments for senior citizens to ice skating races for the more sprightly. A federal grand jury looked into charges that some Soldier Field rock concert contracts looked a little funny, but nothing came of it. The closest Kelly seems to have come to scandal was *Sun-Times* columnist Mike Royko's discovery that he made private steam rooms in the stadium available to friends and political cronies. Kelly got out of that one, uh, clean.

4. Degnan & Company

If the stunning defeat of Michael Bilandic proved anything after the great snows of '79, it was that the Department of Streets and Sanitation could be even more of a political liability to a mayor than the Police Department. For a while, it looked as though Francis "Bud" Degnan, a forty-year veteran and head of the department, was going to bear the blame for the snow removal fiasco.

But Jane executed a political pirouette after her election and said that Degnan had been hampered by the Bilandic administration and that she wanted him to continue to head the department. She also hinted that Robert Marzullo, whose father, Alderman Vito, was among the very first to pledge his fealty to Jane, would be next in line, but then gave the job to Degnan's son, Tim.

A native of the South Side, Degnan still lives at 71st Street and Sacramento. His father was from the 14th Ward and his father-in-law from the 11th Ward. He had a reputation in the Hall for integrity and conscientiousness. His job was mainly to repair and salt the streets, fix the potholes, cement the crumbling curbs, make certain the street lights work, and keep the trees trimmed. If his department has kept the Better Government Association anti-loafer patrol busy over the years, it still performs better than most cities'.

To help Degnan improve efficiency a little, Jane fired three ward superintendents and suspended several others she claimed were not cleaning their wards adequately. Later, she was compelled to move Tim Degnan out of the job because of gambling debts, replacing him with career man, John Donovan.

5. Tom Kapsalis

Lewis Hill, a talented, arrogant, and politically clever fellow, remained a most powerful bureaucrat even after Daley's death. As boss of the Department of Planning and Development, he could demolish entire blocks with a single order, and have considerable say about what went up in their place. "If Chicago works because the business, labor, and political establishments can all get together," said one City Hall observer, "then the place they met was in Lew Hill's office."

But the end for Hill came in October, 1978, when he was rewarded with, or exiled to, the chairmanship of the Regional Transportation Authority, in which post he could supervise the transfer of tax dollars from the pockets of McHenry County farmers to those of Chicago Transit Authority motormen. Anyway, the job gave him a $35,000 raise over his old $46,000 city salary, and much less to worry about.

Hill had little to do with the selection of his successor, Tom Kapsalis, who worked in various planning and public works positions for twenty years. Kapsalis' future was uncertain after Byrne's primary victory, but a delegation from Chicago's Greek community visited her new nibs at City Hall and expressed their desire that Kapsalis remain a key figure. Kapsalis stayed.

But the power of Planning and Development may be downgraded and diffused somewhat by Byrne's creation of a strange new Department of Neighborhoods. The grandiose schemes and plans of the likes of Hill may become things of the past in a period of marked austerity, if Byrne shifts all the spare cash she can to the city's outlying neighborhoods.

6. Richard Albrecht

Of all the ethnic names bandied about in Chicago politics, none is so important as "Chinaman." The "Chinaman" has nothing to do with Orientals; it is Chicagoese for a political sponsor, a person who promotes someone's career and sees to it that the road to success remains unobstructed.

There were two questions asked when former Mayor Bilandic picked Richard Albrecht to replace the late Robert Quinn as fire commissioner: Who is he? And, who's his Chinaman?

(Albrecht's name, incidentally, was not pronounced in the normal way. He called himself "Allbright," which sounded Irish and thus made him seem like someone qualified to run the fire department.)

As far as anyone knows, he doesn't have a Chinaman. He is just another of the faceless, up-by-the-bootstraps bureaucrats who worked every job in the department and seemed an ideally apolitical substitute for the aging, erratic Quinn when it came time for Bilandic to retire him.

Quinn had few known goals in life aside from pleasing Richard Daley. He created a fire department band after Daley remarked how much he liked parades. When Quinn set off all the air raid sirens after the White Sox won the pennant in 1959, he probably thought it would please Daley. A physical fitness enthusiast and one of the best handball players in the city, Quinn set squads of firemen to jogging down the median strip of the Kennedy Expressway to demonstrate the joys of running to commuters. All they did was stop traffic.

Quinn was admired by his men, though. He never failed to show up at a major blaze if he was in town, always wearing the charred and ragged fireman's hat that was his trademark for years. He never hesitated to go into burning buildings if his men were inside and he wouldn't stand around watching if they needed help dragging lines.

He is believed to be responsible for Chicago's only contract to provide fire protection to a suburb. The suburb of Lincolnwood, just north of the city, entered into an agreement with the Chicago Fire Department shortly after Quinn moved his elderly mother to a home there.

The fire department generally is praised by Chicagoans. It doesn't have much potential for scandal, as there isn't much to steal there. Many firemen have obtained trade union cards and use their off-days to work as carpenters, painters, or electricians. It isn't unusual to see a division fire marshall standing on a ladder with a bucket of paint on his day off. However, some union groups have grown increasingly irritated with firemen who have dropped their memberships but continue doing part-time work.

Albrecht lives in the Northwest Side neighborhood of Edgebrook, which harbors legions of bureaucracy and government bosses. He came through his first leadership test with winning marks in 1978, when he resolved a threatened strike by firemen demanding, as always, collective bargaining rights. One thing he can't do anything about is their continuing demand for permission to live outside the city. Maybe they all want to go to Lincolnwood.

7. Joseph Hannon

During the unhappy open housing demonstrations of the 1960's, the late Martin Luther King and the late Richard Daley held a summit meeting. King tried to stress the plight of blacks by asking if Daley knew there were thousands of people starving in his city. The mayor, ever serious, replied: "Give me a list of their names."

King also noted at the time that Chicago was the most segregated city in the United States. That's why Joseph Hannon, superintendent of Chicago schools and 500,000 school children, is never going to have an easy time of it.

Neither of Hannon's predecessors was popular in Chicago because they could not adequately cope with the integration dilemma. Hannon, a Massachusetts native and one of the few outsiders to hold a top government post in Chicago, is trying desperately to make voluntary integration, his Access to Excellence plan, work. But so far, the threat that the federal government and state authorities will withhold funds remains. The feds are in the process of suing the city for failure to integrate, although a final decision by the courts could be a decade away.

Hannon was one of the few top city officials to win praise from Jane Byrne, probably because she understood he could not work miracles and more likely because she realized that one of the shrewder political decisions ever made by her mentor, Daley, was to never ever get involved with school problems.

Hannon, in his forties, won another four-year contract in 1978 and has won plaudits for improving the basic reading skills of Chicago school children. He has also improved the financial condition of the school system, which has 50,000 employees and a $1.3 billion budget. He has little to do with politics. Although the mayor hand-picks Board of Education members through the charade of a nominating committee, the superintendent is traditionally on his own. Whites resent Hannon because he is the man who must devise integration schemes, and most whites are not fond of integration. Blacks are cool to him because they want one of their own installed as superintendent. But Hannon, a resident of the Hancock Center, has been able to keep the fires banked and has avoided any reoccurrence of the costly and troublesome turmoil that plagued his first few years as school boss.

8. *Eugene Barnes*

The blizzard that cost so many people their city jobs gave Eugene Barnes his. Barnes, a former bus driver who once led a strike against the CTA and a veteran member of the Illinois House, was Jane's choice to replace James McDonough as Chairman of the CTA. An effective legislator who often debated against regular Democrats, Barnes was among Byrne's first black appointees and an obvious choice to show the black community that she, too, felt the CTA operation (or lack of it) in the black community during the great snows was reprehensible.

Though shoving McDonough out of the CTA chairmanship as she had promised to do, she kept him on the board, a signal that she may have mended fences with one of the city's more influential men. While Barnes has the opportunity to become a vital part of Byrne's bureaucratic machinery, it is doubtful that he will ever match the power and influence of McDonough, who is well connected throughout the city power structure.

McDonough is an 11th Ward native whose late father was Richard Daley's political sponsor. Now president of C. F. Murphy Engineering, McDonough moves with equal familiarity through board rooms and ward rooms. He formerly headed the Streets and Sanitation Department. Byrne cited his part-time role as CTA chairman while president of the Murphy firm as one major reason for his removal.

9. William Griffin

During the first three months of the Jane Byrne administration, the man to see in Chicago's City Hall was William Griffin, the press secretary who emerged as chief of staff for politics, police department shuffling, etc. The job is now permanent.

Griffin, just into his thirties, left the Chicago *Tribune* political beat to take the $37,000-a-year post as press secretary. As ex-seminarian, he comes from a long line of Chicago policemen, including a father and brother, but resisted family efforts to enlist him in the profession. "I knew that 20 years down the road the last thing Chicago needed was another potato-faced Irish cop," he said.

Now he's in City Hall, up at the top of the team. In addition to such not-always-pleasant task as dealing with the Chicago news media, Griffin functions as advisor, confidante, and trouble-shooter. He has undertaken such varied tasks as negotiating city contracts and ordering Rosalynn Carter's favorite rosé wine for the dinner she had with Byrne.

Griffin came to know Jane as a reporter covering the taxi deal scandal, refusing at one point to put her accusations into print without attribution. She has come to lean heavily on his advice, especially as regards state and county politics. It was his suggestion that she name Michael Brady, a state representative from the city's Far North Side, as her liaison with the General Assembly and with Congress.

This position never existed before. Daley either simply gave orders to the troops or had "thoughts" that the legislative leaders somehow were to divine. Bilandic and his boys tried to operate the same way. Brady built a reputation as an expert on education, finance, and tax matters. He knows all about ward politics and is particularly skillful at settling disputes between large groups. He has ten children.

10. Paul McGrath

McGrath began the Byrne administration as her chief administrative aide, but moved into a role of office manager and community affairs advisor while Griffin operated in the political sphere. McGrath's predecessor, Thomas Donovan, was easily the most powerful man in government during the Bilandic regime, but the keys to patronage were not given to McGrath. Still, he is the mayor's top aide for some city functions, and to understand them better he spent three weeks at Harvard in the summer of 1979.

McGrath, in his early forties, signed on more or less to run Byrne's campaign after a brief stint of free-lance writing that followed years of employment with the Chicago *Sun-Times* and, before that, with the *Tribune*. Although he holds a good staff job with a salary of $48,000 a year, he has not been inordinately involved in many of Janey's early major decisions and has settled into a role as a liaison rather than policy maker.

He caused Byrne some embarrassment when it was disclosed that his girl friend, another Byrne supporter, had been given a fat job on the payroll.

17

Sports

In the century or so that professional sports have been played in Chicago ball parks, the nation's second city has had its share of memorable athletic events, most of them memorable for the wrong reasons.

Chicago and its sporting life is not to be compared with New York, where the Yankees and Babe Ruth created the most successful and storied legend of American sports. It is not to be compared with Boston and its Celtics or Los Angeles and its Dodgers or Philadelphia and its Flyers. It is not even to be compared with tiny Green Bay, Wisconsin, a professional sports base only because of the richness of a history filled with names like Don Hutson, Vince Lombardi, and Paul Hornung.

Chicago is different. It is a city of losers. Of perpetual losers, zany losers, shabby losers and happy losers. In many ways, it might as well be Omaha or Toledo. Soldier's Field is not the Astrodome. Chicago Stadium is not Madison Square Garden, the old or the new. Billy Goat's Tavern is not Toots Shor's.

But Chicago has had its legends. There were the 1919 "Black Sox" who were enshrined as the only team ever to throw a World Series, or for that matter, ever to fix a major sporting event, but that must be rated a hollow honor as no one before or since has tried.

Chicago was the setting for the Dempsey-Tunney heavyweight championship fight in 1927. There have been hundreds of such contests staged in cities from Shelby, Montana, to Kinshasa, Zaire, but only in Chicago did the referee screw up the count. Depending on which drunken sportswriter's memoirs one can believe, the count over a fallen Tunney was delayed between four and twelve seconds while the referee chased Dempsey to a neutral corner.

And there was the moment in 1959 when the White Sox won the American League pennant they had been chasing futilely ever since their Black Sox predecessors threw it away. But the city fire commissioner turned on all the air-raid sirens and instead of the populace cheering the pennant clinchers, they ran to their basements in terror of Russian bombers. By the time they crawled out again, the Dodgers had creamed the Sox in the World Series.

And there's the Cubs. And the Bulls. And the Black Hawks. And always the Bears. Lately there's something called the Sting and over the years there have been teams called the Rockets, the Wind, and the Fire; the Cardinals, the Packers, and the Zephyrs. The Zephyrs and the Wind were not related to the best of anyone's knowledge. They didn't even play the same sport, although from the records they compiled, it wasn't always easy to tell what sports they were playing.

Whatever they were, they all lost. Of all the institutions associated with sports in Chicago, Billy Goat's bar is the single winner and it had to move the franchise from across the street from the Chicago Stadium to a dark corner under Michigan Avenue where only newspapermen and delivery truck drivers can find it. Even Toots Shor's wall decor couldn't match one Billy Goat sign, which reads: "Pressmen do not sit on stools with greasy trousers."

If Chicago fans are reconciled to losing teams, they grow unrealistically ecstatic about superstars when on those rare occasions they have appeared in Chicago uniforms. They never booed Ernie Banks; they were in awe of Gale Sayers.

They braved the smoky heights of Chicago Stadium stands to shriek with delight at Bobby Hull sweeping up the ice; they recounted all through the week the sight of Dick Butkus crawling out from a tangle of players with the blood of someone's thumb dribbling down his chin. Four genuine superstars in thirty years isn't much of an autograph collection—especially when the Hawks said good-bye to Hull without even opening the door for him, and Sayers' career was abbreviated by injuries. Even in Ernie Banks' final days, there were more stories about Manager Leo Durocher hinting that Banks should quit than items about Banks' home runs, which came fewer and farther between.

Superstars never made winners in Chicago, probably because they never had any help. Chicago owners always appeared so startled to discover a gifted player on their teams that they remained in a catatonic trance—except when it came time to take the box-office receipts to the bank.

Only Hull's presence led to a major championship and the Hawks could win the Stanley Cup only once in his time. The Bears were always mediocre despite Sayers and Butkus. Their sole championship season in modern memory, 1963, was fashioned with people named Whitsell, Leggett, and Wade. The Sox of 1959 were such an undistinguished group that most of them were traded in two years.

Even the Cubbies of '69, those blunderers of summer, were a team of non-superstars. The Chicago fan has come to expect that the fingers of his heroes will never be cluttered with World Series or Super Bowl rings. He recalls the misery of Luke Appling playing two decades for a team that never once occupied first place, let alone win it. Chicago fans watched Jerry Sloan, a superstar of desire, bang his way up and down the Bulls' court eighty games a year only to hear every summer that he might be traded. They remember Butkus crashing, crushing, diving, kicking, and doing everything he could to convince his fellow Bears that football was a game you were supposed to win.

Most of all they remember the ones that got away.

"Remember when we traded Lou Brock for Ernie Broglio? Boy, was that dumb. . . . How about when the Bears had the three "L's," Luckman, Lujack, and Layne. We traded Layne and the other two retired."

There was Phil Esposito, whom the Hawks sent over to Boston, where he set all-time scoring records and led the Bruins to several titles. There were the Cub pitchers, Ken Holtzman and Burt Hooton, who have spent several autumns in the World Series since leaving Wrigley Field. And the Sox established some sort of a sports first in 1978. They fired Bob Lemon as manager. Lemon went to the Yankees where he became the American League manager of the year.

No team better exemplified the plight of Chicago sports better than the Cubs of 1969. They led the league all summer. They led by ten games with a month to go and even in Chicago, where they should have known better, some people actually expected them to win. They didn't, of course. And it's just as well. Truly dedicated fans take a perverse enjoyment in spending their winters moaning over the clumsiness of the Bears and their summers wincing and hooting at the Cubs and Sox. The Cubs surprising showing in 1979 traumatized them.

The fans are often commended for supporting their professional teams without regard to won and lost records, but that support is somewhat exaggerated.

Chicagoans, and particularly suburbanites, who rarely shell out the fifty it takes to bring a few kids to a hockey game, like to boast they are the most loyal fans in the nation. But they aren't. Chicago turnstiles don't click with the speed some civic boosters would have everyone believe. The Chicago area has a population of about seven million people who are no farther than thirty miles from any of the city's sports arenas. This is much larger than Detroit's or Philadelphia's available sports audience, and far greater than Cincinnati's or Kansas City's.

Yet Chicago teams only rarely outdraw their counterparts from those other cities. The sole exception is the Bears, who sell out every game because of professional football's current status as the class national game, and because every other NFL team sells out as well. Moreover, the people who buy football tickets are usually businessmen who pass them out as deductible enticements to associates. Judging from the amount of ticket-holders who don't bother to show up later in the season, it's likely that if Chicago ever does build a seventy-thousand-seat stadium, the Bears won't sell it out.

The Cubs are supposedly big draws in their ivy-covered Wrigley Field, where they have never had night lights or a good left-handed pitcher. But their lofty attendance figures of 1.6 million are a far cry from the 3.2 million the Dodgers drew in 1978 or the 2 million little Cincinnati jams in every year. But then the Dodgers and Reds have a habit of winning pennants, sometimes even World Series titles.

Nobody even bothers to brag about White Sox loyalty. The team was about ready to leave town in financial desperation when Bill Veeck showed up to bail it out four years ago. And despite all the promotions staged by master showman Veeck, the Sox don't draw unless they win. Their 1977 team, which had a strange penchant for hitting home runs in 1978 shrunk to Texas League singles and the attendance took a comparable dive.

Perhaps most satisfying to the fan who feels he has been gouged and deprived is the recent fate of the once-proud Black Hawks, whose pride disappeared when Hull left town. In the Golden Jet era of the 1960's, the standard attendance at the Stadium was 16,999, because that was all the fire laws permitted. But everyone knew those thousands of people standing in the aisles to watch Hull's slapshot ran to 20,000 or so. A Hawks' ticket in those days was tougher to find than a Republican.

Now, anyone can walk up to the Stadium gate at face-off time and buy one, and most people don't.

Black sports enthusiasts seem somewhat brighter than white ones. They are not so eager to squander their money on the quality of athletics displayed in Chicago. Comiskey Park, aging home of the White Sox, suffers from the myth that it is located in a "bad neighborhood," which means a black neighborhood. But its proximity to the Dan Ryan Expressway and public transportation makes it more accessible than most of the sports palaces, and the average Sox crowd indicates blacks prefer to wait for good baseball before buying tickets. Few blacks are seen at hockey games, probably because they weren't cultivated back in the days when the tickets were hoarded as items of great social esteem, and the prices are high. Even the Bulls, whose percentage of black athletes is higher than any team, are not overwhelmed by black spectators. If Jimmy Carter had tried to take sports tickets off expense accounts instead of the three-martini lunch, the Stadium's only sellouts would be ice shows and rock concerts.

Part of the problem is the quality of teams, part of it is the quality of the stadiums, and most of the problem is the odd and varied attitudes of the men who run Chicago sports.

In most cities, the great sports entrepreneurs either became financial successes or were driven out of the business. They were often replaced by men with the bank accounts of giants and the imaginations of little boys who wanted nothing more than to own a winning team. In many instances, they simply bought one. In so doing, they made even more money.

But Chicago is different. Its sports moguls are anachronisms. For a variety of reasons, they are unable to equate financial success with winning teams. In the case of Arthur Wirtz, who controls the Hawks and the Bulls, it is generally agreed that he doesn't really care. In the case of George Halas, who has been the only owner the Bears ever had, it has been said he was too tightfisted. In the case of the Wrigley family, which runs the Cubs, it was suspected that the team was a hobby, and in the case of Bill Veeck, who operates the Sox, it is agreed he doesn't have the dough.

But most fans who are disgruntled just simply say they are all too cheap. Whether the Chicago owners are in fact more interested in dollars than championships is impossible to prove, but the way they spend their money is clearly reflected in the caliber of the teams who play here.

And they are answerable to no one.

THE TOP TEN SPORTS FIGURES IN CHICAGO

1. George Halas

George Halas is Chicago sports. In a world where success counts in dollars, and dollars don't mean as much as they did yesterday, George Halas still counts his. He is not the wealthiest professional-sports-team owner in the country, or in Chicago. But he is the most powerful.

Other sports entrepreneurs can make money or buy an occasional championship, but George Halas is the only man alive who helped create a sport, and no one ever forgets that.

Halas, now in his eighties, didn't invent professional football, but he wet-nursed it, put up with its adolescent illnesses, went broke caring for it, and gave it integrity, excitement, and the love of a proud father. Then he sat back and watched it grow to a maturity he never believed possible, a success he had never imagined when he and a few friends sat on the running board of a touring car in Canton, Ohio, and decided that Americans would pay to see grown men play football.

Halas started out with a team called the Decatur Staleys. He owned, coached, and starred for the Staleys, whom he moved to Chicago in 1921 and named the Bears. It was Halas and his Bears who provided sports with a half-century of Sunday-afternoon excitement and Chicago fans with their proudest moments.

On Thanksgiving Day, 1925, Halas started professional football on its spiraling climb to the top of the sports world. He brought college football's most celebrated player, Harold "Red" Grange of Illinois, into Wrigley Field and thirty-six thousand people came out to watch him. He then barnstormed across the country taking Grange and the sport on a whirlwind tour that established both of them. Crowds showed up at train stations to see Grange and went away talking about professional football.

During the Depression, Halas kept the fledgling league alive by helping other owners with loans and players, and he created the first of his championship teams with such sports legends as Bronko Nagurski.

In 1940, Halas revolutionized the game with the introduction of the T-formation that added the glamour of the touchdown pass. In a playoff game that year, the Bears produced the most efficient display of offensive football ever seen with a 73 to 0 whitewash of the Washington Redskins. The next time the two teams played, the Redskins won.

The Bears of that era were also awarded the only nickname of prowess ever held with any longevity by a Chicago team. They were called the Monsters of the Midway and no one seemed to care that they had little to do with either the University of Chicago or the airport.

Television then brought the NFL to its peak and Halas was among the league owners who made certain that television paid for the right. The sport became so successful it grew into two leagues and eventually into the twenty-eight-team financial success it is today.

The years were good to the sport Halas created, but not so good to the team he owned. After forty years of running the Bears from the sidelines, Halas stepped down from coaching. He subsequently proved that while he knew how to coach, he didn't know much about hiring those who claimed they did. At the same time, the man who built a sport without a dime in his pocket wasn't about to spend millions on unproved collegians when the bidding wars began with the then-rival American Football League.

Many of Halas' aging colleagues felt the same way and the great young players of the 1960's wound up creating championship teams for the New York Jets, Miami Dolphins, Kansas City Chiefs, and Oakland Raiders. And the Bears, buoyed here and there by a Butkus, Sayers, or Walter Payton, won enough to be promising, but never enough to be contenders.

Halas finally gave up and turned the entire operation over to Jim Finks, the general manager who had been part of the Minnesota Vikings success. But after five years, and one brief flirtation with glory in the 1977 playoffs, the Bears seemed no closer to traveling the victory road they once knew so well.

Finks did move the Bears from their archaic offices to some fancy new digs, and he did convince Halas that Payton, the league's most valuable player in 1977, deserved to earn $500,000 a year. But Halas still must be wondering how he can be paying a man five-hundred dollars for every yard gained when he used to pay players that much for an entire game.

Halas is wealthy. He has a variety of investments and his notorious stinginess toward his football team is scoffed at by intimates who recall all the favors and dollars Halas made available to friends and players.

He never abandoned such close cohorts as Phil Handler and Luke Johnsos, who helped coach the Bears for as many years as they could stand up on the sidelines. His annual old-timers party is crowded by the men who played for him in the 1930's and 1940's, but there aren't too many old grads from recent years. Like most paternalistic rulers, "Papa Bear" Halas demanded loyalty and when he didn't get it, even from his most valuable aides and assets, he was an unforgiving man. He took George Allen to court rather than let him go free to become head coach of the Los Angeles Rams. He argued bitterly over paying Dick Butkus for the remaining years of his contract when Butkus insisted his knees were shot and his tackles were a thing of the past.

To younger fans and win-hungry supporters, George Halas also may be a thing of the past. But he owned a football team while Al Capone was still bouncing drunks at a South Side club. George Halas won a world championship while Richard Daley was still going to law school at night, and as long as he is around, George Halas will be Chicago sports.

2. Arthur Wirtz

Probably the richest professional owner in Chicago is Arthur
Wirtz, but he doesn't make his money hosting championship games.
Wirtz has never done anything to indicate that he has much interest
in whether the teams he operates, the Hawks and the Bulls, achieve
anything more than paying the rent.

The solitary Stanley Cup the Hawks won in 1961 doubtless never
cheered him as much as those signs on 1800 West Madison Street
that said "Sold Out." Rooms-to-let is his business and he's got the
only place in town that will seat twenty-thousand. But the Ice
Follies fill it easier than the Canadiens.

Many sportswriters don't like to talk about Wirtz in front of
small children. But businessmen and politicians say that he's a
pleasure to deal with. Everyone agrees the statistic that charms him
most is an earnings statement. Unlike a Halas or a Bill Veeck, who
will leave their sports with a lasting impression, if Wirtz attended
a league meeting he might be mistaken for the hotel owner, especially if the meeting were held in the Bismarck Hotel, which he
owns. He is a virtually invisible power in Chicago sports. He lives
at 1420 Lake Shore Drive, dresses in the manner of a man who is
worth many millions, and is the chairman of eight companies.
When it comes to controlling sports entertainment, Wirtz is easily
one of the most powerful men in Chicago.

But Wirtz, the son of a Chicago policeman, did not grow up
with any desire to create a sport or invent exploding scoreboards.
Wirtz wanted to fill rooms. In the 1930's, using his real-estate savvy
to purchase properties, Wirtz began accumulating a variety of
buildings. One that caught his eye was the Chicago Stadium, a
hulking piece of concrete stuck two miles directly west of the Loop
in an area of urban decay that few suburbanites would ever see
if pals didn't offer them a pair of Hawk tickets.

His partner was James Norris, the owner of the Black Hawks,
and the two men combined to get the team out of its doldrums.
Norris enjoyed the victories. Wirtz enjoyed the rent.

But the Hawks didn't play every night, and to make the Stadium
a profitable property, Wirtz used the national infatuation of the
1940's with ice skating. The shows starring Sonja Henie paid the

mortgage on the stadium and over the years, Wirtz has provided Chicago with the opportunity of watching Barbara Ann Scott, Peggy Fleming, Janet Lynn, and Dorothy Hamill.

And ice shows are always more pleasant than other events at the stadium because the lights are out much of the time.

There were other ways to put people in the stadium. Wirtz and Norris formed the International Boxing Corporation that promoted nearly fifty championship fights and a variety of others in the 1950's.

Still, the stadium had vacant seats. Professional basketball teams always struggled in Chicago, and usually disappeared. But with the help of national television in the 1960's, the National Basketball Association seemed solvent. Wirtz decided that if the Chicago Bulls were here to stay, they ought to be staying at the stadium, so he bought a piece of the team.

Wirtz splits gate receipts. The business of dealing with players and finding winners Wirtz leaves to other people.

3. Bill Veeck

In his "Second Coming" at Chicago, Bill Veeck is as unpredictable, popular, and dedicated to turning a buck as ever, but this time, there have been no sirens in the night. Bill Veeck loves baseball and he probably is the most knowledgeable owner in the game when it comes to players' skills and filling ball parks. And once or twice every thirty years, he manages to bring the two together.

Veeck is a promoter first of all. Baseball is merely the product he happens to be selling. His father, William Veeck, Sr., was general manager of the Cubs in the 1920's when they were actually pennant contenders. Veeck grew up inside ball parks. He operated teams in Milwaukee; the long departed St. Louis Browns (who still have a fan club in Chicago), and the Cleveland Indians. He's owned the White Sox twice. He knows baseball.

Better than baseball, he knows brass bands and fireworks artists, drummer boys and organists, and bat days and jacket days and helmet days, creaking legends and memorable midgets.

Veeck is somewhat of a legend of his own, not in a baseball sense like LeRoy "Satchel" Paige was when Veeck brought him to the majors in 1948 at the age of forty-five, long after his fastest pitches had been thrown in the Negro leagues. Nor is he as legendary as

Eddie Gaedel, the midget he sent up to pinch-hit for the Browns against Detroit one Sunday in 1951.

But Bill Veeck is the guy who keeps trying to fill ball parks. He is the guy who wouldn't wear neckties long before everyone decided that knit jerseys were socially acceptable; a guy who walks on one wooden leg with a hole carved in it to deposit the cigarettes he chain smokes throughout the day. He told writer William Brashler he estimates that four and a half years of his life have been spent in hospitals where he has undergone thirty-three operations on his legs, back, ear, knee and other spots. Everyone begins to die the moment they are born, but Bill Veeck seems to do it in bigger pieces than most people.

He spent the years between his White Sox days operating race tracks on the East Coast. If he had been raised in the shadow of Churchill Downs instead of Wrigley Field, the nation would probably have exploding parimutuel boards at every track.

When he left the White Sox the first time, Veeck's legacy included the 1959 pennant and the scoreboard in centerfield which goes into incendiary panic each time a Sox player drills one into the seats. But in Chicago, it is often left to a foreigner to create memorable moments, and the day the White Sox scoreboard really became a piece of baseball legend was when Casey Stengel of the Yankees responded to one of his player's homers by trotting out of the visitors' dugout waving a tiny, flashing sparkler.

Veeck's second time around with the Sox began in 1975, when Chicago feared their South Side team was in danger of becoming the Seattle Sox. Veeck came hustling to the rescue and the Hertz-Avis era of baseball began.

Working short of cash with a team destined to excite no one, Veeck shuddered at the salaries being demanded by players, who in 1976 were declared by the courts to be free from contracts binding them to one team. Veeck invented rent-a-player. Other owners let players depart if they couldn't afford them or spent millions to buy championships. Veeck simply rented his players, cheap.

He swapped the players whose salary demands he could not afford to teams similarly deadlocked with their stars. But he didn't sign his new players to contracts. Such clouters as Richie Zisk and Oscar Gamble, who contributed more than sixty home runs to the 1977 team, played that year for less than they earned in 1976, until by 1978 they were free at last to sign million-dollar pacts with teams who could afford them. In the spring of 1978, Veeck tried the same thing by getting Bobby Bonds in a trade, but when Bonds didn't bring anyone to the ball park, he and his free-agent status were quickly peddled to the Texas Rangers.

Since many of the game's best players took advantage of the free-agent status to sign lucrative, long-term contracts, few are now available and the Veeck era of rent-a-player is over.

Veeck began 1979, however, with a bullpen full of young, live arms and there were no assurances that some of the more promising pitchers wouldn't be sold for cash. Sox loyalists understand that Veeck is neither a Wrigley, nor a George Steinbrenner of the Yankees, nor a Walter O'Malley of the Dodgers, who in various ways have become millionaires. They know Veeck is back to hustle, have fun, make a buck, and hope the Sox can win more than they lose.

Veeck doesn't always hire managers for their genius at making out batting orders. When Lemon was fired in mid-season, Veeck didn't expect Larry Doby to transform a bunch of Punch-and-Judy hitters into Murderer's Row. He just hoped a few black fans might turn out to see baseball's only black manager. When Doby was given his farewell in October, it was probably because Veeck had counted the house at Don Kessinger's Fan Appreciation Night in September. If thirty thousand could show up to see a thirty-seven-year-old shortstop play, think how many might come back to see him play and manage, too.

Billy Martin, the volatile former and present manager of the New York Yankees, once defined winning numbers in baseball by observing that every team would lose fifty games and win fifty games. "It's what you do in the rest of the games that counts."

Veeck's winning numbers are up on the scoreboard, too. But they don't get there until after the seventh inning and they're marked, "Attendance."

4. William Wrigley

There are no exploding scoreboards at ivy-covered Wrigley Field. In fact, there is not even a modest, simple electrical scoreboard at Wrigley Field. There is a man who sits high up overlooking center-field who replaces cardboard numbers at the end of every inning, keeping track of all the zeroes. For all its charm and beauty, the major problem with Wrigley Field has been that the Cubs who live there accumulate more zeroes than their opponents.

William Wrigley III hopes that will change for good. But the latest of the Wrigleys to own the Cubs doesn't want much else to change. He believes his father, Philip K. Wrigley, was absolutely right in his refusal to install lights at Wrigley Field, the only major league park that plays all its games during daylight hours.

Wrigley, in his mid-forties, inherited the Cubs after his father's death in 1977. He's given no indication in that brief time that he will be any more visible than was his father, who usually watched the Cubs on television in his Lake Geneva estate. But that didn't deter P.K. Wrigley from involving himself with the team. Much of his involvement dealt with the hiring and firing of managers who consistently won less than they lost. But P.K. always added an interesting twist.

One year, he decided the Cubs should be treated the way colleges treat varsity teams, so he did away with the standard general-manager operation and created a post of athletic director. The Cubs still lost.

And there was his college of coaches. Instead of installing a single manager, Wrigley selected ten coaches to run the club on a rotating basis. The Cubs still lost.

The last time the Cubs won a pennant was 1945 and their World Series with Detroit is not so much remembered for its outcome as it is for the famous prediction made by the late sportswriter, Warren Brown, who said, "I don't think either team can win it."

Wrigley III is another of the unusual sports owners in Chicago. He grew up as a kid going to spring training and meeting just about everyone he wanted to in the world of baseball, yet he never had any favorite players. He is president of the Wrigley Gum Company, and expects his leadership of that firm to be demanding more of him than his role as a professional sports owner.

Like Halas, Wrigley's father had a paternalistic attitude toward Cub players, but he too was accused of being cheap when it came to buying winners. His son views the Cubs as a business and if winning teams means higher profits, his view on investments might change.

Much of Wrigley's private time was lately taken up by a divorce suit in which he tried to have his second marriage annulled on the grounds that his wife had not been properly divorced. A major issue was whether Wrigley would have to pay alimony from what his wife claimed was a $400,000 income. That much money doesn't even pay for a good utility infielder these days.

Whatever else the Cubs have done in Chicago, they still offer the best sports bargain in town with $1.25 seats in the grandstand and reductions for senior citizens. Whether P.K. Wrigley liked night baseball or winners is probably irrelevant to the millions of people able to watch the Cubs on television.

P.K. Wrigley pioneered baseball broadcasting and believed it created fan interest. As a result, almost every Cub game, home and away, is televised, and the White Sox follow the pattern. Nowhere else in America can baseball fans see their home teams so often without going to the ball park. They can watch them from saloons, with all that beer to cry into.

5. Lee Stern

Lee Stern is a rich man who thought that what Chicago sports fans needed was a winning team. So he went out and bought a soccer team. He did it at the same time that other rich men bought similar teams in New York, Minneapolis, and Los Angeles. But Stern's team was in Chicago and it immediately began to lose. Chicago may take to its heart any team that loses, but so far Stern's team has not created as much excitement as he found in the Board of Trade and Chicago Mercantile Exchange, where high-rolling in commodities made him a millionaire.

Chicago fans like players with names like Zeke, Gus, Hank and Mike. Stern's players have names like Gerhardt and Deiter and Helmut. Almost no one went to see them. But Stern deserves some credit. Joe Cappo, editor-at-large of *Crain's Chicago Business*, says he never understood why the sports nicknames in Chicago didn't reflect the nature of the city. "We have all these furry animal names like Cubs and Bears and Bulls." Why didn't anyone name a team the Chicago Pols? Maybe Stern came the closest. The Chicago Sting.

6. Jack Brickhouse

For thirty years, Jack Brickhouse has been rooting for the Chicago Cubs. The only trouble, according to his critics, is that he does it on television where everybody can hear him. Brickhouse's critics also complain that he gets the score wrong too often, doesn't keep track of which players are in the game, and overlooks any clumsy play that would draw the wrath of an objective observer. Brickhouse is strictly a house man.

But that makes no difference. His admirers far outnumber his critics, and the long-suffering Cub fans identify with Brickhouse's exuberance, his anxieties, his cheers, and the pathetic way he starts talking about next April every September.

For years, the balding Brickhouse was the radio voice of the Chicago Bears, for which he was even more soundly criticized, and he has been a special announcer from time to time for just about every major sporting event in the country.

But Brickhouse is mostly with the Cubs these days, and his often-heard clichés are sometimes the only reason for watching the late innings of Cubs games. Cub fans shiver with glee in an extra-inning game when the opposing side is retired and Jack shouts happily as the Cubs wait to bat, "Any old kind of a run wins it." Not to mention his "Hey! Hey!" cheer for the infrequent Cub homer, or a disconsolate sigh that precedes, "Oh, brother," when an opponent whacks one out of "the friendly confines of Wrigley Field."

Brickhouse is a Chicago sports institution. He's completely partisan. He urges people to come on out to the old ball park, to sit in the beautiful sunshine on a glorious day in Wrigley Field. Some people go so they won't have to listen to Brickhouse.

7. Harry Caray

Harry Caray, the voice of the White Sox, is about as opposite from Brickhouse as can be. Gravelly-voiced, graying, and feisty, Caray has only been around Chicago for a few years, after doing most of his verbal criticism of the national pastime in St. Louis. He put in a brief tour at Oakland, but his loyalties to the Cardinals were still evident in his first few Chicago years. That changed, and Caray became a rabid Sox fan and critic. Unlike Brickhouse, who always believes the players should get credit for trying, Caray gets mad at players who don't produce. Especially the ones paid the most to produce the most. "What are they paying him? One hundred thousand dollars?" Caray asks in disgust when some big hitter pops out with the bases loaded.

Caray is also a super salesman for baseball and beer. He always seems to have a Falstaff handy and his iconoclastic style of reporting makes him a favorite of fans who shout at him throughout his post-game visits to a variety of North Side saloons.

Caray makes everyone believe he's having fun at the ball game, broadcasting sometimes from the center-field bleachers, or sticking his head under the makeshift shower in the grandstand.

And his seventh-inning stretch rendition of "Take Me Out to the Ball Game" has become a tradition in Comiskey Park where everyone stands and turns toward the broadcast booth to join in. At most Sox games, this moment is the only thing worth waiting for.

Caray also has become a controversial sports character. In the few years of his residence in Chicago, the question of whether the stations or the ball club would renew his contract draws as much interest as the signing of a player. But Caray earns more than most of the players and most fans think he's worth it.

8. Roland Harper

Bears linebacker Doug Buffone told sportswriter Don Pierson about his first encounter with Roland Harper: "The first time I lined up against him in a scrimmage when he was a rookie, I said to myself, 'This shouldn't be too hard.' Then he comes out on me and almost tore my legs off. I said, 'Who is this?'"

Fullback Harper is the surprise star of the Chicago Bears. In a team that often looks like it's auditioning for a slapstick routine, Harper does things right. The five foot eleven inch, 210-pound fullback runs, blocks, carries, co-captains, and leads repentant teammates in prayers before and after games.

Harper has convinced players and fans that he's something more than Walter Payton's sidekick. Payton and Harper form the No. 1 rushing combination in the NFL. While Payton belongs to the O.J. Simpson razzle-dazzle run school, Harper works like a draft horse, plowing through linemen, always trudging toward that first down. Harper is paid like a draft horse too. Payton gets $500,000 a year; Harper, something like $47,000.

Payton is superstar; Harper is spirit. Roland is the most reliable team player. Harper has fumbled only eight times in his career. Quarterback Bob Avellini counts on Harper. Said Avellini in an interview: "When he's supposed to block someone, you know the guy is blocked."

Bears General Manager Jim Finks may be plagued by recurrent nightmares, one stemming from the fact that the Bears almost turned down Harper. In 1975, Harper, the blocker from Louisiana Tech, was the 420th player in a draft of 442. The Bears picked him on the seventeenth round—after Finks had left the screening room. Bears college scout Jim Parmer chose him. Said Parmer: "When Finks came back into the room, I told him I had taken a kid from Louisiana Tech. He said, 'Tell me about him.' I said, 'He's a blocker and he won't embarrass us.'"

9. Johnny (and Jeannie) Morris

What Payton and Harper are to rushing, Johnny and Jeannie are to sportsbroadcasting. The dynamic duo of *Channel Two News* in Chicago works like the NFL rushing stars: Johnny is the up-front face, beaming in a choirboy way as he describes the day's carnage; Jeannie does the fieldwork of interviewing coaches and stars and zeroing in on sports features.

Johnny and Jeannie get along well with the Bears. It probably helps that Johnny was a Bears receiver himself. As No. 47, he stunned fans with his pass receptions in the early 1960's, and played in the fabled 1963 season, in which the Bears clinched the NFL title. Johnny's old teammate, Doug Buffone, is still on the field (though he's done pretty well off the field as well, with his ownership of popular night-spot Sweetwater and his friendship with well-connected people like Congressman Henry Hyde). Johnny retired from football and went into broadcasting where he's set new records for affability and for preserving a shockingly innocent face.

Both Johnny and Jeannie have a knack for getting tight-lipped sports players to open up. After the debacle in the 1978 season in which Lionel Antoine taunted the opposition while spiking the touchdown ball, thus costing the Bears fifteen yards and losing them the game, Johnny asked Antoine if he was sorry about getting the call of "unnecessary intimidation." Antoine considered, and then drawled: "That's what I thought football was all about."

10. Artis Gilmore

The Chicago Bulls are widely considered the worst team in professional basketball, but Bull fans remain bullish. Chicago fans learn to savor victory as a rare vintage; as sportswriter Don Pierson holds: "In Chicago, any victory, any way, any time, any place, any sport, is a big deal."

Bulls fans are bucked up by the presence of seven foot two inch center Artis Gilmore, the strong man who can be counted on for the right stuff at the right time. As Gilmore has learned, it's tough carrying a team and the expectations of violently caring fans. Gilmore was the great black hope of the Bulls in 1976 when Chicago latched on to the pivotman from Jacksonville University in the dispersal draft of ABA players. But after a thirteen-game losing streak, Chicago fans felt betrayed by Artis, and Artis still didn't like Chicago. Artis thinks Chicago is too cold, and his reception in some snob bastions, like the BBC, a Rush Street disco which refused him admission in 1976, has been less than warm. The losing streak, especially, got to Gilmore. Gilmore once confided: "It was about the time when that fellow Gary Gilmore was being executed out West and I heard some talk about 'the Gilmore who's killing the Bulls.' It seemed horribly unfair to me, almost like I was being executed by the Chicago media."

All was forgiven in 1977, when Gilmore led the Bulls in one of the most amazing stretch runs in NBA history, in which they won twenty of their last twenty-four games. Artis Gilmore, of the twenty-seven-inch thighs and thirty-one-inch waist, may be the strongest man ever to play professional basketball; certainly he's the NBA's best all-around center.

If only he could play for the Bears and the Sox in his spare time.

18

Corporations

On children's maps of the United States, Illinois always seems to be colored yellow and Chicago is a tiny cluster of buildings, smokestacks, and a miniature railroad engine. This signifies business, manufacturing, and transportation, the soul of Chicago.

Carl Sandburg labeled the town "hog butcher of the world" and F. Scott Fitzgerald depicted it in many stories as the gleaming rail gateway to the rest of the country with its myriad lights and splendid train depots. That was the Chicago of the past. The city as a home of the stockyards and bustling train terminals has vanished. The last time anyone in Chicago saw a live pig was in 1968 when the Yippies let loose a squealing animal called Pigasus on the Daley (Civic) Center Plaza.

The great years of the passenger trains are only a memory, although the vital freights still chug through the city and its outskirts. The glamour of the Twentieth Century Limited and the Broadway Limited has been replaced by the so-called efficiency of Amtrak with its Saran-Wrapped meals and economy fares.

The city still remains America's greatest transportation hub and one of its big seaports. But it is also the leader in heavy manufacturing of steel and machinery, and a leader in finance with its newly burgeoning commodities markets. Chicago is the home of the world's giant retailers, Sears Roebuck and Montgomery Ward; of the major food processors like Esmark, which used to be Swift. Much of the world's money ends up in Chicago.

Unemployment rarely creates the problems in Chicago that it does in other cities because the labor market is so vast and diversified. And, Chicago's economic climate is stable. Companies like International Harvester and Sears have made major investments in Chicago, not only to prevent inner city blight, but to protect the massive stake they have compiled here over the decades.

Helping them is the fact that the major industry in Chicago is politics. "The companies who do best here are the companies who learn to deal with City Hall," one business expert said. There is virtually nothing the business community cannot do in Chicago, providing they ask the right people in the right way.

What many companies have asked for over the years is zoning variances. City government imposes strict codes for building, remodeling, and supplemental construction. Like many of the city's rules, they can be changed.

"There probably hasn't been one downtown building in the last twenty-five years that didn't ask for and get some sort of zoning variance for its construction," one business leader said. "Imagine major companies like IBM and Standard Oil having to go hat in hand to a city council so they can put up multimillion-dollar structures that other cities would love to have.

"On the other hand, what other city closes down sidewalks and intersections for builders? What other city lets companies build massive downtown hotels without any provisions for parking?" The same kind of glue that knits everything else together in Chicago clings to corporations. They have the responsibility to provide the capital, while labor provides the workers and City Hall provides the opportunities. But business at least does not have to feel it would never have gotten started without the political machine.

Chicago was destined to be one of the great commerce centers of the world by nature. Its location at the tip of one of the Great Lakes, in the center of the nation, and an overnight truck ride from two thousand American communities, provide a combination of transportation links unique in America. "Chicago is a hemisphere city," says Frank Considine, president of National Can

Corporation and head of the Chicago Association of Commerce and Industry.

The city moves more manufactured goods by rail than any other in the United States with thirty-seven thousand freight cars passing through daily. More trucks drive in and out of Chicago than any other city in the nation: 20 million tons of products are shipped annually down the Illinois and Mississippi rivers from Chicago: seven hundred ships from foreign ports sail down the St. Lawrence Seaway into Chicago every year. And then there's O'Hare, the world's busiest passenger airport with nearly two thousand operations every day, bringing 44 million people through Chicago every year.

Even Richard Daley couldn't take credit for Chicago's location. A third of the U.S. population lives within five hundred miles of the city, providing a market for 40 percent of all American merchandise and $100 billion a year in retail sales.

"O'Hare puts us around the corner from the world," says Considine. The mushrooming business complex that has been built around O'Hare in the past decade is both a source of pride and anxiety for city leaders. It allows corporate managers to utilize the swift connections between New York, Minneapolis, Boston, and other cities for brief business sessions that do not require overnight stays so costly in time and money. At the same time, many Chicago establishments decided in the 1960's that they should relocate their headquarters in the suburban sprawl, depriving the city of vitally needed taxes, and threatening to remove the commitment of many companies to remain in and expand in the city.

That suburban trend seems to have been slowed, if not halted, by a combination of government, corporate, and media concern. The erection of big new downtown buildings like the Sears Tower helped.

One of the disadvantages Chicago faced because of the diversification of its business interests was that there was no single corporate personality or industry to lead the others. It remained for the politicians to create a common interest. Thus Daley set about creating his various committees and enticing as many corporate bosses as he could find to join them. A pattern has emerged that divides the key business leaders in Chicago into two categories: those that are politically astute and involved with the governmental branch, and those who remain apart from it.

Chicago has more than fifty of the Fortune 500 companies in its midst but only about a dozen of them are tightly woven into the establishment pattern that connects business, government, and labor. "More and more companies are beginning to look for chief executive officers who can understand how the system works, and how they can implement their own objectives by using it," one corporate official said. In many instances, the nature of business dictates the amount of interest a corporation has in local affairs. In other cases, the personality of the chairman or chief executive officer determines the company's ties to the local establishment.

The business establishment breaks down into five key areas: utilities, retailers, manufacturers, big conglomerates, and transportation specialists.

In the utilities, Commonwealth Edison and Illinois Bell Telephone have become influential and are widely involved with the political and social structure of the city. People's Gas has been less entwined with City Hall.

Both Sears and Montgomery Ward executives have been highly visible and active with the powers that run the city. The local retail giants, Marshall Field and Carson Pirie Scott, have played a much smaller role.

Conglomerates and service industries have moved into positions of strength. Esmark's top men and Ben Heineman of Northwest Industries are particularly influential.

Santa Fe remains the premier local railroad by virtue of its freight success. The Milwaukee Road and Rock Island lines have gone through financial problems in recent years, but IC Industries, which owned great sections of land used for air-rights development, remains a force in the city. United Airlines is the only major aircarrier with headquarters in the Chicago area and its base is in Elk Grove Village. Still, United's stewardesses come into the Loop.

The traditional estrangement between businessmen and the Democratic Party kept the political and corporate communities at arm's length for many years. But by the middle of the Daley era, the corporate captains began to realize that in strengthening Chicago, Daley was strengthening them.

This transition occurred almost simultaneously with the creation of a new breed of corporate chairmen and presidents. These men for the most part are not family members who inherited their jobs, but men who worked their way up through various companies to positions of top management. They brought with them none of the high-handed nineteenth-century attitudes of corporate aristocracy. They also knew Chicago and its politics.

There are still a few of the old prominent Chicago names in the business world. William Wrigley heads the chewing-gum empire created by his grandfather, and Brooks McCormick is chairman of International Harvester, the giant farm-machinery manufacturer that grew from Cyrus McCormick's invention of the reaper.

Chicago's mercantile princes left little of their personal stamp on the city and even less of their names. Of the major Chicago skyscrapers, only Sears and Standard Oil have Chicago heritages. The others all seem to be named after insurance companies.

Aside from the Palmer House Hotel, named after Potter Palmer, the most identifiably Chicago business edifice is the Wrigley Building. Perhaps because of its location at the corner of Michigan Avenue and the Chicago River, or its name, or the fact that it is included in a Frank Sinatra rendition of *My Kind of Town*, the Wrigley Building has a special niche in Chicago. For many Chicagoans, the most dismaying feature of the energy crisis of 1973 was that the nighttime floodlights that shine so brightly on the Wrigley Building were temporarily turned off.

Perhaps because most of their origins are not very regal, Chicago's business leaders are a hard-working and relatively unpretentious group. Few of them extend personal luxury beyond their homes or the car and driver which await them each morning. They often schedule civic affairs meetings at 7 A.M.—breakfast gatherings that won't interfere with company business. Most of them belong to the same clubs and seemingly serve on all the same boards of directors.

The First National Bank board reads like a guide to Chicago businessmen: Thomas Ayers of Commonwealth Edison; Marshall Field; John Gray of Hart, Schaffner and Marx; Ben Heineman of Northwest Industries; Frederick Jaicks of Inland Steel; Brooks McCormick of International Harvester; John Nevin of Zenith; Dean Swift of Sears; and Robert D. Stuart, Jr. of Quaker Oats.

McCormick is also a director of Commonwealth Edison and Esmark; Ayers is a director of Sears, Zenith, and Northwest Industries; Robert Reneker, former chairman of Esmark, is a director of Continental Bank, Trans Union Corporation, and U.S. Gypsum.

Graham Morgan of U.S. Gypsum is a director of Illinois Central, and Harvester. And so it goes.

Their favorite clubs are the Chicago, Commercial, and the Tavern; and almost all the top corporate executives belong to at least one of them.

The racial unrest of the 1960's stirred the business community more than any other social upheaval. The awareness that blacks must be given broader roles in the city, and might soon be in the majority, led to the creation of a high-powered business committee to opening communication between themselves and the black community.

Thirteen companies, including Sears, the top banks, Edison, Bell, and Inland Steel, contributed $641,000 to form a Black Strategy Center. The Center eventually failed, but it led to a regular dialog session between black and white business leaders. They subsequently formed the organization called Chicago United, a group that includes just about every major business interest in Chicago.

That reliance on teamwork and a dependence on committees, boards, and consensus decisions rather than individual power plays has largely prevented a rigid pecking order from emerging in Chicago's business community. But, as always, some are more important than others.

THE TOP FIFTEEN BUSINESS LEADERS IN CHICAGO

1. Thomas Ayers

It has nothing to do with his position as Chicago's top-ranked business leader, but Thomas Ayers lives in the western suburb of Glen Ellyn, which is nice, but not posh. Ayers drives himself around in a compact car to save the kind of energy that his company is extremely efficient at producing.

Ayers, who has been chairman and chief executive officer of Edison since 1973, is the closest thing to "glue" in the business community. He was described by *Fortune* magazine as the top of the inner circle consulted by ex-Mayor Bilandic: "The first on all lists is Tom Ayers . . . who appears to have won both the affection and admiration of his peers and politicians."

In 1977, Ayers was the only corporate businessman listed by an Associated Press survey of the ten most powerful men in Illinois. He is the sort of fellow who knows the first names of cleaning ladies and checks up on the welfare of long-retired employees. Beyond that, he is the highest-paid utility-company executive in the country, with an aggregate earning of $331,000 in 1977.

Ayers is a premier proponent of nuclear energy; his advocacy has helped make Commonwealth Edison the leader in that exploding field. After Three Mile Island, President Carter noted that half the city of Chicago received its power from nuclear reactors.

Like many of his local peers, Ayers is neither a native Chicagoan nor was born to a silver spoon executive. He was born in Detroit, and went to work in the trenches with Edison in 1938, moving through a variety of management positions until his emergence in the 1960's as president. Ayers was named chairman and chief executive officer of the company in 1973.

Ayers was one of the very first Chicago business leaders to become involved with the problems of Chicago minorities. He's gotten several awards from black civic groups. Ayers was a key mediator during the racial conflicts of the 1960's and a leader in the open-housing crusade that touched off some protest marches, but eventually led to better race relations in Chicago.

Ayers, like other top business executives, serves on all the right civic committees and has memberships in all of Chicago's influential clubs.

One businessman attributes a considerable portion of Ayers' influence to his efforts to attract new industry to the city. Ayers heads the city's Economic Development Commission. Even more crucial is Commonwealth Edison's record for delivering power with a reliability found in few other regions; a key enticement for manufacturing and industrial firms.

2. Frank Considine

One reason that Ayers is Chicago's most influential businessman is that his reach cuts across all political and corporate barriers. Frank Considine, president of National Can Corporation, and head of the Chicago Association of Commerce and Industry, falls in the same category. While some businessmen have maintained close ties with the Democratic-controlled City Hall, and others have maintained the traditional alliance with Republicans, Considine has access to a wide array of civic, labor, and business leaders, and has gained acceptance in both political parties.

Considine, in his mid-sixties, is another of those chief executives who started at the bottom. He was, of all things, a theatrical booking agent in Chicago in the 1930's and 1940's and worked in several firms, including his own, before he moved to National Can in 1961. Considine was named president in 1969.

A soft-spoken executive who likes to schedule breakfast work sessions, Considine keeps track of the hours he works a week by consulting his chauffeur's hours. Considine claims that he averages about sixty-four.

Considine is a director of Loyola University and Barat College. Perhaps what makes Considine proudest is the view of seemingly all of Chicago that he has from his office at the extreme northwestern edge of the city.

3. *The Pritzkers*

For pure financial power, the Pritzker family tops everyone in Chicago. Keeping it all in the family is a major Pritzker effort. Their financial empire is a wonder of the city. The mainstay of the entire structure, of course, is Abram Nicholas Pritzker, lawyer, negotiator, financial genius, and millionaire many times over.

The Pritzkers deal in private partnerships rather than public stock corporations. Their rare partners have included the Murchisons of Texas, banker David Rockefeller, the Ford Motor Company, and Prudential Insurance.

There are about twenty-seven Pritzkers involved in the various family enterprises. A.N.'s son, Jay, is considered the financial wizard. Jay takes an active interest in culture. Jay was also a contributor to Republican Governor James Thompson's campaign. One chief executive active in civic affairs says, "You can always count on A.N. and Jay."

4. *Brooks McCormick*

One of the few Chicago business giants around whose family has been prominent a century or more, Brooks McCormick, chairman of

International Harvester Company, remains one of the city's most-involved businessmen.

Now in his early sixties, McCormick was president and chief executive officer of Harvester for a decade until he moved himself upstairs to the chairmanship and brought in Archie McCardell from Xerox to handle the giant farm-manufacturing firm. Harvester employs ninety thousand and, in 1977, had net revenues of nearly $6 billion.

McCardell got a whopping $1.5 million bonus and a salary in excess of $400,000 to join Harvester. He immediately instituted cost-saving steps that trimmed the payroll—by twenty-five hundred persons.

McCormick is still the visible head of Harvester in Chicago and presumably will be freer to operate such ventures as fund-raising drives for hospitals and the United Negro College Fund, a favorite charity of his that raised more than $1 million in 1977 for forty-one predominantly black American colleges.

Because of Harvester's great interest in overseas sales, McCormick has been a world traveler. Brooks is a great-grandson of William Deering, founder of the Deering Harvester Company, and of William McCormick, who was associated with the old McCormick Harvesting Machine Company. The two firms were predecessors of International Harvester, formed in 1902. McCormick graduated from Groton and Yale, and then served in various Harvester positions before becoming its president. He is, as noted, a director for various other big, big companies, including the First National Bank, Esmark, and Commonwealth Edison.

McCormick is not completely woven into the business-government fabric of Chicago, but his firm is an important employer and a historical base for the heavy manufacturing industry which Chicago must retain to secure its tax revenues.

5. James O'Connor

If his boss, Tom Ayers, is clearly No. 1 among business leaders, Jim O'Connor, president of Commonwealth Edison, ranks among the most influential.

O'Connor's rise in business has been faster than a speeding bullet. He joined Edison in 1963, and seven year later was appointed a vice-president. He has responsibility for Edison's seven operating stations, fifteen generating stations, three nuclear plants, a $5-billion plant construction program, and all engineering and public relations activities.

O'Connor is a native of the South Side; he still lives there. He was the youngest of three children. O'Connor likes to boast about the kind of education he received at St. Ignatius High School, a "college prep" institution run by the Jesuits.

"That was the real world," O'Connor says. "I would trade the degrees I got from Holy Cross College, Harvard, and Georgetown law school for the St. Ignatius diploma."

Like all good Chicago corporation heads, O'Connor is involved in many organizations outside Edison. He's a director of Borg Warner Corporation, and serves with twenty-five civic, industrial, and Catholic groups—many of which mirror Ayers' involvement in race relations, open housing, and health conditions.

O'Connor is a voluble critic of government interference in big business. He's also down on critics of nuclear energy and Chicago businessmen who don't contribute enough to community interests. "There aren't more than about two dozen businessmen who are truly effective in the civic and charity field," O'Connor says, noting that his boss Ayers is clearly the leader.

6. The Sears Squad

Chicago's Second City syndrome got a big setback when Sears, Roebuck, and Co., the world's largest merchandising company, put up the world's tallest building on the western edge of the Loop. The Sears Tower not only made Chicago First Skyscraper City, it contributed a major impetus to the city's renovation of downtown.

Arthur Wood, who recently retired as Sears' chairman, is considered one of the behind-the-scenes powers of the town. Edward Telling, a senior vice-president, was tapped in 1978 to succeed Wood, but hasn't busied himself much with civic and government matters. Wood preferred to let the company president, Dean Swift, act as Sears' public conduit to other parts of the establishment.

But Sears has been an active participant in city growth and Wood, a native Chicago blueblood, still serves on the most prestigious civic and corporate boards. He was a prime mover in the

Chicago United effort to break the barrier between business and the blacks.

Wood attended Princeton and Harvard Law. He married the daughter of Potter Palmer, Jr., and then practiced law privately until he went to Sears in 1941 at the request of General Robert Wood, then chairman of the giant store chain, but no relation of Arthur's. After serving in slots like general counsel and comptroller, Arthur Wood became president in 1968 and chairman, chief executive officer in 1973.

7. John Swearingen

John Swearingen, chairman of Standard Oil Company of Indiana, probably has more international and national power than he wields in Chicago, but Swearingen is considered by his peers and by the politicians as one of Chicago's most important men.

Swearingen and Daley were very influential forces behind Standard's decision to maintain its headquarters in Chicago and, more importantly, to build the eighty-story marble tower east of Michigan Avenue, creating the wedge for the $4-billion IC air-rights-development project, another integral part of the effort to bring back downtown.

Swearingen, who became chief executive officer of Standard Oil in 1960 at the age of forty-two, is also one of the toughest, most blunt-speaking executives in the city. He insists that profits are the name of the game and his peers rate him as one of the slickest oilmen in the business. Paid more than $500,000 a year, Swearingen heads one of the world's largest petroleum organizations and the largest domestic oil refiner. Its return on equity surpasses its five top competitors.

Swearingen started out as a chemical engineer. He joined Standard Oil in 1939, and was made director of the Amoco Production Company at the age of thirty-one. Swearingen's road has not always been easy—he has been a chief defender of the oil industry during the recurring energy crises, when critics attacked especially big oil's big profit margins. But Swearingen's position as the oil industry's chief spokesman (and as head of the American Petroleum Institute) gives him some national and local stature, in board rooms if not in the lines at the gas pumps.

Back home, the Swearingens, who both came out of the South (John from Columbia, South Carolina and Bonnie from Alabama) live fashionably at 1420 Lake Shore Drive.

8. *Edward Donnell*

Although Montgomery Ward does not compare with its giant competitor, Sears, in terms of total business volume, its chairman, Edward Donnell, ranks high in the corporate hierarchy in terms of Chicago clout. A low-key chief executive officer who presided over the acquisition of Wards, and its parent, Marcor, Inc., by Mobil Corporation in 1976, Donnell helped bring Wards back as a major merchandise retailer.

Wards lost a big battle with Sears when Sears decided, in the late 1920's, to stop dealing exclusively as a mail-order-catalog operation and opened a network of retail stores throughout the country. Wards did not do this until after World War II, and by that time Sears had garnered the lion's share of the general merchandise market. However, under Donnell's stewardship, Wards has generated three quarters of its business from retail stores, located in almost every state. Wards now ranks fifth behind Sears, J.C. Penney, K-Mart, and Woolworth's.

Donnell used to belong to the Sears staff (it helps to know the competition in Chicago business). He joined Wards in 1967 at the age of forty-eight and became president in 1968.

Donnell was one of the top executives who testified in favor of the Franklin Street subway project (while critics claim that the Franklin Street is the "subway that won't go anywhere" business and government officials like to think in terms of the $500-million that would be spent on it).

Donnell is a member of the usual boards and civic groups, and, with several years yet remaining before he retires, is expected to continue to exert his quiet influence on city affairs for some time.

9. *Edward Carlson and Richard Ferris*

"When O'Hare hiccups, every other airport in the country gets a bellyache," a federal official moaned in 1978.

O'Hare is the world's busiest airport, and United Airlines, Inc., the busiest airline of them all, is run from Chicago's suburban Elk Grove Village.

Edward Carlson has retained the chairmanship of UAL, the holding company which owns United and Western International hotels, but in 1979 he turned over the chief executive position to Richard Ferris.

Ferris, who has been described as a typically dynamic young corporate boss, came from a business career in hotel management with Western International, where he was first spotted by Carlson. His first association with Chicago was in the 1960's when he managed the Continental Plaza Hotel for Western. His relationship with Michigan Avenue and the downtown business boys has spurred his involvement in far more civic affairs than previous airline chiefs in Chicago.

One of Ferris' biggest challenges after becoming the airline's top man was the machinists strike which grounded United's fleet for more than a month in the spring of 1979. He won kudos from his business peers for his tough bargaining position and his willingness to personally involve himself in negotiations. Ferris, in his early forties, lives in Northbrook, which makes his commute to UAL's corporate offices in Elk Grove Village a short run on the expressways. He is a graduate of Cornell University's school of hotel administration, the best in the country. Although his background was hotels, he decided his role as chief executive of the nation's biggest airline demanded some practical experience so he began taking flying lessons every Sunday in 1979.

Carlson was working for Western International Hotels as corporate chairman when United Airlines picked him to sail them into the friendly skies and out of the red ink. United plays a pivotal role in O'Hare's operation, which is more than of passing concern to Chicago business.

Carlson's influence stems more from his position at United than from any widespread involvement in civic functions. He commutes out to Elk Grove Village every day from his Lake Shore Drive home, and spend vacations sailing off Seattle.

10. Frederick Jaicks

Frederick Jaicks has been working for Inland Steel Company for nearly forty years (since he was twenty-one) and, for most of the 1970's, he has been chairman and chief executive officer of the nation's sixth largest producer of steel. Inland's Indiana Harbor Works is the third-largest steel mill in the country. It's also a major industrial employer for Chicago, especially for the southeastern corner of the city.

Jaicks and the various members of the Block family who have operated Inland for several decades have been major influences on Chicago. The Block family has been greatly involved in civic and philanthropic efforts, while Jaicks is a behind-the-scenes man. The Inland board includes Abboud of First National, Don Kelly of Esmark, and Don Perkins of Jewel Foods.

Jaicks is a past chairman of the American Iron and Steel Institute. He graduated as a mechanical engineer from Cornell. Frederick's uncle brought him into Inland. When Jaicks was appointed to the presidency in 1966, he became, besides an extremely powerful man, the youngest president in the steel industry.

11. Daryl Grisham

Daryl Grisham is one of those Chicago corporate heads whose reach extends everywhere. As president of Parker House Sausage Company, Grisham is one of a handful of black business leaders prominent in both the black community and throughout Chicago. With John Johnson of Johnson Publishing, and Ernie Collins of Seaway Bank, Grisham is part of a powerful black leadership that has been a force in creating better relations between blacks and business.

Grisham is chairman of the PUSH Foundation and a director of the United Negro College Fund.

12. Donald Kelly

If Esmark still were still called Swift, Don Kelly would be a lot more identifiable as the head of the world's largest meat-packing company. Esmark, the conglomerate that owns Swift and Company, was put together by Kelly and the man who preceded him in the chairman post, Robert Reneker.

Kelly, in his mid-fifties, succeeded Reneker in 1978 after serving five years as president and chief executive. Reneker ended many of Swift's Chicago packing operations. That caused some job loss, but Esmark's subsequent growth as a corporation allowed it to maintain its prominence in the city.

Kelly had been somewhat obscured by Reneker's many far-flung activities in government, civic, and corporate affairs, but with his ascension to the chairman post, Kelly is starting to move in similar directions. He is a director of Harris Bank, Inland, and TransOcean Oil, Inc., and is on the board of the Lyric Opera.

13. Ben W. Heineman

Ben W. Heineman made the trains run on time. Chairman of the diversified Northwest Industries, he is a former lawyer who joined the Chicago and North Western Railway in 1956 as chairman and put the struggling carrier back on the right track before he sold the concern to employees in 1972. The sale gave the new conglomerate, Northwest Industries, $200 million in working capital, which Heineman has used to create a company with eleven subsidiaries and forty-three thousand employees.

His decision to sell the railroad stemmed from the industry's inability to control external factors such as government regulations and union demands. Northwest Industries now owns companies that produce underwear, scotch whiskey, and steel, and the Coca-Cola Bottling Company of Los Angeles, its most recent acquisition.

Heineman, in his mid-sixties, does not plan on retiring until he's seventy. He fits in time for sailing and photography between his business duties. He has long had close ties with the Democratic Party and has been a national convention delegate as well as major contributor to candidates. However, Heineman supported one of Mayor Daley's opponents in 1975, a move that confirmed his eccentricity.

Heineman belongs to several yachting clubs, the prestigious Casino Club, and is one of the few corporate commandants living in the Hyde Park area on the South Side.

Some observers believe that Heineman's impact on Chicago has lessened somewhat since he relinquished control of the railway that is such a vital link for Chicago's North Shore and northwestern suburbs, but he is an extremely astute businessman and civic leader.

14. The State Street Boys

Chicago's major local retailers, Marshall Field & Co. and Carson Pirie Scott, do a bit of this and that to attract business downtown, but have been generally less than influential on matters not directly relating to State Street, the retail heart of downtown Chicago whose entire future rests on the good health of these two old-line retailers. "Under the clock at Field's" has been a Chicago meeting place for ages and the business and governmental powers want to keep it that way.

Leading businessmen are hopeful that the new boss at Field's, Angelo Arena, who joined the firm in 1977 at $300,000 a year, will take an increasingly active civic role.

Norbert Armour, sixty-four, a native of South Dakota who started in the shipping room of Carson's in the middle of the Depression, was named president of the company in 1968 and became chairman and chief executive officer in 1972. Carson's has sent some satellite stores to suburban shopping malls, and has even gone into the food-service biz at O'Hare Airport. But there is no Carson's on the Michigan Avenue "Magnificent Mile" where Field's has set up a glittering showcase for shoppers.

15. Patrick O'Malley

Unlike many businessmen, Patrick O'Malley, president of Canteen Corporation, has never minded being out in front. O'Malley, who also is a member of the Regional Transportation Authority and the chairman of the Chicago Park District, has probably served on more civic committees than any other business leader in Chicago.

During Daley's reign, O'Malley was unquestionably the City Hall link to the business establishment in the same way that William Lee was Daley's conduit to labor. O'Malley was so entrenched in Daley's City Hall that a year after Daley's death he chaired a dinner for Bilandic and introduced him as "Mayor Richard Bilandic."

O'Malley did not seem to be as much in evidence during the Bilandic era and the election of Jane Byrne threatened to eliminate him as a link between the business community and City Hall.

Mrs. Byrne's first political objective was to take control of patronage in the Park District and she immediately plotted to remove O'Malley from the chairmanship of that board as a means to install her own general superintendent. O'Malley obviously fell into disfavor with Mayor Byrne when her stunning primary victory caused him to blurt that Chicago would be in for chaos. Technically, though, his term lasts into the 1980's.

Media

Hollywood has its film stars.
New York has its Beautiful People. Chicago has its news media.
Like all the other cities in the Doubleknitsville that is Middle
America, its only real celebrities are newspaper columnists and
television news anchors. But it's in keeping with the spirit of the
place. Newspapers and broadcasting in Chicago have long been
associated with the two things the city admires most: power and
money.

In the old days, the newspapers were mostly associated with
lurid crime stories and cheap reporters' whiskey. Ben Hecht's and
Charlie MacArthur's *Front Page* was for all its laughs something
of a documentary. Reporters actually did do and say those things
in the 1920's. As old men, many of them were still doing and saying
them in the 1960's.

But not anymore. No longer do newsmen start fires on doorsteps
to gain access to suspected murderers they want to interview, or
sabotage the competition's telephone in the City Hall pressroom.
John Danovich of the late *Daily News* is now the late John Danovich, his passing lamented much in the Stage Door saloon where
he used to down boilermakers by the dozen and terrify young

reporters with the .44-caliber pocket cannon he called his "nigger pistol."

They no longer have shootouts between drunken reporters in the pressroom of police headquarters. Reporters no longer pose as cops, or dress like cops, or think like cops, as did the *Tribune*'s immortal, if deceased, Joe Morang. The equally unkempt Ed Rooney of the late *Daily News* is now a college professor.

In the old days, there were two kinds of crime stories: crime that was "news" and crime that was "cheap"—the latter usually a synonym for "black." Nowadays, most crime stories are "cheap." What fills the pages besides all those columnists, fun features, and rock-star biographies is in large part the hard-hitting investigative exposé.

Both the *Tribune* and the *Sun-Times* have developed a mania for this kind of reporting—and for the many Pulitzer Prizes it has sent both their ways. The *Tribune*'s Bill Mullen cracked the Chicago Board of Election Commissioners and helped make an honest institution out of it. The *Trib*'s Bill Recktenwald spent a week working as a guard in one of the state's most dangerous prisons and made Governor Thompson pay some long overdue attention to it. The *Sun-Times*' wonder woman, Pam Zekman, led the team that exposed all those city shakedown artists in the Mirage Tavern scandal, and the team that reported the horrors of a high priced abortion factory.

The two papers also find room for heaps of politics and government reporting, but that is, after all, the city's major industry. In some respects, the papers really haven't changed. Frequently, in Chicago, the political beat and the crime beat are the same.

The evolutionary process that reduced Chicago from a wide open town with a dozen or more newspapers to one with only two great big ones was a noisy and, in the 1920's and 1930's, often violent one. In recent years, it has shaped up mostly as a war between two major institutions: the Tribune Company and Field Enterprises. The war is over, and the *Tribune* won. Its Sunday circulation is way over a million and climbing. Daily circulation exceeds 780,000 and is climbing. It has had a long list of advertisers it had to keep turning away for lack of room, and classified ads roll off its presses like dollar bills from the mint.

The *Sun-Times* is no joke. With Sunday circulation over 750,000 and daily running at around 690,000, its the sixth-largest paper in the country. But it never beat the *Tribune*. In the late 1960's, many people thought it inevitable that the *Sun-Times* would, but it never happened.

In the 1960's, the struggle had a decidedly ideological flavor. With the late Don Maxwell as editor, the *Tribune* stood for the Republican Party, the Vietnam War, Richard Nixon, and Fiscal Responsibility. The police participants in the 1968 Chicago convention riots often came off as heroic Boy Scouts. Politicians to the left of Dwight Eisenhower were routinely described in political copy as "ultra liberal."

The Field Papers were just as bad—in the other direction. At the height of the mid-1960's racial turmoil, the death of a year-old black baby (later found to have been the result of malnutrition and maternal neglect) prompted a *Daily News* lady reporter to stir up a controversy by going around the West Side telling people the child had been eaten by rats. During the Chicago 7 Conspiracy trial, Alice Hoge, then wife of *Sun-Times* Editor Jim Hoge, had Abbie Hoffman to a party at the house. Reports had it he danced in his underwear.

All that dramatically changed. New management at the *Tribune* realized that ideology in the news columns was a nineteenth-century anachronism that no modern big-city daily could afford. Enlightenment also came to the *Tribune*'s editorial page. It discovered that there actually were Democrats worthy of being supported for office. The *Sun-Times*' editorial page still has a liberal tone, but the strident, raucous crusading against The Right has ceased. The only place readers of both papers find any ideological hooting and hollering is in the columns, and they come in all flavors. Before 1970, the *Tribune* wouldn't even use outside columns.

Both papers wield enormous power—especially where politicians are concerned. The *Tribune* got McCormick Place put up and is still crusading for a downtown stadium, if somewhat forlornly. It helped enact the state's first income tax and elect two liberal Democrats, of all people—Bill Singer as alderman and Abner Mikva as 10th District congressman. It even helped knock Richard Nixon out of commission by turning on him at a key point in the Watergate saga.

The *Sun-Times* destroyed the political careers of chaps like former Republican State School Superintendent Ray Page. It has been as effective as the *Tribune* with the lawmakers in Springfield and has been in the vanguard of almost every reform drive. Both papers are strong supporters of merit selection of judges and both may take credit for the failure of two big machine judicial powers—Judge Joseph Power and Judge John Boyle—to win retention.

As a matter of fact, the election endorsements of both papers these days are usually much the same. Democratic politicians court both papers and are most respectful to their editorial boards. Governor Thompson is slavish to them. When one or the other writes something negative about him, he's said to often sit brooding for hours.

Until 1974, the *Tribune* operated a tabloid afternoon-sidekick paper called *Chicago Today*. Mildly liberal, irreverent, and frequently fun, it proved a drag on the ad market and had to be killed. The execution was swift and surgically neat, if painful for about half the *Today* staff. The other half was taken aboard the *Tribune*. No *Tribune* personnel were removed in this merger, and the amalgamation worked out happily.

In 1978, Marshall Field decided that his *Daily News*, while universally admired, had cost too much money for too long. Its demise was less a surgical stroke than an ax murder. The staffs of both the *News* and the *Sun-Times* were merged, but with wholesale firings on both sides. For months, the morale on the surviving paper was on a par with that in the Confederate Army. In 1866. It has improved only slightly.

In the 1930's and 1940's, Chicago was a big radio town, its studios broadcasting popular network shows like *Sky King* and *Jack Armstrong*. In the late 1940's and early 1950's, before cable and microwave linked the nation, it was a big television center. In fact, it was television's class act in those days.

What came to be widely admired as "the Chicago School" of television produced brilliant improvisations like Dave Garroway's *Garroway At Large*, Burr Tilstrom's *Kukla, Fran, and Ollie*, and Fred Kilian's *Penthouse Players* and *Super Circus*, the show that set blonde Mary Hartline on the road to a mansion in Palm Beach. It started with a weekly budget for circus acts of five hundred dollars. Studs Terkel's brilliant *Studs' Place* was performed every week without scripts.

With Clint Yule, Chicago pioneered the TV weatherman (his wife would bring cookies to him at the end of the forecast). It was one of the first cities with TV movies, featuring Jim Moran the Courtesy Man selling snazzy new Hudsons with commercials that some-times lasted fourteen minutes each. Perhaps the funniest and certainly most innovative half hour ever on television was an early production of the Chicago School. It consisted of nothing more—or less—than three chimpanzees let loose in a roomful of toys.

In those days, news was sacred. Except for Clint and his cookies, every minute of news was full of news. Actual news. News shows were regarded as public service time. They had no other purpose than to inform. Two forces combined to kill that and all the other admirable aspects of the Chicago School. Both involved money. The first was the lure of New York and Hollywood salaries. As both these cities became production centers, Chicago's talent pool evap-orated. The most classic example was Dave Garroway's moving to New York to do something called *The Today Show*.

The other factor was greed. As sponsors became more and more interested in television, and more and more generous with their ad dollars, the money men became more influential. In the case of ABC, in its bloody merger with Paramount Theaters in 1953, the money men took over an entire network in one swoop.

Soon everything was ratings and cost-per-thousand. News was in prime time, and so, too valuable to waste as mere public service. It had to draw ratings. It had to make money. It had to become enter-tainment. With each extra rating point earning a station an addi-tional $1 million in revenue now, the news shows have become battlegrounds—especially between the ABC, CBS, and NBC sta-tions in Chicago, which are all owned and operated by their networks.

That's why so many of the general managers New York sends to Chicago to run these three stations seem to have sales instead of news or programming in their backgrounds. That's why CBS's all-news radio is such a success in Chicago. The broadcast audience has to find out what's happening somewhere.

Though some of its reporters sometimes look and sound as though they were hired off the first CTA bus to come along, WGN television puts on a thorough-going, news-filled news show. The others often look as though their news director is Sam Goldwyn. Hard-hitting coverage for *Channel Two News*, the top-rated of the network three, has often meant something like sending Bill Kurtis to Africa to put on a khaki correspondent's suit and ride in a truck with the Rhodesian army. One of his reports from Africa featured about five minutes of footage of him taking a picture of an elephant. Although Kurtis scored brilliantly in exposing the use of "Agent Orange" in Vietnam.

Channel Two's John Drummond, who frequently wears striped gangster suits, is one of the few really street-smart TV reporters around. Yet they have him doing "news" features like great sex murders in Chicago history and interviews with Elizabeth Taylor.

A huge TV page ad for Channel Two was boldly headlined: "SEX AND MARRIAGE. The Myths and Realities. Watch Channel 2, THE 10 O'Clock News." One for Channel Five began: "THIS WOMAN WAS RAPED FOUR YEARS AGO. LAST NIGHT, SHE WOKE UP SCREAMING." Channel Seven's ads have featured nasty digs about the supposed negative personality of opposition anchormen. Channel Seven pioneered "happy talk" and long has had one of the most asinine weather reports in television.

Chicago radio has its bright spots. WFMT functions as a virtual monopoly of cultural broadcasting, and is one of the best three or four classical-music stations in the country. Except for the midday ramblings of its Bob and Betty Sanders, WBBM's all-news station performs brilliantly and is a fixture of the Chicago airwaves, despite the news-talk competition it's now receiving from WIND. WGN radio is strong on news, top-grade talk shows, sports, and public service. Otherwise, you mostly get rock, more rock, country, elevator music, occasional jazz, and, on FM, polkas, Bible-thumping and ethnic pop tunes.

Chicago is home to some good trade magazines, notably *Advertising Age* and *Crain's Chicago Business*, and some profitable and surprisingly powerful neighborhood and suburban newspaper chains, such as the Lerner outfit and *Pioneer Press*.

Like its affiliate organization, WFMT, *Chicago* magazine is a monopoly. It keeps getting imitators and competitors, but they never go very far; not even Jon and Abra's *Chicagoan*, which *Chicago* magazine bought up.

Put out mostly by a gang of antiestablishment refugees from Chicago's newspapers, *Chicago* magazine is nothing at all like the sophisticated *New Yorker* or the slick *New York* and *New West*. Like the city itself, it's rough-edged, irreverent—and very rich. If it did have some meaningful competition, it might try to organize its pages a little better. It's quite tiring having to thumb through all those ads.

THE TOP FIFTEEN MEDIA PEOPLE IN CHICAGO

1. Stanton R. Cook

As publisher of the *Chicago Tribune*, Stan Cook is the head of the most powerful media institution in the city. As chairman of the Tribune Company, he runs what is in terms of newspaper circulation, broadcast audience, and ad revenue the most powerful communications empire in the country. In its fold are the *Tribune*, the New York *Daily News* (the country's largest-circulation daily newspaper), and a string of rich papers in Florida and California. In addition to WGN, there's a string of radio and television stations. There are Canadian forests, paper mills, and ships to bring the paper home in. There are some valuable chunks of real estate.

For all this power, Cook is not aloof. Quite the contrary. Many's the young reporter who's been astonished if not unnerved to find Cook standing beside him in his shirtsleeves with a question. Cook calls this "walking the floors." He walks all of them. He's flown in little airplanes to the depths of the *Tribune*'s forests, accompanied reporters on election night to South Side precinct headquarters, and even undertaken a photo assignment in China. Callers at his home have found him in a sweatshirt, tootling on his old high-school French horn.

Glad of hand, and affable to the point of calling people "Tiger," Cook came up through the ranks, starting as a production engineer at the *Tribune* in 1951. Now just past fifty, he was named publisher in 1973. A World War II Army Air Corps navigator, he was a mechanical engineering graduate of Northwestern University. He is a member of the executive committee of Chicago United and has been named to the boards of the University of Chicago, the Symphony, and the Field Museum.

Cook is known and respected for ruling with a guiding rather than a heavy hand. It's not at all like the days when Colonel McCormick would call up in the middle of the night to have a reporter come out to his country estate and fix his water pipes.

2. Mike Royko

A Polish-Ukrainian kid who grew up in and around his father's Near Northwest Side saloon, Mike Royko came out of the army in the 1950's with some sergeant's stripes, no college degree, and the notion that he might become a newspaperman. He became one by starting out where the best Chicago newspapermen have always started out—the penurious *City News Bureau,* a local wire service whose editors have traditionally been as mean and nasty as basic training sergeants. As mean and nasty as Attila the Hun's basic training sergeants. Mike then went to the *Daily News* and the county beat. His acerbic musings on politicians led to what has become the best and most devotedly-read newspaper column in the city.

The *Tribune* had a chance to get Royko as a green reporter, but declined. He periodically gets his revenge by offering to switch sides, backing out of the negotiations at the last minute. He could probably command an office anywhere he wanted in Tribune Tower and a Rolls-Royce to take him to Billy Goat's Tavern, even though it's right across the street from the *Tribune* basement.

Royko was the principal attraction that kept the *Daily News* going for as long as it did, and has been the main attraction of the *Sun-Times* since the big merger. He could doubtless get the *Sun-Times* to provide him with a Rolls-Royce to take him from his desk to the men's room. He swings enough weight to be involved in many policy, editorial, and personnel decisions (the rank and file at his paper look up to him as a sort of champion), but his chief power comes from the popularity of his column and the skill with which he makes use of it. No one else in town can make a politician or establishment poobah feel so much pain. No one else can so snickeringly get away with it.

Though he's now a middle-aged man in his forties, you imagine Royko bouncing up and down in his chair like a kid, cackling with fiendish glee over one of his funny and telling lines. Though the *Tribune* and the *Sun-Times* have a couple of guys who try, no one in Chicago is funnier than Royko. Beyond that, he is so effective as a columnist because he speaks and writes with the rough street-corner voice of Chicago, and always knows whereof he speaks and writes, especially as concerns the way they run City Hall. He also has the skilled columnist's technique of shooting only at big, fat, juicy sitting targets—as abound in City Hall. The Republicans once wanted him to run for mayor.

Royko's long staying power may also be attributed to the fact that he's something of a misanthrope, and plays no favorites. Conservative *Tribune* executives, lakefront liberals, black leaders like

Jesse Jackson, and stars like Frank Sinatra get shot at by him as much as the cigar and fedora set. He did get a little cuddly with Jimmy Carter for a while, but quickly discovered he was being romanced. Soon after he called Carter "that pious little ice cube."

A Pulitzer Prize winner, Royko is the author of *Boss*, a nationally best-selling and extremely unauthorized biography of Da Mare that Mrs. Mare tried to have taken off supermarket shelves.

Royko still lives on the Northwest Side, though in a much nicer neighborhood, and still hangs out in the Billy Goat. He enjoys his refreshment, and once got into an altercation with a young lady in a much swankier joint that ended with his splattering her with ketchup. He apologized in print.

3. Ray Nordstrand

In terms of having an immense personal imprint on the city, and personal control over two of its most important institutions, Ray Nordstrand must be rated one of the most powerful individuals in the Chicago media.

He is publisher of *Chicago* magazine, which is to local magazinedom what A.T.&T. is to the telephone business. With no significant competition—and as the repository of much of Chicago's literary output—*Chicago* mag has a circulation of two hundred thousand. It carries about 2,100 pages of advertising a year. According to the *Tribune*, *Chicago* has more ad pages in one month than *New York* magazine carries in four issues.

Nordstrand is also president of WFMT radio, the repository of much of Chicago's other cultural productivity, especially the musical kind. The iconoclastic Studs Terkel operates from a WFMT base. The station's *Midnight Special* program on Saturday nights has for years been a must for nearly everybody in the city who thinks. The station's advertising salesmen have very easy lives.

In fact—to extend the cultural monopoly a little further—WFMT kicks back some $250,000 a year to its parent organization, the Chicago Educational Television Association, which operates WTTW-Channel 11.

A somewhat rumpled, bespectacled fellow who ran the college radio station at Northwestern when he was a student there, Nordstrand comes across as something of a Midwest small-town boy, but few of those sleek moguls in New York broadcasting have anything like his independence and personal power.

4. Clayton Kirkpatrick and Maxwell McCrohon

Clayton Kirkpatrick, editor of the *Tribune* since 1969, was promoted to the position of Chicago Tribune Company president in June, 1979, replacing Robert Hunt, who took over the troubled *New York Daily News*. To no one's surprise, Managing Editor Maxwell McCrohon became editor of the *Tribune* at the same time.

Though possibly the most dignified-looking man in Chicago (an interviewer once described him as someone who would look comfortable in a high, starched collar), Kirkpatrick worked in his youth as a freight handler, museum attendant, waiter, door-to-door stove-lid salesman, radio announcer, and lumber camp mess attendant. He came to the *Tribune* in 1938 via the *City News Bureau*, caught the eye of Colonel McCormick as a star reporter, and, with brief stops along the way at practically every editor's job in the newsroom, became The Editor in January, 1969.

Despite a pronounced fondness for the Republicanism of the late Robert Taft, Kirkpatrick is the man most responsible for leading the *Trib* out of its reactionary cocoon. In the 1968 election, upholding a long-standing tradition, *Tribune* endorsements said simply: vote Republican. In March 1969, shortly after Kirkpatrick took over as editor, a *Tribune* endorsement elected liberal independent Bill Singer as an alderman. The *Tribune's* attack against Nixon in 1974 came as no surprise to those who knew Kirkpatrick well.

McCrohon, the man who continued and completed the job of modernizing the *Tribune* and deserves much of the credit for the *Tribune's* circulation triumph over Field Enterprises, is a soft-spoken Australian with the impeccable manners and speech of a London clubman. He helped take the *Tribune* a quantum leap from the nineteenth century to the latter part of the twentieth, and is preparing it for the twenty-first. Whatever the newspaper of the next century will look like, it will look like the *Tribune*.

A survivor of assignments that took him to forlorn reaches of the Australian Outback in dangerously piloted small planes, McCrohon was a New York and Washington correspondent for the

Sydney Morning Herald. He went American in 1959 and ultimately became managing editor of *Chicago Today.* He was promoted to the same position at the *Tribune* in 1972.

Bill Jones, McCrohon's ex-Marine protégé who won a Pulitzer Prize for exposing a cruel ambulance racket, has been promoted to managing editor. As city editor, head of the *Tribune*'s Task Force, Criminal Court reporter, assistant political editor, and the neighborhood news reporter who invented the *Tribune*'s Ellison the Elf, Jones has dealt with the Chicago news scene from every conceivable angle. Barely past forty, he is the man to watch in Chicago journalism.

5. *Jim Hoge*

James Fulton Hoge, Jr. editor-in-chief of the *Chicago Sun-Times,* looks like an actor, and not the *Lou Grant* show's Ed Asner. As handsome as Robert Redford, and now divorced from his newspaper heiress wife, Alice, Hoge has a reputation as a Chicago ladies' man, perhaps as *the* Chicago ladies' man. He also has a reputation as one of Chicago's keener minds. The product of the best Eastern Establishment society and schools, he has never finished his novel, but writes poetry. Though he's only in his forties, he is at the top of his profession, having leaped to command of both Field papers (while the *Daily News* lasted) in a mere decade.

It was Hoge who took the *Sun-Times* from a provincial tabloid to national prominence in the 1960's, and gave the *Tribune* such a run for its money. It was Hoge who took the last stab at saving the *Daily News,* and who might have succeeded if he had been given just a little more time and money. It is Hoge who keeps getting mentioned when the editorships of more major American newspapers or big broadcast jobs are discussed.

There is not a snob menu in the world that could intimidate this elegantly well-bred fellow, yet Hoge wears frayed shirts and goes to places like the Billy Goat for nothing more elegant than a cheeseburger and a beer. He has generously and sometimes courageously intervened to save the careers, marriages, and even lives of his staff members, and certainly has inspired more personal loyalty and devotion than most Chicago newspaper editors. Yet many of his reporters and writers, though admiring him, find him cold and aloof, a sort of textbook military officer who cares intensely for his men but never permits himself to become one of them.

There is something of Alexander the Great's "no more worlds to conquer" in Hoge. Field apparently trusts him completely with the running of his remaining newspaper, and it's difficult to imagine anyone else running it. His job is doubtless his for life.

There are other worlds to conquer. They're just not in Chicago.

6. Marshall and Teddy Field

Unlike Cook, Kirkpatrick, McCrohon, and Jim Hoge, Marshall Field V is not a true-blue, ink-in-the-veins newspaperman. As he told *The Wall Street Journal*, he sees his mission in life as "to continue publishing the *Sun-Times*, provide my brother and myself with money to live and pay taxes, and enable us to pass on what we have to our children."

While that may seem like simple common sense in the gentlemen's lounge of the Chicago Club, that attitude has not endeared young (late-thirtyish) Field to the *Sun-Times*' staffers who keep the bar at Riccardo's so well polished with their elbows. They seem crushed every time a rumor that Field's about to sell the *Sun-Times* falls through. Many of them talk of his scuttling of the *Daily News* as though it were a war crime, as though losing $8 million a year was a required form of public service.

Still, the Field staff seems to be putting out a much better paper than it did under his father. (The *Sun-Times*' Lisa Meyer is on *Washington Week in Review* all the time.) Field has returned the paper to the straight and narrow, and kept it on course. He should get a great deal of credit for backing Hoge against some of the paper's high-level graybeards, and for backing him on such things as Pam Zekman's City Hall-rattling exposés.

Teddy, Marshall's half-brother, automatically got a big say in running the family businesses—the *Sun-Times*, five television stations, coal mines, paper mills, and real estate—on his twenty-fifth birthday. The department stores were sold off some time ago. But Teddy seems willing to defer to his big brother in many matters. The way things are going, they get to share some $1.6 million a year just in dividends.

Marshall and his knock-out blonde wife, the former Jamee

Jacobs, have residences at the right addresses and memberships in all the right clubs and on all the right boards. He probably doesn't even have his old National Guard enlisted man's uniform hanging in the closet.

Teddy stays mostly out in California, racing cars and running a chain of barbecue restaurants he started up called "Four Guys From Texas." Some *Sun-Times* men wish he would take a hand in the paper, and some don't.

7. Walter Jacobson

Gravel-voiced and street-wise old Len O'Connor is a venerable Chicago institution and the dean of the city's radio and television commentators. Young Peter Nolan is very, very good. But the honors for most powerful and preeminent commentator have to go to CBS's Walter Jacobson—especially since O'Connor left NBC's Channel 5 for the less-watched WGN.

A onetime Chicago Cubs batboy (Mike Royko delights in recalling in print how Cubs players used to throw their dirty underwear at him), Jacobson grubbed his way to the top. A low-paid reporter on *Chicago's American* (the predecessor to *Chicago Today*), he went to Channel Two as a political hotshot, and got bounced. Picked up by Channel Five as a sort of understudy to Len O'Connor, who goes on forever, he seemed to face a dismal future. But in early 1973, new management at CBS decided he was just what they needed as a co-anchor for star Bill Kurtis, and took him aboard for some fifty thousand dollars a year. He clicked, especially with his nightly commentaries.

No one throws dirty underwear at Walter Jacobson now. Not at a salary in the neighborhood of $250,000 a year. There have been jokes about how Walter's smarts are possibly on a par with Gerald Ford's—including one legendary one about his going into a control room to see how he looked on camera—but no one dares repeat them to his face.

Jacobson needs a Red Flyer wagon to haul his Emmys home every year. His secret to success as a commentator is much the same as Royko's: He's a quintessential Chicagoan and he aims his shots at big fat sitting targets. It also helps to have all sorts of legmen and camera crews at one's disposal.

Divorced, and slightly paranoid over the extraordinary number of traffic tickets he seems to attract, Jacobson is a Great Presence on the Near North Side, especially in Lakefront Lib circles. His role as Kurtis' curly-haired, smart-aleck kid sidekick belies the fact that he's not only in his forties but two years older than Kurtis.

8. Wally Phillips

WGN Radio's early-morning presence, Wally Phillips once told a reporter that people's first concern in the morning is "whether they're going to make it through the day."

Phillips is the first link many Chicagoans have with everyday reality, whether it's a ten-car pileup on the Dan Ryan or a wind chill of thirty below. Phillips tries to ease people into the day; he gives the hard facts about getting to work and back alive and then a smorgasbord of news stories, quizzes, traffic and weather conditions, and a stream of pleasant patter. And strange phone calls.

Phillips is more a phone jockey than a disc jockey. "Call me anything but just don't call me a disc jockey," he once advised writer Cliff Terry. "Some mornings I don't play music at all. People are wonderful. Every time I mention this on the air, a guy will phone and say, 'Hey, is this the disc jockey?'"

More often, people call in to answer Wally's trivia questions. Sometimes they report fires or accidents. The information flow on the Phillips show is so fast and frequent that other stations have been known to call up Phillips to find out what's going on.

Before the FCC ruled that a person had to reveal his identity when making calls on the air, Phillips was the scourge of the early morning unwary. April 1 always had Phillips calling the Brookfield Zoo and asking for Mr. Fox. He once called up Ben Gingiss, the owner of a large chain of rented formal-wear stores, who was on vacation in Hawaii. "We're down at the store," Phillips said excitedly. "Where do you keep the fire extinguisher?" Phillips also interrupted a Chicago pharmacist's honeymoon in Arizona by complaining that when he took apart a Contac capsule, expecting to find six hundred tiny time-released particles, he found only 594.

Phillips was fired from a deejay spot in Ohio when he tried to liven up the news broadcast. Phillips slipped a phony item into the script of a pompous news announcer. According to Phillips, he wrote: "'All members of infantry company so-and-so report immediately to your draft board' and I described an insurrection in some phony country. He read it on the air." When Phillips was relieved of his deejay duties, he was told "This isn't your field."

For somebody in the wrong field, the fiftyish Phillips is doing pretty well. *The Wally Phillips Show*, which wakes up the city between 5:30 A.M. and 10 A.M., has about 1.4 million listeners a day. Phillips earns, as he says, "too much"—around $200,000 a year.

Phillips has realized one great ambition, that of creating an "instant world all around me." But Phillips, who uses two alarm clocks in his Winnetka home to make sure that he gets up at 3:30 A.M., has one constant unrealized dream—"Sleep."

9. *John H. Johnson*

John Johnson heads the nation's second-largest black business after Motown Records: Johnson Publishing Company, which turns out *Ebony, Jet, Black Stars*, and *Black World*. Besides handling a publishing empire, Johnson is chairman of the board of Supreme Life Insurance Company (Johnson's first job was as a Supreme office boy), is president of Fashion Flair cosmetics, and chairman of WJPC, Chicago's only black-owned radio station.

In the late 1960's, *Ebony* magazine popularized the term "black power." Publisher Johnson embodies it. "I never think of myself as a millionaire," says Johnson, "because I know I am not that far from the days when we were on relief." Johnson grew up in the sawmill town of Arkansas City, in southeast Arkansas, the son of a mill worker and a housemaid. Johnson's widowed mother took him to see the Century of Progress Exposition in 1933, and Johnson and his mother decided to stay in Chicago. They stayed on the relief rolls here for two years.

Johnson describes his rise simply: "I thought my way out of poverty." Johnson swears by W. Clement Stone's "Positive Mental Attitude" approach. The two most important books that the young Johnson read were, he claims, Dale Carnegie's *How to Win Friends and Influence People* and Napoleon Hill's *Think and Grow Rich*.

Johnson has always been adept at getting around obstacles. When he launched his first magazine, *Negro Digest*, in 1943, he organized his friends into shifts, and they plagued news vendors night and day with requests for the new publication. Johnson started *Ebony* in 1945 by getting a five-hundred-dollar mortgage for his mother's furniture. When *Ebony* needed additional space in

1949, Johnson tried to buy an old funeral parlor on South Michigan Avenue. The mortician who owned the place refused to sell to a black, especially a black who published magazines. So Johnson hired a white lawyer to pose as an independent agent representing a large Eastern publishing house that wanted to set up a Chicago office. The deal was closed for $52,000 (Johnson had offered the owner $60,000), the lawyer asked if he could send a maintenance man around to check out the building, and Johnson entered his new domain, outfitted in work clothes and carrying a flashlight.

Today, in his early sixties, Johnson commands his publishing empire from an office equipped with an eleven-foot-long burl-wood desk, topped by four phones and the first Picture Phone sold in Illinois. The walls of his office are suede-covered, and just off his office is an exercise room with a barber's chair in the center— Johnson has his woman barber come to him so he can shave some time off his schedule.

The Johnson Publishing Company building at 820 South Michigan Avenue is a monument to the PMA philosophy and its rewards: it contains a priceless collection of African and black American art; alligator-covered telephones and marble conference tables abound, and the carpeting in the elevators changes with the seasons.

A minister once said of Johnson's publishing house: "Now I know what God would have done if he hadn't run out of money."

10. Irv Kupcinet

It's relatively easy for a newspaper columnist to spin off into lucrative sidelines like broadcasting and personal appearances (especially in celebrity-starved Chicago), but none has ever managed to spin off into as many things as Kup—or as successfully.

He is *the* gossip columnist in Chicago—his *Sun-Times* column is an even bigger draw than Royko for some readers. Though not the Big Event it used to be in the 1960's, his television coffee-table talk show remains a Chicago institution. Until recently, he even did color for the Bears' radio broadcasts.

Certainly one of the best liked and most popular public speakers and emcees in Chicago, he, his foot-long cigar, and his wife Essie show up at everything: movie previews, gala receptions, political dinners, grand openings, sports luncheons. No celebrity party in Chicago is complete without him (though, for that matter, no celebrity party in Chicago is complete without Barbara Rush). The secret to successful spin-offing is a matter of knowing the right people, and Kup knows EVERYBODY. When in Washington, he regularly lunched with J. Edgar Hoover. And, of course, he was a pal of Da Mare.

Kup and Essie live in one of those ritzy palaces on Lake Shore Drive just up from the Drake. They could certainly afford Lake Forest, but it's a bit off the banquet circuit.

11. Gary Deeb

With the exception of titans like the *Tribune*'s immortal Claudia Cassidy, Chicago newspaper critics generally don't wield much clout. It's hard to make ballet criticism very meaningful to the average reader, and rock-music critics have to face the fact that most rock fans don't read newspapers—if they read at all.

Movie critics Roger Ebert of the *Sun-Times* and Gene Siskel of the *Tribune* are celebrities in their own right. Siskel is a regular performer on *Channel Two News* and a frequent face on Channel Eleven. Ebert actually won a Pulitzer Prize for movie criticism, and wrote the screenplay for the ultimate in disaster movies, *Beyond the Valley of the Dolls*. Both host a fun show called *Sneak Previews*, which is seen around the country on public television. But both have little to say about what movies Chicagoans see. The theater owners and distributors make all those decisions, and they have such a grip on things that Chicago moviegoers have very little to choose from after you subtract all the violence and sex films from the schedule.

It's fine that Gene and Roger approve of the flicks at the Cinema Theater, but they stay at the Cinema for months and months—even if Gene and Roger don't approve of them. Besides the Cinema, there's not much else besides the Carnegie, the Esquire, Water Tower Place, and the Biograph (where Dillinger got it).

Gary Deeb, the *Tribune*'s television critic, has clout. Television executives tremble before him. The *Sun-Times* has specialized in thoughtful television critics (its Ron Powers also won a Pulitzer Prize). Deeb is mean. He's been called "the Wolf Man," and "Fang." His tone can get a little zealously righteous at times, but he treats television as the crap most of it is, and rages at producers to do better.

A former disc jockey and reporter who went to the *Tribune* via the Buffalo *Evening News*, Deeb is noted for his continuous scoops and the close attention he pays to all the behind-the-scenes stuff going on within station management. He makes good guys and breaks bad guys all the time. He does have a tendency to deal with performers as though they were war criminals sometimes, such as when he heaped abuse on Channel Five's Jane Pauley— apparently, just because she was pretty and knew nothing about Chicago when she first came to Chicago. Jane got her revenge. She was promoted to *The Today Show* and has now probably forgotten who Gary Deeb is.

12. Milt Rosenberg

Chicago's best evening talk-show host is, of all things, a University of Chicago professor. WGN's *Extension 720*, a two-hour discussion show with an hour reserved for call-ins, is conducted by Milton Rosenberg, a professor of psychology at the University of Chicago, and author of several books, including *Vietnam and the Silent Majority*. He is multi-lingual, a remarkably good broadcaster, and may be the best read man in Chicago.

Rosenberg's show has been on the air since 1968 (the less erudite Jack Brickhouse was its first moderator) and is aired every Tuesday through Friday nights, although the show is always subject to preemption by WGN's sports coverage.

As many as 250,000 listeners from thirty-eight states tune in to hear such Rosenberg guests as Jesse Jackson, Mayor Teddy Kollek of Jerusalem, the cast of Watergate, and a succession of journalists and authors. The subjects vary from politics to religious cults, the arts, entertainment, literature, and American attitudes. If you want to complain about commies or talk about UFO's, call elsewhere.

13. Ann Landers

Ann Landers has a terrific perquisite that comes with her job: she gets to tell people exactly what she thinks of them. In no uncertain terms, either. Ann's method is to collar the suffering, cut away to the core of their misery, and tell them to stop it, get rid of the bum, or take themselves to a therapist. Ann Landers sounds like a cross between a drill sergeant and the Oracle of Delphi.

Ann Landers is the syndicated advice columnist and a major power at Field Enterprises, where she has been dispensing wisdom for twenty-four years from her well-staffed office at the *Sun-Times*. Ann probably gets more requests for help than Vito Marzullo, averaging one thousand letters a day from people worried about everything from funeral arrangements (should the departed's fifth wife be allowed at the service?) to what to do until the vasectomy comes.

Ann has a staff of letter openers and sorters, people specially trained to recognize both representative and oddball dilemmas and to weed out prank pleas. Ann also has one of the most enviable Rollodexes in town—when Ann comes up against a touchy problem in ethics, she can call up her old pal Father Ted Hesburgh, president of Notre Dame; when the question is one of psychology, she can ask one of the Menninger boys.

What appears in the syndicated column, however, is pure Ann Landers. Ann once confided in a television interview, "I may be wrong, but I am never without an opinion."

Landers' column is one of the most popular in the nation and certainly the one with the most day-to-day impact. Surveys have shown that many people (and there are some 60 million of them who daily look up Ann Landers in 910 papers) consult Ann Landers before they read anything else in the paper.

Before Ann Landers became part of the question "Hey, did you hear what Ann Landers had to say this morning?" she was Eppie Lederer, well-to-do wife of Dr. Jules Lederer, and a Chicago matron with time and money on her hands. In 1955, the original Ann Landers (the *Sun-Times* editor who conceived of the column thought that Ann Landers had a reassuring ring to it) died, leaving the *Sun-Times* advisor-lorn. A competition was held, and Eppie won out over twenty-eight other would-be oracles.

Nine months later, another advice column was born, *Dear Abby*, headed by Ann's twin sister Pauline. (The sisters have always been closely linked. Their yearbook from Central High School in Sioux City, Iowa, identified Eppie Friedman as "peppy and cute" and Pauline Friedman as "cute and peppy.") Perhaps some day one of the columns will carry a letter about the pangs of sibling rivalry.

Ann Landers lives the kind of life she might advise her readers to try for. Now divorced (gosh) from Jules after thirty-six years of marriage, Ann lives in a fourteen-room apartment on the lakefront. She sets off her tiny frame in designer clothes. She graces the speakers' tables of fund-raisers for Governor Thompson, meetings for the League of Women Voters, and for the Menninger Foundation and the Mayo Clinic.

Bruce Vilanch, a *Tribune* feature writer since gone to Hollywood, once attended a party at the home of Chicago writer and Glamorous Person Margo Coleman. He is said to have shrieked with delight at finding a huge picture of Ann Landers in Margo's bedroom, proclaiming it the very ultimate in camp. Margo didn't find it so campy. As Vilanch apparently did not know, Margo is Ann's daughter.

14. Rance Crain

The business of Crain Communications is business. The Chicago publishing house, founded by the late G. D. Crain, Jr., chaired by his widow, Gertrude, and run by son Rance, churns out papers keyed to special financial and consumer interest groups: like *Business Insurance, Pensions and Investments, Automotive News,* and *Rubber and Plastics News.*

Advertising Age is one long-standing Crain publication that not only reports what's going on in that most frenetic business, but helps shape events. *Ad Age* is part reportage, part market report, and part obituary. Ad people comb it for jobs, for accounts, to find out what agency is losing what account, what copywriter is losing his touch, what account executive has driven yet another agency into bankruptcy.

At the core of Crain Communications is president Rance Crain. Rance—destined for publishing like a Field—always wanted to be a disc jockey. In his travels around the country for Crain Communications, Rance would sometimes manage to appear, late at night, in radio stations in obscure towns in North Dakota, billing himself "The Boss Jock from the Windy City."

But Rance eventually became a full-fledged Crain. After attending Northwestern University's Medill School of Journalism, where he first broke into print as sports editor for the *Daily Northwestern,*

Crain spent the 1960's working in *Ad Age*'s Washington, New York, and Chicago offices. He was editorial director of *Business Insurance* and *Industrial Marketing* and editorial director of *Ad Age* in the early 1970's. In 1973, Crain became the president of Crain Communications.

Rance Crain's coup was the launching of *Crain's Chicago Business* in the spring of 1978, a weekly tabloid that reveals as much about the inner workings of Chicago as an alderman's private phone line. Financial news, as treated in *Crain's*, is hot. Since *Crain's* success, other tabloids, like Murray Weil's *Chicago Business Review*, are scampering to cover the Chicago business beat too. As Crain said in a *Sun-Times* interview, "It's kind of a throwback to the old *Front Page* with people battling for a scoop. Now it's shifted to the business arena."

15. John Madigan

Some ten years ago, WBBM Radio's political editor John Madigan, was czar of everything at CBS's Chicago news operation—TV news, radio news, and even host of a TV talk show competing with the great Irv Kupcinet's.

But one by one, like a French Foreign Legion officer humiliated before his troops, he was stripped of these powers and honors. He's been reduced to a daily news and political commentary on WBBM Radio, along with a daily "John Madigan views the press" harangue against his colleagues in the news media. Still, no one else gets a daily-news commentary and harangue against the press. He's even chewed out CBS's own queenly Susan Anderson on the air.

A former old-time newspaperman and Washington correspondent, who was chased out of his beloved South Shore neighborhood when it went suddenly black, Madigan is a quintessential Chicago Irishman. The kind Mayor Daley loved so well. He loved John especially. WTTW's Joel Weisman summed up his opinion of Madigan's objectivity on things City Hall with three words: "Radio Free Machine." Still, it's nice to have an honorary member of the Daley family mingling with the news folk.

And it's useful to know that, when John talks about Democratic politics, he knows whereof he speaks.

20

Where They Live: The City

Many of the people who run Chicago can't seem to bring themselves to live there, preferring more seemly residence in opulent suburbs like lofty Lake Forest, where the only vestige of the urban experience is an occasional bit of sewage floating down the lake from Milwaukee. That's how it is with aristocrats, even the Chicago kind.

But a significant portion of the elite hangs out in town, and the neighborhoods they inhabit are the city's best. There are only ten of them worth ranking, but some cities have only one. Detroit may not have any.

The demographics of Chicago are pretty simple—visible from any jetliner flying across the city to O'Hare, when the wind isn't blowing the green smog in from Gary. The rich and powerful live in a narrow band of high-rise prosperity along the lake, and in a couple of suburbanesque outposts on the Far Northwest and Far Southwest Sides. The mere masses live every place else.

Actually, there are some rich and powerful who live out among the masses, but only because their jobs require them to. Street-gang leaders, for example—who surely could afford most any Lake Shore Drive condominium—have to stick to their turf to keep control over it. As street gangs flourish mostly in the worst neighborhoods, you seldom see the chieftains of the Stones lounging about the Racquet Club, although that would be fun. Back in the fun 1960's, gang leaders did enjoy a certain cachet in liberal Hyde Park salons, but it proved a fleeting fashion.

Chicago's mob bosses are certainly an affluent and influential group, but most tend to shun the ostentatious and luxurious for the nondescript and anonymous. Hoodlum Manny Skar lived a wild and crazy extravagant existence both on Rush Street and in a nifty Lake Shore Drive pad. Not godfatherly Sam De Stefano. He lived unpretentiously in a quiet section of Oak Park. They gunned Manny down in his Lake Shore Drive driveway while he was still a reasonably young man. Sam also got it in his driveway, but he had lived to be an old man.

The city's ward bosses and other politicians are somewhat more respectable and could move into the Gold Coast or similarly posh districts without too many complaints from the neighbors. But most prefer to quarter where the votes are. Alderman Thomas E. Keane, who made millions while City Council floor leader, never resided anywhere but the Northwest Side 31st Ward, except when he went to jail.

Unlike the unfortunate Mayor Martin Kennelly, who perished politically a resident of Lake Shore Drive, the late Richard Daley stayed in Bridgeport. As we have seen, Bilandic stayed in Bridgeport, even though it meant moving Heather from her Michigan Avenue area digs to a two flat, and a long dreary drive from the ballet. If Jane Byrne is smart, she'll get out of her high-rise and into a bungalow, too.

Few in Heather's set are so inconvenienced. For most of them, running Chicago means being able to live where they bloody well please, even if that also means living on top of each other.

The following ranking of the city's best neighborhoods takes into account such criteria as average income, educational levels, housing value, and population density, as well as such factors as proximity to the lake and the park, neighborhood character, characters in the neighborhood, and nearby amenities. Emphasis is also placed on such indices as the number of Social Register listings and memberships in important clubs.

As a consequence, even with Heather, Bridgeport doesn't make the list.

THE TEN BEST NEIGHBORHOODS IN CHICAGO

1. The Drive (Near North)

Chicago is basically a tank town. It does have that world-renowned symphony and those glittering stores, and fashions that are only a year behind New York's. But, basically, it's just a big St. Louis or Indianapolis. The only big difference is the lake, and more particularly, the lakefront.

Milwaukee and Cleveland are on lakes and have lakefronts, but those are strewn with factories, grunge heaps, and other urban junk. Chicago's Lake Michigan shoreline is principally parkland, beaches, and yacht harbors, with that fantastic skyline just behind. The late Ian Fleming called it one of the world's great waterfronts.

Lake Shore Drive, with only a few interruptions, runs along most of that lakefront on the North Side. The name has been sanctified. When former Alderman Paul Wigoda, who later got convicted for something or other, suggested changing the name of Lake Shore Drive to Apollo 11 Drive to commemorate the first manned moon landing, the rich people all but took to the streets and rioted. "Lake Shore Drive" means something.

The most prestigious section of the Drive runs north from Lake Point Tower around the two bends of Oak Street Beach and then north again to the southern boundary of Lincoln Park. This is the classiest real estate in town and qualifies as the single-best neighborhood in Chicago.

It might be argued that a single street can't be a neighborhood; that, in fact, Lake Shore Drive (Near North) runs alongside two: the Gold Coast and Streeterville. But that is nonsense. You either live on the Drive or you don't, and if you don't, you're just not in the same neighborhood. To live on the Drive is to not merely be near Lake Michigan but to take possession of it. An apartment on the Drive commands an unimpeded view of the lake. It also sits in a building that impedes the view of others. What better way to feel sure of one's place?

The high-rise buildings on the Drive (Near North) range from the Miami Beach glitzy to 1930's Robber Baron, but they're all very, very expensive. The apartments tend to be large enough for a decent game of jai alai, and, if a faucet shouldn't work, the buildings are quite labor intensive. There's a "little man" for the most trifling whim and errand.

The most socially esteemed addresses on the Drive are some great stone WASP palaces at 1242, 1500, and 1540 North Lake Shore Drive and 209 and 229 East Lake Shore Drive, opposite Oak Street Beach. The East Lake Shore Drive apartments are really the best, because they face north up the shoreline and give the gazer something to see besides a flat, dull expanse of empty water.

Probably the best building is 179 East Lake Shore Drive, right next to the Drake Hotel. It's the one with Abra (Rockefeller) Prentice Anderson's charming penthouse on the top.

The great thing about living on the Drive (Near North) is that you're quite literally next to everything. The best Michigan Avenue shops, the Oak Street boutiques, fancy Rush Street groceries and wineries, and the Casino Club are all within a few blocks of Abra's. If you live a bit farther up the Drive, you have the advantage of the Racquet Club, and if you live a bit farther down, you have the advantage of the Filtration Plant. Everything else that matters in town is just a short cab or limousine ride away. Living on the Drive means being just minutes from bedroom to beach, beach to boardroom, and boardroom to bedroom. And, depending on your proclivities, bedroom to bedroom.

And there are always cabs on the Drive.

2. The Gold Coast

If there were no lakeshore and Lake Shore Drive, the No. 1 neighborhood in Chicago would be the Gold Coast. It is now No. 2, but how long it can maintain that status is open to question. Its residents are not at all what one would call impoverished, but the population density is approaching that of the Warsaw ghetto.

Settled by rich people trying to live as close as possible to the Potter Palmers' little place on the lake, the Gold Coast runs roughly from Lincoln Park down to Division Street, and from the rear of the Lake Shore Drive apartments west to the alley behind Dearborn Street. Its principal thoroughfares are Dearborn, State Parkway, and Astor Street, which was made into a historical district in a much-too-belated effort to stop the awful growth of high rises in the area.

The "nicest" Chicago folk lived on the Gold Coast in the days of carriages and Pierce Arrow town cars. There are still "nice" people to be found, but many of them drive Volkswagens and little BMWs and still can't find a place to park.

In the robber baron days, the Gold Coast consisted almost entirely of single-family dwellings (if you could call the Swift or Potter Palmer mansions single-family dwellings) featuring coach houses, stables, and giggling servant girls in the rear.

But in the last twenty years, the neighborhood has been beset by two unfortunate trends characteristic of Chicago real estate: the subdivision of old homes into apartments, and the erection of towering, pack-'em-in high rises with intimate views of each other.

The former have lately been curbed through zoning and establishment clout downtown. The latter were in part halted by the Astor Street landmark district, but it came much too late. If Chicago had the same stringent, tow-'em-off parking law enforcement that New York does, there'd be rioting and bloodshed in the Gold Coast every night.

The Gold Coast isn't quite so convenient to things as Abra's penthouse. It is near North Street Beach, which is just as nice as Oak Street Beach, except for the murders.

Cardinal Cody lives in the Gold Coast, in a Charles Addams' architectural notion of gracious urban living. The esteemed British and French consuls-general are Gold Coasters as well, as is seemingly half the Social Register.

Hugh Hefner, whose Christmas cards aren't nearly so tasteful as Abra (Rockefeller) Prentice Anderson's, finally closed his ridiculous Playboy Mansion on North State Parkway, but there's always the dread that, like the alewives, he may come back.

The Racquet Club and the Junior League are in the Gold Coast, which is just super, as are St. Chrysostrom's ever-so-exclusive Church and the Ambassador East, where theatrical stars stay.

But airline stewardesses and apprentice advertising executives are infesting the place, like root-feeding mealy bugs, and bringing their boisterous life-styles with them.

3. Streeterville

Chicago's No. 3 neighborhood is Streeterville, which sounds vaguely like a whorehouse district, but is not. At least, not the kind where you can readily tell.

Extending south from Oak Street to the Chicago River and west from Lake Michigan to just past Michigan Avenue (actually, you probably ought to call it Greater Streeterville), this expanding Near Downtown residential district still has a few warehouses and raunchy saloons among its more glittering addresses, but it glitters more and more year after year.

It was named for Cap Streeter, a bewhiskered and bewhiskeyed late-nineteenth-century loon who set up housekeeping on a sandbar at the east end of the area and proclaimed it his own private kingdom. He was ultimately run off as a public nuisance. There are still a few winos carrying on his tradition among the warehouses at the neighborhood's south end.

Streeterville is very much a high-rise district, but unlike the Gold Coast, the population density is not oppressive. The posher parts are still mostly north of Chicago Avenue, but the southern end, what with the Time-Life Building and those restored townhouses, is becoming quite nice. That's where Harry Weese wants to put boutiques and sidewalk cafés.

The most convenient of Chicago's "best" neighborhoods, Streeterville is perhaps excessively convenient. It has the Hancock Center and Water Tower Place, of course, and all those Michigan Avenue stores. It also contains a branch of Northwestern University, a post office, the sprawling CBS studios, the sprawling Northwestern Memorial hospital complex, the city's best movie theater (the Cinema), some good hotels, some not-so-good hotels, a small park with a clogged jogging track, and the national guard armory where young Marshall Field served dutifully in the riotous 1960's as an enlisted man.

In some ways, living in Streeterville is rather like living over a store, but Bonwit's is no fish market, and the Casino Club is no corner tavern. If it's still somewhat hard to tell the debutantes from the call girls, there are debutantes, which is more than you can say about Rogers Park.

4. Lincoln Park-Lakeview

If one could combine London's Regents Park with Bloomsbury, with a touch of Mayfair and Soho thrown in, one would have a neighborhood something like Lincoln Park-Lakeview—only much better. Chicago, alas, is no London.

Occupying a long and increasingly wide swath of the city's Near North Side along the western boundary of Lincoln Park, LPL is where you'll find most of Chicago's artistic and intellectual life now, such as it is. Chicago must always ask itself why Nelson Algren moved to New Jersey. LPL is also the major breeding ground for the city's independent liberal political activity, such as it now is —hence the name "lakefront liberal."

In LPL, the accent is on charm, Chicago style. This often means the merely kitsch, or the slick mass-produced quaintness that makes one wonder if all those cutesy restaurants on Lincoln Avenue aren't secretly owned by the McDonald's chain.

There are some really classic old apartment high rises directly facing the park, with many a shiny new one rising among them. What the area is most famous for, though, is its houses: restored row houses, new townhouses, and huge old Victorian houses, many of them with spacious lawns and large trees. Great fortunes are being poured into the renovation of these structures, with interior decorators toiling like German slave laborers at the height of World War II.

LPL has some lingering seedy sections. Not long ago, much of the neighborhood was seedy. The St. Valentine's Day Massacre garage and Nelson Algren's favorite saloon were major neighborhood landmarks. But the Urban Renewal Department took care of that.

Immediately to the south of LPL is the vast clip joint that is Old Town. To the north is the noisy but less expensive New Town. LPL's stretch of Lincoln Park contains the zoo, the conservatory, two museums, assorted lagoons, and abundant flower gardens. LPL also contains some good private schools like Francis Parker, where little Warwick or Samantha need not fear being done in by some second-grade fiend.

A wonderful assortment of important people live or lived in LPL— everyone from the William W. Princes and Don Reuben to Governor Jim Thompson and *Sun-Times* Editor Jim Hoge to Lakefront Libs like the Rosners. The only time Daley ever seemed to visit was to go to the zoo. He may have thought the whole neighborhood was a zoo.

5. The Drive (Not Near North)

Running north along the lake from just above Belmont Avenue to Irving Park Road is a stretch of Lake Shore Drive that greatly resembles that ritzy segment to the south—Lake Shore Drive (Near North)—that constitutes Chicago's best neighborhood.

The Drive (Not Near North) has the same imposing high rises, old and new, as the Drive (Near North). It has doormen and Social Register listings and magnificent views—much better than most of the Drive (Near North) views because there is also park to look at and not just dull empty water.

But the Drive (Not Near North) is ever so far from everything and—as some Social Register people might put it—the people there aren't quite so "nice." There are a lot of little old widows in fur coats living there whose husbands used to own drugstores. They ride the buses in packs and chatter endlessly about their relatives and vacations. They are not quite so vexsome, though, as the neighborhood's infinite number of dog owners, who in snowy winters amount to a criminal class.

The Drive (Not Near North) really isn't very convenient to anything, except Belmont Harbor yachting, some public tennis courts, and a really good Treasure Island supermarket on nearby Broadway. Temple Shalom, the wealthiest synagogue in Chicago, is on the Drive (Not Near North).

The better addresses on the Drive (Not Near North) are in the older buildings down toward Belmont Avenue—and there are some magnificent houses on Hawthorne and a few other splendidly maintained adjoining side streets.

One of the Drive (Not Near North)'s more illustrious residents is Lili Schenck, Chicago's wealthy, blonde and certainly most attractive lady barber.

6. Belmont Harbor

This is a very charming neighborhood—an enclave of older high rises and handsome houses nestled against Lincoln Park between Diversey and Belmont Avenue. There's an adjoining stretch of Lake Shore Drive here as well that, at this point, functions more as a country lane than a major thoroughfare. Belmont Harbor's main streets are Belmont Avenue and Sheridan Road.

The area is a trifle close to raucous New Town, and too audibly near the Lincoln Park gun club, with all its mindless shotgunners blasting away over the lake on Sunday mornings. A large portion of the neighborhood's park frontage is taken up with the St. Joseph Hospital complex and an enormous nunnery, complete with vegetable garden, facing Lake Shore Drive. But at leeast the vegetables and nuns are quiet.

Not so quiet is the nearby intersection of Clark and Diversey, so infamous for its teenage boy prostitution and other such aspects of the Gay Life that the police refer to it as Clark and Perversity.

7. Marine Drive

For the elite of Chicago who are recently married and just starting out, or who have found themselves in "reduced circumstances," Marine Drive makes for some pleasant and respectable digs at a relatively reasonable cost. A northern extension of Lake Shore Drive, it runs from Irving Park Road up to Foster Avenue, where the exclusive Saddle and Cycle Club hides behind its barbed wire.

So inconvenient as to seem almost Siberian in the winter, Marine Drive's only link with the city's business and social center five miles to the south is some infrequent express bus service and the Outer Drive—the broad lakefront expressway that was another of Mayor Daley's notions of pastoral loveliness. To live on Marine Drive is to drive. One must have a car even to get to the grocery and the liquor store. Many of the liquor stores near Marine Drive specialize in very small bottles of very cheap wine.

Of the city's "best" neighborhoods, Marine Drive is the most happily integrated and probably the most ethnically diverse. They must speak twenty different languages in the WaterFord Condominium there alone. The black people you see waiting for buses on Marine Drive are usually going to work—not home.

A lot of judges and well-heeled politicians live on Marine Drive. One of the Rolls-Royces there is owned by a black rock impresario. One of the battered Volkswagens, by a powerful member of the Union League Club. The best nudie photographer at *Playboy* lives on Marine Drive. An actual DuPont lady lived on Marine Drive, but she moved to Philadelphia.

8. Hyde Park

At the turn of the century, Hyde Park and environs came close to being the city's best neighborhood. The turn of the century was a very long time ago.

Hyde Park does, of course, contain the University of Chicago (or is it the other way around?), with all those Great Minds. But the university is much more concerned with the known universe than Chicago. For many, the surrounding city exists as a vague theoretical concept.

This is not their attitude toward the surrounding black ghetto, which has been Hyde Park's principal obsession in recent years. The University has exerted immense power in trying to control the racial situation—more than Daley ever dared apply to neighborhoods in the rest of the city—but not with totally satisfactory results. Integration has succeeded in that a lot of middle-class black people are living there, but they seem as paranoid about the surrounding ghetto as the white folk. This fortress mentality has drained the community of much of its vitality, and some of its population. Even though the quality of scholarly life is somewhat inferior at Northwestern, those relatively crime-free and tree-lined streets in Evanston are so much more relaxing.

Hyde Park used to be a political hotbed, for political radicalism, that is, but the sheets are growing a little cold. Daley's first opponent in a mayoral election was a Hyde Park liberal, and the community used to send entire teams of them to Springfield. But now the most radical politician in power there is State Senator Richard Newhouse, a rather gentlemanly black fellow. Abner Mikva, as the world knows, moved to Evanston.

A few society grande dames are still clinging to Hyde Park, most notably Mrs. C. Phillip Miller, a Pullman still living on Kimbark Avenue of all places. But the zing has gone out of their cling.

9. Forest Glen and All That

A mere three weeks' drive during rush hour up the Kennedy and Edens Expressways from the Loop are a group of bedroom communities within the city limits on the Far Northwest Side. One of them, Forest Glen, is listed by the Metropolitan Council for Community Services as the top ranking "community area" in Chicago. According to such sociological data as median family income and home value, it undoubtedly is. But, it must be remembered that the sociological "community area" that takes in the Gold Coast also takes in heaps of slum.

Forest Glen and All That is a lovely place. The houses and trees are very pretty. The schools are good. The children are happy, and the doggies go bow wow. There are many people of substance there, especially of political substance. But it is so terribly terribly far. If you want to live in a suburban area, the train service from Evanston is much better. But if you must live in the city, as so many city officials must and do, this place does nicely.

10. Beverly

The Far Southwest Side is just like the Far Northwest Side, only older, and crumbling around the edges. The best of these far-flung neighborhoods is elegant old elitist Beverly—a sort of South Side urban Winnetka, with hills, curving roads and driveways, and large houses, even mansions.

But the ghetto is on the rear doorstep, and on Saturday nights it can sound as if it's trying to get in. White families willing to buy into Beverly are treated like royalty by local savings and loans associations. White families wishing to sell out don't have to worry much about excessive capital-gains taxes.

Beverly used to be a Republican kingdom. The only GOP office-holder left is State Representative Ted Meyer, nephew of the celebrated Cardinal Meyer. Meyer is well known for his many legislative efforts on behalf of endangered species. He is one.

21

Where They Live: The Suburbs

Periodically, University of Illinois urbanologist Pierre de Vise irritates the hell out of people by issuing another of his "socioeconomic rankings" of the 201 suburban communities (with populations exceeding 2,500) in the eight-county metropolitan area. These lists naturally produce a lot of pride and gloating. But there's always irritation. With good reason.

De Vise correctly identifies the "best" Chicago suburbs as those along the North Shore, several of those woodsy communities just to the west of the North Shore, some horsey places in northwest Cook County and west suburban Du Page County, and a couple of the old railroad baronages in the far south suburbs.

But the order in which he ranks them takes many people aback. In his 1977 survey, he put the horsey, manurey Barrington Hills as No. 1. Next were Kenilworth, horsey Oak Brook, Olympia Fields in the far, far, far south suburbs, and the North Shore's Glencoe.

Lake Forest, which is to Chicago suburbia what Queen Victoria was to English peerage, was relegated to eighth place by de Vise. Something like half the Social Register people in the metropolitan area live in Lake Forest. You could put all the society queens who live in Barrington in a single stableyard.

Venerable, leafy old Evanston, which is home to some of the

finest names on LaSalle Street and contains the third-highest number of Social Register listings of any Chicago suburb, de Vise put down at eighty-third. His analyses are based only on median family income, families with incomes exceeding $25,000, and median home value.

Among other things, this penalizes communities such as Lake Forest, which of necessity contains poor people. How can a community of the truly rich and powerful function without some convenient poor people? Who is to do the dishes?

In the following ranking of Chicago's suburbs, we take into account all the socioeconomic data used by de Vise. We also consider such statistics as per capita income, the percentage of white-collar workers in the population, and median education level.

Our criteria also include natural beauty, proximity to the lake (very important except near Gary), convenient shopping (can one buy fresh crab meat?), convenience to downtown (the people who run Chicago can't spend all their time on trains), and amenities (such as the North Shore's Ravinia Park or Oak Brook's polo fields).

As de Vise seems never to have done, we also subtract points for obvious detractions, such as glue works or any racial or religious discord in the community, or noisy airports.

And we've made quite a point to check out club memberships, *Who's Who* listings, and Social Register listings to see who actually lives where. Prosperous dentists in $150,000 homes may rank high in de Vise's listings, but they don't have much to do with the running of Chicago.

THE TOP TWENTY SUBURBS IN CHICAGO

1. Lake Forest

Situated on wooded highlands along Lake Michigan some twenty-eight miles north of the Loop, Lake Forest is the only place similar to Newport or Southampton in the Midwest. Its most prominent characteristics are its parklike setting and its robber-baron, old-money wealth. The mansions there rival Czar Nicholas' summer palace. Indeed, a walk along the suburb's Lake Avenue on the lakeshore is enough to turn most anyone socialist.

Lake Forest has more than four hundred entries in the most

recent Chicago Social Register. This is not only the highest total for any Chicago suburb but is more than twice as many as the next-ranking community, Winnetka.

Lake Forest is just full of old-money names—Swift, Armour, Blair. It has Pullmans and Palmers, Hutchins and Byron Smiths. It even has the Chicago Bears' Doug Buffone. With the possible exceptions of the smaller Winnetka and much smaller Kenilworth, there is simply no place like Lake Forest for money and power in the Chicago area.

Lake Forest is also a college town, though catering more to Reginald College than to Joe. Its institutions include the exclusive Lake Forest College, Lake Forest Academy, Ferry Hall for girls, Barat College, and Woodlands Academy. All abound in ivy. Barat College's Academy Festival Theater is one of the best designed playhouses in the Midwest and gets some really good non-dinner theater, without Barbara Rush.

In addition to its sizable aristocracy, Lake Forest can also claim an upper-middle class, a middle class, a working and shopkeeping class, and an actual colony of actual black people, much cherished by the local rich folk and dating back to the nineteenth century.

There is the problem of Fort Sheridan on the southern edge of town, but the soldiers have learned not to walk on the grass and to take their pleasure elsewhere—such as at the beer bars and dirty movies in nearby Highwood. But it's nice to have the soldiers around. One never knows when the revolution might come.

Lake Forest's shopping district has its own Marshall Field's, and a number of expensive if not au courant boutiques. As Jon Anderson has noted, the Margaret Rutherford look is considered quite au courant there. The shopping district is not merely quaint, but was designed to look like a sixteenth-century English village that caught someone's fancy. The sixteenth century is also considered au courant in Lake Forest.

2. Winnetka

There really aren't any big noises in Winnetka, but there is lots and lots of money. Down the lake from Lake Forest some eighteen miles north of Chicago's Loop, Winnetka ranks very high with the *Town & Country* set, with homes running frequently around $350,000. Its name means "beautiful land" in Potawatomi. The land is no longer zoned for Potawatomi, but has remained rather scenic, with wooded hills and deep, curving ravines running back from the lakefront bluffs.

With nearly two hundred Social Register listings and scads of really big corporation names, Winnetka is not exactly Elk Grove Village, but it does tend to be slightly more arriviste than Lake Forest. You'll find heaps of $300,000-a-year lawyers there. You'll also find W. Clement Stone, who lives in a house that would have made Citizen Kane feel warm and cuddly, and TV talk-show star Phil Donahue.

Despite its wealth and educated populace, Winnetka remains something of a cultural desert, especially in comparison with Lake Forest. We've been to Winnetka lawn parties where the host has cavorted in his wife's wig—at four in the afternoon!

Winnetka is the center of New Trier Township, which is named after the old Roman city of Trier in Germany, which was the birthplace of Karl Marx. Irony is everywhere.

3. Kenilworth

A tiny little lakeshore commuting town with barely three thousand population, Kenilworth is a bedroom community for people who feel the need for ten bedrooms. It seems zoned for mansions.

Kenilworth ranks ninth in the number of Social Register listings, which is remarkable for its small size. It is first in the Chicago metropolitan area in college education, median income, and per capita income.

The *Tribune*'s Stanton R. Cook lives there, as does Dick Thomas, president of the First National Bank; William Graham of Baxter Labs; lawyer Bert Jenner; and no one from the Chicago Bears. Senator Percy used to live there, but left after his daughter was murdered in the family's lakefront mansion in 1966.

Tucked between Winnetka and Wilmette just sixteen miles from downtown Chicago, Kenilworth is a swift commute and near such conveniences as the Plaza del Lago Shopping Center with its Burhop's Fish Store. You can get fresh crab meat! If Kenilworth has a problem, it's sterility. Though *Town & Country* magazine claims there's a Chinese neurologist living there, he's undoubtedly the only non-WASP, and he's said to drive a Rolls. In years of driving through Kenilworth, the authors can recall seeing a minority person only once—a black man riding a bicycle. Doubtless passing through.

4. Wilmette

Wilmette has its mansions and Social Register types, but it's much less pretentious and more relaxed than the suburbs that precede it on this list, having much more in common with its more egalitarian neighbor to the south, Evanston. Indeed, some houses in Wilmette are downright grungy, although you'd never know it from the astronomical tax bills.

A lakeshore community with splendid old homes and tree-lined streets, Wilmette has three things that add greatly to its value: the extraordinary and breathtaking white-domed Baha'i Temple, the only yacht harbor of consequence on the North Shore, and the excellent Plaza del Lago shopping center with its fresh crab legs.

Only fifteen miles from the Loop on the Chicago and North Western commuter line, Wilmette is getting some residential overflow from Evanston, a lot of it from Northwestern University. In its western reaches, Wilmette is developing a largish Jewish community. Its New Trier public high schools are considered among the very best in the country.

Wilmette is named for Antoine Ouilmette, a French trader who once was the only white man in Chicago. There are people in Wilmette who would be pleased at that.

5. Barrington

Chicago's answer to the horse country of Northern Virginia, Barrington and Barrington Hills have a lot of people with money, although not really a lot of people with a lot of money. The area is one of thick woods, innumerable fields and meadows, expensive and secluded country homes, and more horses than you'd care to count, let alone shovel up after.

There was a dreadful murder there in 1972. Some black youths from the Chicago ghetto went for a long drive in the country, broke into a Barrington home, and shot all the occupants. After that, it seemed like everyone in Barrington was carrying a gun, although few switched to western saddles.

The Barringtons, which do have a railroad station, some supermarkets, and other vestiges of civilization, are nearly forty miles from the Loop. The train ride takes two forevers, and it's even longer by horse.

The fabled Arthur Wirtz has a big place in Barrington, as does architect Harry Weese. So does *Tribune* photographer Val Mazzenga and the First National Bank's Bob Abboud. Everyone loves the country, if not horses.

6. Glencoe

Glencoe is just north of Winnetka and has the same kind of fine old houses, lakefront bluffs, and wooded hills and ravines as its neighboring North Shore suburbs. Though not quite so well favored by the high society and captain of industry set, it rates close to the top in nearly all the socioeconomic statistics. Lawyers seem quite fond of it. Howard Trienens of Sidley and Austin lives there, as does Barbara Austin Foote, whose father was the Austin of Sidley and Austin. Poet Archibald Macleish was born in Glencoe, but he moved to more stimulating climes.

Glencoe does have something of a split personality. As a community, it has parts that are intensely WASP and parts that are intensely Jewish. There are seven Christian churches there, and there is the temple of North Shore Congregation Israel, a huge structure of striking design set on sprawling grounds overlooking the lake. Many in Glencoe are quite proud of it and some are not so proud of it.

7. Oak Brook

Though only eighteen miles west of the Loop in Du Page County, Oak Brook for decades was nothing but a polo club. Then millionaire developer Paul Butler and others attempted to create on its sixteen square miles an exclusive residential community devoted to "the gentlemanly outdoor sports." More recently than that, it has been swarmed over by a huge shopping center and countless office complexes, including the global headquarters of the McDonald's empire. Some of its many modern homes must be counted among the most extravagant in the Midwest.

Much too new a suburb to attract the Social Register sort of family, Oak Brook does have all those Butlers and the McDonald's folk, and members of the Union League and Chicago Athletic Clubs abound. For those interested, the "gentlemanly outdoor sports" Oak Brook features are: polo, tennis, archery, soccer, horseback riding, flying, shooting, fox hunting, swimming, badminton, croquet, shuffleboard, and (naturally) horseshoes. Should it rain, there's always billiards, bourbon, and sex.

Unique among supposedly sylvan suburbs, Oak Brook has actual oak trees and an actual brook named Oak Brook.

8. Northbrook

Formerly called Shermerville, Northbrook was for decades a sleepy little village in the woods west of Glencoe that after World War II began awakening to the hammers and saws of subdivision development. But the subdivisions in Northbrook are more elegant than most.

For some reason, it has a fair number of Social Register people living in it and its nearby shopping center includes a Nieman Marcus, which is better than you'll find in Schaumburg.

Situated along the Edens Expressway and Milwaukee Road commuter line, Northbrook has some clean, light industry. But mostly, it seems to have golf courses—more perhaps than some states do. There are three pleasant watercourses around it: the Des Plaines River, the north branch of the Chicago River, and the Skokie River with its lovely lagoons.

9. Evanston

On Lake Michigan just north of the Chicago city limits, Evanston functions as something of a city in itself. Its population now exceeds eighty thousand, with fifteen thousand of that black. Its sizable downtown section has department stores, first class hotels, and everything else you might imagine, including limousine service to O'Hare. Its rail and rapid-transit lines make quick runs to downtown Chicago.

If de Vise rates Evanston so low, it's in large part because of the alleged ghetto on Evanston's southwest side (which must be the nicest ghetto in the country) and because of all the apartment buildings clustered down by the Chicago city line (although those apartments, initially rental units, are now selling in some cases for eighty thousand dollars and more).

What Evanston mostly is, though, is a place of great old trees and great old houses, a place that combines the cultural and civil amenities of big city life with the relaxing comforts of the suburbs, while minimizing the negative points of both city and suburb. In some respects, it seems an old ladies' town, which may account for its abundance of Social Register listings. It was for years home to the Women's Christian Temperance Union (though you can now buy booze in Evanston) and seems to have more garden clubs than all of England. It does have the Northwestern kids, which means it also has Northwestern—a fine university but one that tends to relate to the community the way the Vatican does to Rome.

Evanston has abundant numbers of both liberals and conservatives which is why Abner Mikva was elected to congress and why his victory margins were always so small.

Evanston has excellent schools—and a crime problem (attributable mostly to the kind of traffic the elevated brings in). On one recent occasion, the daughter of a Northwestern University professor was stabbed to death on an elevated platform right in downtown Evanston in the early evening. Some insecure residents suggested sealing up an underpass that connects Evanston with a crummier section of Chicago, but that only provoked a collective gasp. No Berlin Walls, please. Not in Evanston.

10. Lake Bluff

The most northern of the posh North Shore suburbs, Lake Bluff is just beyond Lake Forest and some thirty-three miles from downtown Chicago. It sits on an actual bluff overlooking the actual lake, and has a nice sandy beach. Its extremely exclusive Shoreacres Club is very popular with the more exclusive Lake Foresters, if not with the guys on the wharf at Waukegan.

A great many Lake Forest types actually live in Lake Bluff, including ones with names like Armour, but it still has more "nice" homes than actual mansions.

Lake Bluff ranks third in the metropolitan area for median education college education, which may be attributable to the fact that there's little to do there but read and go for walks on the beach. It's so very quiet.

Just to the north of Lake Bluff is Great Lakes Naval Training Center, which would be totally useless come the revolution and which congressmen and senators keep promising to turn into sylvan parkland, but never do. If the naval base is not terribly popular in Lake Bluff, it at least separates the town from Waukegan and North Chicago.

In the old days, Lake Bluff was the site of religious retreats and camp meetings, but you hardly ever hear a "hallelujah" anymore. Or anything else.

11. Glenview

Glenview, twenty miles from the Loop and just south of Northbrook, is very much like Northbrook, only a modicum less ritzy. Maybe two modicums. It is served by the Milwaukee Road railroad and the Edens Expressway, with the Milwaukee Road serving as a divider of sorts between chic Glenview and the not-so.

Attorney Robert Bergstrom and *Tribune* Columnist Jack Mabley are Glenview guys and both served as village president. Actress Linda Darnell died in Glenview in a terrible fire.

The suburb has had some terrible airplane crashes, because it adjoins the Glenview Naval Air Station, which in the old days used to stage productions like the Battle of Midway, especially on weekends. But all that reservist stuff has been somewhat curtailed and the skies are a little quieter now.

Glenview is extremely proud of its many parks. It has thirty— a ratio of about one to every one thousand residents. There is also golf—everywhere one looks. One of the main highways through Glenview is called Golf Road.

12. Flossmoor-Olympia Fields

Flossmoor and Olympia Fields sit adjoining one another in the far, far, far south suburbs some thirty miles distant from the Loop. Both were founded by Illinois Central Railroad executives who wanted a place where they could hear train whistles in the night. Both are exceedingly Republican.

Olympia Fields, the smaller of the two, is the wealthier in crass statistical terms. The town surrounds a country club and four golf courses. There's also polo, tennis, swimming, shooting, and other "gentlemanly outdoor sports." They also go in for shooting in nearby Chicago Heights, but not in such gentlemanly fashion.

Flossmoor, though less wealthy, is considered more classy. Its age or something. Its residents include a surprising number of intellectuals, including Elisabeth Kübler-Ross, and, of course, Congressman Edward Derwinski and his wife Pat.

The same house that costs you $500,000 in Lake Forest you might get for $250,000 in Flossmoor-Olympia Fields. As one resident told *Town & Country* magazine: "We don't live outside Chicago. We live fifteen miles from Kankakee."

Football coaching immortal Amos Alonzo Stagg was Olympia Field's first village president in 1915. Is football a gentlemanly outdoor sport?

13. *Highland Park*

Highland Park sits just across the Lake County line from Glencoe, amidst all those trees and ravines and overlooking the beauteous waters. It has very expensive homes, four beaches (permit only), and the incomparable Ravinia Park, which really is incomparable. They don't play Berlioz out at Great America.

There are a dozen or so Social Register names in Highland Park, and an address there usually means you have money.

Highland Park has even more of a split personality than Glencoe, however. It has eight Christian churches and five Jewish temples. According to some residents, the two communities can at times be quite abrasive as concerns one another.

14. *Deerfield*

Just west of Highland Park and just north of Northbrook, Deerfield is twenty-seven miles from the Loop by Milwaukee Road commuter train and quite popular with the people who ride those things.

A picture-perfect bedroom suburb, it was in the 1960's one of the top ten Chicago suburbs in terms of median college education, income, percentage of white-collar workers, and all that. It has since begun to slip in the statistics.

It was never in the top ten in terms of social prestige, but people who live there can feel superior to Arlington Heights.

Deerfield has attracted some light industry, like Sara Lee Kitchens and Baxter Labs (where they develop Baxters?). It has also become quite popular with upward bound Chicago Jewish families in recent years.

15. River Forest

Located just west of Oak Park, River Forest has five mansions designed by Frank Lloyd Wright, and a number of other grand old homes done by lesser geniuses.

It adjoins an enormous forest preserve along the Des Plaines River and has some six thousand trees of its own. That's a ratio of about two trees for each resident. As some of the residents have names like Tony "Big Tuna" Accardo, the privacy they provide is no doubt welcome.

Contrary to some opinions, gangsters do not predominate in River Forest. A few Social Register people still live there. Before his death—and unfortunate experience with the criminal justice system—former Governor Otto Kerner did, too.

16. Oak Park

De Vise had Oak Park listed as 110th, which is a trifle off the mark. Oak Park is one of the oldest, pleasantest, and most respectable suburbs around Chicago. If it is getting a little dingy around the edges, it is still regarded as the Evanston of the West. Its trees are as big and its homes as stately as Evanston's. Its Marshall Field and Company store is even prettier. Ernest Hemingway may have left Oak Park, but Frank Lloyd Wright found it very attractive. Twenty-five of his houses and buildings remain there, including his studio.

Oak Park's problem remains the great West Side Chicago slum that lies just across its border at Austin Avenue, but it has devised some artful means of controlling integration and maintaining property values, and may well survive. The pressure from within the black ghetto is easing as other western suburbs are opening up to blacks. Still, there is a crime problem in Oak Park. The village sits on an elevated line that runs right through the West Side to the Loop. Not long after the Evanston elevated platform murder, a young woman medical student was stabbed to death in an Oak Park rapid transit station.

17. Lincolnwood

Lincolnwood is one of the best-kept secrets in the metropolitan area. Though only nine miles from the Loop and right next to Skokie, Lincolnwood is just opposite Chicago's expensive Northwest Side communities of Sauganash and Edgebrook and contains some of the most opulent homes in the north suburbs. And some of the best-groomed lawns.

Founded by a group of immigrant Luxembourgers, many of whose descendants still reside there, Lincolnwood was a major stop for Luxembourg's Grand Duchess Charlotte on her last tour of the United States. She was doubtless enchanted by the suburb's sweeping views of the Edens Expressway.

The closest thing Lincolnwood has to a grand duchess of its own is high society's and the Republican Party's Mary MacDonald, whose home does have a sweeping view of the expressway. Lincolnwood is otherwise much favored by high-income doctors and lawyers who like to live close in.

18. Park Ridge

This middle to upper-middle class and very Republican suburb is eighteen miles northwest of the Loop via the line of the North Western and the Kennedy Expressway. It is also quite close to O'Hare. In fact, the best way to beat the airport traffic crush these days is to have a home in Park Ridge.

According to the *Illinois Guide and Gazetteer*, Park Ridge was settled by refugees from the 1871 Chicago Fire. They found the local clay good for making fireproof bricks, for which they had developed a fondness.

Park Ridge was the home of the first Cub Scout pack in the United States, and was where Frederick W. Goudy invented Goudy type. The *Tribune*'s Stanton Cook spent much of his life here. Congressman Henry Hyde lives here when he's not in Washington, or off finding facts.

19. Hinsdale

Another little conservative Republican bastion, west suburban Hinsdale sits just south of Oak Brook and just off the Tri-State Tollway. It was founded by Burlington Railroad barons in 1862 as a luxury suburb, and it still is.

An old-fashioned place, which goes in big for restored Victorian houses, it features a late nineteenth-century shopping district and a great many late-nineteenth-century social attitudes. And it loves parades.

Hinsdale annexed an enchanting place called Fullersburg in 1923. More recently, it has fleshed itself out with townhouse and apartment developments filled with frolicking young people. But the Old Guard still carries on, and it could not possibly be denied a place in the top twenty.

20. Western Springs

Four miles south of the Eisenhower Expressway and sixteen miles west of the Loop, Western Springs sounds like a stagecoach stop. But, as many are surprised to learn, it is quite affluent. Someone took a survey once and found that one third of the people in Western Springs owned stocks. It's also high in terms of median college education, although, if they're that smart, why are they buying stocks?

Though Western Springs has a lot of rich people, its two most illustrious citizens did not become affluent until they left town. In fact, they became affluent because they left town.

According to the *Illinois Guide and Gazetteer*, one was bank robber John Dillinger, who drove a taxi in Western Springs until he tired of honest labor and took up a life of crime.

The other was pastor at the Village Church in Western Springs. During World War II, he used to evangelize every week on a small-time radio Bible show. In 1943, the church elders told him they could no longer afford the eighty-five dollars it cost to broadcast the show. So the pastor took a walk, and went on to bigger and better things. His name was Billy Graham.

22

Their Clubs

Chicago loves clubs. There may be only a couple dozen or so listed in the Social Register, but the Chicago Yellow Pages list hundreds of them. The Casino, of course, and the almighty Chicago, but also the Rotarians and the Shriners, the Playboy and the Gaslight, the Analytical Psychology Club and the Commonwealth Edison Rifle and Revolver Club, and the Bucktown Hotshots of West Cortland Avenue. Some Chicago clubs have even attained great historical significance, such as Mayor Daley's Hamburg Athletic Association in Bridgeport.

Clubs are intended to bring people with common backgrounds together to pursue common interests. For the Hamburgs in Bridgeport, this meant baseball, patronage jobs, and beating up the non-Irish. Clubs also serve to keep away people from other backgrounds. Chicago's Society of Danube Swabians, for example, may turn away Elbe Swabians.

For the people who run Chicago, though, there are not hundreds of clubs. There are only a few, a very few, and the fewer the better. They are to be found in great gray piles of stone along the lakeshore and downtown, up in shimmering new office high rises, and surrounded by barbed wire in Lincoln Park. They range from ladies' clubs to business-oriented clubs to English-style gentlemen's clubs to very artsy clubs.

"Clubs are the centers of economic power," the First National Bank's Lucius P. Gregg once told an interviewer. "They are the places where the one-on-one interaction takes place, where the soul-searching goes on, where the policy is often made. Anyone who wants access to the resources there wants to belong." Gregg, a bank vice-president, is a member of the University Club. He is also black. Very few Chicago club members are.

Clubs are useful for excluding people, and for cutting deals. Excluding people often makes it easier to cut deals. Clubs are male-oriented cigar and whiskey hideaways, places to sleep, places to hole up when the wife has thrown you out of the mansion. They are also places for the ladies to get away from the men.

The hardest part about getting into a club traditionally has been the fact that you can't get in unless you are a somebody, and you can't be a somebody unless you're a member of the club. But these strictures are being relaxed, somewhat. Clubs are very expensive establishments to operate, and rising costs are prompting membership committees to worry only about the color of a prospective member's money. Also, the old WASP establishment is slipping out of control of thngs. If they want the really big deals to continue to be cut in their clubs, they have to bring in the outsiders.

The University of Pennsylvania's Professor Digby Baltzell, a longtime apologist for the WASP rich and the American class system, explained the phenomenon this way for an interviewer:

"Today you do business with a man," he said. "And you entertain him in your house; you may be a very good friend and you may even fall in love with his wife, but you can't get him into your club. What I'm talking about is the dysfunction of club exclusiveness in a society where more and more people of non-WASP background are rising into leadership positions."

As more and more Chicago non-WASPs have gained power in the city establishment, Chicago's clubs have tended to lose power. In some cases, it's all they can do to keep their properties out of the clutches of Arthur Rubloff and other developers. But the clubs would really have no power at all today if they continued to treat non-WASPs the way their ancestors did. Fifty years ago, the likes of Mayor Daley would not have been allowed to set foot in the Chicago Club.

But that has changed. Though they didn't have their wedding reception there, Michael Bilandic, thanks to Heather, is a member of the Casino Club. Mayor Daley was, and good old Mike Howlett is, a member of the Tavern Club. Jane Byrne had lunch at the Union League Club immediately after her election.

The need for new members is increasing, as long as they've got money. Initiation fees range from $500 to $1,000 and more. Monthly dues can exceed $250. Still, the clubs keep up their standards. For example, there's no wandering around in leisure suits or blue jeans at the Union League Club. As the rules explain:

> Members and their guests are required to wear appropriate attire in the Clubhouse and males of 12 years of age are requested to wear coats and neckties in the Main Dining Room, Crystal Room, Wigwam, Ladies Cocktail Lounge, Rendezvous, and in all private dining rooms used for Club committee meetings or other Club functions.
>
> On Saturday and Sunday, casual attire is acceptable in the Rendezvous, and in the Wigwam for breakfast and luncheon. Ladies and minors are not admitted to the Rendezvous at any time.
>
> Shorts may not be worn by adults in the Rendezvous, the Ladies Cocktail Lounge, or in the dining rooms of the Clubhouse.

The trend now is for clubs to accept women members, and most do—though with some restrictions. The Chicago and Union League Clubs allow them in the building, but proscribe some areas and hours. They will not accept them as members.

Governor Thompson, the TV camera-happy champion of the Equal Rights Amendment and such like, found himself attacked for his membership in the men-only Union League. He promised to "work from within" for change. A year later, newsmen found the rules unchanged and Thompson still a member. Did he stick by his club? He tried. "I'm not sure the women are all that hot to use the men's bar anyway," Thompson said. "My wife tells me that the women's bar is much better than the men's bar."

This prompted *Chicago Sun-Times* columnist Roger Simon to write: "Yassuh, dat sho is nice ob the governor. He gwine to make sho dat all the wimmen-chillin get separate but equal bars." Thomp-

son swiftly resigned from the club and went on to win reelection.
He said he hoped it would one day be possible for him to rejoin.
Perhaps when he leaves politics.

THE TOP FIFTEEN CLUBS IN CHICAGO

1. The Chicago Club

There are some society matrons who would rank the Casino
Club over the Chicago, but hell, you can't make many deals sitting
around playing bridge with a lot of old biddies.

The Chicago Club is *the* center of power in Chicago, and has
been almost always. It is mandatory for the city's biggest executives
to join it, unless they want to be considered not-so-big executives.

Manufacturers like International Harvester's Brooks McCormick
and Inland Steel's Leigh Block, stockbrokers like William Hutchins,
investors like William W. Prince, bankers like Edward Byron Smith
and A. Robert Abboud, and lawyers like Justin Stanley, Howard
Trienens, and Don Reuben are members. Charles Percy, of the
Senate, is a member.

A great, dark pile of stone on Van Buren Street with entrance
just west of Michigan Avenue, the Chicago is quintessentially a
gentlemen's club, complete with natty awning and imperious doorman. It predates the 1871 Chicago Fire (as some of its members
seem to), during which a group of members repaired hastily to the
beach with a club couch and large quantities of club whiskey,
brandy, and cigars.

Until recently, the Chicago Club would not even allow women
across its threshold, even when that compelled it to turn a female
Tribune reporter away from a press conference being held within.
But then Dr. Hannah Gray was made president of the University
of Chicago, and by long-standing tradition the president of the
University of Chicago is made a member of the Commercial Club,
and the Commercial Club meets in the Chicago Club. Now, in
certain select areas, women are admitted—though not as members.

Curiously, it's the younger members who seem most against admitting women members, not the old curmudgeons—as the vote
on the Dr. Gray matter indicates. The younger ones may not ap-

preciate what a sweet young thing might do to liven things up
in a gentlemen's lounge.

2. The Casino

Located just around the corner from the Hancock Center, the
Casino Club is *the* society club in Chicago. Not all of its members
are old biddies, however. Some are young biddies. Nearly all are
"nice" people. The ones who aren't have friends who are "nice"
people. The Bucktown Hotshots probably would not be considered
"nice" people.

The interior of the Casino runs to pastel walls and black marble,
as do rooms in Henry James novels. As is true of many things the
very rich arrange exclusively for themselves, it's not all that expensive. The food is very good. The menus are fixé—like so much
of Chicago—and on Friday nights the club sets out an elegant buffet
for before concert and such.

For high society's party givers, going first class has always meant
the Casino. Its December Ball was the really big society dance of
the year, but the band got sacked for nibbling mushrooms or something and the event was moved up to the Onwentsia Country Club
in Lake Forest, where it became known simply as The Dance.

The Casino was founded by the nice Mrs. Howard Lynn, sister
of Astor Street's nice William McCormick Blair, the stocks-and-
bonds man. Mrs. Lynn also founded the Chicago Junior League,
which is also nice.

The Casino is for all practical purposes a one-story building,
and sits on some of the most expensive real estate in town. It is
unthinkable that anyone—even in Chicago—should ever have the
clout to be able to tear it down.

3. Shoreacres Club

Chicago has hundreds of country clubs and practically none of
them would merit inclusion on this list. The leading exception is
the Shoreacres in Lake Bluff, which may be the most exclusive
in the Chicago area. A beach, tennis, and golf club handsomely
situated on a bluff overlooking the lake, the Shoreacres features a
very small membership and a cozy old frame clubhouse to match.
According to one member, it hasn't a room large enough for a

debutante party, except for an extremely unpopular debutante. To name the members of the Shoreacres is to repeat the better pages of the Social Register—Swifts. Donnelleys, Mitchells, Hutchins, Smiths, etcetera.

Just to the south of the Shoreacres is the beautiful Lester Armour mansion that his widow loaned to director Robert Altman for that peculiar movie, *A Wedding*. To the north is a peculiar indoor tennis thing erected by a peculiar rich lady from Texas.

That's all that's peculiar about the Shoreacres.

4. The Onwentsia

The No. 4 club in the area is also a country club, the Onwentsia, on Lake Forest's Green Bay Road. This is where the aristocrats come to frolic at tennis, golf, swimming, and tea dancing in large numbers. There are almost always parties going on at the Onwentsia. During the day during the week, there are almost always to be found grande dames playing bridge and swilling gin.

A much grander place than the Shoreacres, the Onwentsia has a very elaborate clubhouse. It used to have a polo field and stables, but that's been sold off to buy more silver or something. It still has indoor tennis and squash and that.

Despite the equally elaborate dues, many Lake Foresters like to belong to both the Onwentsia and the Shoreacres so that, if the golf course of one is tied up, they can try the other. The same may hold true for the bathrooms.

5. The Racquet Club

Occupying an outsized building on North Dearborn Parkway in the Gold Coast, the Racquet Club serves the rich sections of the Near North Side the same way the boys' clubs and the Y do the not-so-rich sections.

It has every athletic facility imaginable, including a huge swimming pool and indoor tennis courts that even women are allowed to use. It's very popular with young people, and fun couples like Adlai and Nancy Stevenson, who live just up the street. It's also popular with men who are on the outs with their wives. Many of Chicago's more-succulent divorce rumors get started just by some well-heeled chap's moving into the Racquet for a few days.

The Racquet's New Year's Eve parties are supposed to be the best in Chicago, depending on what sort of New Year's Eve party you favor. Frank Sinatra probably wouldn't like the broads. Actually, he might have trouble getting in.

Senator Percy took a nice black young man from the South Side to the Racquet as part of Percy's effort to enlist him as the Republican candidate for Congress in the late Ralph Metcalfe's district. The effort failed. Few things are so terribly relevant to the black community as the Racquet Club.

In the summertime, the Racquet is opened to members of other chic clubs which may be closed down for the season. One lady visiting from the Casino complained to us that the Racquet was full of fat women and men wearing double knits. Worse, she said, there were no dessert spoons.

6. Indian Hill

Winnetka's Indian Hill Country Club tries very had to be the most exclusive in the Chicago area. It certainly must be the hardest to join. Its waiting list is many light-years long and, rumor has it that the sons (and possibly great-grandsons) of members get shoehorned in at the head of the list. But what does rumor know?

But Indian Hill will never be *the* most exclusive, even if they reduce the membership to five. It isn't in or even near Lake Forest, and, for all the august personages on the membership list from Winnetka and Kenilworth, that just won't do.

Sometimes it isn't who you let in that counts, but who wants to be let in.

7. Saddle and Cycle

The Saddle and Cycle Club is a lovely old Henry Jamesian place on Chicago's lakefront where Foster Avenue collides with Lincoln Park. It is the only real country club left in the city, now that the South Shore Country Club has been turned into a stable for police horses, and a gunnery range for street gangs.

The extension of the Outer Drive north to Hollywood Avenue some years back has separated the Saddle and Cycle from its former beach frontage. Subsequent hard times forced some real estate sell-off and the reduction of the club golf course to three rather close-together holes.

But it's still there, thanks to barbed-wire fences. It will probably always be there, even if it means tank traps and snarling guard dogs.

Outsiders seem to have always caused problems with the Saddle and Cycle, even before World War II. The late Duke of Windsor, visiting as the Prince of Wales, swept scads of Chicago society ladies off their feet, and, one of them—according to legend—under some bushes out where the barbed wire now stands. Coincidentally, she later became, as they say, enceinte. Her husband moved the family to New York and there was a subsequent and unpleasant divorce. The latest Prince of Wales, it should be noted, conducted himself as a perfect gentleman on his recent visit.

With raffish Uptown so close, there are still things going on under the bushes, but mostly to the tune of Johnny Cash records and on the other side of the wire.

A more recent and less publicly whispered-about scandal concerned a lady from a prominent Eastern family who resided for a time in Chicago. She was bounced from the Saddle and Cycle, according to this legend, because some bills piled up—but really because she allowed her dog to do his thing in the club pool. As the legend really, really had it, though, she was bounced because she never, never bathed—especially around the neck. Well, Gustav Swift may never have bathed either, especially when he was pushing that raw meat around in a cart.

8. The Tavern Club

Walk into the main dining room of the Tavern Club high above Michigan Avenue at any noon hour and you're likely to find corporation chairmen, painters, architects, newspapermen (the kind with six-figure salaries), broadcast executives, senior partners in law firms, the Irish Consul General, and high-ranking politicians. Daley loved this club.

Women do not find it quite so convivial, however, until after 4 P.M. That's when they're allowed out of their restricted areas.

Established during those wild, carefree days of the 1920's, the Tavern remains a quite lighthearted club. There are always parties in progress on one of the levels, and such fun events as the artists'

and models' ball. Some of the models have been in their nakeds.
Hoo Hoo!

Situated atop the 333 North Michigan Avenue Building, the club
has maintained strong ties to the city's artistic communities, and
its corridors function as galleries. Its views are not as sweeping
as they were before the superbuildings went up, but they're certainly among the most interesting of any top club in the city.

Numerous high-ranking politicians, numerous high-ranking *Tribune* executives, numerous lawyers like Bert Jenner and Don Reuben, and even convicted Lake Forest swindler William Rentschler
hang out at the Tavern. Rentschler was a leading Republican figure until Jim Thompson did him in, and is rather a decent chap
for all that.

The Tavern is extremely nice to widows of members, who spend
a lot of money there hosting dinner parties. After 4 P.M.

9. *The Union League*

On social standing alone, the Union League might not rank quite
so high—being favored more by fellows from Oak Brook and Evanston than Lake Forest and Kenilworth. But it is *the* Republican
club in Chicago, especially for the kind of Republicans who like to
do things their own way, not City Hall's.

Founded in 1879, the club grew out of the Union League of
America—a Civil War bunch that was not exactly crawling with
Confederate sympathizers. The club's heroes include Abraham Lin-
coln, Ulysses Grant, and John C. Fremont. The Union League
counts among its members such high-ranking Republicans as "High
Collar" Sam Witwer, president of the 1970 Illinois Constitutional
Convention; former State Senate President Pro Tem W. Russell
Arrington; and William Fetridge, long the guiding spirit of the
United Republican Fund. The highly influential Bob Bergstrom
remains among the club's guiding spirits as well.

Occupying a twenty-three-story building on Jackson Boulevard
(named after a Democrat) at the darkest end of the financial district, the Union League is opposite the federal courts and, so, daily
host to a slew of federal judges and hordes of lawyers.

As wood-paneled and leathery as any club in the city, the Union
League prides itself on its art collection, which includes a genuine

Reubens and lots of Frederick Remington Wild West stuff. But, for Republicans, the West was never as wild as Chicago, and the most genuine Reuben is named Don.

10. The Standard Club

In a city where anti-Semitism was once such that even the aristocratic Mary Lasker Block was not very welcome in some WASP clubs, a Jewish club like the Standard still rates—and at the top. It has what all the other clubs do: money and power, and more than most.

Something of the Jewish equivalent of the Chicago Club, it has to be the most expensive club in the city. Its initiation fees, depending on the applicants' ages, range up to $4,000. The Standard charges $90 a month in dues, compared to $55 a month for the Union League and only $35 a month at the Mid-America.

The Standard is expensive in less open ways. It's commonly understood that you have to spread the bread in vast heaps to Jewish charities before you can be seriously considered for membership. And, once admitted, it's reportedly understood that you have to keep spreading the bread.

It's unfortunate that Jews in Chicago have been so discriminated against socially. It's just as unfortunate that so many of them feel inclined to practice the same game. There are many successful lawyers and businessmen along LaSalle Street whose money, position, and good works ought to suffice for membership in the Standard, but, as one lawyer complained, it's hard to get in if "you're the wrong kind of Jew." English, French, and German Jews are very much the right kind of Jews. Polish and other Eastern European Jews sometimes find themselves less exalted.

But the creamed spinach in the Standard is very good. Judge Reginald Holzer, a Republican and one of the club's more typical members, always recommends it for lunch.

11. The Arts Club

The Arts is an odd, extremely avant-garde, very establishment, and very chic club. Once located in the Wrigley Building, it now occupies an entire floor of a modernistic walk-up on Ontario Street, just down from the voluptuous Lili Schenck's barber shop and around the corner from Michigan Avenue.

Members of the Arts Club seem to fall into two groups: high-society types (Mrs. Edward Byron Smith and the William W. Princes are members), and local musicians, painters, and writers. The latter, in fact, get to pay smaller dues—except for Nelson Algren, who moved to New Jersey and doesn't care. If something seems rather patronizing about this arrangement, you get the idea.

The Arts Club frequently exhibits paintings and sculptures by members, ranging in price from $75 to $1,200 and more. But the club's big thing is serving as the first exhibition place for artistic rages brought in from the rest of the country.

Though really a sort of museum, with highly polished floors and excellent lighting, the Arts Club has a lovely dining room and serves up some really elegant eats.

The club has had only three presidents in more than fifty years, and in 1978 had a secretary named Franklin Trueblood.

12. The Women's Athletic Club

The Women's Athletic Club is not to be confused with the YWCA, as a glance at its imposing entrance makes clear. More than eighty years old, it was formerly located in the Loop and now occupies a great gray pile of stone at Michigan Avenue and Ontario Street—on the other side of the street from Lili Schenck's.

Many of the club's members are at an age where they'd barely survive a volleyball game, but there are a number of athletic types bounding through its corridors. Abra (Rockefeller) Prentice Anderson is one of the more visible. Though a women's club, men are granted swimming and eating privileges. In fact, one of the club's reigning swim champs is a man.

The club is famous among Chicago duck and coconut lovers for its duck dinners and coconut cake. If your cook is sick, the club will be happy to whip you up a casserole or something to go. If your cook is drunk, it will still be happy to do it.

13. The University Club

Society ladies we have talked to refer to the University as "a nice club," but not with the same inflection as when they talked about "nice" people. In fact, one of them got real low-down and called the University "Grand Central Station," which seems to be the Midwestern term for New York's Grand Central Terminal. The Tudor decor of the club's East Monroe Street clubhouse certainly is as classic as an old railroad station. The vaulted ceiling is painted with the coats of arms of famed universities (but not Loop College).

The idea is that anybody who went to college can join. And, indeed, there are decorations from the less-than Ivy League Chicago Circle Campus and Beloit College. Until recently, it didn't quite work that way, of course. Now that it is that way, not everyone who went to college wants to join.

14. *The Fortnightly*

This really elegant old place on Bellevue Place just off Lake Shore Drive belongs on this list by sheer dint of its social prestige. Hand a Rush Street floozy $100 million, and it would still be five generations before she could get an offspring in. The Fortnightly is certainly no place to go to have a chat with someone from the City Council Finance Committee, but if you'd like to meet a nice elderly lady worth a few million, it's the best place in Chicago to start.

A beautifully and tastefully, if somewhat archaically furnished establishment, the Fortnightly is the kind of place Henry James would be happy in—probably the only place in Chicago he would be happy in.

Many of the club's members could not survive thirty seconds on a volleyball court—if they could make it out onto the court. But they do their best. Even so, most of the club's elegant furnishings seem to be bequeathed by deceased members.

Many of the members belong to other fun organizations like the National Society of Colonial Dames and the Mayflower Descendents. The Scribblers and the Contemporary (ha!) Club meet in the Fortnightly as well.

You can't help but wish that Abra (Rockefeller) Prentice Anderson might join the Fortnightly and, in a moment of mad whimsy inspired by her Christmas card posing, go off for a run through its hallways in one of her thigh-high split "evening costumes."

15. The Chicago Athletic

The Mid-America and Mid-Day Clubs, which in terms of status come in somewhere around this level, are edged out by the Chicago Athletic because they're merely luncheon and dinner clubs and not club clubs.

Something like the Chicago, Union League, and University Clubs —though not at all like them when it comes to service, especially on holidays and weekends—the Chicago Athletic is a grand old place with paneled walls, bronze statues, and swimming pool.

P. Sveinbjorn Johnson, the Icelandic consul, and James Fletcher, former deputy governor, are typical members.

Honorable Mention: The Bucktown Hotshots

Judging by its name, it has to be the most fun club in town. And one presumes you can wear leisure suits whenever you want.

Afterword

All power has limits. Not even Mayor Daley ruled absolutely. The most basic rule about effective use of power in a city like Chicago is that it should be used sparingly, if at all. The appearance or threat of power can accomplish much; indeed, in the case of someone like Richard J. Daley, it can regularly perform miracles. But the raw, naked exercise of power is usually counterproductive. It exposes the power wielder to the risk of being revealed as not having so much power after all. And it can provoke the kind of confrontation in which the supposed power wielder loses everything he or she hoped to gain.

Wealthy society people are presumed to have power, even though they really don't. That is why so many doors are opened for them and so many things are conveniently arranged for them. But as soon as they attempt to play Czar Nicholas, their lack of power is exposed and they are undone. Bonnie Swearingen said: "Yes, I suppose I do have power." Yet when she got into an altercation with a chauffeur, she and the chauffeur received the same treatment from the police. Hope McCormick would never get into an altercation with a chauffeur.

News people are supposed to have a lot of power, because of the

412

huge numbers of people they reach every day. But they would never dare use this power in a personal way, as so many politicians fear or hope they might, because they'd instantly lose their jobs. The power of the press lies with the institution, never the journalist.

Don Reuben is considered the most powerful attorney in Chicago. He probably is. But it's because of his record and reputation; not because of his barking orders. No one has ever been able to cite a single instance in which Don Reuben ever put the arm on someone.

Mayor Daley, the most powerful man in the history of Chicago, almost never ruled as a monarch or dictator. He used subtle ways, such as when he totally outmaneuvered the late Martin Luther King during the open housing marches of the middle 1960s, or when he totally destroyed the Lakefront Lib revolt of the late 1960s by simply going to a picnic and putting his arm around Adlai Stevenson. When he did try to pull a Czar Nicholas, with his 1968 shoot-to-kill-arsonists, shoot-to-maim-looters order, it accomplished little and cost him plenty. He very seldom did that. The reason his legislative leaders worked so arduously and effectively for him in Springfield is not that they did what he told them to do, but that they did what they thought and hoped he wanted them to do.

Jane Byrne has not learned this lesson. She's a Czar Nicholas type, and it may prove her undoing. She blurted out at a *Sun-Times'* cocktail party in Washington that she was going to fire Park District Superintendent Ed Kelly. Daley would never have done that. If he had wanted Kelly fired, he would have said nothing. Kelly would have simply found himself without a job one day. Daley would only have mumbled something about the fine city parks.

Jane shook up the higher echelons of the police department, but got stiff-armed in her attempt to immediately install her own favorite choice as chief. She purged some ward superintendents, but the ward war lords hardly quivered.

Her worst mistake, though, was her attempt to obliterate Michael and Heather Bilandic's highly popular ChicagoFest music festival. It represented everything Jane seemed to hate, mostly Mike and Heather, but also the lakefront establishment, suburbanites, and just plain fun. And, in some strange way, probably that "cabal of evil men," such as they are fond of rock music and Italian ices. Shortly after taking office, she pronounced: "I never thought the city should be involved in the entertainment field. There's a big question in my mind." A few days later, Karen Conner, the mayor's special events coordinator, opined: "You can safely say that there will not be a ten-day music festival on Navy Pier this year."

The problem Jane immediately ran into was that almost everyone in Chicago liked the idea of ChicagoFest, and no one but Janey's crowd didn't. The Tribune took a thoroughgoing poll that found ChicagoFest ranking right up there with Santa Claus, motherhood, and summertime. In her first big powerplay with the establishment she suposedly had vanquished, she found herself facing a cannon with a squirtgun. The people, embarrassingly, were not on her side. There was no snow.

There was some shuffling and mumbling about providing more neighborhood participation, raising ticket prices, seeking state financial aid, and renaming the event the "Cook County Fair." Ha ha. But the lakefront was not without its crowds and music in the summer of 1979. Jane lost her power play.

"We're going ahead with ChicagoFest," Janey was finally compelled to say, "and we never said we weren't."

Ha ha. If Richard Daley had not wanted ChicagoFest, he would never have said a word. Some terrible safety hazard might have been suddenly discovered at Navy Pier, or a schedule conflict might have arisen because the fire department majong team needed the space for practice. Or else Navy Pier might just have sunk to the bottom of the lake one night, with Daley quickly appointing a committee to study the need for a new one.

But there is one big difference between politicians of Daley's caliber and of Janey's. ChicagoFest was demonstrably popular. It was probably the only real positive achievement of the Bilandic administration. No matter how much he might have hated it, Richard Daley would not have not wanted it.

Authors' Note

Like its authors, readers of a work as topical and contemporary as this must contend with a certain reality: the mechanical process of publishing a book requires at least a few weeks, and it is not always possible in that time to accommodate all the last minute changes that might occur in people's circumstance in a city as big and active as Chicago. Jane Byrne does have that penchant for leaping up and shouting, "Off with his head!"—and the crime syndicate still terminates careers with the abrupt click of a .45 automatic safety, and without a care to publishing deadlines. Even in so sedate a field as advertising or commodities trading the chairs can get suddenly moved around.

The authors have done their very best to make this book as up to date as possible. If there are a few post deadline changes, we think the readers will at least find the bodies or the leather executive desk chairs in question still warm.

Index